T0246128

SUSA YOUNG GATES

Susa Young Gates

SUSA YOUNG GATES

DAUGHTER OF MORMONISM

ROMNEY BURKE

SIGNATURE BOOKS | 2022 | SALT LAKE CITY

*To Mary Susan Wilkinson Burke, love and light of my life,
and to the memory of our mothers,
Hannah Romney Burke and Lurene Kealiilalanikulani Gates Wilkinson*

The opinions expressed in this book are not necessarily those of the publisher. Photographs
are from the private collection of Lurene Gates Wilkinson, except as noted. Frontispiece
courtesy of Utah State Historical Society.

Cover design by Jason Francis

FIRST EDITION | 2022

LIBRARY OF CONGRESS CATALOGING-IN-PUBLICATION DATA

Names:	Burke, Romney, author.
Title:	Susa Young Gates : daughter of Mormonism / Romney Burke.
Description:	First edition.	Salt Lake City : Signature Books, 2022.	Includes bibliographical references and index.	Summary: "Brigham Young had dozens of wives and numerous children, but none have better name recognition than Susa Young Gates. Yet she, like so many women of Mormonism's past, has remained a mystery to most church members. In Susa Young Gates, Romney Burke paints a portrait of a strong woman who rose to prominence within the church, fought for the rights of women throughout the country, yet dealt with personal trials and her share of heartbreak. After divorcing her first husband, Alma Dunford, the trauma associated with that union was such that she steadfastly refused to mention it ever again. She also lost some of her children over the course of her life and was unable to reconcile her older sister's departure from the LDS Church and conversion to Catholicism. Yet despite her trials, Susa found fulfillment in her faith through service, as a prolific writer-co-authoring with her daughter Leah Dunford Widtsoe the 1930 biography of her father, *Life Story of Brigham Young*, founding the *Young Women's Journal* in 1889, the *Relief Society Magazine* in 1915, and in her associations with such prominent women's advocates such as Susan B. Anthony"—Provided by publisher.
Identifiers:	LCCN 2021058669 (print)	LCCN 2021058670 (ebook)	ISBN 9781560854463 (hardback)	ISBN 9781560854173 (ebook)
Subjects:	LCSH: Gates, Susa Young, 1856-1933.	Mormon women—Biography.	Mormon authors—Biography.	LCGFT: Biographies.
Classification:	LCC BX8695.G37 B87 2022 (print)	LCC BX8695.G37 (ebook)	DDC 305.48/6893—dc23/eng/20220113

LC record available at https://lccn.loc.gov/2021058669
LC ebook record available at https://lccn.loc.gov/2021058670

Contents

Introduction

When I met my wife in 1966, I learned that she was a great-great-granddaughter of Brigham Young. What I did not know until later was that her great-grandmother was Susa Young Gates, Brigham's most famous and dynamic daughter. Through Susa's youngest surviving son, Franklin, I heard stories that intrigued me. And Franklin's daughter, Lurene, who became my mother-in-law, served as a secretary to Susa during the last year of Susa's life and brought her alive in my mind's eye.

Knowing of my love of Mormon history and my increasing fascination with Susa, my wife, early in our marriage, extracted a promise from me that I would someday write Susa's biography. There had been a master's degree thesis written about Susa at the University of Utah in 1951 by Paul Cracroft. In the 1970s short sketches about Susa's life had appeared in two collections of famous early Latter-day Saint women. In 1976 Carolyn W. D. Person, also a great-granddaughter of Susa, wrote a chapter in *Mormon Sisters*, and in 1978 Rebecca Cornwall contributed a chapter to *Sister Saints*. Recently, Lisa Olsen Tait's chapter on Susa's life appeared in the third volume of *Women of Faith in the Latter Days*.

Several myths existed within the Gates family regarding Susa's personal papers. One was that Susa's son Harvey, a productive Hollywood screenwriter, author of more than 200 movie scripts in the 1930s and 1940s, had taken Susa's papers to California to write her biography—and lost them. Another was that Susa was so disillusioned by her divorce from her first husband that she had destroyed all the paperwork relating to that marriage. Both turned out to be false. In the early 1980s, after the death of Franklin Young Gates, Susa's last surviving child, Franklin's daughters, Lurene K. Gates Wilkinson and Florence Marie "Florie" Gates Stamm, discovered over 100 boxes of materials in Franklin's garage. This material was donated to the LDS Church History Library in the 1980s by Lurene and Florie and constitutes almost the entire Susa Young Gates collection there. Many years were spent by Church History Library employees in cataloging this material. Almost all of it has now been digitized and is available on the internet. (Several folders, which deal with the church's temple rites, are classified and unavailable to researchers.) And although Susa never wrote about her first husband in any of the biographical information she furnished during her lifetime, she did leave a "smoking gun," a letter to her half-sister, Zina Young Card, the daughter of another of Brigham's wives, Zina Huntington Young, written shortly after her divorce. After it was written, Susa assiduously avoided any mention of him ever again.

Fast forward forty years from my promise to my wife. A busy surgical career, marriage and ten children, and involvement in a host of professional, educational, civic, business, ecclesiastical, and administrative responsibilities made for a hectic life until I retired. After retirement, two years of teaching English at Ocean University of China in Qingdao, through the Brigham Young University China Teachers Program, and eighteen months as an area medical adviser for Latter-day Saint missionaries in Brazil, have further delayed work on a project which has otherwise consumed almost every waking moment, as it seemed, since 2010.

Finally, the first full book-length biography of Susa Young Gates has come to fruition. I believe that history should be honest, and I have tried to portray Susa as I think she was—impressive, articulate, commanding, capable, loving, accepting, adaptable, but also, at times, prickly, imperious, and impatient. Susa was a human whirlwind; it is amazing to consider everything she accomplished in a single lifetime. She was a devoted member of her church, which she influenced in important ways; she was a caring wife and mother of thirteen children; she walked among the great feminist figures of her day; she hobnobbed with the glitterati of the world; she was a prolific writer of novels, poems, editorials, journal articles, and short stories. She lived her personal life amid great personal tragedy and afflictions, but she remained optimistic and hopeful. She believed that an individual life could change the world.

Susa had flaws and foibles, as we all do. I have not tried to emphasize these, nor to whitewash them, but to recount them in a charitable fashion, since they are an important part of who she was. And Susa certainly recognized and lamented her shortcomings and spent a lifetime trying to overcome them. I have pored over the papers Susa left behind and have tried to allow her to speak for herself. She was, after all, a writer. She jotted diary entries, dashed off letters, sent telegrams, and kept ledgers. She penned articles for local and national magazines and journals. She wrote books. Her papers are filled with scribbles, ideas, notes, and rough drafts of articles and biographies she planned to write. She founded two magazines, and, as editor, she wrote columns for nearly every issue of those magazines. Words seemed to pour out of this prolific genealogist, family historian, and chronicler of Mormonism.

I am uncomfortable with much of the speculation I see in biographies. As close I have come to knowing Susa and her family, she is gone and I cannot begin to guess intelligently at the complex, overlapping motivations that drove her day-to-day choices and decisions. The characters of the past were not one-dimensional people, easy to discern from a letter here, a diary entry there. What motivated them one day may not have motivated them the next. Why, for example, after Susa's husband, Jacob Gates, wrote to George Q. Cannon in 1882, asking for him to intercede on Susa's behalf in a deeply personal matter, did both Susa and Jacob let the matter drop? Were they distracted by another family matter? Was reading Cannon's sympathetic reply comfort enough? Were they disappointed by his response? Or did they, in fact, do more, but now those actions are lost to history? Rather than attempt to tease out possibilities in the text, I am usually content to let these matters hang, unresolved. Threads that lead to dark rooms are inevitable when we dive into the past, and I trust readers to know that reliable answers are not always available.

This is not to suggest that I take everything Susa says at face value, and I trust readers to know something about human nature. Susa, prodigious biographer and autobiographer, was, like all of us, a sometimes unreliable narrator of her own story. She was the loyal daughter of an LDS prophet, and she was fiercely Mormon to her bones. I hope that Susa will accept my account of her life in the spirit in which it is written.

The quotes in this book are unaltered from their originals. Apart from an occasional misspelled word, or the absence of an apostrophe here or a comma there, Susa's writing is clear and easy to follow, if not always grammatically correct according to our twenty-first-century rules. Therefore, with rare exception, I have avoided the use of "sic" and the use of brackets to supplement quotes.

Finally, it is hard enough to keep track of all the Youngs and Smiths and Kimballs in the church, but add in the practice of polygamy and keeping track of names becomes labyrinthine. What's more, Susa wed the cousin of her sister's husband: two Youngs married two Dunfords. Rather than try to maintain a formal use of last names, or even first and last names, I frequently use given names to identify the characters in Susa's story. I hope my choice allows readers to follow the threads of Susa's life more easily, and I hope it makes the people in that life a little more human.

ACKNOWLEDGMENTS

Gratitude is due, first and foremost, to my wife, Mary Sue. She has encouraged, advised, revised, suggested, wheedled, threatened, cajoled, and facilitated at every step along the way. The skills she learned as an editorial assistant at Doubleday over fifty years ago have stood her in good stead. She has read and reread every word of every draft of this manuscript; her help and insights have been invaluable.

Franklin Y. Gates, last surviving child of Susa Young Gates and my grandfather-in-law, was a delight to know. He introduced me to the sense of humor of the Young family, and he provided me with a vital and important understanding of Susa's personality.

Likewise, Franklin's two daughters, Lurene K. Gates Wilkinson, my mother-in-law, and her sister, Florence Marie Gates Stamm, wisely preserved the multiple boxes of material from Susa that they found in their father's garage. These records they providently provided to the LDS Church History Library in Salt Lake City. Lurene carefully guarded during her lifetime the photographs which grace this book, which since her death have been taken care of by her daughter, Heidi Wilkinson Lords.

The unsung heroes of this story include the tireless workers at the LDS Church History Library who carefully arranged and catalogued Susa's papers over a period of at least a decade. The directors and managers at the Church History Library have overseen the digitization of this collection, which has changed research from a horse-and-buggy approach to a modern twenty-first-century endeavor. At the beginning of this research I had to physically sit in the special reading room at the Church History Library; now I can press a few computer keys and up comes virtually the entire collection while I sit in my study at home.

Of special help at the Church History Library was Jill Mulvay Derr, a friend of over half a century, who walked me through the workings of the library. Brittany Chapman Nash kindly provided me with a PDF of the Susa Young Gates catalog. Numerous other staff members rendered invaluable help.

Walter Jones of the University of Utah Marriott Library Special Collections provided me with a copy of the Paul Cracroft thesis of Susa's life. Other librarians, most of them unknown to me by name, at the Utah State Historical Society Library, L. Tom Perry Special Collections at the Harold B. Lee Library at Brigham Young University, and my own local City of West Linn Public Library have been kind and generous with their time.

The two women who probably know more about Susa than anyone, Rebecca Cornwall Bartholomew and Lisa Olson Tait, graciously shared their thoughts about Susa and the import of her life. They were a wellspring of understanding and insight. At the beginning of my labors, Becky generously gave me all the materials and notes she had used for the vignette she wrote in the 1970s regarding Susa.

I am indebted to the staff of Signature Books for believing in a neophyte historian and accepting this manuscript. In particular, John Hatch took an imperfect manuscript and made it, I believe, into a tribute worthy of Susa Young Gates. I also benefited from Jeffery Ogden Johnson's careful review of and insightful comments on each of the chapters.

Rob and Ann Dunford kindly furnished me with transcriptions of Alma B. Dunford's missionary letters from England, 1877-78.

Thanks are also due to my parents, who provided me not only

with a first-class education, but a first-class upbringing also. I have never met a smarter woman than my mother, and my father's off-the-chart "emotional quotient" has allowed me to get through life with whatever grace I might possess.

My ten children (Caroline, Kimberly, Suzanne, Brendan, Juliana, Kevin, Christopher, Katie, Brynn, and David) and multiple grandchildren have not only been an inspiration for me to achieve, but kindly gave up time with me and allowed me the space and solitude I needed to complete this project.

Two special teachers have remained a part of me over the years. Alma Blunck, my fourth-grade teacher in Palmer, Alaska, always encouraged me to take a book with me wherever I went. "You never know when you might have a few extra moments to read." And Christine Smith of Austin Lathrop High School in Fairbanks, told me I had a talent for writing, but my efforts needed more "gusto." I may not have achieved the "gusto," but she did teach me to write with precision.

Abbreviations and Note on Sources

CHL   Church History Library, Church of Jesus Christ of
Latter-day Saints, Salt Lake City

JD   *Journal of Discourses*

SYGP   Susa Young Gates Papers, CHL

USDH   Utah State Division of History, Salt Lake City

The Susa Young Gates papers held by CHL number 113 boxes. While I rely on these as the primary source of information on Susa's life, other valuable collections include the Relief Society papers at CHL, the Susa Young Gates papers at USDH, and the Widtsoe family papers, also at USDH.

I draw heavily from Susa's voluminous correspondence. Unless otherwise noted, all of Susa's letters come from her papers at CHL. Throughout the book I cite whom a letter is to or from and where in the collection it may be found. Her second husband Jacob's papers are also a part of Susa's papers and, like Susa's correspondence, unless otherwise noted, all of Jacob's papers come from that collection.

Brigham's Daughter

In explaining the origin of her unusual first name, Susa Amelia Young Dunford Gates wrote the following "sad, mournful tale" for one of her *Young Woman's Journal* girls "in the southern part of the State [of Utah]."[1] Susa had started life as "simple and sensible Susanne" (or Susanna), but through a cascade of events eventually became known variously as Susannah, Susie, Susan, and eventually Susa.

Susa's mother, Lucy Bigelow Young, was the thirteenth of sixteen wives who would bear children in a polygamous relationship with the great Mormon prophet and pioneer, Brigham Young. At Susa's birth, Lucy asked Brigham what they should name their new daughter, to which he replied, "It did not matter so much, and left mother [Lucy] to make her own choice."[2] Susanne (or Susanna) Liptrot Richards, Brigham's cousin by marriage[3] and a well-known nurse in "old Utah days," was present at Susa's birth and importuned Lucy for the chance to name the child in the event Brigham did not do so. Hence, Susa became Susanne Young.

Several of Susa's sisters and friends abridged their names at the time of their baptisms into the church, so at age eight, Susa, a somewhat fanciful child given to literature and romance, asked her father when he confirmed her if he would add a middle name

---

1. Susa Young Gates, "The Editor Presumes to Talk about Herself," *Young Woman's Journal*, Jan. 1896, 200–03.
2. Gates, "Editor Presumes," 201.
3. Susa Young Gates, "My Recollections 2," box 1, fd. 2, SYGP (USDH).

because of her "plain name ... plainer face, and a passion for music and books."[4] The name she chose was Amelia, in honor of her father's elegant new wife, the talented and beautiful Harriet "Amelia" Folsom, who would become Young's travel companion, nurse, consort, and chief hostess during the last years of his life. Susanne Amelia Young was often called "Susie," or, to her "infinite disgust," "Sus" or "Sukey,"[5] and she reports that clerks and recorders often wrote her name as Susannah.

Years passed, and about the time of the dedication of the St. George temple on January 1, 1877, Lucy and all three of her daughters were in a room with Brigham. Talk turned to the names of Brigham's children, and he complained that several of them had altered their names. He was particularly concerned that, except for Nabbie, none of his daughters had kept the names of his sisters, which he had given them. Eunice was called "Luna"; Louisa was "Punk."[6] He then reportedly remarked, "And here is Susan, even she has had to be called Susie, as if Susan was not good enough for her."[7] (Brigham's sister Susannah was often called Susan.)

At that time both Lucy and Susa recounted the story of Susa's being named Susanne at birth, to which Brigham, who by now was seventy-five years old, retorted, "Nonsense, don't you suppose I know what she was named? She was named Susan after my sister Susan." Susa dutifully replied, "If you think my name ought to be Susan—Susan it shall be to the end of the chapter ... I will change the temple records."[8]

Brigham died eight months later. At the reading of his will, it was found that one of the clerks had mistakenly written the name Susa instead of Susan. So it was insisted that Susa sign all the legal documents as Susa. Thus, Susa explained, she was "Susan in the temples, Susa in my ordinary signatures and in legal documents, Su to my dearest and nearest, Suz to those who retain that grating memory of my childish name, Sister Suey to one old quaint friend, Aunty

---

4. Gates, "Editor Presumes," 201.
5. Gates, "My Recollections 2."
6. Gates.
7. Gates, "Editor Presumes," 202.
8. Gates.

Gates to the children of my dear brother Jos. F. Smith,[9] Susannah and Susanne variously in early records, and Aunt Susa to all my dear and beloved girls," including those girls who read the *Young Woman's Journal*, which she edited from 1889 to 1900.[10]

Brigham Young and Lucy Bigelow already had a four-year old daughter, Eudora Lovinia "Dora," at the time Susa was born, and Lucy was disappointed that she had not borne a son. She asked Aunt Zina Huntington, another of Brigham's plural wives also present at Susa's birth, "What is it?" When informed that it was a little girl, Lucy reportedly said, "Oh, shucks!" The reply from Aunt Zina was, "'No, it isn't shucks, its all wheat and full weight at that."[11]

Susa arrived on March 18, 1856, a Tuesday and a workday. She was Brigham Young's forty-second child, the first to be born in the not-quite-finished Lion House where eventually up to twelve of Brigham's wives and families would live at a time. Susa joined, besides Dora, a houseful of half-siblings who in a given week might number four babes in arms, six toddlers, five or six preschoolers, thirteen or more school-aged children between six and fourteen years, several older offspring in their late teens to early twenties, and often a young guest or two staying with the president's family. Lion House children did not include senior wife Mary Ann Angell's six children (aged twelve to twenty-two) nor, after 1860, Lucy Decker's seven (aged one to eleven). Mary Ann decided she preferred living in the White House (the first home built in the family compound), so Lucy Decker, next in seniority, moved into the Beehive House and became hostess of Young's official residence. Emmeline Free, with her brood of five ranging from one to eleven years (and about to include Lorenzo Dow Young, born six months after Susa), may have lived in the Lion House temporarily. But Emmeline soon moved into the nearby Grant House vacated upon Salt Lake City Mayor Jedediah Grant's death in December 1856. In time Emmeline would bear Brigham a total of ten children, more than any other

9. Smith, the nephew of LDS founder Joseph Smith, would become sixth president of the LDS Church and lifelong friend of the Young family.

10. Gates, "Editor Presumes," 202.

11. That is, corn cob shucks. Susa Young Gates, "Lucy Bigelow Young" (unpublished manuscript in author's possession, n.d.), typescript, 40.

of his wives. Perhaps it was felt that, with her large family, she deserved her own dwelling.[12]

No doubt Susa's mother, Lucy Bigelow, had been eager to leave her previous quarters, where she enjoyed little privacy and rarely a room of her own, often sharing a bed with a sister wife or sleeping on the floor.[13] Lucy had determined early in her marriage to refrain from criticism; Susa reported never hearing her mother complain about any member of the family.[14] Still, Lucy's and little Dora's living circumstances greatly improved upon moving into the Lion House.

Brigham's families lived in relative splendor in the family compound in the third quarter of the nineteenth century, becoming the closest thing to royalty the Latter-day Saints would ever know. The compound occupied a fifty-acre plot next to Temple Square in the heart of the city. It was well-appointed, self-sufficient, and included a carpentry shop, store, blacksmith shop, flour mill, barns, corrals, gardens and orchards, pigeon house, gymnasium, small cemetery, and even a family swimming pool. Initially, the children were taught in a classroom in the northwest corner of the Lion House, but in 1862 Brigham completed a private school across the street on the northeast corner of South Temple and State Streets. The compound's three stately main structures included the Lion House and the Beehive House, connected by the governor's and the church president's offices. Third was the White House, located one block farther east, also on South Temple Street.

The Lion House looked modest enough from the front, despite the lion statue carved by William Ward that came to adorn its portico. However, from a side perspective, its three stories and deep length graced by twenty gables (ten on each side) stood out among Great Salt Lake City architecture of the 1850s. Indeed, a stroll past the Lion and Beehive Houses seemed to have been compulsory for journalists and other visitors traveling through the city, no doubt

---

12. "Emmeline Free," *Partridge Nest—Partridge Genealogy and History*, www.partridge-nest.com, accessed Jan. 15, 2020. This blog article cites "Brigham Young: His Wives and Family" in Carter, *Our Pioneer Heritage*, vol. 1, but also draws from a family recollection that the Grant House stood on upper Main Street, a stone's throw from the Lion House and where ZCMI later stood across the street from the Hotel Utah.

13. Whitley, *Brigham Young's Homes*, 82.

14. Whitley.

hoping to catch a glimpse of the controversial Mormon leader himself. To protect his family's privacy, Brigham had an adobe wall built around the compound.[15]

In various writings, Susa left detailed descriptions of the interior of the Lion House. On the ground floor (a long, walk-in basement with more than several outside doors) were the dining room, kitchens, and storage rooms. On the elevated main floor were the private rooms of each wife together with the family prayer room. Lucy Bigelow lived on this floor in No. 7, just south of the hall. Her apartment was immediately north of the rooms Clara Decker shared with her two little daughters, her baby son Jedediah having died only two months before Susa was born, and in close proximity to the quarters of Lucy Decker (before 1860) and Emily Partridge.[16] On the third floor, under the gables, were twenty bedrooms for the older boys and girls.

At the time of Susa's birth, Brigham Young was president of the LDS Church, governor of Utah territory, and Superintendent of Indian Affairs, having been appointed to the latter two positions by US President Millard Fillmore. To give himself a maximum of time with his family despite these heavy public responsibilities, he saw that life in the Lion House was both regimented and communal. This was especially so for meals and prayers. He realized this arrangement was not perfect, once commenting to Susa, "Every mother should have a home of her own, with a deed to it. She should have her own income. She could thus be independent and retain a degree of self-respect impossible where a wife is completely dependent on her husband. In a home owned by herself she can teach her children to better advantage. ... If I had my life to live over I should give each wife a home of her own."[17] In his will he would, in fact, provide a home for each wife. By the time of his death, Brigham had provided each of his wives a place to live.

Each of the wives took responsibility for her own living quarters. Lucy, for example, tidied up her own sitting room and bedroom and,

---

15. The Brigham Young complex played an important role in both civic and religious affairs of Utah Territory.

16. Whitley, 138.

17. Gates, "How Brigham Young," 31. This was the second of a two-part series Susa wrote in 1925 for *Physical Culture*, a magazine published between 1899 and 1955 on health and fitness. The first part was entitled "A Physical Culture Race."

in addition, the prayer room. Because of her interests and talents, she also milked the family's eleven cows. "All the wives had equal rights and privileges and each was, in turn, expected to do her share in keeping the establishment running smoothly. Each wife took care of her own apartment and her own children and assisted in doing other necessary work around the place. Those who had no children … naturally took a heavier part in the running of the entire establishment."[18] "Aunt Twiss"—Naamah Kendel Jenkins Carter Young—with her staff, had charge of the kitchen, feeding up to eighty people at a meal, including family, workers, extended guests, and drop-ins.

The wives were fortunate in that Brigham believed firmly in "conservation of time and energy," filling his homes with a multiplicity of labor-saving devices. Inhabitants of the Lion House had access to a sewing machine, knitting machines, and "built-in cupboards, sinks, drains, stationary washtubs, stationary wash-boilers, outside garbage barrels, and chairs specially constructed to fit the needs of women and children."[19] Susa later wrote that "every new machine, domestic gadget, however expensive or cheap it might be, father bought some and his wives benefited by his thoughtful care."[20]

Their roles in the household led to the wives acquiring nicknames: Clara Decker, who had been with Brigham in the first party to enter Salt Lake Valley on July 24, 1847, was called "the pioneer wife"; Mary Ann Angell, "Mother Young," because of her seniority among the wives; Eliza R. Snow, "the Presidentess," due to her spiritual ascendancy in the family; Zina D. Huntington, "the Doctor," in acknowledgment of her medical skills; Harriet Cook, "the school teacher," because of her background in education; and both Emmeline Free and Amelia Folsom, "the favorite wife," the former because she bore Brigham more children than any other wife, the latter because in his later years she became the aging Brigham's youthful, beautiful, ever-present companion and nurse.

Prayer time, although variable, usually occurred about 7:00 p.m. Brigham would ring the prayer bell, and sickness, generally, was the only acceptable excuse for absence. It was said he had a unique way of

18. Spencer and Harmer, *Brigham Young at Home*, 65.
19. Gates, "How Brigham Young," 31.
20. Gates, "Lucy Bigelow Young," 68.

sounding the prayer bell that no one else in the family could duplicate. Years later in St. George, he commented to Susa: "Were it possible for me to suddenly step into my home in Salt Lake City to-night and ring the prayer-bell, every one in the Lion House would know I was at home without any announcement of my arrival."[21] Brigham usually offered the prayer, described as "short, simple, earnest."[22] Occasionally, however, particularly if a young man were visiting one of the Young daughters, he might be asked to act as voice for the family. After prayers there would be a brief evening devotional, with Brigham frequently commenting on current events.

Sleep too was closely supervised. Lights were out by 10:00 p.m. Brigham loved "fresh air, sunlight, and beauty."[23] All the buildings he was associated with had an abundance of windows, and everyone in the household had the windows open in both summer and winter. There were fireplaces in all living rooms and some bedrooms. Brigham was cautious about fire and would make nightly room checks to be sure there were no live coals. The outer gates to the Lion House were locked by 10:00 p.m. Anybody entering the premises after that hour would have to pass by the guard, who took careful watch and had a close reporting system with Brigham.

The family was up by 7:00 or 7:30 a.m. Breakfast was served at 8:00 a.m. in summer and 8:30 in winter. The usual fare was eggs, toast, milk, and fruit (in season), with potatoes or squash in the winter. Occasionally there were buckwheat cakes. Dinner, the main meal of the day, was served at 12:30 p.m. and included meat (beef, mutton, chicken, or fish, but never pork) and, when available, "venison, bear steak, or wild fowl."[24] Pie was favored by the children. Because of its relative scarcity, it often became a "medium of exchange." Supper was served at 5:00 p.m., usually consisting of mush and milk with bread, cheese, and fresh or preserved fruit.[25]

According to Susa, the family was "largely free from the white [refined] sugar curse," with sweetening generally derived from molasses,

---

21. Gates, "Family Life among the Mormons," 341.
22. Gates, 342.
23. Spencer and Harmer, *Brigham Young at Home*, 56.
24. Gates, "How Brigham Young," 140.
25. Gates.

brown sugar, and maple syrup.[26] However, a great favorite of the children was doughnuts made by a young Native American girl named Sally and called "Indian Sally" by the Young family. She had been saved from death by Paiute Indians and adopted into the Young household.[27] Meals were always announced with a five-minute warning bell. "The penalty for not arriving at the table on time was that you didn't get your meal."[28]

Both Susa and Clarissa Young Spencer, the other child of Brigham Young who left a published account of the Youngs' private life, remembered it as more or less idyllic.[29] Susa asserted, "Our home life was the very happiest domestic drama ever enacted. There wasn't one unhappy or neglected child among us, and we began our earthly career in an ideal environment."[30] Half-sister Clarissa agreed: "Undoubtedly at times there were small frictions and jealousies, but they very seldom showed on the surface, and our home was as peaceful and serene as any home could be."[31] Susa affirmed, "Be sure, these young wives were all of them too busy to bother much with the vices of jealousy and suspicion which are the usual outgrowths of idleness and luxury."[32] According to Susa, her father's treatment of his wives and their treatment of each other were beyond reproach. She recalled, "I never heard a quarrel between my father's wives; I never heard one wife correct another wife's child. Much less did I ever hear or see anything but the utmost courtesy and kindliness between my father and his wives. Correct his children he did, but ever with that dignity and deliberation that neither humiliated the child nor lowered his own self-respect."[33]

Despite Susa and Clarissa's rhapsodic portrayal, surely there were some flaws in this familial bliss. Indeed, in her unpublished memoirs

26. Gates, 141.

27. The story of "Indian Sally" is both interesting and tragic. See Turner, *Brigham Young*, 215–17, and Mueller, *Race and the Making of the Mormon People*, 186–88. Later in life she married Chief Kanosh.

28. Gates, "How Brigham Young," 140.

29. Spencer and Harmer, *Brigham Young at Home*.

30. Susa Young Gates, "My Father's 46 Children," box 1, fd. 5, SYGP (USDH).

31. Spencer and Harmer, *Brigham Young at Home*, 64.

32. Gates, *Lucy Bigelow Young*, 35.

33. Gates, "Brigham Young and His Family," undated typescript in box 12, fd. 3, SYGP (USDH).

Susa made revealing comments about some of her "aunts" that are enlightening, not infrequently entertaining, and often at variance with public perceptions. "I do not say that even I, as a child love all my fathers wives alike," she admitted. "Some of them were queer even sarchastic and a few of them I had only respect for."[34] For example, Susa commented, Mother Young (Mary Ann Angell) was "courteous to us all but she did not encourage us to tramp on her spacious lawns nor to make freely in her sitting rooms. ... There was an invisible line that we children rarely crossed." Perhaps it was to protect herself from the raucous noise of a huge family that Mother Young sequestered her own family away in the White House.[35] Susa also observed that Lucy Decker Young, hostess of the Beehive House, although an "excellent housekeeper and an accomplished cook ... was sometimes very sharp tongued if tired or bothered."[36] Lucy Decker kept her distance, and children "had to have a very good excuse before you invaded the sanctuary of repose over which ... [she] watched."[37]

Harriet Cook came under Susa's particular opprobrium. Harriet was "some grenadier of a woman ... with a tongue as sharp as a razor," her mind "a little uncertain and wobbly ... Aunt Harriet was the one great terror of our young lives. ... Her wit was ... bitting as an acid on steel." In Susa's memory, Harriet Cook prided herself on a "terrible frankness," sometimes wounding her sister wives quite cruelly. Although not physically abusive to children other than her own Oscar (ten years older than Susa), she often "made fun of us," which in Susa's eyes was sometimes worse.[38] "She loved to startle and shock people with rough words and vulgar references." Harriet once instructed workers to paint her room in the Lion House "in a color between piss-brindle and shit-brown." Hearing this, Brigham Young told the painters to follow her directions. According to Susa, Harriet ended up with the ugliest room in the house.[39]

Susa's private recollections extended to Susan Snively Young, "a

---

34. Gates, "My Recollections," undated typescript in box 12, fd. 3, SYGP (USDH).

35. Gates, "Brigham Young and his Nineteen Wives," undated typescript in box 12, fd. 2, SYGP (USDH).

36. Gates, "My Recollections."

37. Gates, "Nineteen Wives."

38. Gates.

39. Gates, "My Recollections."

worker and a good manager." Susan Snively, while "not outwardly aggressive," was a "whiner,"[40] got whatever she went after, and "even Aunt Harriet Cook rarely risked an encounter with her."[41] Susan, Susa said, "could extract more things out of father through complaint than Aunt Clara could through her sweet tact."[42] Susa portrayed Emmeline Free Young as "handsome" and having "a commanding presence," but said she also had "some what of a selfish vain temprament." Emmeline "breezed her way across our domestic horizon never, never quite submissive to fathers counsel, never quite fair to the other women, but always so charmingly subtle about her favors and or appearance that she won out by reason of her superior finesse." Aunt Emmeline became addicted later in her life to morphine, which Susa ascribes to her not following her husband's counsel.[43]

In Susa's memory, even Aunt Amelia Folsom Young, whose name eight-year-old Susa had adopted as her own middle name, had her flaws. Despite a "refined and loyal presence" and "being cheerful and bright company," she "had very little religion about her." Aunt Eliza Burgess, who would later move to St. George at the same time as Susa's mother, was "of excellent qualities and housewifely arts," but had a "sharp tongue" and "just enough faith in the Gospel to keep her feet on the right path." Susa remembered Eliza Burgess's one son, Alfales, as the "unkindest brother" in the family.[44]

Susa reserved her most vitriolic comments for Aunt Ann Eliza Webb Young who, Susa claimed, had hectored Brigham into marrying her. Eliza Webb divorced Brigham in a very public, scandalous, embarrassing legal proceeding and then attempted to support herself later in life by mounting a national lecture tour that, in Susa's eyes, "commercialize[d] her soul," and "gave garbled and lurid accounts of life in ... dear Father's family." Susa felt the family was partially vindicated when Eliza eventually "died in great distress, poverty and obscurity."[45]

---

40. Gates.
41. Gates, "Nineteen Wives.
42. Gates, "Recollections."
43. Gates.
44. Gates.
45. Gates. While Ann Eliza may not have been destitute at the time of her death in 1917, she was, in fact, estranged from her two sons by her first marriage and had long since divorced her third husband.

With these private musings, Susa admitted to "telling tales out of school," but she warned that "if any body suspect that human nature wasn't human nature in the Lion House as well as outside of it he is very much mistaken." Still, she could not recall any open ruptures in the family beyond Eliza Webb. Once, in exasperation at the behavior of some family members—wives and children—Brigham Young "wondered, he said, if he would have to go into the Kingdom of Heaven, wifeless and childless."[46]

Susa naturally had her favorites among the wives. Of course, her mother was in the favored group, which also included Eliza R. Snow, Zina Huntington, and Clara Decker, the latter described as a friend to "every chick and child in the house." Eliza, Zina, and Susa's mother, Lucy Bigelow, were the "spiritual props and guides," while Clara, who loaned Susa books from her "private library," was "our social mentor." As noted, Clara had a gift of wheedling from Brigham Young almost anything she wanted, an ability she also used in behalf of the children. She "was as efficient as most any guardian angel in getting prayers answered."[47]

Susa's infancy might have been one of luxury if not for a series of natural disasters around the period of her birth. In 1855 grasshoppers destroyed a good portion of area crops, causing food shortages here and there across the territory. The winter that followed was unusually mild, providing less than normal snow melt and canyon runoff. This unseasonable warmth meant "many seeds did not germinate; those that did were stunted in their growth."[48] A good percentage of surviving seedlings were either mowed down by an April 1856 grasshopper infestation or burned up in the hot, dry summer made worse by the scarcity of irrigation water. Finally, before the year's grain could be brought in, a third grasshopper plague—one that would prove to be the worst of the century—destroyed between two-thirds and four-fifths (depending on where one lived) of the already-reduced harvest.[49]

One can imagine Lucy Bigelow, a month after giving birth to Susa,

---

46. Gates.

47. Gates, "Nineteen Wives."

48. Carter, "Fish and the Famine," 96.

49. Bitton and Wilcox, "Pestiferous Ironclads," 336–55.

out in the Young orchards with her sister-wives, wielding rags and pieces of brush to knock the grasshoppers out of the trees into waiting bushel baskets, then driving the remainder into ditches to be burned. Perhaps the women followed a *Deseret News* recommendation to re-plant the decimated summer vegetables with potatoes and peas "since the insects seemed to bother them less than other crops."[50]

This infestation was much worse than the memorable one of 1848. Despite desperate efforts, Heber C. Kimball, Brigham's counselor in the First Presidency, reported from a tour of the settlements, "There is not fifty acres now standing of any kind of grain in Salt Lake Valley, and what is now standing, [the grasshoppers] are cutting it down as fast as possible." Things in other parts of the state were no better. "In Utah county the fields are pretty much desolate; in Juab Valley not a green spear of grain is to be seen, nor in Sanpete, nor in Fillmore."[51] A great many Salt Lake City gardens were ruined, Kimball continued. This included some 500,000 apple saplings only just planted by professional gardener William C. Staines, who kept his orchards and gardens a few blocks west of the Lion House.[52]

With spring providing too little grass and autumn too little feed grain, the settlements lost between 50 and 80 percent of their cattle. The result was predictable: many families reported insufficient flour and meat to last the coming winter and some no more than a month's supply. Utah was in a state of famine. The year 1856 would come to stand out as a year of crippling loss.

Brigham Young and other church officials responded by impos-ing rations of a half-pound of breadstuffs per household per day, with any surplus to be turned over to the church for distribution to the season's immigrants and the poor. Undoubtedly, the residents of the Lion House, more affluent than some of their neighbors, wanted and were expected to share what they had with others.[53] Surely Brigham Young, like fathers throughout the kingdom, did all in his power to buffer his family from hunger. His family was privileged to draw supplies directly from the church stores. Yet the Youngs must

50. Carter, "Fish and the Famine," 97.
51. Bitton and Wilcox, "Pestiferous Ironclads," 342.
52. Bitton and Wilcox.
53. Arrington, *Great Basin Kingdom*, 534.

have felt keenly the plight of others. Regardless, if there was no fresh produce to be bought or charged, they too may have resorted to foraging in the foothills for sego lily bulbs and thistle roots and, as that supply dwindled, have fallen back on salt and potatoes.

The famine had more than physical consequences. Historians have speculated another of its repercussions was the Mormon Reformation of 1856–57.[54] Church leaders feared that members had become somewhat complacent in their religious lives. To inspire increased dedication to the faith, Brigham Young sent Jedediah M. Grant, a counselor in the First Presidency, to preach reform in northern Utah in a series of three-day, revival-style meetings. A few weeks before Susa's birth, Brigham himself stood in the old adobe tabernacle on Temple Square and preached a sermon "the like of which the saints had seldom heard," according to Apostle Wilford Woodruff.[55] It was no longer a day for "smooth, beautiful, sweet ... silk-velvet-lipped preaching," President Young said, but a time for "sermons like peals of thunder." The Saints had committed grievous sins.

Elder Grant followed President Young at the pulpit, proclaiming members of the church must confess their sins and reform their lives. Despite the rhetorical nature of the preaching, specially appointed "home missionaries" and ward teachers went house to house, catechizing individuals on twenty-seven points of conduct—"Have you committed murder? Have you committed adultery? Have you made use of property not your own," etc.—and following up by rebaptizing the members.[56] "For many Latter-day Saints, the Reformation was a period of spiritual rejuvenation. Attending meetings, paying tithing and other free-will offerings, and showing other outward indicators of renewal increased dramatically."[57]

Questions about polygamy were not in the questionnaire, so authorities separately addressed complacency over this requirement.

---

54. Among other scholars, Leonard Arrington writes that "there is a good case for the hypothesis that the Reformation itself was an outgrowth of the famine of 1855–1856," *Great Basin Kingdom*, 459n88.

55. Woodruff called it "one of the strongest addresses ... ever delivered to this Church," adding Brigham Young's "voice and words were like the thundering of Mount Sinai." Peterson, "Mormon Reformation," 62.

56. Peterson, 70.

57. Paul H. Peterson, "Reformation (LDS) of 1856–1857," in Ludlow, *Encyclopedia of Mormonism*, 3:1197.

The result was a 65 percent increase in plural marriages during the next two years.[58] Brigham himself took another wife on March 14, 1856, four days before Susa's birth. He married Harriet Barney, a twenty-six-year-old divorcee who had lost a baby daughter during the exodus from Illinois but now brought with her three surviving children ages five, three, and one. In 1862 Harriet would produce another son, Phineas, with Brigham.[59]

As for the city's ex-Mormons and "gentiles," who heard hard talk against themselves for allegedly violating women, drinking in the streets, and verbally abusing the locals and church authorities, Salt Lake City policeman Hosea Stout claimed, "The fire of the reformation is burning many out who flee from the Territory, afraid of their lives. ... The wicked flee when no one pursues, and so with an apostate Mormon; he always believes his life is in danger and flees accordingly."[60]

Military historian Robert Coakley noted specific incidents of intimidation of several of the more disreputable federal government appointees who had earned themselves hostility among Utah's citizenry through behavior that was less than circumspect.[61] However, the key words in Stout's recollection are "when no one pursues"— most gentiles and "apostates" knew their lives were in no actual danger, and relatively few fled the territory.

This reform movement did have a winnowing effect, with some church members and non-members alike choosing to exit the territory. But some of the fierceness went out of the Reformation after Jedediah Grant's death in December 1856. By then, other Saints had wearied of overwrought religion, apparently among them Jacob

---

58. "The number of plural marriages in relation to population was 65 percent higher in 1856–57 than in any other two-year period in Utah history." Ivins, "Notes on Mormon Polygamy," 231. Ivins attributed this burst of plural marriages to the religious reformation of 1856.

59. Harriet Barney Young Death Certificate, "Utah State Archives Indexes," Series 81448, Department of Health, Office of Vital Records and Statistics, Utah State Archives, Salt Lake City.

60. Peterson, "Reformation," in Ludlow, *Encyclopedia of Mormonism*, 3:1197.

61. Coakley, *Role of Federal Military*, 196. Coakley referred specifically to "the profligate Judge W. W. Drummond, who brought a Washington prostitute along with him as consort" and earned considerable hostility from locals for attempting to take over the probate courts.

Gates, father of Susa's future husband. Gates had served several church missions and would go on to serve several more, mostly to England, where he was a mission and emigration leader. In 1862 Brigham would appoint him to the First Council of Seventies. But in May 1857, Gates, clearly cautious of fanaticism but just as clearly a diplomat, said from the pulpit he was sorry some preachers had not followed the example of church leaders by being "more merciful and kind to the human family. I tell you, we should learn to deal with people with a gentle hand whom we know to be tender, such as new converts to the faith that they may have time to learn and grow strong in the knowledge of God."[62]

After suffering through the famine and the reformation, there was a third public trauma marking Susa's infancy: the Utah War. One-fifth of the armed forces of the United States would invade Utah territory on allegations of rampant insurrection on the part of the Mormons.[63] After the formation of the Territory of Utah in 1850, government officials tended to be federal appointees, many of them new to Utah and not LDS. President James Buchanan, upon taking office one year after Susa's birth, immediately began to hear complaints from former Utah appointees of Mormon disrespect, even rebellion, against the United States government.

A charge Buchanan frequently heard was that too much power resided in the hands of a single man, Brigham Young, who kept a tight rein on both territorial and ecclesiastical matters. Buchanan decided to replace Young as governor of Utah with a Georgian named Alfred Cumming. Buchanan, just in case the Mormons should, in fact, be in outright rebellion, ordered General William S. Harney, later replaced by future Confederate general Albert S. Johnston, to escort Cumming to Utah to ensure his safety. Because of "muddled" planning, Johnston's army was slow to assemble but eventually numbered 2,500 soldiers. This so-called Utah Expedition started west in July 1857.[64]

On July 24, several thousand Saints had gathered in Big Cottonwood Canyon near Salt Lake City to celebrate the tenth anniversary

---

62. Jacob Gates, "Discourse," *Deseret News*, May 27, 1857, 3.

63. For more on the Utah War, see MacKinnon, *At Sword's Point*.

64. Coakley, *Role of Federal Military*, 196–200.

of the Mormons' settlement of the valley. The merriment was abruptly shattered by the arrival of Salt Lake City Mayor Abraham O. Smoot, who had learned of Buchanan's plans when he went to pick up the westbound mail in Independence, Missouri. There he had been informed the government had terminated the mail service contracted out to the Brigham Young Express and Carrying Company, for which Smoot worked. Smoot had been able to glean details about the army contingent then still mustering. Whether Lucy, Dora, and baby Susa attended the Big Cottonwood celebration is unknown, but it is likely they were there.

Brigham resolved that neither Colonel Johnston's soldiers nor Governor Cumming would enter the valley that fall or winter. The Saints felt that they had endured enough government persecution in their brief history, and they would protect themselves. Young deployed guerrilla fighters to sabotage the army's supply wagons plodding their way through the Wyoming region. Army livestock were stampeded, and, from small fortresses hastily erected in the canyons east of the valley, rocks were fashioned to shower down upon unsuspecting troops. These strategies succeeded so well that Cumming and the army were forced to winter at Fort Bridger, approximately 115 miles from Salt Lake City.

In April 1858, when it became apparent troops would indeed enter the valley, Brigham ordered a "scorched earth policy." All but a skeleton contingent of Salt Lake City residents prepared to leave their homes and relocate to points south. Homes and buildings were readied for burning, if necessary, and the foundation of the Salt Lake temple, which had been under construction for four years, was covered with dirt. The plan was for the army to be unable to sustain itself in the valley.

When Brigham announced the "move south," Lucy, with her two daughters, "was the first one of the wives ready."[65] With sister-wife Aunt Zina, who had an eight-year-old daughter as well as two sons from a previous marriage, Lucy traveled forty-five miles to Provo in Utah Valley. However, there they found every house and barn already occupied by some 30,000 other evacuees. With the

---

65. Gates, "Lucy Bigelow Young," 45.

help of a local ward bishop, Lucy and Zina were able to clean out what they believed was a bear cave, where they stayed temporarily. In her biography of her mother, Susa wrote, "It was not long before father came down and with all his family leaving the Lion House boarded up. He himself built a long, many-roomed lumber, shanty row, where his dear wives gathered in and made themselves cosy and comfortable."[66]

Lucy, Zina, and their children returned to Salt Lake that fall. When it became apparent that the Mormons were not in a state of rebellion, the Utah War ended without a single battle. Peaceful negotiations ensued, and in late-spring Alfred Cumming became the second governor of Utah territory. He served four years, earning the esteem of his constituents.[67]

A half-year later, in the spring of 1859, Lucy returned to Provo to stay in the home of one of her brothers. She had suffered "birth-mishaps" and needed a respite from household and child-care responsibilities. Susa, three years old by now, and Dora, nearly seven, remained in Salt Lake in the hands of their "aunts."[68] During her teen and young adult years, Susa might chafe under her father's strict governance. However, in middle age she looked back on the Lion House as "the loved home of as healthy and happy a family of women and men as ever lived under one roof. In all my life in that home," she claimed, "I never heard my father speak an unkind or irritable word to one of his wives; nor did I ever hear a quarrel between the wives. They were ladies. All but one of them were of New England parentage, and they possessed that training of restraint, mingled with a strong religious impulse, which is so much a part of the Puritan inheritance. ... We were not a contentious family and my father's spirit and example reached us all."[69]

---

66. Gates, 47.

67. Elizabeth Randall Cumming, accompanying her husband to become Utah's new First Lady, found that, in the light of firsthand observation, she had to abandon preconceptions she had formed about the overland trek and the Mormons through reading the popular press. She left a sympathetic account of her Utah experience in letters to Boston family members. See Beeton and Canning, *Genteel Gentile.*

68. Gates, "Lucy Bigelow Young," 49. In the Young household, children referred to their mothers' sister-wives as "aunts."

69. Gates, "How Brigham Young," 138. The Young family's Puritan New England background would become one of Susa's common themes as an adult.

More than once Susa called attention to her parents' New England heritage. In her day, the Puritans had not yet come to be associated with unhealthy repression and inhibition. Thus, although relations between her father's wives did sometimes grow strained, and Aunt Zina might have felt it wise to gather them into her sitting room to sing hymns and pray until peaceful feeling once again prevailed, Susa did not see this as suppression of natural feeling so much as schooling it. Prayer was the women's means of re-centering and refocusing on priorities. And perhaps it enabled them to fall back on the self-restraint, strong-mindedness, and persistence one has come to associate with the Puritans and the Mormon pioneers.

2
New England Grit

The consuming occupation of the last quarter of Susa Young Gates's life—even eclipsing her biography of her father—was genealogical research and temple work for her ancestors. Typically, for Susa, she made sure this personal absorption touched the church at large, benefiting peers and subsequent generations of genealogists alike through her campaigns for better order and collaboration in the collection of ancestral records and more systematic recording and sharing of rites performed for the salvation of the dead in all LDS temples.[1]

Susa was acutely cognizant of her parents' New England heritage. She grew up with stories told by her mother and an assortment of aunts, uncles, and cousins, as well as those told from the pulpit by her father. Susa referenced her Puritan roots not only in her biography of Brigham Young but in unpublished recollections of her mother and the Young and Bigelow families, as well as in various essays and articles.

But this heritage was equally Susa's own. Perhaps she alluded to it as a way of establishing her bona fides and obtaining common ground with women's rights associates from back East. But what, precisely, were those bona fides? What did she write of Puritan New England values? More importantly, how did she perceive those values to have influenced the evolution of the Young family in the American West?

---

1. For more, see chapter 17, herein.

THE YOUNG FAMILY

Susa's first definitive ancestor in America was her great-great-grand-father, William Young (ca. 1698–1747). William was born in Boston, Massachusetts; his father may have been the Boston glazier of the same name. William himself started life as an apprentice cordwainer (shoemaker) and ended up, according to Susa, "not a poor man, nor one without friends and influence."[2] Town records show William Young, Cordwainer, was appointed to a succession of positions of public trust, including scavenger (street commissioner), sealer of leather (supervisor of the tanning industry), hog reeve (constable assigned to prevent and appraise damages by stray swine—a frequent problem in English and New English villages), and clerk of the market (controller of weights, measures, and market prices). He married his master's daughter, Martha Emmons, in 1717 and for several years worshipped with her as respectable members of the Old South Church.

William's shoemaking was interrupted by service in at least one of the many native Indian skirmishes marking his century, where he emerged "with a record of faithfulness and bravery."[3] At about the same time, in 1720 or 1721, all references to Martha Emmons Young end, suggesting that she had died, possibly in childbirth. William, wifeless and childless, moved to New Hampshire where he met Susannah Cotton and married her in the North Church in the nearby town of Portsmouth. They had two children, Elizabeth (1723–87) and Joseph (1729–63), before Susannah's untimely death in 1730. William married a third time and continued to prosper. At his death in 1747, William left an estate of about $10,000, perhaps more than $400,000 in today's dollar value. It was a significant enough sum that his death apparently spurred a years-long quarrel over it among some of his surviving relatives.[4]

Thus, Puritan ethics were already personified in Susa's first known New England ancestor. William Young was apparently god-fearing (as evidenced by his church memberships and the pious preface to his will); public spirited (demonstrated in the roster of his service to the community); faithful and brave in patriotism; equally brave

---

2. Gates, "Young Family," 66–70.
3. Sessions, *Latter-day Patriots*, 25.
4. Gates, "Young Family," 68–69.

and resourceful in colonizing; a mixture of prudent, ambitious, and successful as a landowner; and tender hearted as a spouse, father, friend, and modest benefactor of the town's widows (intimated by the will's careful provision and diction). William was, in other words, the seeming prototype of his great-grandson Brigham Young—and, Susa no doubt wished it to be noted, his great-great-granddaughter.

William's son Joseph Young (1729–69) was, like his father, born in Boston and, unlike his father, lived a short, tragic life. Indeed, for three generations, until Brigham himself amassed great wealth in Salt Lake City, the Young family endured crippling poverty. Joseph was a year old when his mother died and yet a teenager at his father's death. Perhaps he had worried his parents, for in the will William put his son "under the care, direction, government, and discretion of the Rev. Samuel Barrett … till he come of age."[5] Four years passed and, at age twenty-one, Joseph came into his inheritance and was able to undertake an apprenticeship in medicine. With no medical school yet existing in the Colonies, he must have studied and observed under a local physician for the customary term of three years. Perhaps it was during this period—being "Furnish'd … with plenty of money"[6]—that he took to serious gambling and alcohol. These activities did not, apparently, interfere with the completion of his studies. Just as he would have been setting up his practice in Hopkinton while farming on the side, the French and Indian War broke out. Joseph enlisted in the British–American army and in his twenty-eighth year barely survived the 1757 siege of Fort William Henry. His work as an army surgeon could not have been pretty and may have been so traumatic as to contribute to his later troubles, for it involved the treatment of wounds, amputations, and extraction of arrows and bullets.[7] A fair number of his patients must have survived, for he "began to get a great name."[8]

---

5. Gates.

6. "Fanny Young Carr Murray Letter" Jan. 1, 1845, online transcript at young. parkinsonfamily.org, accessed Feb. 1, 2020. Family historian Ben Parkinson notes that "LDS Archives has an earlier transcript [of the letter], which appears to be the basis of a third, partial transcript. … This transcript corrects numerous small errors in both." Fanny was Brigham's third oldest sister. She died in Salt Lake City in 1859.

7. Sessions, *Latter-day Patriots*, 24.

8. "Fanny Murray Letter," 2.

After war service, Joseph Young resumed his practice back in Hopkinton. While paying a house call to John Hayden, a man with advanced cancer, he met Hayden's daughter, Elizabeth "Betsy" Hayden (Treadway) (1728–1810). Betsy was a widow with four children; in 1759 she married Joseph, and they went on to produce six children of their own. The third child was John, father of Brigham Young.

Unfortunately, Joseph's gambling and drinking caught up with him. He squandered his inheritance and likely was under the influence when he died in an accident at the age of forty. Brigham Young said his grandfather was killed "by the fall of a pole from a fence."[9] Brigham's brother Phineas claimed Joseph was killed by a falling tree. Either way, their older sister Fanny wrote in 1845 that their grandfather went missing after leaving the local tavern and the next morning was found by a neighbor dead "at the far side of a field not far from their home."[10] Joseph had outstanding debts, and Betsy's "farm was sold; and every article which the law would allow, was taken from her." Following common practice at the time, "the select men of the Town found places for most of her children, and bound them out."[11]

John Young (1763–1839), Susa Young Gates's grandfather, no more than seven or eight years old, was placed in the home of Colonel John Jones, a wealthy Hopkinton landowner whose wife disliked the boy and, following Bible instruction, frequently had him flogged. Young John seems to have withstood this treatment for nearly ten years before escaping to the relative amiability of soldiering. He completed three enlistments in the Revolutionary War, serving in Massachusetts and New Jersey, though the dates of his military service are somewhat sketchy.[12] When in 1832 he appeared before the court of Monroe County, New York, to apply for a pension as a Revolutionary War hero, he certified that he had enlisted, first, in June 1780 (when he was seventeen) for a period of six months; second, in August 1781 for three months; and third, in March 1782 for six weeks.[13]

John was described as short, "nimble, wiry,"[14] an unimpressive

9. Gates, "Notes on Young and Howe Families," 180–81.
10. "Fanny Murray Letter," 6.
11. "Murray Letter."
12. Sessions, *Latter-day Patriots*, 25.
13. Cannon, "Pension Office Note," 83–84.
14. Arrington, *Brigham Young*, 8.

young man yet confident enough to woo and eventually win the hand of Abigail "Nabby" Howe (1765–1815) of Hopkinton. Nabby's father, Phineas Howe (1735–1817), came from a substantial New England family that counted among its members Elias Howe Jr., inventor of the sewing machine, and Samuel Gridley Howe, prominent social reformer and husband of Julia Ward Howe, author of "The Battle Hymn of the Republic." Phineas was active in community affairs and had signed, along with other Hopkinton town fathers, a letter to the Continental Congress.[15] Nabby's mother, Susanna Goddard Howe (1742–1837), was the daughter of Ebenezar Goddard (1713/14–1762), "sherriff of the County, a man much respected and beloved of his upright conduct, and benevolent principles and disposition,"[16] and Ebenezar's wife, Sybil Brigham, from whom Brigham Young received his first name.

Nabby was one of five Howe sisters born between 1762 and 1770. People spoke of them as musically talented, charming, kind, and attractive. Eventually four brothers and two younger sisters joined them. Nabby was pretty, vivacious, and popular, with blue eyes and "yellowish brown hair, folded in natural waves and ringlets across her shapely brow."[17]

Nabby's parents saw that their eleven children were christened at Christ Church (Congregational) in Hopkinton and sent to "subscription school, singing school, and church socials." Nabby's mother seems to have been the more religious of the couple; she interpreted the Bible literally, whereas Phineas was somewhat more skeptical in both political and ecclesiastical matters.[18]

Nabby had a mind of her own, for against her parents' wishes she married at age twenty "the little orphan," John Young.[19] After their marriage they remained in Hopkinton, where two daughters were born, Nancy (1786–1860) and Fanny (1787–1859). Early on, they converted to Methodism from the Congregationalist background of virtually all their ancestors. Also from the start, John and Nabby

---

15. Arrington, Madsen, and Jones, *Mothers of the Prophets*, 30.
16. "Fanny Murray Letter," 14.
17. Susan Evans McCloud, "Nabby Howe Young," *Mormon Times*, July 16, 2011, 5.
18. Arrington, Madsen, and Jones, *Mothers of the Prophets*, 31.
19. Arrington, *Brigham Young*, 8.

Young led a hardscrabble existence that persisted throughout their lives, John barely eking out a living from the soil.

In 1787 the family moved 130 miles west to the Platauva District near present-day Durham, New York, in an attempt to own land, establish their independence, and improve their fortunes. Their third daughter, Rhoda (1789–1841), was born during this brief stay in New York. John Young's children, grandchildren, and clear down to great-grandson Franklin W. Young liked to tell a story that occurred just before Rhoda's birth and serves to reveal John's pluck and ingenuity:

> One Sunday [John] was walking in the woods with one of his very few neighbors, when his faithful dogs began barking not far distant, and on going toward the sound they found the dogs had "treed" a very large black bear. He tried in vain to get his neighbor to stay and keep the bear up the tree, whilst he, being more active than his neighbor, would run home for his gun. Neighbor did not care to stay with the bear, but would go for the gun. Accordingly, Mr. Young remained. Though of what he should do if Mr. Bruin should take a notion to come down occurred to him; so he cut a hickory sapling and sharpened one end to probe bruin with should he attempt a descent before the arrival of the gun. And sure enough, down came the bear. All the probing with the hickory stick was of no avail. Bruin let all holds loosed, and down he fell to the ground; he lit upon his feet, but broke down, and the dog caught him by the end of the nose, causing him to open his mouth, when Mr. Young pushed his sharp stick down his throat, killing him almost instantly. The neighbor went leisurely home, ate his dinner, and then returned with a gun. To his great surprise he found the bear nicely dressed and ready for roasting.[20]

Bear slayer or not, John could not please his father-in-law. John thought he was doing well in New York: "everything he put his hand to, prosper'd—he had got in a good crop of wheat, they had a good cow, and two heifers that would come in the next year; a good yoke of young Cattle, and provisions for the winter."[21] But Phineas never particularly approved of John, and he missed his daughter Nabby. Shortly after Rhoda's birth, when there was adequate snow on the ground, he sent two sleighs to bring the family back to Hopkinton. Perhaps he wanted Nabby closer to decent medical care for her

---

20. Susa also recounted this tale in "Notes on Young and Howe Families," 180–81.
21. "Fanny Murray Letter," 43.

consumption (tuberculosis); perhaps this latest pregnancy had aggravated her illness. Regardless, Phineas Howe seemed to think it his prerogative to recall his daughter's family to the relative luxury of Hopkinton. Fanny recalled, "I have heard my Father [John] say, he never saw so unhappy a night, before, in his life, as the one after these men arriv'd to carry them back to their native place."[22]

Their brief stint in New York state was probably as close to self-sufficiency as the family would ever get. They remained in Hopkinton until the beginning of 1801. During this period five additional children were born: John Jr. (1791–1870), Nabby (1793–1807), Susannah (1795–1852), Joseph (1797–1881), and Phineas Howe (1799–1879). Finally, after eleven or so years, John determined to make another effort at independence, this time in southern Vermont, where Brigham (1801–77) was born. But the Vermont soil proved rocky and uninviting, and three years later they relocated again, to Sherburne, New York, where their tenth and eleventh children were born, Louisa (1804–33) and Lorenzo Dow (1807–95).

Wherever they stopped—Massachusetts, Vermont, or New York—John was a strict disciplinarian. Brigham would say of his father, "With [him] it was a word and a blow, but the blow came first."[23] Nabby was the gentling influence in the family, acting as an emotional lightning rod for John's sternness with the children. However, both parents held to a rigid code of frontier Methodism; Brigham described his parents as "some of the most strict religionists that lived upon the earth." He was taught that if he found a pin in the road, his clear duty was to find its owner. "When I was young, I was kept within very strict bounds, and was not allowed to walk more than half an hour on Sunday for exercise."[24] About his mother he said, "Would she countenance one of her children in the least act that was wrong, according to her traditions? No, not in the least degree."[25] Amusements such as dancing, listening to the fiddle, and novel reading were forbidden. Historian Leonard Arrington asserted that "the only improvement of the mind [in the Young family] came from reading the Bible."[26]

22. "Murray Letter."
23. *JD* 4:112.
24. *JD* 2:94.
25. *JD* 6:290.
26. Arrington, *Brigham Young*, 21.

Susa, studying her grandfather's family, might have concluded with historian John Turner that Brigham proved to be more Howe and Goddard in spirit than Young. Turner has observed, "Brigham's Goddard and Howe relatives bequeathed to their descendants a robust belief in supernatural phenomena."[27] But in another respect, too, her father aligned himself not with his parents' Methodism but with his maternal relatives somewhat less exacting Congregationalism:

> I had not a chance to dance when I was young, and never heard the enchanting tones of the violin, until I was eleven years of age; and then I thought I was on the high way to hell, if I suffered myself to linger and listen to it. I shall not subject my little children to such a course of … unnatural training, but they shall go to the dance, study music, read novels, and do anything else that will tend to expand their frames, add fire to their spirit, improve their minds, and make them free and untrammeled in body and mind.[28]

John and Nabby Young followed a brand of Methodism.

Through the rigors of life on the frontier and his family's poverty, Brigham Young became self-sufficient at a young age. He helped with clearing land and planting, cultivating, and harvesting crops; trapping for fur; fishing; building sheds and cellars; and caring for his mother, who was an invalid for several years before her death from tuberculosis in 1815 at age forty-nine. The five older siblings—Nancy, Fanny, Rhoda, John Jr., and Susannah—were married by that time. Brigham's sister, also named Nabby, had died in 1807 of tuberculosis contracted from her mother. Brigham was fourteen years old when his mother died.[29]

Although not unexpected, the loss of Mother Nabby devastated the family members still at home. In later years Brigham spoke of her, "I can say, no better woman ever lived in the world than she was."[30] More than a hundred years after the fact, his talented daughter Susa wrote this encomium to the grandmother she never knew:

27. Turner, *Brigham Young*, 10. At the same time, both Brigham and Susa were cautious about relying too much on spiritual gifts such as dreams and speaking in tongues.
28. *JD* 2:94.
29. Leonard J. Arrington, "Brigham Young," in Ludlow, *Encyclopedia of Mormonism*, 4:1601.
30. *JD* 6:290.

Abigail Howe Young was a born reformer, so we are told. She was an invalid the last few years of her life, troubled with the frequent New England complaint of consumption [tuberculosis], but she kept an active finger on the pulse of the neighborhood. Her sympathies were so broad, her vision was so clear, her grasp of human values so perfect that friends would come for her when their children married and take her in wagon or sleigh to spend a few days in counsel and assistance to young couples who were starting out in life. She was greatly beloved by her associates. Her children are her noblest monument.[31]

After Nabby's death, the family never lived all together again. Brigham moved with his father and two older brothers, Joseph, eighteen, and Phineas, sixteen, to "Sugar Hill," located thirty-five miles west of Genoa. Lorenzo, eight, was sent to live with Rhoda and her husband, John P. Greene, and Louisa, eleven, also likely went to live with one of her sisters.

In 1817 Brigham's father remarried, to a widow named Hannah Brown; in 1823 they would have a son named Edward. About this time John informed Brigham, now sixteen, that it was time he provided for himself. So Brigham left for the nearby city of Auburn, New York, where he was apprenticed to John C. Jeffries to learn carpentry, painting, and glaziering. After three or four years, having become a "skilled artisan,"[32] he moved north to Buckville, now Port Byron, on the Erie Canal, where he painted and built boats.

During this time Brigham met Miriam Works, whom he married on October 5, 1824. He was twenty-three, she eighteen. For the next nine years they moved frequently, undoubtedly following job commissions. (All of these moves occurred within a roughly eighty-mile radius in the Finger Lakes district of northwestern New York.) Their first daughter, Elizabeth, was born on September 26, 1825, in Port Byron. After three years they relocated twenty-eight miles north to Oswego and, less than a year later, to Mendon, where seven of Brigham's siblings were living. His small family stayed briefly in his father's home while he built a house of their own on John's land. The Youngs persisted through grinding poverty. A second daughter, Vilate, was born on her father's birthday, June 1, 1830. Brigham

31. Susa Young Gates, "Abigail Howe," *Juvenile Instructor*, Jan. 1924, 5.
32. Whitley, *Brigham Young's Homes*, 38.

moved briefly some fifty miles east to a rural village near Canandaigua[33] but in 1832 returned to Mendon. There his wife, afflicted with the same disease that had felled his mother and his sister, died while living in the home of their close friends, Heber and Vilate Kimball.

By then Brigham, despite lacking a formal education, "had become an expert farmer, gardener, carpenter, glazier, mason, cabinetmaker, painter and boatbuilder."[34] He had also converted to Mormonism. In 1830 Samuel Smith, brother of Joseph and considered the church's first missionary, met Brigham's older brother Phineas while passing through Mendon. Phineas obtained a copy of the Book of Mormon, which had been published only the preceding month in Palmyra, a village twelve miles northeast of Mendon. Phineas intended to prove the book wrong but ended up feeling it represented truth. He passed the book to his father and then to his sister Fanny, who ultimately gave it to Brigham, who determined to make a careful study of it. Not until two years later was Brigham baptized into The Church of Christ, later The Church of Latter-day Saints, and, after 1838, The Church of Jesus Christ of Latter-day Saints.

All of Brigham's immediate family joined the church, including his father, John, stepmother, Hannah, and all nine siblings. In April 1832 John and Hannah were baptized along with six of John's children (Fanny, Rhoda, Joseph, Phineas, Brigham, and Lorenzo) and their spouses, except for older brother Joseph's. Later in 1832, Susannah and Louisa and their husbands joined the church, followed in 1833 by Nancy and her husband and, in October of that year, John Jr.[35] Surely this monumental shift by the entire family from orthodox Protestantism to "Mormonism" resulted in large part from the strict and earnest observance of biblical religion in John and Nabby Howe Young's home.

Once Brigham joined the church, he all but gave himself over to preaching the gospel taught by Joseph Smith and to establishing the "Kingdom of God." After Miriam's death, in the fall of 1832 he traveled with Heber Kimball to Kirtland, Ohio, where he met for the

---

33. Whitley.
34. Arrington, *Brigham Young*, 18.
35. Arrington, 20.

first time Joseph Smith, the Mormon prophet. By the next summer Brigham was living in Kirtland, where he met Mary Ann Angell of Seneca, New York. They were married on February 18, 1834.

In May and June 1834, Brigham participated in the Army of Israel or Zion's Camp, an ill-fated, 900-mile march under adverse conditions from Kirtland to Clay County, Missouri. Its purpose was to assist the Missouri militia in reinstating Mormon settlers on their lands in adjacent Jackson County, Missouri, from which they had been driven out the previous fall by non-Mormon elements. When Missouri's governor reneged on militia assistance, the goal turned to "rescuing Zion" by bringing money, supplies, and moral support to the destitute Missouri Saints.[36]

Although Zion's Camp did not recapture the Missouri Saints' lands, it demonstrated to Joseph Smith which of the 200 participants were proven trustworthy. In February 1835, nine of the original twelve apostles for the church were drawn from Zion's Camp participants. The Council of the Twelve was arranged in order of seniority by age, with Brigham third in line. The apostles' calling was to act as "traveling councilors ... or special witnesses of the name of Christ in all the world," equal in authority to and subject only to the presidency of the Church (D&C 107:23). For the next several years, Brigham balanced his church and family duties by traveling on preaching missions in the summer and caring for his family in Kirtland in the winter.

By the late 1830s he had moved his family to be with the Saints in Nauvoo, Illinois, the new Mormon settlement on the banks of the Mississippi River. Then Brigham and several other apostles were called to undertake a mission to Great Britain. Brigham was now the senior apostle. Despite being ill, he and Heber Kimball departed Nauvoo on September 14, 1839, leaving their families also ill and in dire straits for care and food. After several months of missionary work in the Eastern states, they sailed from New York City in March 1840 and arrived in Liverpool on April 6.

The mission to Great Britain brought a bounteous harvest for the troubled young church. By April 1841, when Brigham left Liverpool,

---

36. Lance D. Chase, "Zion's Camp," in Ludlow, *Encyclopedia of Mormonism*, 4:1627–29.

the Twelve had made between 7,000 and 8,000 converts, printed and distributed 5,000 copies of the Book of Mormon, and assisted 1,000 new Saints in emigrating to Nauvoo.[37]

In 1841, while the Twelve were still in Great Britain, Joseph Smith secretly introduced plural marriage to select church leaders in Nauvoo (it would not be taught publicly until 1852 in Salt Lake City). On Brigham's return from England, he was directed to take a plural wife; he did so on June 17, 1842, marrying twenty-year old Lucy Ann Decker. Before he went on to become the most famous polygamist in the world, he would recall his initial aversion to the doctrine in 1855 in an oft-quoted talk in Provo.[38] From Nauvoo Brigham resumed his practice of proselytizing summers and providing for his families over the winters.

Brigham was in Massachusetts during the summer of 1844 when, on June 27, Joseph Smith and his brother Hyrum were murdered in the Carthage, Illinois, jail. Brigham did not hear the news until July 16. He immediately started for Nauvoo, arriving August 6. Sidney Rigdon, first counselor to Joseph in the First Presidency before disaffecting over polygamy, also hurried back from Pittsburgh, where he had been living for several months. A "dramatic confrontation" occurred in a public meeting on August 8.[39]

At this meeting, Rigdon offered himself as "guardian of the Church."[40] Brigham, on the other hand, argued that "the keys of the Kingdom" had been given to and so rightly belonged with the Twelve Apostles. A majority of the church's members sustained the Twelve as their leaders, with Brigham Young at the head. A three-and-a-half-year interregnum began; the First Presidency was not reconstituted until December 1847. These three years brought escalating violence on the part of non-Mormon factions (along with, by some accounts, spotty retaliation by some victims) such that, ultimately, church and civil leaders alike concluded the only solution was for the Mormons to go elsewhere.

---

37. Arrington, "Brigham Young," 4:1604.
38. *JD* 3:266.
39. Arrington, "Brigham Young," 4:1604.
40. Bruce A. Van Orden, "Sidney Rigdon," in Ludlow, *Encyclopedia of Mormonism,* 3:1235.

THE BIGELOW FAMILY

Susa researched and wrote much of the available information regarding her ancestors, the Youngs, Howes, and Bigelows. Again, their old, proud, New England Puritan backgrounds appear to have been important to her. Given her later attachment to the Republican Party, the National and International Councils of Women, and the Daughters of the Revolution, Susa no doubt viewed New England as the cradle of the nation to which she was so devoted.

One family historian writes, "The immigrant ancestor of nearly all persons in North America bearing the surname Bigelow in any of its several variants, is John Biglo of Watertown, Massachusetts [a suburb of Boston]."[41] He was Susa's five-greats-grandfather. In a civil court case in Watertown, John Biglo (1617–1703) would aver that he was from Wrentham, England. Indeed, the rector of Wrentham parish in John's birth year was the same Rev. John Phillips who later immigrated to Dedham, Massachusetts, and testified that "the blacksmith John Biglo of Watertown, Massachusetts was the same infant whom he had baptized in 1617 as the son of Randall Beageley" and that he (Phillips) had "known John Biglo from earliest youth upward."[42]

John's marriage to Mary Warren on October 30, 1642, was the first union recorded in the Watertown public records. John and Mary proceeded to have thirteen children between 1643 and 1668, the last two dying in infancy. Meanwhile, John appeared again in the records after he agreed to donate ten trees to "the towne" so that he could "set up his trade" with a smith forge.[43] Biglo (the surname was spelled variously as Biglo, Bigelow, Biglow, Biggilo, and Biggalough) would be chosen surveyor of highways in 1652 and 1660, tax collector in 1663, and selectman (town councilman) in 1665, 1670, and 1671. John had served in the Pequot War of 1636, then in King Philip's War in 1675, when he was in his late fifties. His service as a militiaman no doubt contributed to his being named a freeman in 1690 at

41. Rod Bigelow, "Bigelow History," Bigelow Society Home Page, bigelowsociety. com, accessed Feb. 3, 2020.

42. Rod Bigelow, "John Biglo, Immigrant Ancestor," Bigelow Society Home Page, accessed Feb. 3, 2020.

43. Watertown town records, Mar. 4, 1651, qtd. in Rod Bigelow, "John Biglo."

age seventy-three. This meant he was no longer a "common" worker, indentured servant, or still indebted for his passage from England, but now a full citizen: he could attend and vote in the annual town meetings, act as an officially chartered member of the church, and own the prescribed amount of land for his number of dependents.

In 1694, after his first wife died, John married Sarah Bemis. They lived into their eighties, she surviving him. In his will John bequeathed to his widow 80£ and each of his children between 10–25£, for a total of 250£. He also left Sarah the land she had brought to the marriage, as well as to her and his children several hundred pounds in pork, barley, corn, butter, cheese, flax, and land parcels.[44]

Four generations of Bigelows "of old New England stock" succeeded John.[45] His sixth child, Joshua Bigelow (1655–1745), lived in Watertown most of his life, married Elizabeth Flagg, and had twelve children. Joshua was named an executor of his father's will. He too had fought in King Phillip's War and, for being wounded, was granted land in what is now Westminster, Massachusetts. Joshua outlived all his siblings except the youngest, Abigail.[46]

Joshua's namesake, Joshua Bigelow (1677–1728), also was born in and died in Watertown. At twenty-four, Joshua Jr. married Hannah Fiske; they lived four miles west of the town proper in a section set apart in 1713 under the name Weston. Joshua and Hannah had eight children. Two of their daughters married and settled in Mendon (Massachusetts, not New York), about twenty-eight miles southwest of Watertown.

Joshua Jr.'s sixth child was John Bigelow (1715–ca. 1787), again born in Weston (formerly Watertown). At twenty-four, this John married a county girl, Grace Allen of nearby Sudbury. They produced nine children, their last, Eunice, dying in infancy. Prosperity was never as obtainable for these subsequent generations of Puritans. Not only was good land and timber increasingly limited, but large family sizes led to smaller and smaller shares of inherited property and money. John, in other words, was born at the wrong time. He

44. Bigelow, "John Biglo." Other than Susa's research, virtually all we know about John Bigelow, his son Joshua, grandson Joshua, and great-grandson John derives from Rod Bigelow's research on the Bigelow Family Home Page.

45. Gates, "Lucy Bigelow Young," 1.

46. Rod Bigelow, "Simeon Bigelow," Bigelow Society Home Page, accessed Feb. 3, 2020.

was the first in his line to establish the habit of frequent moves—from Weston to Stow (further west of Grace's hometown, Sudbury) to Acton (eight miles north of Sudbury), then back to Weston. Despite John's service in 1757 under Captain Samuel Davis, presumably in the French and Indian War, in 1762 he, Grace, and their eight children were "warned out of town" by the Weston constable. Since the family did not actually leave, this suggests the warning was merely official notice that the family could not be "chargeable" to the town; that is, they were ineligible for public aid to the poor. Being warned out was not a terrible disgrace, but it was no honor, either.[47] At some point John and Grace did move again, this time thirty-five miles north to Ashburnham, on the border with New Hampshire. There, in her sixties, Grace died. Two years later John, together with his son Silas, Silas's wife, and ten grandchildren, moved across the border to New Ipswich, New Hampshire, where John died at an unknown date.

John's youngest son, Simeon, was Susa's great-grandfather. Simeon Bigelow (1752–1837) was born during the family's stay in Acton, and he did a modest amount of migrating himself—from Ashburnham to Conway, Massachusetts, and finally to Brandon, Vermont. Simeon married three times and was widowed twice. The wife of his youth was Sarah Foster, whom he wed in Ashburnham in 1780 and who gave him five children before her death in 1789. He married his second wife, Elizabeth Avery, in Brandon in 1790; she bore him eight additional children before she and their five-year-old daughter died from smallpox in 1804. Simeon lastly wed Sarah Bump Avery, also in Brandon. They were together from 1804 until his death at age eighty-five in 1837. Sarah applied for a pension based on her first husband's Revolutionary War service, although Simeon too had served briefly at Shelburne, Massachusetts.

Of Simeon's thirteen offspring, it was his third child and Susa's grandfather, Nahum Bigelow (1785–1851), who would travel far and establish a whole new Bigelow line in the American West. Born in Brandon on February 19, 1785, "he was trained in all those sturdy habits of mind and body common to the New Englanders of the last

47. Mark Bushnell, "Then Again: Early Vermont Towns 'Warned Out' Undesirable Settlers," *VT Digger News*, Sep. 23, 2008.

[eighteenth] century. His people were farmers and stock raisers, but with true Yankee restlessness he determined when a grown man to try something with greater promise of speedy wealth. With a peddler's pack he started out and he traveled from place to place for a number of years."[48]

Little is known of this period of his life, although Nahum told his children that a French Canadian trapper once offered him his mixed-race daughter in addition to her weight in gold if Nahum would marry her. But, said Susa, "neither the dark charms of the black-eyed French girl nor the bright glitter of her father's precious gold could tempt the sturdy New Englander to sell his birthright or lend himself to anything unworthy of his name and manhood."[49]

At age thirty-six, traveling through southeast Illinois, Nahum stopped at a house where, "working about," was a twelve-year-old girl named Mary Foster Gibbs, whom he decided then and there to marry, if ever he married. Mary, born in 1809 in Lisle, Broom County, New York, was one of seven children of Benjamin Gibbs, a cooper, and Adobe Hubbard. The Gibbses had moved from New York to Ohio and then to Lawrence County, Illinois. Mary's grandfather, Benjamin Gibbs, had given yeoman's service in the Revolutionary War, having been "drafted for three years and enlisted four years."[50]

A bright girl, Mary had begun reading at age four. By seven she was taking four lessons a day, two in reading and two in spelling, in addition to studying a chapter from the New Testament. Nahum must have stayed in Lawrence County, or, at least, visited frequently, for he was the one who took Mary, now thirteen, to school on horseback. Five years after their first meeting, Mary, now seventeen, wed forty-one-year-old Nahum, in Lawrenceville, Illinois.

After the births of a daughter and son, Nahum and Mary moved about fifty miles northwest to Coles County, Illinois, where they remained ten years. The remainder of their ten children would be born in Mercer County, forty miles north of Nauvoo on the other side of the state.

---

48. Susa Young Gates, "A Sketch of Nahum Bigelow," *Juvenile Instructor*, Apr. 15, 1891, 253.

49. Gates.

50. Gibbs, "Autobiography of Mary Gibbs Bigelow."

The Bigelow children knew their father to be "frank, [and of] sturdy independence. Honest, to a fault, generous, quick-tempered and affectionate." He was not only a good provider, but the children, Susa was told, "were familiar with a huge tool chest" that held "strange and unknown tools and instruments"; Father Nahum was an inventor who spent years trying to solve the problem of perpetual motion. "His success was that of others who wasted time in this direction, but at least it cultivated the reasoning faculty, developed the mind, trained the hand, and interested the thoughts. This faculty was visible in a hundred handy ways," Susa continued, for the Bigelow household boasted many comforts and conveniences other frontier homesteads did not.[51]

Susa's mother, Lucy Bigelow (1830–1905), the third of Nahum and Mary Foster Gibbs Bigelow's ten children, was born on October 3, 1830, in a rural area near Charleston, Coles County, Illinois. At the time, the family was living in "a small two-roomed cabin with white-scrubbed floors and shining clean glass windows."[52] Lucy was described as "always a bright, lovely, lovable child—whose powers of attraction were early displayed and whom more than one man would have given his weight in gold to possess as his wife, so much she inherited from her father."[53]

When Lucy was seven years old, two Mormon missionaries appeared at the family's doorstep asking for a night's lodging. Susa's account of how her grandparents initially wrestled with Joseph Smith's message of "a golden Bible," angels appearing to modern man, and God himself speaking to latter-day prophets, is worth reading not only for its poignancy (if also a touch of grandiloquence), but as typical of the process of conversion apparently experienced by many early Mormon converts.[54] After a period of intense study, Nahum agreed to be baptized, trusting the Lord to make it known if this step was acceptable. Lucy, not yet eight years old (the prescribed age for baptism in the church), stayed at home with the younger

---

51. Gates, "Sketch of Nahum Bigelow."

52. Gates, "Lucy Bigelow Young," 1.

53. Gates. Susa described more than one young lady as being pursued by many suitors who would pay her weight in gold to have her as their own.

54. Susa Young Gates, "Auto-bio—Mary Bigelow," undated typescript, box 14, fd. 2, SYGP (USDH).

children while her parents and two older siblings, Mary Jane, eleven, and Hiram, nine, were baptized in a nearby stream. The family's conversion would put Lucy Bigelow on a life course so extraordinarily different from that of her ancestors as to defy expectation.

Lucy's parents became faithful Latter-day Saints. Cole County meetings of the new church were held in their home.[55] Nahum dove into Mormonism with the same enthusiasm and persistence he gave all his life pursuits. With the encouragement of his half-brother Daniel,[56] Nahum decided to move to Mercer County, forty miles north of Nauvoo, and from there they finally moved to Nauvoo proper.

In 1845 Nauvoo was one of Illinois's largest towns, with 20,000 residents.[57] Still, non-Mormon antipathy continued to plague the Mormons. In spring 1845 the family relocated again to the safer environs of a farm eighteen miles outside Nauvoo, and Lucy's father continued to prove his mettle and loyalty by supplying city residents with goods from his farm.

In the meantime, Lucy grew into a tall young lady, "womanly in her looks," with "dark brown lustrous locks and bright blue eyes," and "correct almost classic features." Her personality was "joyous, impetuous, and impulsive." Reportedly, she attracted many suitors, among them a young man named Merlin Plum, who accompanied her several times to church conferences and the theater in Nauvoo. It was there Lucy first saw Brigham Young, who was playing the part of Pythias in the play *Damon and Pythias*. For reasons now unknown, Lucy was forbidden by her parents to see young Plum again.[58]

At about this time different events occurred that must have terrified Lucy, now fourteen, and her younger siblings, and which led to Nahum having to stand trial in Carthage. Both Nahum's and Mary's

---

55. Gates, "Lucy Bigelow Young," 2.

56. It is not clear why Nahum would seek advice from his younger half-brother, Daniel Post Bigelow, in such a matter, Daniel being a farmer residing in western New York State. Perhaps Daniel's location—Barre, New York, only twenty-five miles from Rochester, in close proximity to many sites associated with Brigham Young's and Joseph Smith's early histories—and his experience as a major in his local militia, qualified him as having special knowledge of Mormon-gentile relations.

57. Black, "How Large Was the Population of Nauvoo?" Compare this to Chicago's 1840 census population of 4,470—although by 1850 Chicago's number had ballooned to 30,000.

58. Gates, "Lucy Bigelow Young," 4–6.

personal histories describe the occasion but with somewhat differing details. While these later recollections may not recount events precisely as they occurred, they are a testament to the family's fear and their trust in God to get them through.

Hostilities against the Mormons had reached such an intensity that regional and state civil leaders and the church authorities concluded the only solution was for the Mormons to evacuate. Brigham Young had reached an agreement with Governor Thomas Ford in which Young promised the Saints would leave Illinois the following spring (1846) in exchange for being left alone while they harvested their crops. A tentative peace was agreed upon, and Nahum was one of the first to return to his farm outside Nauvoo.

Shortly thereafter, a mob broke into the Bigelow home and threatened to burn it down. After Mary grabbed a hot poker and brandished it at one of the intruders, the mob left, but they promised to return in three days. The family sent Hiram, sixteen, to confer with Brigham, whose counsel was for Nahum to file an affidavit requesting protection and send it to Governor Ford in Carthage. Hiram went back home with a pistol given him by either Brigham[59] or Brigham's brother, Joseph Young.[60] Hiram hurried on to Carthage with his father's affidavit requesting military help, which was refused by either Major Warren[61] or the governor himself. Nahum was advised to seek assistance from the Nauvoo militia instead.

Hiram was again sent to Nauvoo to report this development. But meanwhile the Carthage officials recanted and sent a force to protect the Bigelows and their farm. Soon after Hiram returned, these state troops, egged on by a member of the mob that had previously accosted the family and had been given directions to the home, decided to impersonate the mob and give "the old man [Nahum] ... a good scare." The state militiamen forced their way into the Bigelow home, and Nahum's pistol accidentally, as Nahum told the story, discharged. Lt. Everett, wounded in the breast and hip, later confessed his responsibility in the incident, but Nahum was forced to stand trial in Carthage.[62]

---

59. Gates, 274.
60. Bigelow, "Autobiography."
61. Bigelow.
62. Bigelow.

The trip to and from the courthouse in Carthage was risky, for Nahum was already weak from sickness, and hostile elements followed his wagon. Mother Bigelow, riding alongside and ever courageous, told the harassers they would have to take Nahum over her dead body. The couple reached Carthage safely and the trial proved anticlimactic once Lt. Everett's complicity in the prank was made evident.

Two other episodes that winter of 1845–46 define the difficulties between the Mormons and Illinoisans. One day fourteen-year-old Asa, the second Bigelow son, was sent to the spring for water. He found a green scum on it; acting on a premonition and after collecting a sample of the water, he moved on to a more distant spring. Later the sample was analyzed by Dr. Willard Richards, a Nauvoo physician and church apostle, and found to contain lethal doses of arsenic.[63] A second attempt was made to poison Nahum, this one occurring on a return trip from Nauvoo to his farm where he hoped to save his crops. He passed the home of a known Mormon apostate, who invited him to breakfast. Offered coffee by the man's wife, and while the couple drank tea, Nahum drank it, complaining that it was bitter. Within hours Nahum was in severe pain. This presumed poisoning affected his health not only throughout that winter but the rest of his life.[64] He would die just two years after reaching Utah, leaving his family convinced that his demise had been hastened by the poisoning.

These experiences were traumatic for Lucy and her siblings. However, rather than weaken their faith, opposition served to entrench it, to alienate them further from non-Mormon society, and to promote a sense of connection and solidarity with fellow Mormons.

When the first group of Saints departed Nauvoo in February 1846, the Bigelows were not able to go with them. Nahum spent the winter in poor health. By early spring he had recovered enough to begin preparations for joining a company that would leave in late spring. The family, with three wagons, abandoned Nauvoo in June 1846. They were well-provisioned, avoiding much of the distress of inadequate food and transportation that plagued many others.

Despite its difficulties, the journey through Iowa must have been

---

63. Gates, "Sketch of Nahum Bigelow," 344.
64. Gates.

an adventure for the younger Bigelow children and perhaps for Lucy herself. Reaching the Mormon encampment at Winter Quarters (near present-day Omaha, Nebraska), they involved themselves in church activities. The two older girls, Mary Jane and Lucy, attended a free school. They approached their studies eagerly, especially since their only other opportunity for education had been in Nauvoo where, according to Susa, "Lucy learned all that she ever got from books, save from after reading and studying on her own part." Susa remembered that her mother "was never in her life able to read or write except with great labor and patience, yet she was remarkably well educated and surprisingly intelligent in the school of experience, observation, knowledge of human nature and of faith."[65]

Susa may well have been justified in her emphasis on her ancestors' Puritan backgrounds. It is easy to see in Nahum Bigelow and his wife and family that same tenacity that moved the Pilgrims to face danger, starvation, illness, death, and defeat, purely because they felt God called them to do so.

During the sisters' stay in Winter Quarters, Mary Jane and Lucy, both of them young women, continued to attract (according to Susa) the attention of young men. However, not just young ones—in autumn 1846, a Brother Wicks told Nahum how much he admired his daughters and asked him for their hands in plural marriage. Nahum, clearly no dictator as a father, responded, "Oh, yes ... you are welcome to my consent. What you will have to get though, will be theirs."[66] Mary Jane had expressed no overt disapproval of plural marriage, but spunky Lucy had "resolved long ago not to be sealed in plural marriage."[67] The girls appear to have been free to make up their own minds about the doctrine. As a devout believer and an associate of both Joseph Smith and Brigham Young, Nahum accepted the practice as God's truth. So did the girls' mother, presumably, though exactly how she may have counseled her daughters Susa neither recorded nor speculated on. That the girls might be predisposed to early marriages to older men is believable given their parents'

---

65. Gates, "Lucy Bigelow Young," 14–15.
66. Gates, 15.
67. Gates, 17.

history. That Nahum did not take a plural wife himself might have been due to his age and poor health.[68]

Wicks's courting efforts were so persistent, along with the sisters' refusals, that Nahum eventually asked his friend and ecclesiastical leader, Brigham Young, what he should do as a father, since Wicks was interested in his daughters. Brother Brigham replied, "Oh, he is, eh? Well, so far as anything I know, Brother Wicks is a very good man, but his wife is a high-strung piece." Nahum replied that he was willing to follow Brigham's counsel, but mostly he wanted "the matter settled one way or another."[69] Brigham promised to drop by the Bigelow home to interview the girls.

The above conversation, instigated by Nahum, may have been a tacit request for Brigham Young to take care of his daughters. Nahum was now sixty-one. His health was poor, and a presumably grueling journey lay ahead. He had already scared off at least one suitor of Lucy's; how many others did he and his wife deem irreligious, too religious, or outright irresponsible? Moreover, if either girl married into the Young family, Nahum's wife and younger children probably would be taken care of as a matter of course. Finally, as researcher Gary James Bergera has pointed out, marrying (or giving one's daughter) in polygamy was "a show of loyalty, obedience, and sacrifice," in reward for which "blessings unimaginable awaited" for all concerned.[70]

Brigham kept his promise to Nahum several days later. Family members must have understood the nature of the visit, for they cleared out of the way, leaving Mary Jane alone with Brigham. Brigham asked if she wanted to marry Brother Wicks.

"No, sir; I don't think that I do," the girl replied.

"Well, is there any one you do want? The Sisters ought to have their choice in the matter for they can choose but one; and they have a right to select that one. So if you know of any you would like, tell me who it is."

"I don't know of any one, thank you, Pres. Young."

"Well, now then; how would you like me for a husband, Mary?"

---

68. Or Nahum Bigelow may have been an incurable romantic.
69. Gates, "Lucy Bigelow Young," 15.
70. Bergera, "Identifying the Earliest Mormon Polygamists," 4.

40

"I can't tell, sir."[71]

Brigham advised Mary to take whatever time she needed, to think about the matter, and to ask her sister Lucy "the same questions I have asked you." In Susa's eyes, Brigham's dignified manner indicated his personal motto in regard to romance: "Marry first and spark after." She wrote, "When the Spirit of the Lord whispered to him that he should seek such and such a one for a wife, he did so in a quiet, manly, grave way, never with any spirit of co-ercion on his part."[72]

Several times during that winter, Brigham dropped by the Bigelow home. Almost always Lucy absented herself, for she had determined that she had no interest in a man her senior despite, or perhaps because of, her parents' own large age gap. Yet when queried by Mary Jane, Lucy was evasive, being somewhat reluctant to say no to the president of the church.

Early in March the issue came to a head. Brigham dropped by the Bigelow home and asked Mary if she or both girls had decided to accept his proposal of marriage. "Lucy," said Mary Jane afterwards, "President Young wants you to make up your mind now; I am to be sealed to him next week, and you, too, if you want to. So what do you say?"

"I don't know," answered the puzzled girl. "I'll tell you what it is, Mary, I don't feel as if I could marry him. He's got such lots of wives now, and it don't seem like he could ever be my husband."

Another week passed by, and Brigham dropped by again. He found Mary and Lucy alone in the living room. He faced Lucy and asked her directly, "Well, Lucy have you made up your mind whether to be sealed to me or not?"

"Y-es sir," she replied. Susa later wrote that her mother's "fate was sealed forever."[73]

The next week Brigham appeared at the humble Bigelow home in the company of three apostles: Heber C. Kimball, Willard Richards, and Ezra T. Benson. Heber officiated, sealing both girls to Brigham "for time and all eternity," Mary first, followed by Lucy. It was March 20, 1847. Mary was nineteen, Lucy sixteen. These marriages were

---

71. Gates, "Lucy Bigelow Young," 16–17.
72. Gates.
73. Gates, 19.

kept secret for the time being, known only to those present. They were also in name only. Lucy's sealing to Brigham would be repeated in 1850, by which time she had turned nineteen. This sealing would take place in Salt Lake City in the Council House. From that time on, the union was presumably conjugal.

For now, Mary and Lucy continued to live with their parents. Brigham saw Lucy three times before he left for the west, twice while Lucy was ice skating and once while she was playing games with friends. On the third occasion, as she was skating, Brigham passed by in his stately carriage and doffed his hat at Lucy "with one of his princely bows." Lucy said she felt quite foolish.[74]

In early spring 1847, Brigham departed with the advance company of pioneers bound west. Only one of his polygamous wives, Clarissa (Clara) Decker, traveled with him in the first company to the Great Salt Lake Valley. In most cases, the other wives came west later with relatives. Mary Jane and Lucy stayed with their parents, who would not make the trek for another two years. Sometime after Brigham's party had gone, Lucy, her mother, and a brother back-tracked to St. Louis to obtain temporary employment and replenish the family's supplies. When Brigham returned the next spring and found Lucy gone, he said "he would rather have given the last coat off his back than to have her down there."[75] Lucy's father informed her of Brigham's displeasure by letter and Lucy, a little uneasy, hurried back to Winter Quarters with the other family members.

She intended merely to visit, then return to St. Louis to earn more money for her family. However, she was about to learn one of the lessons of wifehood to Brigham Young. He ran a tight ship and did not want any wife of his flitting between Mormon and gentile (non-Mormon) territories under her own steam. "I am very thankful to say that I have heard a very good report of you while you stayed in St. Louis," he told her mildly. "But I don't wish you to go down there again," he added, asking if she wouldn't prefer traveling to Utah that summer instead. His own wagons had been diverted to urgent church business, but he would find places in other men's wagons for those of his family he wished to emigrate that season.

---

74. Gates, 21.
75. Gates, 23.

So, in exchange for a yoke of oxen, 300 pounds of flour, and Lucy's service as an aide to his wife, an invalid, Willard McMullen took Lucy under his wing.

Lucy's journey to the Salt Lake Valley started in May 1848. Her frequent companion was a sister-wife of Brigham Young, Ellen Rockwood, sixteen, whose parents were in the same company. Somewhere along the trail, Lucy became quite ill with measles, at that time an often fatal disease. Brigham, hearing she was sick, administered to her, and she quickly healed. At another point in the journey, Lucy was informed that she was to work for her board that winter for Vilate Young Decker, one of Brigham's two daughters by his first wife, Miriam. Vilate was the same age as Lucy, married, and known for having a "proud, haughty disposition." Lucy replied, "Well, I won't do it, let me tell you," only to relent under Brigham's pleadings as he expressed concern that because of Vilate's "delicate health" she might die prematurely as her mother had.[76] Otherwise, Lucy's experience of the Mormon Trail seems to have been uneventful.

As it turned out, Vilate and Lucy grew as close as sisters. They shared the first adobe house ever built in Utah, located on Brigham's Great Salt Lake City property near City Creek. This rudimentary structure, provided by Brigham, housed the Deckers (Vilate, husband Charlie, and daughter) in two rooms; a combined kitchen, dining, and sitting area in which Lucy insinuated herself; and a fourth room occupied by two other of Brigham's young wives, Margaret Alley and Emmeline Free. Lucy was kept very busy with housework, cooking, washing, and ironing not only for the Deckers but also for the hired men working in Charlie's sawmill.[77]

In fall 1848, Brigham built a long log cabin called Log Row next to City Creek, just east of State Street along today's First Avenue.[78] There were seven or eight bedrooms that housed several of the younger wives. Lucy B., as she came to be called since there was also a Lucy Decker, roomed with Clara D. (also Decker) as distinguished from Clara C. (Chase). Some years later the Young schoolhouse would be built on this site. Lucy wrote to her sister Mary, who at

---

76. Gates, 28–29.
77. Gates, 29–30.
78. Whitley, *Brigham Young's Homes*, 92.

the time was still married to Brigham but was traveling to the valley with their parents, that she was currently living in the house of Lorenzo Young, "but we expect to move shortly in to the Row. Mr. Young is having the kitchen finished today."[79]

Life in the Row involved "hard manual labor"—cooking, baking, candle-dipping, matchmaking, soap making, washing, ironing, quilting, sewing, knitting, cloth weaving (involving shearing, carding, and dyeing the wool), and milking, the latter of which Lucy excelled in and performed with enthusiasm. According to Susa, the young wives lived in harmony, "all of them too busy to bother much with the vices of jealousy and suspicion which are the usual outgrowths of idleness and luxury." The men and boys built houses, gardened and planted grain, gathered wood from the canyons, and made fences, along with other tasks.[80]

The rest of the Bigelow family arrived the next autumn, 1849, settling initially in Farmington, a one or two days' ride north. By now Mary Jane had had a change of heart, for she asked Brigham to release her from her marriage vow. One of Young's biographers wrote, "Although not an advocate of divorce, Brigham was nevertheless fairly liberal in granting it, especially in cases of plural marriages."[81] Mary Jane did not marry again until 1852, at age twenty-five, and then it was in polygamy again, to an older man. In divorcing Brigham, Mary Jane set a precedent that would reemerge among her nieces, Lucy's daughters, of hastily entered, less-than-successful marriages that eventually failed.[82]

While living in Log Row, on May 12, 1852, Lucy gave birth to her first child, a daughter who was named Eudora Lovina. Within

79. Gates, "Lucy Bigelow Young," 32.
80. Gates, 33–35.
81. Arrington, *Brigham Young*, 318–19. At least ten of Brigham's wives eventually divorced him (see Whitley, *Brigham Young's Homes*, 219–24).
82. In 1852, Nahum Bigelow having died, Mary Jane moved with her mother and siblings to Provo where she married Horace Ephraim Roberts, a Provo potter. She was Roberts' second wife and the marriage did not last. In 1856 she wed John Bair as Bair's fifth wife. That marriage too must have failed, for in 1857 or 1858 she wed Daniel Durham Hunt as Hunt's fourth wife. In 1868 she married Philander Bell, to whom I have been able to find very few references. In 1868, at age forty, Mary Jane bore her only child and died six months later, the baby following soon thereafter. Mary Jane was described as warm hearted, kind, impulsive, and of delicate health. See Gates, "Nahum Bigelow."

44

five days Lucy, ever active, was up and back to work. Brigham, in the meantime was busy building homes for his several families. The White House, more formally known as the "Mansion House," was finished in 1854, located just south of the Log Row. It was reported to be the "first house in the state with a shingled roof" and the "only white-washed building in the territory in that early period."[83] It was the center of both the territorial government and the church until the completion of the Beehive House the following year. The Lion House was intended to replace the Log Row as home for the preponderance of Brigham's wives. By late 1855 the Lion House was not yet finished, but anxious wives and families began to move in anyway.

---

83. Whitley, *Brigham Young's Homes*, 96.

Life in the Lion House

3

Susa Young lived her first fourteen years in the Lion House except for a stay at her father's farm when she was five and six. So many travelers through Great Salt Lake City peered into Brigham Young's compound that life there may have seemed sometimes like a fish bowl. Brigham took steps to protect his family from the "inordinate amount of scrutiny and ridicule in the public press." Besides building the privacy wall, in 1857 he instructed clerks in the Church Historian's Office that he wanted very little about his personal family included in the public record.[1] These attempts may have resulted in too little information about the Youngs' home life, but fortunately Susa, her half-sister Clarissa Young Spencer, and others left extensive recollections.

Among the polygamous culture of pioneer Utah's leading families, Susa's preschool years were not extraordinary. As a toddler, she felt her father's daily presence unless he was traveling, but in the main she was supervised by her mother, with assistance from her various "aunts."[2] Susa's mother described her with "an all-pervading spiritual light in her eyes, lingering in her smile and casting its halo over her whole personality." There was "the calm dignity of a self-controlled spirit in her walk, the quiet repose of a soul who laid her all upon the altar of prayer."[3] From Susa's several reminiscences,

---

1. Historian's Office, Journal, Jan. 31, 1857. See also Jessee, "Man of God," 23.

2. Brigham Young's children referred to his other wives as "aunts."

3. Gates, "Lucy Bigelow Young," 53; and Gates, "From Impulsive Girl." This article was taken from a biography Susa wrote of her mother, "Lucy Bigelow Young," a 249-page typescript, box 14, fd. 5, SYGP (USDH).

a portrait emerges of Lucy Bigelow as a private person (unlike the prominent Zina Huntington Young and Eliza R. Snow), dutiful in the extreme (she reportedly refused to eat any of the cream and butter she herself skimmed and churned, reserving these luxuries exclusively for the babies and invalids), and of a charitable and sympathetic spirit. One story recalled that during the drought of 1856 "her heart bled for the hungry workmen who were crowding the completion of the Lion House, and many days she carried over her share of the scanty rations of bread and skim milk, to the weakened carpenters and painters who labored all winter to finish this unique dwelling-place."[4]

Susa further portrayed her mother as joyous, a lover of music and dancing, and an enthusiastic and gifted seamstress; she became the de facto assistant to Sister Bowring, lead costumer for the Salt Lake Theater. But Lucy Bigelow's dominant trait was conscientiousness. On returning home after the 1858 move South, "she had worked so hard plunging into the primitive tasks with her youthful dynamic energy during that hard year [1857–58] and especially the winter following, that she was flat on her back in the early part of the spring of 1859." Even though Lucy suffered miscarriages and "premature birth-mishaps," she could not bring herself to refrain from doing her chores and "she too often overdid her share."[5]

Thus, Susa's formative years and socialization progressed under the influence of lively, engaged parents in a lively, engaged household. Not only did she have the company of her older sister but also of her extended family of half-siblings and substitute mothers. There was, in addition, her church family—on Sundays Lucy took her to meetings: morning meetings in the Old Tabernacle[6] and evening ward meetings. One Thursday each month was set aside for fast meeting, when members of the Youngs' assigned ward "poured out their testimonies, of healings, of answers to prayers and of heavenly dreams and manifestations." Usually Lucy did not participate, not being a forward personality and probably absorbed in keeping

---

4. Gates, "Impulsive Girl," 276.

5. Gates, 278–79.

6. The Old Tabernacle was a rectangular adobe building with a pitched roof, built in 1852. The "new" Tabernacle that still sits on Temple Square was first used in 1867. See Jenson, *Encyclopedic History*, 860.

her little girls quiet. Eventually one child would lay her head on Lucy's lap while another curled against her shoulder. If they grew too restless, Lucy would pacify them with a sugar cube or a piece of cracker. In addition to formal worship, Lucy, like her sister-wives, held morning prayers with her children in her private sitting room. Susa recalled her mother practicing this "simple prayer-ceremony" with characteristic diligence.[7]

Judging by later events, Lucy may have been somewhat permissive in her mothering. Neither, contrary to his reputation today, was Susa's father overly strict. Brigham expatiated on his child-rearing experiences, or at least his philosophy, in numerous sermons recorded in the *Journal of Discourses*. He was stern and organized with his families, but he evidenced kindness, self-control, and general acceptance of his children. In 1861 he said, "I do not rule my family with an iron hand, as many do, but in kindness and with pleasant words." However, he added, "See that your children are taught every principle of goodness and virtue, and do not let them run uncontrolled in the streets."[8] In 1861 he said—almost certainly as a reaction to his own father's emotional barrenness—"I believe in indulging children in a reasonable way."[9] Discipline necessarily played a vital role in the upbringing of the Young children, but it appears that Brigham, although a taskmaster with high expectations, handled his paternal responsibilities with control, calm, and perhaps kindness. "I seldom give a child a cross word; I seldom give a wife a cross word."[10] "Bring up your children in the love and fear of the Lord; study their dispositions and their temperaments, and deal with them accordingly, never allowing yourself to correct them in the heat of passion."[11]

Example, example, example was Brigham's mantra for teaching his children and a doctrine that he preached repeatedly from the pulpit. "In training our children ... a most effective way is to do it by example. If we wish our children to be faithful to us, let us be faithful to God and to one another. ... Parents should manifest before their children all that they wish to see exhibited in them. ... Example is

7. Gates, 280.
8. Brigham Young, Apr. 7, 1861, *JD* 9:39.
9. Young, Jan. 26, 1862, *JD* 9:173.
10. Young, Apr. 22, 1860, *JD* 8:74.
11. Young, Apr. 22, 1877, *JD* 19:221.

better than precept."[12] Susa's recollections of her father bear out his preaching on parenting.

Of course, by the time Susa was born Brigham was fifty-five; maturity and long experience may have mellowed his parenting reflexes. Also, because of time constraints, most of his children's day-to-day supervision was carried out by their mothers, allowing him the luxury of patience and forbearance. Brigham believed firmly in the primacy of mothers: "It is the mothers, after all, that rule the nations of the earth. They form, dictate, and direct the minds of statesmen, and the feelings, course, life, notions, and sentiments of the great and the small, of kings, rulers, governors, and of the people in general."[13]

Yet both Susa and Clarissa Young Spencer claimed that—the regimentation governing the Lion House notwithstanding—Brigham enjoyed a close relationship with each of his children. According to Clarissa, "The bond between my father and me was as close as if I had been his only child, and I am sure that each of the other children felt the same way."[14] It is difficult to know how earnestly to take such claims. Susa received only one letter from her father in her life.[15] With forty-six surviving offspring (plus adopted children and stepchildren), Brigham could not have spent a great amount of time with any one child. Young also traveled a lot and had church and territorial affairs to attend to, but he still took pains to provide for the group and individual needs of his children.

Susa described herself as a sickly child, "fragile and delicate."[16] At a young age she developed whooping cough, which led to "asthma [which would improve dramatically after she moved to St. George, some 300 miles to the south, at age fourteen] and heart disease."[17] In either 1861 or 1862, at age five or six, Susa and her mother were moved to the Brigham Young farm where they remained for at least a year.[18] This farm, lying about four miles from downtown Salt Lake

---

12. Young, July 1, 1865, *JD* 11:117.
13. Young, Apr. 7, 1861, *JD* 9:38.
14. Spencer and Harmer, *Brigham Young at Home*, 35–36.
15. Susa was twenty-one years old when her father died.
16. Gates, "Lucy Bigelow Young," 59.
17. Susa Young Gates, "Life Items," box 1, fd. 2, SYGP (USDH).
18. Susa gave 1862 as the year she and her mother went to the Forest Farm; more likely it was 1861, since while Lucy and Susa lived on the farm, it had barely begun construction. Susa remembered "two log houses, one the cook house and [the other the]

City, comprised roughly a square-mile swath between today's 2100 South and 2700 South Streets as one approached, and 500 East and 1300 East Streets on its lower and upper reaches.[19] Susa's sister Dora, ten at the time, stayed with Aunt Twiss[20] in the Lion House to continue her schooling. Susa recalled,

> [Mother] went down to father's farm house which was later called the Forest Farm, to take care of the men who worked there and to make cheese and butter for the family in the Lion House. Mother was a splendid milker and she milked all the cows of the family in the first days in the Log Row and in the Lion House. That might have been one reason why father arranged for her to go to the farm. She loved churning and cheese-making, yet by this time, men did the milking.[21]

Ann Eliza Webb, the most notorious of Brigham's many wives, lived at the farmhouse some years later and afterward complained that "Brigham Young only sent wives there who were in disfavor and then he worked them to exhaustion."[22] That seems unlikely, for Lucy does not appear to have been under opprobrium from Brigham, nor would she have viewed supervision of the milking operation as punishment. At this time, Ann Eliza made her living lecturing against Mormonism, so her testimony was not entirely disinterested.[23]

In the 1850s, church ledgers referred to this farm as "the Church Farm." By 1857 it was being called "the Prest's dairy farm." Under

---

dining room, separated by a roofed-in passage way from the milk and cheese house, and there was a chamber above which was mother's bed-room." Gates, "Impulsive Girl," 281; Cornwall, *Brigham Young's Forest Farm*.

19. The farm comprised a portion of Salt Lake Valley's original Ten Acre Big Field Survey. Part of the farm is now the Forest Dale Golf Course (Cornwall, *Brigham Young's Forest Farm*, 14–17). In 1976 the Forest Farmhouse was moved to the This is the Place Heritage Park on Salt Lake City's east bench.

20. Aunt Twiss was Naamah Carter Twiss (1821–1909), who married Brigham in Nauvoo in 1845, four months after the death of her young husband, John Sanderson (or Saunders) Twiss. Upon the opening of the St. George temple, with Brigham in attendance, she and sister-wife Margaret Pierce acted as proxies for the "second anointings" of their deceased first husbands. Naamah was "sealed" (married for eternity) to Twiss after his death. Under LDS policy, Naamah, being female, could be sealed to only one spouse, so her marriage to Brigham Young was for "time" (this life) only. One source says Naamah died in 1868, but she was named in Brigham's 1877 will, and all other sources give her death date as 1909.

21. Gates, "Lucy Bigelow Young," 59.

22. Whitley, *Brigham Young's Homes*, 168.

23. Young, *Wife No. 19*, 532.

either name, it was recognized as Brigham's personal property. In 1862, when it began to be listed as the Forest Farm, workers started tilling portions of its 640 sagebrush-covered acres. Also about this time, a legal change of title was made but without exchange of money, Brigham assuming ownership in lieu of salary.[24] He intended it for his children's inheritance, which eventually was accomplished.

Susa remembered tubs of milk curd and pans of milk standing on shelves in the milk house. There must have been a cheese press. The groves of trees that later graced the grounds had not matured, and to a little girl the flat fields and meadows seemed to stretch for miles. She and her mother were not lonely at the Forest Farm. Other family members visited frequently, and Brigham himself used it as a Sunday afternoon retreat. Aunt Zina's "broth of a boy," Chariton, lived there each summer and kept everyone laughing with his practical jokes.[25]

Susa recalled once witnessing a German workman named Charlie beating a horse. Peeking between the corral boards, she and Lucy watched the horse kick the air in terror and neigh loudly as if screaming. "Mother was wretchedly upset over the whole affair and she must have said something to father for Charlie left the Farm and he certainly never handled horses for father again."[26]

Brigham, his wives, and his workers turned the Forest Farm into a showplace. Not only did it serve as a demonstration farm to the territory, trying out the newest machinery and best dairy and breeding practices, but it served as an experimental station for silkworm culture and testing new varieties of mulberries, sugar beets, and alfalfa. With 240 of its 640 acres cultivated in wheat, oats, Indian corn, potatoes, hay and barley, it became the mainstay of Brigham's farming enterprises. By 1869 the operation would boast forty-five milk cows, produce 3,000 pounds of butter, and keep eighty-four breeding and meat cattle. It had no sheep and only a few pigs.[27] That year it employed thirty-three workmen, paying out $4,500 in wages. Throughout the 1860s and early 1870s, it also served as a

---

24. Cornwall, *Brigham Young's Forest Farm*, 8.
25. Gates, *Impulsive Girl*, 281.
26. Gates.
27. Cornwall, *Brigham Young's Forest Farm*, 9.

social center for family members and their friends, church dignitaries, eastern visitors, and nearby residents. The use of the farmhouse would decline after 1872 as Brigham's health failed and he began spending winters in St. George.[28]

In early winter 1863, when it became apparent Lucy was pregnant, she was brought back to the Lion House for fear the farm work would be too demanding physically. Her place was taken by Susan Snively.[29] Susa was nearly seven when, on February 22, 1863, Lucy gave birth to her youngest daughter. She was called Rhoda, after Brigham's older sister, and in her early years went by that name or by Rhoda Mabel. Later, she went simply by Mabel. She would be a major figure throughout Susa's life, and they would collaborate on at least one genealogical history.

Ensconced back in the Lion House, Susa began attending classes in the family school room overseen by Aunt Harriet. Susa reported being "fanciful in her thinking" as a grade-schooler.[30]

> When I was a young girl all sorts of subjects connected with fortune-telling and magic had a powerful charm for my imaginative mind. In fact, I don't think I shall confess to what an absurd extent these notions of mine were sometimes carried. ... It was not until I was old enough to be ashamed of myself that I lost all apprehension of seeing a fairy jump out of every flower I plucked, or of hearing a genii roar every time I threw down the seed of a date.[31]

Beginning at about age seven, Susa, along with her half-sister Louise,[32] trained under Sara Alexander to be a "child danseuse" and "fairy

---

28. Cornwall, *Brigham Young's Forest Farm*, 10; Gates, "The Home on the Farm," typescript, box 10, fd. 8, SYGP (USDH); Young, *Wife No. 19*, 532; and Stromberg, "Brigham Young's Forest Farmhouse," 72–88.

29. Susan (also written as Susanne and Susannah) Snively Young (1815–92) was a Southerner, born in Virginia. In 1844, at age twenty-nine, she married Brigham Young in Nauvoo. She was known for her positive, determined personality, as expressed in her and her sister's building (or paying to be built from their own earnings) their own house in Nauvoo. Susan was also said to be kind and accommodating to the distressed. See "Brigham Young: His Wives and Family," in Carter, *Our Pioneer Heritage*, vol. 1.

30. Gates, "Life Items."

31. Gates, "Editor's Department," *Young Woman's Journal*, Nov. 1891, 86.

32. Louise probably refers to Susa's half-sister, Louisa Wells Young (1855–1908), daughter of Emmeline Free. At sixteen, Louisa would marry James S. Ferguson. It is possible Louisa and/or James attempted a career on the stage, for three of their children were born in New York City, and there exists a modestly exotic portrait of "Louisa Nell

dancer."[33] In the 1850s and 1860s, almost every frontier town had its own theater proffering a formidable repertory of dramas, melodramas, comedies, and musical and dance entertainments. Weaving its way into these performances was the Victorians' fascination with all things supernatural and fairy-related.[34] Susa's memoirs make it clear the allure of such entertainments reached America's hinterlands. Even before Salt Lake City had a theater, it had the Social Hall, which from 1852 hosted dances, dinners, and theatrical productions. However, from 1862 the Salt Lake Theater shone as the first theater to be built west of the Missouri River. It stood on the northwest corner of State and 100 South Streets—a few-minutes' walk for Susa, who was six at the time of its dedication on January 1, 1863. Built in the style of a European opera house, with a capacity of 1,500, "it was easily the largest and most imposing building in the community" for that time.[35]

What Susa related only in part was how extensive were her father's efforts to expose his children to the arts. It was one of many ways she was remarkably advantaged by being Brigham Young's daughter. She and Louisa danced not only at home for a family audience but were among a troupe of child dancers who performed at the Salt Lake Theater. In 1866, they were chosen to assist their instructor, Sara Alexander, as solo dancers.[36] Six years later Susa and Louisa danced a polka in *The Pride of the Market*, a three-act comic drama, at the Theatre.[37] Almost sixty years later Susa claimed she could still do the "sailor's hornpipe" and Spanish dances.[38] Brigham

Young Ferguson," in perhaps a dancing costume, by pioneer Utah photographer Charles R. Savage taken around the 1870s. Louisa died in Manhattan in 1908 at age fifty-three.

33. Gates, "Lucy Bigelow Young," 65.

34. In an 1867 *New York Times* ad, *The Black Crook* was described as "a story of sorcery, demonism and wickedness generally." Of course, Brigham Young could (and did) bar profanity and wickedness from performances in the Salt Lake Theater.

35. Ronald W. Walker, "Salt Lake Theatre," in *Utah History Encyclopedia*.

36. Sara Alexander was a young St. Louis-trained ballet dancer who converted to Mormonism with her mother and sister and immigrated to Utah in 1859. From 1862 to 1868 she lived in the Lion House as dance instructor to the Young daughters, rejecting several offers of plural marriage and finally leaving to join a San Francisco theater company. In 1871 she took her three-year-old orphaned niece, Lisle, to New York, where she focused mainly on Lisle's quite successful career. From 1916 to 1919, in her seventies, Sara acted in silent pictures. See Maxwell, "Particular Favorite."

37. Harold H. Jenson, "Susa Young Gates—True Pioneer Stories," *Juvenile Instructor*, Mar. 1929, 135. *The Pride of the Market* was first performed in London in 1847.

38. Gates, "How Brigham Young," 142.

himself continued to dance into his seventies, and "communal dancing parties" were often held at the Young home.[39]

In 1862 Brigham Young invited Sara Alexander to live in the Lion
House as his children's dance teacher. (She was also a schoolteacher
and may have instructed the Young children in other subjects.) Sara
remained a Beehive House guest-employee for six years. Clarissa
Young Spencer described the gymnasium where the "Big Ten" (referring to ten of Young's daughters born between 1847 and 1850)
received their dance instruction. "Along the full length of the west
side of the house ran a huge porch, and here Father had placed every contrivance available in that day." There were different teachers
"to instruct us in gymnastics, fencing, and solo dancing." She also
remembered that the lessons prepared them to be "'fairy' or ballet
dancers when the Salt Lake Theater was opened."[40]

Other types of culture were an integral part of life in the Young
household. Brigham himself had a pleasing bass voice and encouraged music among his offspring. He preached, "My little children
... shall go to the dance, study music, read novels, and do anything
else that will tend to expand their frames, add fire to their spirits,
improve their minds, and make them feel free and untrammeled
in body and mind."[41] All the Youngs, boys and girls alike, sang and
played the piano. When Brigham discovered that Lucy and Dora
were giving music lessons to save money for an organ, he bought
them a "Mason and Hamiln" organ.[42] Other instruments in the Lion
House included a piano and harp, and the children were provided
the services of "competent musical teachers."[43]

With the completion of the Salt Lake Theater, the family often
attended performances there once or twice a week, enjoying their own
reserved seating near the front. There was also a small theatre at home;
Susa recalled twelve-year-old Dora writing and producing an original
play entitled either "Love or Prejudice"[44] or "Love and Pride."[45]

39. Gates, 30.
40. Spencer and Harmer, *Brigham Young at Home*, 31.
41. Brigham Young, Feb. 6, 1863, *JD* 2:94.
42. Gates, "Lucy Bigelow Young," 63.
43. Gates, "Family Life," 341.
44. Gates, "How Brigham Young," 139.
45. Gates, "Family Life," 343.

Other than theatre productions and large dance parties, most of the family's entertainment took place at home. In winter the family sometimes popped corn and pulled molasses taffy; in summer they made ice cream with their freezer. Holidays, especially Christmas and New Year's, were festive occasions, "a time of gladness, love, good wishes, stockings full of new toys, and goodies for our innocent but voracious appetites—nuts, candies, raisins and all the time-honored list." The family loved Christmas. It was, Susa remembered, "an indescribable experience." The size of the family only added to the cheerful spirit. "Happiness gained a resistless momentum from sheer force of numbers. We were a joyous mob, and no individual among us could resist the contagion of happiness in the mass around him."[46] Many a holiday, the children would pile into a sleigh and be driven out to the Forest Farm where they slept under feather quilts in the upstairs rooms. The farmhouse had central heating engineered by running the vent pipe from the large wood stove in the downstairs parlor, up and along the entire ceiling, so that it heated the upstairs floor before venting through the bedroom roof.

In Brigham's view, physical health and spiritual well-being were naturally intertwined. Thus, cleanliness, a proper diet, adequate rest, and physical activity were essentials of a well-ordered and happy life. Latter-day Saints believed the body would rise in the resurrection, and it was appropriate that it be kept in the best possible condition. Susa was very proud of the health record of her father and his family and emphasized it numerous times in her writings. "My father, Brigham Young, had fifty-six living children, all born healthy, bright and without 'spot or blemish' in body or mind."[47] Susa declared that "Brigham Young was what would nowadays be called a physical culturist, and required all his family to lead a rigorously physical culture life."[48] In addition to physical activity, Young insisted on cleanliness. Besides regular baths, the children were often taken to swim at Warm Springs three miles north of the city.

In 1862 Hiram Clawson, Brigham's business manager and son-in-law, took a trip to the East, where he first learned about Dio

---

46. Gates, "How Brigham Young," 141.
47. Gates, "Family Life," 340.
48. Gates, "How Brigham Young," 29.

Lewis's gymnastics equipment.[49] Enthused, he came home and discussed his findings with Young. Soon the Young children enjoyed a fully equipped gymnasium on the porch on the west side of the Lion House. There were "wands, hoops, backboards, horizontal bars, climbing poles, a trapeze, sand bags, weights, and the like."[50] Thereafter, gymnastics classes were held daily in both summer and winter. Modest dress was enforced—ankle-length bloomers for the girls and overalls and shirts for the boys.[51]

Probably because of Brigham's lament at having received only eleven days of formal education in his life, his children were well taught. He recommended encouraging both boys and girls in their studies, using "every means in our power to direct their minds in the right direction to the most useful result." To the youths, he said, "I would advise you to read books that are worth reading; read reliable history, and search wisdom out of the best books you can procure."[52] Observing sound educational philosophy, he encouraged Utah's young people not to neglect music studies and also "to read history and the Scriptures, to take up a newspaper, geography ... and make themselves acquainted with the manners and customs of distant kingdoms and nations, with their laws, religion ... climate, natural productions ... commerce, and ... political organization; in fine, let our boys and girls be thoroughly instructed in every useful branch of physical and mental education. Let this education begin early."[53]

Susa's formal schooling began in the Lion House classroom overseen by Aunt Harriet. Harriet Cook Young (1824–98) hailed from Brigham's home region of western New York. At age eleven, she had heard John P. Greene (Brigham's brother-in-law) preach and was converted. However, due to family opposition, she was not baptized. Later she lived with her older sister in Russell, Pennsylvania, while attending school in the home of a local Quaker woman.

---

49. Diocletian Lewis (1823–86) was a homeopathic practitioner and lecturer on temperance, hygiene, and physical culture. He was well known by the 1860s for developing a system of gymnastic exercises that benefited children, women, and the aged instead of athletes only. Loeffelbein, "Dio Lewis."

50. Gates, "How Brigham Young," 31.

51. Gates, 142.

52. Brigham Young, Jan. 26. 1862, *JD* 9:173.

53. Young, 188.

Finishing that, she trained as a tailor and helped to operate a tailoring shop in Utica.

Various sources say Harriet was a schoolmistress by profession, reasonably well-educated for her time. This means she gained at least a common school education, although there is no evidence she obtained advanced training at one of the normal or teaching schools founded in 1840s New England, which certification would have qualified her to teach beyond the primary grades. The Protestant churches and other proponents of the common school movement of the 1830s argued for free public schools on the premise that social harmony and political stability depended on a literate, informed populace. Harriet's parents must have subscribed to this philosophy, for family tradition is that her father insisted that his children pursue both book learning and a practical trade. Harriet would put both sets of skills to use teaching the Young children and sewing suits and coats for the boys. She must have been quick at mathematics, for more than once she was asked to help the bookkeeper at ZCMI to straighten out his accounts.[54]

When she was seventeen, Harriet and her employer encountered the LDS missionaries again and both were baptized. Harriet moved to Nauvoo in 1843 and that fall married Brigham; she was eighteen; he was forty-two. She and Brigham had one child, Oscar, born in 1846.

As a teacher, Aunt Harriet was feared and obeyed. Only later did Susa come to respect her as "a woman of more than ordinary intelligence" (as Harriet's obituary described her in the *Deseret News* for November 5, 1898) but admitted she could be eccentric and sharp tongued. With considerable insight, Susa would speculate on the motives behind her aunt's acerbic behavior:

> [She] was a profound student of the scriptures ... [her] tongue was as a flame of darting fire. But she knew, and all her sister wives knew, that there was no corroding acid of hate here, just an outlet for the flashing genius that might have made her a great general or a mighty organizer

---

54. Zion's Cooperative Mercantile Institute was part of Brigham Young's efforts to move Utah Territory to a cooperative economic system. Young worried that the railroad would bring outsiders and competitive markets which would damage church interests. Over the years, ZCMI, as it came to be known, developed into a popular Utah department store. See Bradley, *ZCMI*.

of human forces, had she been a man. Her sex, her real affection for father, her love of the Gospel, her circumstances, her flashing sharpness of speech kept her from achieving. And so we all watched out for Aunt Harriet whose quick sarcasm whipped us, oftentimes, into the love of our duty more effectively than the gentle reproofs of our own mothers.[55]

In 1864 Susa turned eight, the "age of accountability" according to LDS doctrine, when one is believed to be of sufficient moral awareness to be capable of sinning. Thomas Higgs, one of her father's carpenters and an ordained elder, baptized her a member of the Church of Jesus Christ of Latter-day Saints by immersing her in a pond near City Creek.[56] The next day, in Sunday meeting, her father confirmed her.[57] Susa probably knew Higgs well, for he was her father's master carpenter and machinist and, while working on the Salt Lake Theater and Tabernacle, lived with his family in a small house in the Young compound. He may even have attained hero status in the eyes of the Young children for building the city's first fire engine and serving as its chief engineer.[58]

Brigham must have realized his children required more in the way of formal education than what Aunt Harriet could provide, and in 1862 he had a schoolhouse built across the street from the Beehive House. Other children from the community attended as well as the Youngs. The building was thoughtfully designed. The windows were situated high enough so that light would not stream directly into the students' faces but rather indirectly onto the pages of their books. Desks and chairs were custom made to maximize comfort in sitting. Evidently, nothing was too good, no effort too

---

55. Booth, Phillips, and Allred, "History of Harriet Elizabeth (Cook) Young."

56. Thomas Higgs (1822–95) was an Englishman living in Davenport, Iowa, when his wife became ill and was not expected to live. She asked him to "go and get one of those miracle men"—meaning the LDS missionaries. Thomas already believed in the church, so Edward Bunker and William Walker baptized him and ordained him an elder. He then blessed his wife, after which she converted. They came to Utah in Captain Hodgett's wagon company, which did not arrive in the Salt Lake Valley until mid-December 1856 due to helping the Willie and Martin handcart companies. Forty-two when he baptized Susa, Higgs would later be chief engineer on the Manti temple. In 1875 he was ordained to the Quorum of Seventies. Holzapfel, "Thomas and Elizabeth Higgs."

57. Gates, "Life Items."

58. Christensen, "History of Thomas and Elizabeth Higgs."

great, no opportunity too expensive when knowledge and culture were the possible results.[59]

Susa was a bright and diligent student in the subjects that interested her. In addition to her regular teachers, there were music teachers, as noted, and a French teacher, Mons. Bellereive.[60] About 1865, Karl G. Maeser, a German educator, immigrant, and convert who would become the second principal of Brigham Young Academy (later University) in Provo, was hired to help tutor the Young children in this schoolhouse. Maeser had been a teacher and headmaster in Dresden until being forcibly expelled, reportedly, for joining the LDS Church. He and his family arrived in Utah in 1860. Immediately he was elected a regent of the University of Deseret, where he helped to develop that school's teacher training program. He became an important figure in Utah's developing educational system.

Maeser was gifted at motivating young people. One of his memorable maxims was "Don't be a scrub." He would add, "You cannot afford it. If you would be one, use tobacco and visit saloons, where scrubs graduate. Make yourself a master workman. If you are a first-class tailor, carpenter, or blacksmith, you are better than a professional man who is a scrub in his profession."[61] Susa would be fortunate to come under Maeser's sway twice in her young life: first as one of his child-tutees and later, in her early twenties, as a student at the Brigham Young Academy.

David Evans, before becoming Susa's shorthand professor, recorded Brigham's Tabernacle sermons beginning in October 1865. In 1868 he was hired to teach the Young children phonography. He came twice a day, one hour before school and two hours after, requiring considerable dedication on the part of twelve-year-old Susa. At first there were seventy to eighty students in the class, by Susa's estimate; only seven finished the two-year course, and Susa remembered herself as a star pupil.[62] She became an expert in shorthand and a decade later would record all the dedicatory sessions of the St. George temple.

59. Susa Young Gates, "Brigham Young Schoolhouse," unpublished typescript in box 1, fd. 2, SYGP (USDH).

60. Gates, "Lucy Bigelow Young," 62-A.

61. Karl G. Maeser, "Excelsior," *The Idea*, Feb. 1893, 40.

62. Gates, "Family Life," 340.

As in the Lion House, the Young school had a fixed schedule. From 9:00 a.m. to 10:00 a.m. there were classes, then an hour recess—no mere fifteen-minute breaks for the health-conscious, physically active Young children. Classes were held again from 11:00 a.m. to 12:00 noon, followed by a ninety-minute dinner period, and finally more classes from 1:30 p.m. to 4:00 p.m., with a thirty-minute recess.[63] The students were by and large conscientious and hard-working, although one taciturn teacher complained, "You are a lazy set; can't half appreciate the advantages your father lavishes upon you."[64] There is no doubt that the Young children's education was a cut above that afforded most other pupils in the Salt Lake Valley and Utah territory at that time. However, the Young family school—as with each of Brigham's undertakings—benefited other families both directly through their children being included and indirectly by setting a standard of commitment and curriculum.

On her own time, Susa became a "voracious" reader, eclectic in her choice of literature. Until she was "old enough and rich enough to buy [a book] for myself,"[65] she owned only one, *Golden-Haired Gertrude*, which she read more than once. She had to continually retrieve it from sisters and aunts who borrowed and failed to return it. Susa "would follow its zigzag course" throughout the house, "rescuing it again and again from uncertain oblivion," after which she would read it once again. The book was eventually lost, and Susa "searched and mourned in vain."[66] "I borrowed books too—relentlessly and voraciously. I read everything I could lay my hands on, from the almanac—and that was pretty lively reading in those days—to ... [a] spirit-rapping book which sent ugly shivers of fear rippling down my spine at each perusal."[67] Despite some rather salacious passages in *Arabian Nights*, she reported, "I never found myself injured by the perusal of the Arabian Nights. I read them thirteen

---

63. Gates, "How Brigham Young," 142.

64. Gates, "Family Life," 340.

65. Susa Young Gates, "Lion House Memories," box 1, fd. 2, SYGP (USDH).

66. Gates. The book was by Theodore Tilton, *Golden-haired Gertrude: A Story for Children* (New York: Tibbals & Whiting, 1865). This story, in which a king disguised as a poor glazier woos a golden-haired orphan living with a mean aunt, is available online at archive.org.

67. Gates, "Lion House Memories."

times when I was thirteen years old; and what harm there might be in them made not the slightest impression on me." Instead, Susa felt that "the imagination and invention of my mind, such as it is, was engendered by the beautiful and quaint stories."[68]

In 1868, at the behest of Brigham Young, the University of Deseret was reorganized.[69] Because of her academic prowess Susa, going on thirteen, was sent there to study under the direction of Dr. John R. Park. Park (1869–92) would prove the longest-serving president to date of the University of Utah and its predecessors. A graduate of both Ohio Wesleyan University and New York University School of Medicine, Park grew dissatisfied with his medical practice and headed west, arriving in Utah a year after Karl Maeser. He taught school briefly, converted to the LDS Church, and was promptly appointed president of the revived University of Deseret. Like Maeser, Park believed the end of education was decency and intelligence. He told his normal school graduates of 1885, "Always remember in your teaching that the grand purpose of your labors is to make citizens—active, thinking intelligent, industrious and moral men and women. This you cannot do by any narrow routine of school forms."[70]

Functionally, the University of Deseret was more like today's high schools. Its classes were held in the confines of the "old Council House" but with "such innovations as departments, class-rooms, offices, and a faculty with cheerful adaptation."[71] Susa thrived in this more challenging school environment. Her report card for February–July 1870 indicates that, except for one score of three ("average") in

---

68. Susa Young Gates, "Novel Reading," *Young Women's Journal*, June 1894, 496. Susa probably read the bowdlerized Edward Lane translation, *One Thousand and One Nights*, published in three volumes in 1840, then revised and printed in a single volume in 1859.

69. It had first been created in 1850 through legislative action but failed due to insufficient funding and feeder schools.

70. Inscription on identification plaque on statue of John Rockey Park standing outside the main entrance to the University of Utah main administration building.

71. Gates, "Family Life," 340. The Council House stood at Main and South Temple Streets, again only a stone's throw from the Lion House. It was built in 1850 as official headquarters of the State of Deseret. When Congress declined to recognize Deseret, it was used for various purposes, including an endowment house, church administration building, Deseret University campus, Deseret News offices, and a boarding house. It burned down in 1883.

French, most of her grades were between four and five, with consistent fives in reading and spelling.[72] She had decided years before that she was not a mathematician. "I liked literature, but hated figures."[73]

In 1869, while a student at the University of Deseret, Susa performed a reading for suffragists Susan B. Anthony and Elizabeth Cady Stanton, who were on their way to San Francisco.[74] In later years, she would be closely associated with both of these renowned leaders. In the second year of the university, the students founded a modest newspaper they named *The College Lantern*.[75] Susa and her brother Willard, along with Joseph L. Rawlins and Mary McEwen, worked as student editors in one of the first college newspapers west of the Mississippi.

Susa reveled in an educational environment that demanded excellence. In later years, she would use the Young children's success at the University of Deseret as proof against an argument raised by reformers that polygamous offspring tended to be stunted in their mental and physical development. Ever a proponent of plural marriage for others if not for herself, Susa insisted, "Let any who wishes to know the mental caliber of polygamous children ask the genial and learned Dr. Park ... who have been his brightest and keenest pupils. His unhesitating answer will be a convincing argument for my [pro-polygamy] position."[76] To buttress her claim, she pointed out that five of her half-siblings eventually studied in the East, two graduated from West Point and Annapolis, and another earned a law degree from the University of Michigan. Susa herself would spend the summer of 1892 studying at Harvard University.

The other side of Brigham Young's emphasis on education was his insistence that learning be practical, serve a useful purpose, and prepare the recipient to face the realities of life. In regard to educating daughters, he said, "I delight to see the mother learn her daughters

---

72. Report cards in box 3, fd. 4, SYGP (CHL).

73. Harold H. Jenson, "Susa Young Gates," *Juvenile Instructor*, Mar. 1929, 136.

74. Jenson. Susa may have had her dates wrong since Anthony and Stanton did not visit Utah until 1870, on the occasion of Utah women receiving the right to vote. See Barbara Jones Brown, "Susan B. Anthony and Her Strong Utah Ties," *Better Days 2020*, Dec. 15, 2017, www.betterdays2020.com.

75. Gates, "Family Life," 340.

76. Jenson, "Susa Young Gates."

to be housekeepers, to be particular, clean, and neat; to sew, spin, and weave; to make butter and cheese ... to cultivate flowers, herbs, and useful shrubs, [to] ... rise early in the morning and work in the soil."[77] As for his sons, he stated, "Teach the little boys to [use] the garden hoe, the spade, &c. ... and let them have access to tools that they may learn their use, and develop their mechanical skill while young." For girls and boys, he urged parents to "encourage within them mechanical ingenuity, and seek constantly to understand the world they are in, and what use to make of their existence."[78]

Susa's father stressed the value of work in shaping good moral character and preparing one for life. He put his preaching into practice with his own children, seeing that they worked during their three-month summer vacations from school. Susa wrote, "Father believed in work and plenty of it. He saw to it that his eager boys, keen for fun and action, had a chance to translate their superabundant vitality into productive action."[79] The older boys helped on the Forest Farm, hauling wood, ploughing, tending stock, and caring for the fruit trees. Susa and her sisters learned to "weave, color, spin, sew, and knit."[80] All the children helped with harvesting apples, pears, grapes, plums, peaches, and black walnuts. The girls were allowed to dry and sell the peaches for spending money.[81] It is little surprise, therefore, that Susa developed into a prodigious worker with equal capability in both intellectual and manual labor, as seen in some of her ambitious To Do lists surviving in the archives of her papers.

While Susa was engrossed in her university studies, her mother took on the responsibility of a fourth child. In 1869 Lucy agreed to adopt[82] a child who was one-quarter East Indian, an orphan named Indianna Mary ("Ina") Maybert. Ina was six years old, the same age as Rhoda Mabel, and Susa recalled them growing up like twins.[83] As a toddler, Ina had been brought to Utah by her grandmother,

---

77. Brigham Young, Feb. 2, 1862, *JD* 9:188.

78. Young, 9:189.

79. Gates, "How Brigham Young," 143.

80. Gates, 142.

81. Gates, 140.

82. Whether or not she legally adopted Ina, Lucy became functionally responsible for the young girl and acted as a legal guardian.

83. Gates, "Lucy Bigelow Young," 70.

a Hindustani woman named Emelia Wittenbaker MacMahon.[84] In colonial India, British infantries fought alongside native units and often married native daughters for the sake of good relations. Emelia MacMahon had married an officer or sergeant in the British army, Arthur MacMahon. Their daughter Agnes likewise married a British officer, Captain James Maybert, and upon Agnes's death, baby Ina came under the guardianship of her grandmother.

Emelia and Arthur MacMahon had converted to Mormonism in Calcutta in 1853 through the efforts of the East Indian English Mission. Upon learning of the Mormons' practice of polygamy, Arthur dropped out of the church. He died the next year, but Emelia and their daughter, Agnes Leslie MacMahon Maybert, "remained faithful members ... for more than a decade, with little priesthood support, without regular contact with the Church, with the faith to leave home and trek to Zion."[85]

Once in Salt Lake City, Emelia and little Ina stayed with Apostle Orson Pratt. Pratt's home stood one-and-a-half blocks west of the Lion House; perhaps Emelia and Lucy met at church or through neighbors. Emelia extracted a promise that Lucy would take care of little Ina if anything should happen to her. It was when Emelia died at age fifty-five that Ina came to live in the Lion House where, according to Susa, she and Mabel, born just three months apart, were raised as sisters.[86] In 1870 Ina would accompany Lucy, Susa, and Mabel in their move to St. George, a settlement established in 1861 300 miles south of Salt Lake City. Ina was duly baptized into the church and later endowed in the St. George temple. As she grew

---

84. Some sources spell it McMahon.

85. Arthur and Emily MacMahon had two daughters who converted to the church. The second was named Indianna Mary MacMahon, after whom Agenes's baby, Ina, must have been named. Ardis E. Parshall, "Tracing Emily," *Times and Seasons*, Nov. 27, 2007, www.timesandseasons.org. While still in Calcutta, Emelia MacMahon became close friends with another widow and recent convert, Hannah Peters Booth. Hannah's autobiography details her experience (similar to Emelia MacMahon's) of leaving her luxurious Indian life, with nine servants and a carriage, behind and learning to survive in the harsh Utah desert, tutored by neighbors. Hannah mentions her dark skin attracting "kindly looks from some of the other Mormon colonists." See Hannah Peters reminiscences, online at familysearch.org/tree/person/memories/KWVL-5YM, accessed Feb. 20, 2020.

86. Gates, "Lucy Bigelow Young," 70. The 1870 Census shows Ina Mayburt living with the Youngs.

older and Lucy began to travel on temple duties, the girl was often left in the company of Susa's grandmother, Mary Bigelow.

Ina eventually made her way back to Salt Lake City and, according to Susa, "married a son of James Jack, father's trusted private clerk."[87] No record of such marriage has been found, but at some point things went terribly wrong for Ina. She died when she was barely eighteen in a Butte, Montana, brothel of a self-administered overdose of laudanum (opium), leaving behind a suicide note for a scornful lover.[88]

Susa, now based in her own attic bedroom in the Lion House, began to expand her life further. She enjoyed many extracurricular opportunities to practice the skills she was learning at school. She attended public meetings and joined societies. On January 10, 1870, she was with her father's party celebrating the opening of the Utah Central Railroad branch line connecting the transcontinental line in Ogden to Salt Lake City.[89] On January 8, the *Deseret News* had reported, "The ceremonial last rail to be laid with much to-do on Monday, January 10, 1870."[90] Wilford Woodruff recorded "this great day in Utah" in his journal:

> Some Twelve or Fifte[e]n thousand of the of the Inhabitants of the City of salt Lake & surrounding Country of Men women & children assembled around the Rail Road Depo to Celibrate the Building of the Utah Central Rail Road & to see the last rail laid & the last spike driven By President Brigham Young. ... There were present in the Assemb[l]y The Bands of Music from the City, Camp Duglass Band & many others[.] There were present on the Stand the first Presidency the Twel[v]e Apostles, The officers of the Union & Central Pacific Rail Road & of the Utah Central Rail Road with Many invited guest including the officers of Camp Duglass.[91]

Brigham drove the last spike—not a golden one, as had been used at Promontory Point, but a beehive-engraved spike of Utah-manufactured iron.

---

87. Gates.

88. See "In the Dark Valley," *The Weekly Miner* (Butte, Montana), Nov. 15, 1881. See also Butler, *Daughters of Joy*, 68.

89. The Golden Spike ceremony observing completion of the main, transcontinental, line had been held May 10 the previous year, but on that occasion there had been no official Mormon presence and no representative of the heroic Chinese workers.

90. "The Celebration on Monday," *Deseret Evening News*, Jan. 8, 1870, 3.

91. Woodruff, Journal, Jan. 10, 1870, in Journals and Papers.

On May 27, Susa was made corresponding secretary to the newly established Young Ladies Retrenchment Association. Organized in a parlor meeting with her father directing, this girls' branch of a parallel women's society answered the widespread fear that the imminent completion of the transcontinental railroad would expose Utah's youth to corrupting influences. The stated purpose of the society was to encourage young women to spend "more time in moral, mental and spiritual cultivation, and less upon fashion and the vanities of the world."[92] In its first ten years of existence, it focused mostly on simplicity in dress fashions and on buying Utah-manufactured goods.[93] Brigham appointed his daughter Ella Young Empey, oldest daughter of Emmeline Free, as the society's president. Membership was open not only to single girls but to young married women, and Ella was the second wife of Nelson Adam Empey, a Salt Lake City bishop.

It is not clear how regularly meetings were held, but they were conducted by either Ella or one of six counselors. As the society grew in recognition, up to 200 girls might attend on a given night. The program usually consisted of extemporaneous comments by audience members, perhaps on a topic suggested by the conducting officers. "Timid members were urged to participate, for it was 'as essential for the sisters to learn to preach as for the brethren.'"[94] The Retrenchment Society would expand to wards throughout the city and territory and endure for thirty-five years.[95]

The world grew well beyond the Beehive House for Susa. On August 12, 1870, Susa, now fourteen years old, was among a reported crowd of 11,000 present at the Tabernacle for the final evening of a three-day debate between Apostle Orson Pratt and Dr. John P. Newman on whether the Bible sanctioned polygamy.[96] Pratt was an

---

92. *Woman's Exponent*, Sep. 15, 1882, 59; see also Carol Cornwall Madsen, "Retrenchment Association," in Ludlow, *Encyclopedia of Mormonism*, 3:1224.

93. "Resolutions Adopted by the First Young Ladies' Department of the Ladies' Co-operative Retrenchment Association, S.L. City, Organized May 27, 1870," *Deseret Evening News*, June 20, 1870, 2.

94. Minutes for Feb. 6, 1875, qtd. in Madsen, "Retrenchment Association," 3:1224.

95. "Young Women Organizations," *Church History Topics*, churchofjesuschrist.org, accessed Feb. 24, 2020.

96. This attendance figure may have been exaggerated, for the three-year-old Salt Lake Tabernacle had a capacity of only 7,000. Allowing for standing room may have extended that number by some hundreds.

instructor at the University of Deseret, teaching moral science as well as math and astronomy; he may also have led the "literary society" (debate squad) to which Susa may have belonged. Newman was a prominent bishop of the Methodist Episcopal Church and chaplain to the US Senate who availed himself of the recently completed railroad to visit California and, on the way, answer a perceived challenge to debate the polygamy question in person. Unsurprisingly, Mormon newspapers said Pratt won; non-Mormon papers claimed Newman won.[97] It is no mystery who had prevailed in the mind of the precocious teenager, Susa Amelia Young: she would defend polygamy to the end of her life.

That same month Susa heard Martin Harris speak at her regular Sunday morning ward meeting in the Tabernacle. Harris was the once-wealthy New York farmer who had underwritten the first printing of the Book of Mormon and was one of the Three Witnesses to the Book of Mormon.[98] Harris had been excommunicated from the church during the financial struggles in Kirtland, Ohio, but various missionaries visited him over the years, always urging him to come to Utah, and in 1869 Harris finally agreed. A collection effort had raised $200 (Susa's father donated $25) to pay Harris's fare and buy the eighty-eight year old a decent suit. Harris was rebaptized in the Endowment House and resumed friendly ties with his former wife and a nephew who had immigrated years earlier.[99] Susa's interest in writing history was no doubt influenced by these kinds of encounters.

At fourteen, only two years away from marrying, Susa had probably begun to have suitors. On a Sunday evening, up to ten girls might be entertaining boyfriends in the Lion House parlor. They did not get in much physical affection, with eighteen other "disinterested [or perhaps not so disinterested] eyes observing [them] minutely."[100] If the young men were present when it came time for family prayers, one boy might be asked to say the prayer. If they were still there at 10:00 p.m., Brigham would come in with an armful of hats and ask each young man to find his own and take his leave.

---

97. Hatch, "The Pratt–Newman Debate," 78.

98. For more on Harris, see Walker, "Martin Harris," and Black and Porter, "Martin Harris Comes to Utah."

99. Black and Porter, "Martin Harris Comes to Utah," 157–64.

100. Gates, "Family Life," 344.

Brigham took an active part in the dating lives of his children. He frequently interviewed the young men dating his daughters. He made certain to remember "names, faces, and incidents,"[101] and would question them closely about their families, many of whom he knew. Years later, he might ask them about individual family members by name. The Young children were encouraged not to mingle with "gentiles."[102]

One night someone had dimmed the parlor lamp and stacked books around it to further darken the room. Brigham entered with his candle and, without saying a single word, directed his candle to one couple at a time, carefully scrutinizing the face of each youngster until he had examined them all. He then turned up the lamp and walked silently out of the room.[103] Another night Brigham noticed a young man named Scipio Kenner about to enter the family gate. When Brigham asked if he were a Mormon, the young man, who had left Utah as a child and had just recently returned, stammered, "Slightly." Brigham laughed and always afterwards called him Skippio Sinner.[104]

One daughter Brigham watched with particular alertness was Susa's older sister, Dora. Dora was "a beautiful girl with a reposeful manner and an exceeding bright mind ... very popular with father, with her brothers and sisters and especially with young men, and even some older men who would gladly have offered her marriage."[105] Since age sixteen, Dora had been causing her parents some discomfiture. She had been going around with Moreland "Morley" Dunford, the English-born son of George Dunford, a former Navy seaman who had brought his family to Salt Lake in 1867 and opened the city's first boot and shoe shop on the corner of 100 South and Main Streets. The Dunford home was in the Seventeenth Ward, two blocks west of the Young compound, so Dora might easily have met Morley through friends, at school, or while

---

101. Gates, "Family Life," 343.

102. Latter-day Saints consider themselves to be members of the covenant descendants of the Hebrew Bible prophet Abraham. Latter-day Saints, if not literal descendants of Abraham, are "adopted" into the house of Israel at the time of baptism. Anyone not baptized into the Church of Jesus Christ of Latter-day Saints is thus, by this definition, considered a "gentile."

103. Gates, "Family Life," 344–45.

104. Gates.

105. Gates, "Lucy Bigelow Young," 62-A.

strolling downtown.[106] Susa described Morley as "industrious …
with a sunny disposition," but lacking self-control with regard to
alcohol. This was not a small failing, easy to overlook on the part
of the parents of young women. Alcoholism was a widespread and
serious problem in nineteenth-century America, hence the century-
long temperance push. Women, with few legal rights and almost no
way to support themselves, could be trapped in an abusive marriage
with a violent, alcoholic husband. Men who were thought to have
trouble with alcohol were eyed warily at best, and Susa likely worried deeply about her sister.[107]

To separate the young couple, Dora was sent "to study in Provo at
the Utah University branch school."[108] The separation did not work,
and "Dora returned more in love than ever."[109] Susa later wrote of
her sister: "Dear Dora, so beautiful, so gifted, so adorable, she was
the idol of her father's, mother's and little sisters Susa's and Mabel's
hearts. And yet, with all her love and loyalty to them personally,
there lay in the roots of her character, the corroding weakness of
vanity and selfishness."[110] Back home, Dora persuaded Susa to accompany her not once but "many evenings" to the home of Zina
Pratt Bishop, where Dora would meet her sweetheart, "a drunkard
[their] father had forbidden her to flirt with."[111]

The matter came to a head on October 3, 1870. It was a busy
day for the family: Lucy turned forty and Susa received her temple endowments. That evening Susa attended a party in the Young
schoolhouse. Sometime during the celebration, Dora earned her
sister's imputation of selfishness by luring Susa outside with the intention of using her "as a blind."[112] Dora threatened to take poison
unless Susa accompanied her to either the Methodist or Presbyterian

---

106. The Young compound was in the Salt Lake Eighteenth Ward.
107. Gates, 69.
108. Gates, "Lucy Bigelow Young," 71. It is not clear what school Susa had in mind
but probably Warren Dusenberry's, which he reopened in 1869 in the Lewis Building
on Center and 300 West Streets in Provo and considered to be the first branch of the
University of Deseret. Wilkinson, *Brigham Young University*, 1:39–49.
109. Gates, "Lucy Bigelow Young," 62-A.
110. Gates, 69.
111. Gates, "Life Items."
112. Gates, "Lucy Bigelow Young," 72.

minister's home, where Dora and Morley were married. The girls then returned to the party.[113]

Dora was eighteen, free to make her own marriage choice. But, at least in Susa's later recollections, she received the bulk of the blame. How a fourteen year old came to be held at least partially responsible for her older sister's marriage remains ambiguous, but Susa later wrote that three days after the wedding, both girls were called out of class for an interview with their father. Dora begged Susa "to take all the blame," promising to confess the truth later, perhaps when emotions had settled down. Susa agreed and duly "told the lie—and—I can't tell or recall his [father's] talk to me. Poor dear, betrayed father—and mother! I was shut up in my bedroom 3 weeks alone—then Aunt Zina begged to have me given into her care down at little Zina's—that saved my reason and life."[114] Susa could have remained in Salt Lake City with a sister-wife to continue her studies, but as a consequence of this episode, her father "was determined that Susa must live in St. George and withdrew her from the University of Deseret."[115] Whatever the motives behind his decision, it would alter the course of Susa's life.

113. Susa remembered Methodist in one account, Presbyterian in another. Gates, "Life Items."

114. Gates, "Lucy Bigelow Young," 72.

115. Whitley, *Brigham Young's Homes*, 206.

St. 4 George

As Susa's father approached his seventies and suffered progressively from rheumatism, he preferred the warmer winters of the southern settlements in Utah's "Dixie."[1] In 1866, Brigham sent word to church leaders in St. George that he would like to winter there, but he needed the telegraph line to be finished first to discharge his responsibilities as church president. The line was finished the next year. In 1867 Brigham built a house in nearby Leeds for his wife Harriet Cook, who remained there a year or two,[2] but Brigham did not permanently move other members of his family south until 1870.[3]

Historians have speculated why Lucy Bigelow and Eliza Burgess were the two wives chosen to be sent to St. George. Both women were in their forties, both had small families (Lucy, three daughters; Eliza, one son; all but one teenagers), and both were happy to live their lives in the background, eschewing the high visibility and civic leadership roles of others wives. They were also by inclination and habit hard workers. Eliza worked for several years as a servant in the Young household before becoming a wife.[4]

Did Susa and Dora factor into Young's decision to send the family

---

1. Southern Utah is referred to as Dixie due to its similarity in climate to the US South. A Cotton Mission was even established in southern Utah in an effort to make Utah less dependent on imports. See Georgene Cahoon Evans, "The Cotton Mission," *Utah History Encyclopedia*.

2. Gates, "Lucy Bigelow Young," 71.

3. Whitley, *Brigham Young's Homes*, 205. Harriet's son, Oscar Brigham Cook, was Leeds's first blacksmith. See Mariger, *Saga of Three Towns*.

4. Stenhouse, *Tell It All*, 171.

south? Was the decision made before or after Dora's elopement? Could relocating to St. George have been retribution for Susa's complicity in the betrayal?[5] Would moving Susa away from Dora to a remote, rural area help protect her? Susa even wrote in her diary that Dora and she could not see each other. But all these theories seem oversimplified. While Young undoubtedly considered his daughters in his decision, and he remained angry at Dora's surreptitious marriage, other factors certainly loomed larger. Brigham's health was declining, and Lucy had a reputation for being an expert nurturer and healer. Young may have envisioned Lucy caring for him while he wintered in St. George. Lucy became known "for her ability to treat many ills with herbs and blessings, including blessings using consecrated oil."[6]

Emmeline B. Wells later wrote glowingly of the spiritual side of Lucy's nursing skills. Wherever Lucy was, "the sick, the afflicted and the sorrowing send for her, to bless, to comfort and to assist them in prayer and supplication for the mercy of God in the healing of the sick, and comforting of the distressed."[7] Throughout the nineteenth century, LDS women washed, blessed, and anointed one another for the healing of the sick. It is not hard to imagine Lucy responding to a swift knock at her door, gathering her herbs and oils, throwing on a cloak, and riding off to a distant farmhouse to care for a sick woman. Once there, she would gently wash the woman, anoint her with oil, and place her hands upon the woman's head to pronounce a blessing of healing. Over time, later church leaders decided that this common practice should fall under the purview of the all-male priesthood, and the tradition was phased out.[8]

By the time Brigham regularly traveled to St. George, however, most of his care was provided by Amelia Folsom Young, often rumored to be his favorite wife. Brigham and Amelia were wed in 1863 when he was sixty-one and she was twenty-four. Amelia would come to accompany Young nearly everywhere, including southern Utah. Young's marriage to Amelia may have spurred jealousy among

5. Susa, who was attending the University of Deseret, later lamented that she "had to quit school at fourteen." Jenson, "Susa Young Gates," 137.

6. Whitley, *Brigham Young's Homes*, 206.

7. Emmeline B. Wells, "Lucy Bigelow Young," *Young Woman's Journal*, Jan. 1892, 147.

8. Linda King Newell, "A Gift Given, a Gift Taken: Washing, Anointing, and Blessing the Sick Among Mormon Women," *Sunstone*, Sep.–Oct. 1981, 16–25.

some of his other wives who resented the attention the prophet lavished on the younger woman. He later planned an opulent home for her across the street from the Beehive House, a stately manor to host dignitaries, with Amelia in the role of charming hostess. The home was finished after his death and called the Gardo House, but it was nicknamed Amelia's Palace.[9] Susa later wrote that her father's marriage to Amelia was "surely a love match," and for her part, she denied the rumors of infighting among the wives.[10] If Lucy said anything about Young's attachment to Amelia, it has not survived.

Regardless of why he was moving Lucy and her family to St. George or his initial plans for them, Brigham planned well. He arranged for Lucy and Susa, prior to their departure, to take a course in bread, cake, and candy-making at the Golightly Bakery, where the Young family bought their baked goods. This was Susa's and her mother's first journey to southern Utah, while Brigham had made at least ten such trips. He personally inspected every wagon horse and mule, "peering like a well-intentioned wizard into every nook and cranny pointing out a defect here and there."[11] Lucy loved relics, and so as a parting gift Brigham presented her with the Lion House prayer bell; after she left, he bought a new one to replace it.[12]

Seven weeks after Dora's elopement, on November 25, 1870, the Young party left Salt Lake City in multiple wagons, destined for St. George. In the group were Brigham, his wife Eliza, his wife Lucy and her children—Susa, fourteen, Mabel seven, and presumably adopted daughter Ina. Also in the party were Apostle Brigham Young Jr., his wife Lizzie, and Apostle and counselor in the First Presidency George A. Smith, and his first wife, Bathsheba. The first evening of the trip, Susa confided in her diary:

> I suppose I must tell you, dear journal, that Sister Dora is married. Shall I tell you how? Very well. You see Morley and Dora had been engaged for two years, and loved each other very much, and at last they resolved to get married. Papa was very much opposed to their getting married

9. For more on Amelia Folsom Young and her marriage to Brigham, see Hal Schindler, "Brigham Young's Favorite Wife," *Salt Lake Tribune*, July 30, 1995, J1; Turner, *Brigham Young*, 325–27.

10. Gates, "Recollections," box 12, fd. 3, SYGP (USDH).

11. Kane, *Twelve Mormon Homes*.

12. Gates, "Lucy Bigelow Young," 74.

and so was mama. So they didn't run away but walked away and got married by a gentile priest. I feel very bad about it (as I was with them when they were married) because Dora can't come and see Me and I can't see her. I am going to write to her tonight.[13]

No railroad line yet ran south of Provo, and the requisite ten-day wagon trip from Salt Lake City to St. George was arduous. The party covered twenty to thirty miles each day. After a full day of travel, they were met by her father's friends and church officials, who had been alerted by telegraph. Brigham held meetings at almost every stop with the citizens in each town. Progress of the Youngs' caravan was relayed in regular dispatches sent by George A. Smith to the *Deseret News*. For instance, a December 7 telegram advised that Presidents Young and Smith had addressed a large Payson audience at 4:00 p.m. the previous evening; the message concluded, "To-day the weather is clear and cold, and the roads are dusty."[14] These visits by Young and other prominent church leaders were exciting for the small communities dotting the Utah landscape. When a town would learn of an impending visit from Young, they would "set aside that day as a holiday."[15] The dismissed school children would line the road, and a brass band would accompany a detachment of the town's cavalry on horseback.

Midway through the journey, in the town of Scipio (named after the father of the young Lion House courtier Brigham had once taken to calling Skippio Sinner), Susa penned a self-portrait:

> Let me describe myself. I am about 5 feet 3 inches, weight about 115. I am light complected. Dark blue eyes, some call them blue gray. Light brown hair rather curly. Small mouth, red lips and I must confess my teeth are the only redeeming feature of my face. Small, even, and clear as pearls. Clear skin through not white. Small feet and long though beautifully shaped hands, soft and white. Small ears. You may think I am flattering myself but I have endeavored rather to moderate rather than exaggerate myself. Let me tell you what I heard a gentleman say: I was concealed from him. "She has a winning way with her that you cannot resist."[16]

---

13. Gates, "Transcript of Diary, 1870," Nov. 25, 1870, box 1, fd. 2, SYGP (USDH).
14. "President Young and Party," *Deseret News*, Dec. 7, 1870, 1.
15. Wood, "Brigham Young's Activities," 12.
16. Gates, "Transcript of Diary," Nov. 30, 1870.

Thus began a seminal new stage of life for this fourteen-year-old, fair-complected, doe-eyed young woman with light brown hair, red lips, small ears, clear skin, small feet, and beautiful hands. Her childhood surrounded by family and friends in Salt Lake City had come to an abrupt end.

When Brigham and his retinue reached St. George on December 8, it was obvious to at least one observer that he was not well.[17] Brigham made it clear he intended to spend his future winters here. He gave immediate orders for a major expansion, under the supervision of Miles Romney, of "the Chesney house," which had been built by James Chesney in 1869. Romney was an 1839 convert from England and a talented builder who would oversee not only the remodeling of Brigham's home but also the construction of the St. George Tabernacle and the St. George temple.[18] The house expansion was so extensive it would not be completed for a year.[19]

In the meantime, wives Lucy Bigelow Young and Eliza Burgess Young were installed in more modest settings, but each did have her own home. Lucy's, which is no longer standing, was located on the southwest corner of 100 North and 100 West Streets. It was a relatively roomy, New England-style house with two floors, four bedrooms, a parlor, a wide front porch, and a large yard enclosed by a white picket fence. It had a barn, corrals, garden, fruit trees, and grape arbor.[20] Lucy turned easily to domestic endeavors despite having had only limited housekeeping responsibilities during the preceding fifteen years. Her home was crowded that first winter: Brigham and Lucy occupied one bedroom, Brigham Jr. and wife Lizzie another, and the hired help, men and girls, stayed in the other two. The children slept on the floor.

Because of concern for Brigham's safety, "the Bishops counsellors

---

17. Walker, *Diary of Charles Lowell Walker*, 171. Walker, among the first pioneers to settle St. George, wrote that Young looked ill. Walker was a musician, songwriter, poet, and actor whose long, informative diary often referred to Young's and other church leaders' activities in St. George.

18. Today the "Brigham Young Winter Home" remains a major tourist attraction in St. George.

19. Whitley, *Brigham Young's Homes*, 208–09.

20. Gates, "Lucy Bigelow Young," 75; Reuben Wadsworth, "Pioneer Home Day: Young and Hamblin Homes Stand as Reminders of Early Pioneer Legacy," *St. George News*, Dec. 17, 2017.

and the City Council" arranged for armed guards to be posted at Lucy's home at nights for a brief period of time. Potential threats to Young came from within and without. Brigham had been aggressively pushing his cooperative economic plan,[21] and in doing so he had alienated Mormon and non-Mormon businessmen. This had spurred the founding of what became the non-Mormon *Salt Lake Tribune* newspaper, the Godbeite movement, and the Liberal Party, the first challenge to LDS political dominance of Utah Territory. Pressure from federal officials, especially Judge James McKean, was also growing against church leaders over polygamy. But eventually the guards were discontinued, perhaps deemed unnecessary in so quiet a village.[22]

At first, Brigham reportedly divided his time between Lucy's and Eliza's homes. For six weeks he stayed mostly at home, letting George A. Smith and others speak in his place while he recuperated from the excessive labor of speaking duties and traveling."[23] During these weeks, he "and one of his daughters"—Susa—worked on plans for a St. George temple.[24] Susa read to Brigham "over and over again … the descriptions given In Leviticus of the Tabernacle in the wilderness and the account of Solomon's Temple as given in I and II Chronicles and I and II Kings." Brigham wanted to know it all: how "long was a cubit," how the oxen were built that held "the baptismal font, called the sea of brass," and where the font should be.[25] Unfortunately, Susa and her father were interrupted and Brigham's plans to overwinter in the south were soon preempted by a court summons from Judge McKean, and Brigham soon set out for Salt Lake City, despite his poor health.

When Brigham left on February 10, 1871, Lucy's "heart was both glad and sad!" according to Susa. She proved herself "equal to every domestic occasion" and reveled in her husband's company, which she

---

21. Young envisioned what he called the United Order in smaller communities: a utopian-style economic system where all things were shared and goods were produced locally instead of imported. For more, see chapter eight.

22. Walker, *Wayward Saints*; Turner, *Brigham Young*, 357–65; Walker, *Diary of Charles Lowell Walker*, 322.

23. Walker, 305.

24. Since Mabel was only eight, it was almost certainly Susa who worked with him.

25. Gates and Widtsoe, *Life Story of Brigham Young*, 234–35.

normally had to share with many other wives. She was also delighted to finally have "a home of her very own, deeded to her, and with plenty of means to make herself and children comfortable." On the other hand, after this precious time with Brigham, she was "sad, very sad indeed, to see father go out of her daily life for months—how long?"[26] It also could not have helped Lucy's emotional well-being that one of her daughters remained behind. Dora's elopement, with a husband she disapproved of, cast a further pall on Lucy's spirits. Left alone, Lucy threw herself into an "orgy of house-cleaning!"[27]

Susa, ever social, became fast friends with Elizabeth "Libbie" Snow, daughter of Apostle Erastus Snow and future wife of Anthony W. Ivins, later an apostle and eventually First Counselor in the First Presidency. Libbie showed Susa the ropes of semi-annual housecleaning in the dry, dusty climate and "drew the attention of the neighbor's son, Jake [Jacob] Gates," who helped with the heavy work. This is the first mention of Jacob F. Gates as a figure in Susa's life. Lucy praised the Gateses' apricots, grown from seed brought from England by Jake's father.[28] The Gateses lived one block north and across the street from the Youngs.

St. George in 1871 was not yet a cultural (or economic or social) mecca. However, there were in the city several prominent families, who would eventually loom large in Mormondom, including the Ivinses, Snows, Eyrings, and Romneys. Moreover, the Mormon pioneers knew how to relax after a hard day's work—St. George had parties, dances, dramatic programs, prayer circles, a School of the Prophets, etc., besides quarterly and semi-annual church conferences. Susa lost no time in joining the activities. She performed in two plays in a six-week period, acting in *The Rough Diamond* and *The Charcoal Burner* alongside other locals.[29] When Susa was not acting in plays, she created her own culture. She threw parties, gave

---

26. Gates, "Lucy Bigelow Young," 77.
27. Gates.
28. Gates, 77–78.
29. Walker, *Diary of Charles Lowell Walker*, 171. *The Rough Diamond* is a one-act farce by John Buckstone and was performed several times throughout the territory; *The Charcoal Burner; or, the Dropping Well of Knaresborough*, is a melodrama. Both were mid-nineteenth-century English plays.

recitations, and a few years later she helped to form the Union Club, a "progress club" dedicated to "union, friendship, and learning."[30]

During her first year in St. George, on July 24, 1871, Susa helped the residents celebrate Pioneer Day "after the usual manner, Guns firing in honor of the First Presidency, Procession in which figured a few of the Old Pioneers, a few Battalion Boys, Young Ladies in white, young men, old men, Female Relief Society, Music &c &c." The parade marched through the streets of the town "displaying a variety of Flags, Banners, mottoes, emblems" and "speeches were made" by prominent citizens, including Susa. There was much singing by the choir, and in the evening there was "a Dramatic Performance, singing &c. All went off very peaceable and in good order."[31]

The minutes of Susa's speech that day have survived, and they give a glimpse into who the now-fifteen-year-old girl standing in front of a large crowd was. She was asked to speak as a representative of the Young Ladies Mutual Improvement Association; she was also the only female speaker of the day:

> We, the young ladies of St. George feel *honored* in being allowed to participate in the celebration of this glorious day of days, the twenty-fourth (24th) of July. The day that will be celebrated through countless ages, as that in which our fathers gained a peaceful asylum, where they could worship God according to the dictates of their own hearts and consciences, without fear or molestation.
>
> We feel a deep joy and thankfulness to the Giver of all good in contrasting our circumstances now, to those of our Fathers and Mothers when they entered these valleys.
>
> We cannot help comparing the differences in our position to that of our mothers. They, with a few exceptions, enjoyed none of the educational advantages that we enjoy at the present time. Still, it is but lately that we have had many scholastical priviledges in Dixie. Nevertheless we are *grateful*—truly grateful—for those that we *have* had, and shall strive to make the best use of our time and talents, and hope, in time, to be inferior to none in educational pursuits.
>
> Our Mothers! May we always honor, reverence, and *love* them as they deserve.

---

30. Leah D. Widtsoe, interview by Hollis Scott, Feb. 11, 1965, #UA 155, L. Tom Perry Special Collections, Harold B. Lee Library, Brigham Young University.

31. Walker, *Diary of Charles Lowell Walker*, 322.

Our Mothers! *God bless them*—when other names shall [be] in oblivion, they will be held in honorable and loved remembrance by all future generations, the Pioneers of 1847.[32]

In October 1871 Brigham returned to St. George but remained only until January 1872; he had left Salt Lake City in the middle of the night to avoid an arrest warrant from Judge McKean. Young and other church leaders were charged in the murder of Richard Yates after "Wild Bill" Hickman agreed to cooperate with federal officials.[33] Young would be acquitted (and dozens of polygamists freed after being charged with cohabitation) when the US Supreme Court ruled that McKean's anti-polygamy actions violated the law.[34] Susa, an avid reader and participant in community events, would have heard the news and would have seen McKean as an anti-Mormon persecuting the Saints for their religious beliefs and values. Given that she was entrusted by her father to help him make plans for the St. George temple, it is also reasonable to think that the two discussed his legal difficulties.

During Brigham's abbreviated stay, he announced the construction of a temple on a six-acre plot on the south side of St. George and on November 9, 1871, presided over the groundbreaking ceremony. Susa recorded in shorthand her father's comments and the dedicatory prayer offered by Apostle George A. Smith.[35] Also, as "editress" of the St. George *School Gazette*, Susa wrote,

---

32. "Minutes of the Young Ladies Mutual Improvement Association," box 3, fd. 5, SYGP (CHL), emphasis in original.

33. Hickman joined the church in 1839 and served as a bodyguard to church leaders Joseph Smith and Brigham Young. He also operated a ferry across the Green River and served in the Utah territorial legislature. He later published a sensational autobiography titled *Brigham's Destroying Angel*, which claimed he was ordered by Young to commit multiple murders. Like other ex-Mormon exposé-style memoirs published in the nineteenth century, it is difficult to separate fact from fiction in Hickman's account. See Hilton, *"Wild Bill" Hickman*.

34. The court ruled in its *Engelbrecht* decision that McKean had improperly impaneled juries. For different summaries and perspectives of the Yates murder, the charges by McKean, and the court's *Engelbrecht v. Clinton* decision, see Turner, *Brigham Young*, 364–68; Bigler, *Forgotten Kingdom*, 288–92; Arrington, *Brigham Young*, 371–73; and Alexander, *Brigham Young*, 162–63, 311–14.

35. An immediate need was felt for a temple in which to perform sacred ordinances, for progress on the Salt Lake temple, which had been under construction in fits and starts for eighteen years, had been plagued with multiple difficulties and would not be completed for another twenty-two years.

We wonder if one half of us can realize the importance attached to the building of this temple, here in St. George? If we young folks could but imagine the great blessings and benefits that are to accrue from it, we would feel like endeavoring to render it all the support that lay in our power, and would *try* to become more worthy of the blessings which we are assured will be given to us therein. And to think that it only rests with ourselves, whether we enter in and officiate for ourselves and our dead, and that we have the privilege of choosing what we shall hence-forth be; it is indeed a most solemn thought. For is it not said "Many are called, but few are chosen." It remains with us whether *we* are chosen or not, as the pure in heart are the ones who have their lamps trimmed and burning when the bridegroom cometh.

We feel to say "God bless the workmen, who labor day after day and spend their time and means in erecting this temple to the Lord of Hosts. And never may they lack for the blessings of heaven or earth."[36]

This support of her father's building program, along with her activism in the drama society and YLMIA, are strong indicators that Susa would not be following her mother's pattern of public reticence and private good works. Early in life, Susa seemed to choose for her career model her father and the more public of her "aunts."

Susa's forwardness and intensity seem to have impressed some of her teachers and peers as audacious. She seemed to be one of those people who inspired exasperation and annoyance in some who found her off-putting, but who also inspired fierce loyalty in others who admired her brains and her opinionated spunk. In his study of Susa Young Gates, Paul Cracroft pointed to Susa's feistiness in addition to several other characteristics, including, but not limited to, abruptness, lack of tact, vanity, lack of the common touch, and impatience with wasting time. Over the years these traits would lead her to clash with multiple personalities.[37] In a jesting letter that Susa held onto throughout her life, teacher Richard S. Horne imagined various traits in measurable inches and speculated on how Susa would measure up:

---

36. Notes for St. George School Gazette, box 3, fd. 6, SYGP (CHL), emphasis in original. These early writings demonstrate Susa's experimentation with style—much like a student painter imitating the masters—and exhibit a precocious mimicry if not mastery of adult speeches and editorials she was hearing from the pulpit and reading in territorial newspapers.

37. Cracroft, "Susa Young Gates," 32.

We cant exactly remember how many feet make an inch, but we can call to mind the number of inches that are necessary to measure [Susa's] own estimated grains of etiquette, slang phrases, rattle-brain chatter, common sense, self-conceit, reflections on futurity, respect for good advice, domestic duties, care for others feelings, anxiety to please, pleasure of getting others under her influence, delight in making herself generally ridiculous, and lastly but not leastly, throwing away golden opportunities of becoming worthy of friends and friendship. The dimensions are as follows: Etiquette, one; slang phrases, fifteen thousand; rattle-brain chatter fourteen thousand, nine hundred and ninety-nine, and nine-tenths; common sense, five; self-conceit, twelve thousand; reflections on futurity, one; respect for good advice, one; domestic duties, ten; care for others feelings, two; anxiety to please, one; pleasure of getting others under her influence, thirteen thousand; delight in making herself generally ridiculous, fourteen thousand; and throwing away golden opportunities of becoming worthy of friends and friendship, fifteen thousand. The above is a correct result as [illegible] by careful [illegible], and arithmetical calculation [illegible] Miss Susie Young; the author of this is R. S. Horne.

While things like "rattle-brain chatter" and "self-conceit" earned Susa tens of thousands of inches, etiquette and others earned barely any notice at all.[38]

A letter from her sister hints at dislike from another teacher. Dora wrote Susa and encouraged her not to worry that "Miss Eliza Hinkley" did not like her. "I should think you would consider yourself above such small-fry, and not condescend to notice any thing she can say or do." Susa apparently worried that Miss Hinckley (probably Eliza Jane Hinckley, a twenty-year-old schoolteacher from Cove Fort) was influencing her friends to dislike her. Dora responded to Susa that friends who wouldn't like her because of something a teacher would say are not "worthy of your making yourself miserable over their displeasure." Hinckley had spread the rumor that Susa was

---

38. Letter from R. S. Horne, holograph, n.d., in box 3, fd. 5. Presumably "R. S. Horne" was Richard Stephen Horne (1844–1925), whom Brigham Young sent to "the Muddy" to clerk at the new cotton factory. He lived in St. George, teaching adult night school to the factory workers. If Susa was one of his students, he must have taught day school as well, and two years before Susa arrived, he married another student, fifteen-year-old Elizabeth Price. "Compilation from History written by Eva-Durrant Wilson, Autobiography of Richard S. Horne."

not liked any better in Salt Lake City than she was in St. George, a notion Dora labeled jealousy: "O how I would love to give the lie to such low miserable sneaking persons as dare to assail the good name of *my Darling Sue*."[39]

What Dora considered cattiness on Miss Hinckley's part may just have been an expectation of greater emotional maturity from a precocious student. One of the challenges Susa struggled with throughout her life, even at an early age, appears to be snide comments by people who were less talented and intelligent than she. Dora's label of "small-fry" suggests the two sisters saw themselves as special people, perhaps even superior, as daughters of the prophet. As time passed, Susa retained her strong opinions and her impatience with others, but she showed no inclination to superiority based on her heritage.

If Susa's feelings were hurt by schoolyard barbs from both teachers and students alike, they were about to come to an end. Susa's adolescence itself was about to vanish, and her graduation to adulthood would be harsh and full of disappointment.

It is not clear when Susa met Alma Bailey Dunford, but it was probably after she turned sixteen in March 1872. Virtually nothing is known of their courtship. In fact, perhaps the most notable thing about their relationship is how little remains about it. Gates family legend says that Susa expunged all personal records of the marriage except for a brief entry in her unpublished biography of her mother when she wrote, "Susa was married in December, 1872, to a cousin of Dora's husband, and he too drank and the marriage was a most unfortunate one, only that it gave Susa two fine children."[40] What information remains comes from a letter Susa wrote to her half-sister, Zina Williams (see chapter five), and from a few letters preserved by the Dunford family. Near the end of her life, Susa wrote a damning account of this marriage. The account was likely destroyed shortly before or shortly after Susa's death, and it has never come to light.[41]

Alma Bailey Dunford was the son of Isaac and Leah Bailey Dunford, LDS converts from England. He was born on August 19, 1850,

---

39. Dora Young to Susa Young, Sep. 14, 1871, box 1, fd. 1, emphasis in original.

40. Gates, "Lucy Bigelow Young," 84.

41. Lurene Gates Wilkinson, personal communication, Feb. 2009. The only known record of the marriage by Susa, written shortly after her divorce to Alma was finalized, is in a letter to her half-sister, Zina. The letter is detailed in the next chapter.

in Trowbridge, Wiltshire, and emigrated with his family from England at age three. Before settling permanently in Utah Territory, the Dunfords spent eight years in St. Louis. In September 1864, when Alma was fourteen, the family finally arrived in the Salt Lake Valley. By November of that year, they had moved to the Bear Lake settlement at the Utah–Idaho border, where they had been called to help colonize. The family was greatly impoverished. In early 1866, sixteen-year-old Alma was dispatched to Salt Lake City to stay with his older brother, William, and to find work in order to send flour home to their parents. Alma chose to undertake professional training and apprenticed under Dr. W. H. H. Sharp, a prominent Salt Lake dentist.

By 1872, Alma was practicing dentistry on an itinerant basis, typically traveling from "Beaver to Cedar City, to Toquerville and on to St. George."[42] He often found himself in Dixie, where he apparently met the Young daughters through attending parties in their home. The first mention of his association with Susa comes in a June letter to his parents in which he wrote that "Dora is here—she just came down on a visit to her ma and her sister Susie ... is here and lots of other nice young ladies."[43] Alma's casual reference to Dora suggests the family already knew her, since she had married Alma's cousin Morley.

Presumably after that brief aside about Susa in his letter, a courtship emerged. At some point Alma likely approached Brigham Young to ask for Susa's hand in marriage. Unlike her sister, Susa had permission to get sealed in the Endowment House in Salt Lake City. The couple made their way north and were wed on December 1, 1872.

Shortly after their wedding, Alma opened a dental office in Salt Lake City, and he and Susa moved north. Dora was also living in Salt Lake City, leaving Lucy alone in St. George with her youngest daughter, Mabel. By now Brigham Young was spending winters in his new home in St. George, always accompanied by Amelia. Left alone by her oldest daughters and with her husband's attentions turned toward another wife, it was a difficult time for Lucy. Susa later wrote that "it would be impossible to deny that mother's heart twisted with sorrow at the thought of her dear husband coming down to spend his winters in another wife's home." Her mother was

---

42. Isaac and Leah Dunford Family Association, *Dunford Family Story*, 63.
43. Alma Dunford to Parents, June 22, 1872, qtd. in Dunford Family Association.

"human—she was a woman." But she was also a deeply committed Latter-day Saint and polygamist, so "she just quietly made up her mind to meet the situation with her customary sweet patience and faith." If Lucy was jealous or angry, no one heard "a word from her lips except the usual cheerful, everyday talk. She was fond of Aunt Amelia and that friendship was mutual."[44]

The marriage between Susa and Alma seems to have been happy initially. A handful of early letters Susa wrote to Alma's parents are full of love for him. In her first, she called Alma "one of nature's noble men." Other letters proclaim that "he is my only thought and love," that Alma "has the least faults of any man I have ever heard of," and she thanked her in-laws "for the goodness of heart and gentleness of spirit that you have imparted to my dear husband."[45]

Nearly fifteen months after they were married, on February 25, 1874, Susa gave birth in Salt Lake City to her first child, a daughter they named Leah Eudora—Leah for Alma's mother and Eudora for Susa's older sister. A son followed eighteen months later. In June 1875 Brigham invited Lucy to come with Mabel to Salt Lake City again, as "Dora and Susa expect to be sick [deliver children] in August."[46] Lucy came and helped with both convalescences. Both women delivered boys two weeks apart. Susa and Alma named their second child Alma Bailey Jr., born August 13. Dora and Morley named their second child George Albert. But later that year Dora divorced Morley and ended the first of eventually three marriages. Divorce was no less shameful than a marriage to an alcoholic, and Lucy was troubled at the dissolution of her eldest's union.

Susa and Alma moved back to St. George, either in the fall of 1875[47] or the spring of 1876,[48] and for reasons unknown. Susa bought a lot in St. George from her father for $1,000 so that she and Alma could build a house.[49] Whether money actually changed

44. Gates, "Lucy Bigelow Young," 83.
45. Susa Young Gates to Isaac and Leah Dunford, Jan. 13, 1873, in Dunford, *Letters of Alma Bailey Dunford*; Susa Young Dunford to Leah Dunford, Jan. 30, 1874, qtd. in Isaac and Leah Dunford Family Association, *Dunford Family Story*, 64; and Susa Young Dunford to Leah Dunford, Feb. 11, 1874, copy in my possession.
46. Gates, "Lucy Bigelow Young," 85.
47. Gates.
48. Isaac and Leah Dunford Family Association, *Dunford Family Story*, 64.
49. St. George Property and Bill of Sale, box 3, fd. 1, SYGP (CHL).

hands between Susa and her father is unclear. Alma wrote that after he and Susa arrived in St. George, Brigham gave them "a lot in the center of town, a lot that he paid One Thousand dollars $1000 for about Three or four years ago."[50]

Alma drew up building plans, and construction began on the home.[51] Progress was slow, and the home would become a burden to Susa for years to come. Alma complained numerous times in letters to his parents of the lack of business in St. George and the paucity of money. His father-in-law "encourage[s] me to be contented here, but I tell him business is nothing like as good here as it is in [Salt Lake City], but he said I would have plenty of business after awhile, but I want it to come along soon, as I am in need of it."[52] Alma's letters give no hint of the state of his marriage, which apparently was deteriorating even then, nor of the likelihood that he was drinking away some of his much-needed earnings.

Brigham celebrated his seventy-fifth birthday in St. George, and a grand public celebration was mounted in his honor in the new tabernacle. Susa spoke at the event, suggesting that marriage had not stifled her lust for public life. After the celebration, Brigham was invited for dinner at the home of an elderly citizen, who had invited only men over seventy to attend. When Brigham found himself surrounded only by old men, he remarked, "You will excuse me. I am going home to my family. You have invited all the living tombstones in the country to remind me that I have one foot in the grave; so let them enjoy themselves."[53]

A major motif in Susa's life is how she managed to survive psychologically, for years before and after her marriage, as a literary prodigy stowed away in a frontier town that offered little in the way of intellectual sustenance. In her earliest years, living in Salt Lake City, she was exposed to the best education Utah Territory had to offer, with mental and artistic stimulation provided by the bevy of teachers Brigham brought home to give advantage to his large family. But then from the age of fourteen, with the move to southern

---

50. Alma Dunford to Parents, May 25, 1876, in Dunford, *Letters of Alma Bailey Dunford*.
51. Isaac and Leah Dunford Family Association, *Dunford Family Story*, 65.
52. Alma Dunford to Parents, Nov. 22, 1876, in Dunford, *Letters of Alma Bailey Dunford*.
53. Gates, "Lucy Bigelow Young," 86.

Utah, Susa found herself more or less adrift. St. George was a desert in more ways than one. Time and again, Susa demonstrated that she had within her being an overarching yearning for knowledge and self-improvement. Wherever she went, if opportunities for mental advancement and self-expression did not exist, she made them happen. Throughout her life, she constantly strove to associate with the best and the brightest or, lacking that, to create the brightest and best, beginning with her time in Dixie.

One of Susa's proudest accomplishments during her married life in St. George was her involvement in forming the Union Club on August 2, 1876. Her daughter was two and a half, her son was not yet one year old. The club was a self-improvement group that met weekly and concerned itself with a plethora of interests and subjects. Brigham expressed sufficient interest in this endeavor to attend some of its "public exercises." With humor, if not modesty, Susa later described her achievement: "Organized a literary Club in the southern part of Utah, taking up the rough element of the town and through the refining influences of poetry and music worked a thorough change in the youthful society of the town." On December 20 she was elected secretary and treasurer; the minutes that survive, from October 18, 1876, to January 10, 1877, are almost entirely in her hand.[54] The exception is one week, when they were written by her sister, "Dora L. Young," the assistant secretary, who by now had resumed her maiden name and was living with Lucy in St. George.

The ten rules of the St. George Union Club emphasized appropriate dress, punctuality, and participation. Only those "excused by a medical certificate" would not be expected to read, sing, or otherwise perform. Kindness and encouragement were welcome, while "jest, ridicule, whispering, or unseemly laughter" were forbidden during readings or speeches. Novels "of all kinds" (apparently pulp fiction) were to be avoided; only that which "will tend to refine and instruct" was allowed. Rule eight spared young men lengthy walks: "no gentleman be expected to escort any lady home on foot beyond a distance of three miles unless the gentleman be positive and the lady agreeable." Finally, "rude, ungentlemanly behavior" could lead to

---

54. St. George Union Club, 1875–77, box 3, fd. 8, SYGP (CHL).

expulsion if it continued after a warning. After all, "we are striving to refine our minds and manners."

Meeting agendas included opening and closing prayers, songs, select readings, *extempore* speeches, recitations, essays, "side-splitting letter[s]," sacred readings, chapters from classics, dancing, and refreshments. The only minutes that document attendance show eleven members present. All the meetings for this time period were held at Susa and Alma's home. Susa was an active participant; at one meeting she gave a reading; at another she sang a song; at yet another, she presented an original essay on "Formation of Character" and read a chapter from *Oliver Twist* by Charles Dickens. Her sisters, Dora and Mabel, were likewise heavily involved, performing readings, songs, and recitations. At a "Grand Literary Entertainment" given by the Union Club in St. George Hall in May 1877, Susa sang a duet with J. E. Johnson, participated in a dialogue with three other people, sang in a trio, and played the role of Fanny Grudge in "The Tragical Duel."[55]

Susa's promotion of the Union Club may have struck some St. George citizens as pretentious. However, many locals appreciated Susa's energy, creativity, and willingness to put herself out while benefitting others. On learning of her impending departure from St. George later that summer (because Alma had received a mission call to England), her singing partner J. E. Johnson wrote to Susa:

> Permit me to express my high appreciation of your efforts, through the Union Club, to improve, in letters manner, and polish, the social condition of our young folks, by the careful blending of instruction with amusement. And especially I thank you for the friendly solicitude you have so constantly exhibited towards those of my children who have been associated with you. I have been the recipient of your sisterly counsels and instructions. And believe me, when I say, I much regret that your departure will so soon deprive them of the association that has so much Amused and interested them.[56]

Although the St. George temple was not complete, enough portions were finished to facilitate temple work, and the dedication took place on New Year's Day, 1877, before an estimated throng of 10,000

---

55. The records detailing the creation, rules, minutes, and performances are in St. George Union Club, 1875–77, box 3, fd. 8, SYGP (CHL).

56. J. E. Johnson to Susa Young Dunford, box 3, fd. 8.

people. Using her stenographic skills, Susa acted as recorder for the dedicatory services, a responsibility she would repeat for the Logan temple in 1884 and the Salt Lake temple in 1893. Lucy was called to act as president of the "sister workers" in the St. George temple, and both Dora and Susa served as ordinance workers. Baptisms for the dead commenced on January 9, 1877. Since Susa was the first person ready, she was the first person to be baptized in the pristine font supported by twelve shining brass oxen in the temple basement, with Apostle Wilford Woodruff officiating. She served as proxy for eight women and Alma for twenty-two men.[57] The next day Lucy was the first person to undergo an endowment ordinance for the dead. Brigham declared that, to his knowledge, this was the first endowment ever performed on behalf of a deceased person, "for history does not give us to understand that the ancient Saints ever worked for their dead in the giving of those higher gifts and blessings."[58]

Susa and Alma prepared to leave St. George as Alma readied himself for a mission to England. Alma was shocked by the call and disappointed that he could not finish his house before leaving. He asked his parents if Susa and their children could live with them in northern Utah after he left for England in the summer.[59] What Alma may not have known or, more likely, had not wanted to admit to himself, was that he was being sent on a mission to give him an opportunity to reform his heavy consumption of alcohol. The marriage was already rife with trouble. When Susa and Alma reached Salt Lake City, she and the children moved into the Lion House; he did not. A large part of their differences may have related to money, or in this case, a lack of it.

Susa despaired. She wrote an angry, frustrated letter to Dora who, perhaps she felt, might be the one person who could understand what it was like to be unhappily married and the daughter of the stern prophet at the same time:

> How do you suppose I can go out or receive company? The children and their Mama are decidely out-of-place, in this stylish hell-hole [the Lion House]. ... I get up in the morning, and do but precious little till I go

---

57. Alma Dunford to Parents, Jan. 28, 1877, in Dunford, *Letters of Alma Dunford.*
58. Gates, "Lucy Bigelow Young," 87–89.
59. Alma Dunford to Parents, Apr. 29, 1877, in Dunford, *Letters of Alma Dunford.*

to bed at night, but vainly try to keep my young ones out of other people's way. ... I have done my best to do as Father told me and get away somewhere else, but there is not one soul (with the exception of course of Alma) in all Salt Lake City that will let me stay with them until Sept. I have tried to get reporting, music teaching, and school teaching to do, but all in vain. Father *kindly* offered me in about as rough a way as possible to give me a 100 lbs bag of flour to last me till I went south. Accompanying the offer with the remark that whoever he did for or looked after, he would do nothing for me. ... How *gladly* would I support myself if I could. But what can I do with two children. I have tried every means in the world, to get something to do, but even Father told me I could do *nothing* with two children to tend. I haven't an idea what I shall do for the next three months.

She wanted work so that she could support herself, but as a married mother of two young children, she had no options. She had no intention of going to Bear Lake to live with Alma's parents because "Alma's father felt as though he could not make me comfortable." But St. George was also not an option. "The house is untenantable until door-locks and glass can be got and put in. How can I earn anything down there? What shall, what can I do?"[60]

Alma left Salt Lake City and made his way by train to New York City where, on July 17, he had boarded the steamship *Wisconsin*. A week later the ship was about 500 miles from Liverpool, where all LDS missionaries disembarked and made their way to the mission office for their assignments.[61] Sometime after Alma had departed for England, Susa went to see her father to ask for money. As Susa later wrote, it did not go well:

He [Brigham Young] had been so understanding and so gentle that I perhaps took advantage of his mellow sympathy and went the next morning to ask him for financial help. I was in some considerable trouble at the time, and he had answered me rather sharply because as I found afterwards, several of the girls and one of his own sons had just preceded me with far more insistent requests and demands upon his resources. I said nothing. How could you say anything to father? Nobody ever answered father back.[62]

60. Susa Young Dunford to Dora Dunford, June 13, 1877, box 1, fd. 2.
61. Alma Dunford to Family, July 25, 1877, in Dunford, *Letters of Alma Dunford.*
62. Gates, "Thoughts about Death," box 1, fd. 5, SYGP (USDH).

Susa, miserable in the Lion House and with nowhere else to go, finally agreed that she and the children would live with Alma's parents in Bloomington, Idaho, during the summer of 1877. On the ride north, Susa was glimpsed through the train window by her father in Brigham City, where he was attending a conference. Brigham sent his son John W. to fetch Susa so that he could talk with her outside. Susa, furious at her father's unwillingness to help her find a job or loan her money, refused—twice—until at the third request John informed her he was holding the train and would physically carry her off if she did not come. So, accompanied by her two little children, Susa went to Brigham's carriage where "he drew me up to the seat beside him and took me in his arms and blessed me and healed all the hurt that he had made before although he did not mention [it], nor did I." Neither knew it at the time, but it was the last time Susa would see her father alive.[63]

On August 13, 1877, Brigham wrote to Susa the only letter he ever directed to her personally. He reported, "We have heard of the safe arrival of Alma and the rest of the party at Liverpool, but have not yet learned in what district of Country he has been assigned to labor." Things must have been better with Alma's parents than Susa expected, because Brigham wrote that he was happy to "learn of the comfortable position in which you found yourself, through the kindness of Alma's Father and Mother." He was happy to report that his own health "continues to be excellent." Although much of the letter was formal, with the usual well-wishes of good health, he did report that "I took a bath in the great Salt Lake for the first time in many years, and enjoyed it exceedingly." He signed this only letter he wrote to his daughter, "your affectionate Father."[64]

Sixteen days later, at age seventy-six, Brigham Young died in Salt Lake City as a result of an acute abdominal condition. Whether his death was due to a ruptured appendix, as postulated, or a perforated diverticulum or cancer of the colon, is unclear. Thus passed into history "the Lion of the Lord."

The night before Susa departed Salt Lake City to stay with Alma's parents in Bloomington, her father shared a significant thought

63. Gates.
64. Brigham Young to Susa Young Dunford, Aug. 13, 1877, box 1, fd. 10.

with her that she later recorded. It has become something of a Gates family mantra to the present time. Susa was counseled by her father: "If you were to become the greatest woman in the world, and your name should be known in every land and clime, and you should fail in your duty as wife and mother, you would wake up in the morning of the first resurrection and find that you had failed in everything. But all that you can do after you have satisfied the claims of home and family will redound to your honor and to the glory of God."[65]

---

65. Miscellaneous Notes, box 11, fd. 2, SYGP (USDH).

Divorce

Brigham Young's funeral was held in the Salt Lake Tabernacle on Saturday, September 1, 1877. Approximately 12,000–15,000 people attended the services, including nearly all of his wives and children, and scores of grandchildren.[1] An estimated 50,000 people crowded onto the grounds of the Tabernacle.[2] In accordance with Young's wishes, the services were simple. He was laid to rest in a plain redwood casket and dressed in his temple clothes. The men wore no crepe, and the women bought no black bonnets, dresses, or veils—although Young had permitted mourners to wear them if they already had them.[3]

Young was eulogized by church leaders Wilford Woodruff, Orson Hyde, George Q. Cannon, and John Taylor.[4] Susa accompanied Apostle Charles C. Rich and President William Budge of the Bear Lake Stake from Idaho, where she and her two children, Leah and Bailey, had been living with her mother- and father-in-law since husband Alma's departure to England as a missionary.

Susa's mother, Lucy, and younger sister Mabel began a frantic trip north from St. George to make the funeral services in time. They traveled with Wilford Woodruff, and the trip, which usually took at least a week, took them "three days and nights, telegraphing

---

1. "Brigham Young's Funeral," *New York Times*, Sep. 3, 1877.

2. Susa Young Gates, "Memories BY Death," box 1, fd. 5, SYGP (USDH).

3. Brigham Young, "Funeral Plan," typescript in box 3, fd. 38, SYGP (CHL). Susa requested that Young's plan be mirrored for her own funeral.

4. "Brigham Young's Funeral," *New York Times*, Sep. 3, 1877.

ahead for relays of horses and drivers, sleeping as we could."[5] Lucy and Mabel arrived in Salt Lake City two hours before the services began. Mabel described "how solemn and impressive was that simple service. No pomp nor ceremony. ... Thousands upon thousands of the saints, their eyes and hearts full of grief, crowding to the very doors of the tabernacle, and filling the grounds."[6] Thus ended the life of the man who had once told Susa, "If it were not for Mormonism, I would be a carpenter in a country village."[7] For all the strange circumstances around nineteenth-century Mormon polygamy, Susa had loved her father and Lucy had loved her husband. Both would miss him. Brigham's last words to Lucy had been, "Take care of the girls! Look after the house, and work in the Temple all you can."[8] Lucy would spend the next year or two "taking care of the girls."

In September 1877, while still in Bloomington, Idaho, Susa, always ready with a handy word of advice, had some thoughts for her current town. Susa objected to what, at least, to her mind was, the privileging of Paris, Idaho, over Bloomington. Her criticisms spilled out in public in a lively exchange with the editor of the *Deseret News*, and at least one reader, taking exception, thought Susa "cast a slur on this people." Susa, keen as always to be clear, said she "would like to set myself right." The problem was the availability—or lack thereof—of reliable goods and services. "*All thorough mechanics* are invited to settle in Paris" (emphasis in original). The Bloomington carpenters and butchers, she allowed, may "do something," but they were not "apprenticed tradesmen." If "a shoe is to be mended; not even a cobbler here to do the job. A team must be hitched up, and away we go to Paris to get it sewn up. Perhaps this engenders a trip or two for the shoe before it can be got. It is the same with coopering, blacksmithing, or masonry." Her complaint was "no discredit to Bloomington," but rather she took issue with "a feeling in the people of Paris" that they were entitled to a "monopoly" on tradesmen. "There must be nothing done or allowed that will give any place a rivalry of Paris." Susa preferred Bloomington to Paris; all she wanted,

5. Gates, "Lucy Bigelow Young," 90a.
6. Gates.
7. Susa Young Gates, "What My Faith Means to Me," *Juvenile Instructor*, June 1918, 291.
8. Gates, "Lucy Bigelow Young," 89.

and was quick to suggest, was "a few mechanics coming here in order to set this place on an equality with Paris."

She used the public debate to push another issue: she objected to the co-ed meetings of the Young Mutual Improvement Association. Susa had attended the gatherings of the young men and women, and felt that if meetings were held separately it would compare favorably with meetings elsewhere in the territory. The "joint meeting of the young people ... seemed to me hardly conducted rightly." She suggested that "the Presidency from S[alt] L[ake] City visit them" with "some special instruction given to the youth [on] how to conduct these joint meetings." She concluded that she had "the best of feelings for all" and that she had no interest in giving "offence."[9] Susa's outspokenness and strong opinions, coupled with her apparently sincere desire to cause no umbrage, was a hallmark of her young adult years.

Susa's older sister, Dora, whose precipitous marriage in October 1870 to Morley Dunford had figured in the relocation of Lucy and her younger daughters to St. George, had also moved to Utah's Dixie to be with her mother. Alma Dunford wrote to his parents from Cedar City on July 7, 1876, that "Dora is still with her mother, but her health is improving slowly. ... I receive a letter once in a while from Morley and he don't like it at all his wife being a way from him, but I understand she don't intend going home until she is entirely well." Health was obviously not the major issue in their marriage, since less than a month later Dora filed for divorce in probate court in Washington County. Dora's marriage to Moreland was one of many unwise decisions that ultimately led to her unhappiness. Her choices disappointed and troubled her mother for several years, and the heartache she caused would continue for the rest of Lucy's life.

Dora's divorce complaint, sworn before Adolphus R. Whitehead on August 2, 1876, said that the couple "cannot ... live in peace and union together, more particularly on account of Defendant's [Moreland Dunford] intemperate habits and incompatibility of temper, and that their welfare requires a legal separation."[10] On September 14, 1876, Dora appeared in court, but Moreland, who had been

9. Susa Young Gates to Editor *Deseret News*, Sep. 27, 1877, box 1, fd. 2, SYGP (CHL).

10. "Dunford vs Dunford," Civil and Probate case files, Washington County Probate Court, box 1, fd. 16, Series 26638, Utah State Archives, Salt Lake City.

"thrice called," did not appear, thus defaulting. No attorneys are mentioned in the records, but two witnesses appeared for the plaintiff, Lucy B. Young and Susie Y. Dunford.[11] Lucy swore under oath "that Moreland Dunford is very intemperate in his habits, drinking very excessive and getting intoxicated very often … at times threatening and abusing the inmates" of the home. Susie swore that "she has repeatedly seen the Defendant intoxicated, at times being brought home almost uncontrollable and dangerous, using rough language and threatening those around him."[12]

Dora fared well in court, undoubtedly helped by her husband's refusal to appear. Judge William Snow granted her custody of both sons and possession of their house in Salt Lake City, which had been built on a lot that her father had given her, as well as all household furniture. In addition, Moreland Dunford was ordered to pay $25 for the plaintiff's attorney fees and $20 in court costs—roughly $500 each in today's value.

Within six months Dora became a plural wife of Wilford Woodruff,[13] and received her "second anointing" with him on March 21, 1877.[14] In a show of how intertwined Mormon families could become, Woodruff had previously offered his daughter Phoebe as an additional wife to Brigham Young, who demurred, so Phoebe instead married Lorenzo Snow, who would become the fifth president of the church. Now, Woodruff had married Young's daughter. Dora gave birth to Woodruff's child on April 1, 1878; the baby died the same day. If Lucy Young had hoped her daughter's marriage to an apostle would create lasting happiness, she was soon to be disappointed. Dora and Woodruff divorced shortly after the death of their only child together, and Dora eloped with a married man.[15] Woodruff biographer Thomas G. Alexander wrote that "at least four of [Woodruff's] marriages failed for reasons not entirely clear … perhaps his neglect in Eudora's case."[16]

---

11. Susa was still going by Susie at this time.
12. "Dunford vs Dunford."
13. They married on March 10, 1877.
14. Alexander, *Things in Heaven and Earth*, 230. For more on the second anointing, see Buerger, "Fulness of the Priesthood."
15. Alexander, 404.
16. Alexander, 332.

Her sister's success in her divorce may have given Susa ideas of her own. On February 21, 1878, Susa's missionary husband, Alma Dunford, wrote to his parents from Manchester, England, that he was suffering "the greatest grievance that could fall to a man while on a mission." He had not received any letters from Susa for several weeks after she left Bloomington. Finally a letter came from St. George, dated October 27, 1877. It was "written well, and well put together and *full of love for me*."[17] But on New Year's Day 1878, Alma received another letter "asking for a bill of divorce."[18]

Dunford was shocked and "nearly out of my mind for days." All Susa had said was "she doesn't love me and consequently doesn't wish to live with me." She asked him whether he would rather she pursue the divorce "from the church or courts."[19] Alma conferred with his superiors in the mission and was told to continue to correspond with Susa as though he had not received her letter asking for the divorce. Alma wrote to President Joseph F. Smith and was awaiting word from him whether he should return home to Utah. Alma said the news had made him "unfit" him for the mission. "I can't do justice to myself nor the cause. ... The brethern here ... say they wonder how I stand it as well as I do." Alma found Susa's action particularly painful, since "there was never a man came on a mission with a greater desire to fill an honorable mission than I did." He concluded, "I don't wish to be separated from my Dear Wife and darling babies, and I hope, trust and pray I never shall be, but I pray for all things to be over-ruled for the best."[20] He opted to stay on his mission for the time being.

The mission leaders' advice to act as if nothing had happened showed they did not know Susa Young very well. She had already laid the groundwork to dissolve her marriage. She approached Adolphus Whitehead, the same court clerk who dealt with Dora's divorce, and indicated she too wanted a divorce, but asked for the proceedings

---

17. Dunford to Mother and Father, Feb. 21, 1878, in Dunford, "Letters," emphasis in original.

18. Susa Dunford to Alma Dunford, Dec. 7. 1877, in Dunford, "Letters."

19. Dunford, "Letters," and "Dunford vs Dunford," Civil and Probate case files, Washington County Probate Court, box 1, fd. 24.

20. Dunford to Joseph F. Smith, in Dunford, "Letters."

to be kept private.[21] Whitehead asked if Wilford Woodruff knew of Susa's action, and she said he did. Woodruff, she insisted, approved of the split since the couple "had never been happy together since they were married."[22] Woodruff had, in fact, spoken with Judge William Snow and indicated his desire that the divorce be "done as still as possible."[23] Susa had previously asked President John Taylor about getting the divorce in Salt Lake City when she was visiting there, but Taylor apparently thought she should wait until Alma came home from his mission.

On February 1, 1878, Susa officially filed complaint against Alma in Judge Snow's court, sixteen months after Dora's appearance there to end her own marriage. Susa's complaint said that "in consequence of incompatibility of temper the said Plaintiff and the said Defendant cannot live in peace and union together and their future welfare requires a legal seperation."[24] She added "that she did not wish to expose Almas faults too much, consequently she only complained of Incompatibility of Temper."[25] She would come to regret her unwillingness to be too critical.

When questioned by the clerk about custody of the children and division of property, Susa indicated that she would ask for the children and that "the Property was all hers except a portion of the Furniture and the Organ and Almas Office furniture."[26] Susa wanted the divorce right away, but, with Alma away, it was not so simple. He would need to be informed of the complaint, either by publication or by being served a summons. If Alma would "accept service, sign and return the summons," the divorce could proceed without further delay. Whitehead explained to Alma that there was no desire "to take any advantage of his absence," and three options were offered him: sign the summons accepting the service, employ someone in St. George to defend him in absentia, or appear in court himself.[27]

21. Macfarlane, *Yours Sincerely*, 173.
22. Macfarlane.
23. Macfarlane.
24. "Dunford vs Dunford," Civil and Probate case files, Washington County Probate Court, box 1, fd. 24.
25. Whitehead, "Sketch of Whitehead," 2.
26. Whitehead, 3.
27. Whitehead.

Alma stunned Susa when he chose the third option. He quickly returned home from England, presumably on borrowed funds, since he had written several times in letters to his parents that he had little money. He arrived in Salt Lake City on a Thursday night and by Sunday sent a telegram to Susa, who claims that he "never … hint[ed] … to me that he even had the slightest intention of leaving England."[28] When Susa learned that Alma had returned to Utah, it "completely upset me. I knew of course that Alma was determined to have the children, and knowing as I did his oft-repeated threat to have them in spite of God, angels, devils, or men I scarcely knew what to do." She felt "completely unprotected. No brother, no father, my sister very low, and alone in mother's house with Rhoda and the children."[29] She sent the children to stay with the Nixon family in nearby Trumbull, because she was afraid Alma "would come and take them away."[30] What's more, Alma was no Moreland Dunford. He had "sought legal advice, and was told just what to do in order to make his case good."[31]

Church officials made attempts at reconciliation—attempts that quickly unraveled. Alma visited Susa, bringing local LDS leaders with him. Alma asked about the family's furniture, but Susa had sold it to her mother in payment for room and board during Alma's time in England.[32] Alma "then asked me for both the children, and the deed to the place in [Salt Lake] City."[33] Both requests were beyond the pale for Susa. She and Dora had both been given lots in Salt Lake City by their father with a firm "promise never to deed away our property to our husbands," and Dora had received her Salt Lake property as part of her divorce settlement. Susa's steadfast refusal to give Alma her father's property became a major obstacle in their divorce proceedings.

Instead, Susa, feeling she "could not break my solemn promise to

28. Susa A. Young to Zina Young Williams, May 18, 1878, box 3, fd. 14. This letter was written shortly after the divorce was complete; Susa had dropped Dunford from her name and signed as "Susa A. Young."

29. Young to Williams.

30. Whitehead, "Sketch of Whitehead," 3.

31. Young to Williams.

32. Macfarlane, *Yours Sincerely*, 173.

33. Young to Williams.

my dead father," counter-offered to deed the Salt Lake City property to their children, which would allow Alma the use and benefit of it until Leah and Bailey were of age. Alma would have none of it. Susa then consulted with St. George bishop David H. Cannon, who approached Alma and suggested that the case be handled by arbitration or a church court. Once again, Alma refused, "So after this all that remained was to wait till the court commenced" on April 22, 1878.[34]

Susa was urged by Judge Snow and by John M. Macfarlane, defense attorney, to seek legal counsel,[35] but was unwisely advised by Bishop Cannon to "go there armed with truth, and refuse to empl[o]y lawyers to increase bad feeling and make expense."[36] Whitehead also advised her to seek legal counsel from E. G. Woolley.

Susa steadfastly refused legal counsel and appeared in court with her mother "alone and unattended,"[37] although White later wrote that she brought "three other Witnesses."[38] Based on her sister's favorable treatment in the same court with the same judge just nineteen months earlier, Susa may have felt that "truth" alone would prevail. If so, she did not consider that Dora's divorce had been uncontested and the defendant did not appear. Alma, on the other hand, entered the courtroom with two attorneys and a legal assistant, and they promptly made short work of Susa's homespun proceedings. The defense attorney explained that Susa "was permitted to act as her own advocate." But she was untrained in the law and "being entirely unfamiliar with court procedure ... coached the witnesses, telling them how to answer." Of course, "the defense objected," but Susa "scornfully refused to play by their rules," so that Snow and the defense attorney finally gave up and "abandoned the device of objection as judicially useless." Macfarlane concluded that "Judge Snow, as well as the defense attorney, was lenient with Susie out of consider[ation] for her family, and she was allowed to get away with conduct that would not have been permitted from someone else."[39]

---

34. Young to Williams.
35. Macfarlane, *Yours Sincerely*, 173.
36. Young to Williams.
37. Young to Williams.
38. Whitehead, "Sketch of Whitehead," 4.
39. Macfarlane, *Yours Sincerely*, 173.

Whitehead, the court clerk, concurred with Macfarlane's assessment. "Not being acquainted with the usage of eliciting testimony, she would tell the Witnesses what to say." Whitehead thought that only "one unaccustomed to Courts would think she did not have a fair chance," but Susa was fortunate that "the Court and defense were very lenient with her."[40]

Susa obviously viewed the process differently. "My witnesses were called one after another. Every question I asked was objected to on some ground by the lawyers. ... When I had tried to get the best evidence I could from mother, the lawyer interrupting me constantly, he commenced to cross examine her." When she tried to give her own evidence, "the lawyers immeadiately objected and the court ruled" against her. She felt that "it was impossible to make a remark ... without the lawyer constantly interrupting me." Finally, emotionally exhausted and drained from the proceedings, "feeling outraged at the indignities heaped upon me, I burst into tears and lost all control of myself for a time." Unlike Macfarlane and Whitehead, Susa felt that the judge was against her since he "never once attempted to induce the lawyer to desist from his ungentlemanly course."[41] After this disastrous outcome, several acquaintances of Alma spoke of his "gentlemanly behavior in public, the business reputation he enjoyed &c, but never one denial of the drinking, swearing, and personal abuse inflicted on the plaintiff in private."[42] Alma also presented thirteen letters from Susa, now lost to history, written to Alma while on his mission in England, professing her love for him.[43]

These letters threatened to upend the whole trial. After it went on for two days and both sides had presented their evidence, Snow saw no cause for divorce in view of Susa's letters. But Dunford "in his plea, admitted that now the parties could not live in peace together, in consequence of the course of Susie in commencing the suit, sending off the children, disposing of the furniture &c."[44] Given this admission, the divorce was granted by Snow, but only after two weeks had passed to give Susa and Alma a chance to agree on the

40. Whitehead, "Sketch of Whitehead," 4.
41. Young to Williams.
42. Young to Williams.
43. Whitehead, "Sketch of Whitehead," 2.
44. Whitehead, 5.

division of property. But the two weeks were time wasted. Their relationship had become so contentious that no amount of time would likely resolve any differences.

Susa was granted the divorce she wanted from Alma, but at a very high cost. It was in many ways the opposite outcome of her sister Dora's divorce. Alma was given the Salt Lake City property with all her family furnishings, including "Office furniture, Books, Pictures and papers." But even worse to Susa, Alma was given "the care, custody and control of Leah Eudorah Dunford, Aged Four years, and the guardianship of Alma B. Dunford, Aged two years."[45] Susa would only have "care and custody of the youngest child, Alma," as well as possession of the St. George property.[46]

Division of the St. George and Salt Lake City properties in this way caused Susa two problems: First, she would have to break her promise to her father not to divest the lot he had given her; and second, being deeded the St. George property imposed financial obligations she would struggle to meet. The Dixie property was "built by Alma" only after he received "two thousand dollars" from Susa's father. This "house is not only unfinished, but there is a lien on it, and some ten or eleven hundred dollars due to workmen, and for material—all of which liabilities fall upon the plaintiff"—Susa.[47]

She despaired, "Oh how my heart swelled with indignation. My children torn from me by a man, whose only care is reputation and money. And my word to my father cast aside as naught." But her promise to her father was nothing compared to her feelings as a mother. "Oh my children. Completely overcome, and broken-hearted, ma and I left the court. ... With torn and bleeding heart, I sought my home, and clasped my precious children to my bosom. [Alma's] friends thronged around him to congratulate him on his success, while only God's angels came to bind up my lacerated heart."[48]

Alma appeared at Susa's home, demanding the pictures he had been awarded and even refusing to leave Susa the picture of her father. It had been a gift from Brigham to her. He also took the Bible

45. "Dunford vs Dunford," Civil and Probate case files, Washington County Probate Court, box 1, fd. 24.
46. "Dunford vs Dunford."
47. Young to Williams.
48. Young to Williams.

her father had given her. Susa, however, drew the line at her wax flowers. Alma insisted that his money had paid for the frames, so Susa took down the pictures, broke the glass, removed the flowers, and laid the frames on the rest of the pictures. Then, adding further insult to injury, Alma sent the clerk of the court with the deed to the Salt Lake City property for Susa to sign.[49]

On Friday, May 10, Susa went to the courthouse where she took the deed, wrote the names of her children on it instead of Alma, listed Alma as their guardian, and signed it. Because she had defied the court, Snow ordered her to appear on Monday on charges of contempt of court. Susa once again outlined her reason for refusing to sign the deed to Alma, which she considered a broken promise to her father. She offered to pay Alma the cost of the house; he refused. Losing her temper, she threatened Snow that she would hold him responsible before God, to which the judge replied that he would take the entire blame. Susa then "signed the deed calling upon all present to witness I did it not of my own free will but because Judge Snow compelled me to."[50] The judge insisted that she acknowledge to a notary public that she had signed "freely and voluntarily," which she "positively refused to say." She said she had already lied to her dead father, and she refused to tell another lie by saying she had signed away the property voluntarily. For her obstinance, Susa Young, daughter of Brigham Young, went to jail.

She was incarcerated in Washington County jail until about 10:00 p.m. that evening. Frank Farnsworth, who had come to visit her, became upset and declared that "he never heard of such a thing as a woman's being forced to deed away her property and then ... [say] she did it freely and voluntarily." At Farnsworth's outrage, the notary and judge decided that her signature would suffice, and Susa was discharged. "I walked out in the open air a free woman, but oh with such a sense of burning injustice filling my heart."[51] The ordeal must have devastated her.

Why did Susa so abruptly divorce her husband? The causes have been speculated by family members and historians for well over a

---

49. Young to Williams.
50. Young to Williams.
51. Young to Williams.

century, and multiple theories have been proffered. Susa destroyed almost all records related to her first marriage, making the detective work all the more difficult. Nearly all information has come from Alma's letters to his family and the brief accounts of John Mac-farlane, defense attorney, and Adolphus Whitehead, clerk of the Washington Country Probate Court. The only information extant from Susa is her letter to her half-sister Zina, written just five days after her imprisonment for contempt.

One theory is financial. Alma, particularly in southern Utah, was not as successful as he wanted to be, and he often had difficulty collecting his fees.[52] Another theory is that Susa, married at age sixteen, "was sexually uninformed, psychologically unprepared for the intimacies of married life."[53] This speculation has been perpetuated in at least three other accounts of Susa's life, two of which were written by direct descendants of Alma Dunford.[54] The information for this theory comes mostly from Anne Widtsoe Wallace, a librarian at the University of Utah and granddaughter of Dunford. Other sources are Susa's daughters, Leah Dunford Widtsoe and Lucy Gates Bowen.[55]

Susa herself left no doubt about the cause of the divorce: Alma's heavy drinking and abusive behavior. In virtually her only extant words about her first marriage, there is biting, unmitigated criticism of Alma. Susa's lengthy letter, a transcription of which fills eight single-spaced typewritten pages, began by informing Zina of her intent to relate the events of the preceding four weeks.[56] "I will place before you if possible the simple, plain truth, uncolored by my opinions, and open to through investigation." She asked Zina to recall the many nights Susa spent alone, especially

> one evening, when, frightened out of my own house by the lateness of the hour, and the lonliness of the whole atmosphere, I knocked at your door,

---

52. Robinson, "Susan Amelia 'Susa' Young Dunford Gates," 75.

53. Cracroft, "Susa Young Gates," 8.

54. See, for example, Cornwall, "Susa Young Gates," 68; Person, "Susa Young Gates," 201; and Robinson, "Susan Amelia 'Susa' Young Dunford Gates," 75. Carolyn W. D. Person and Kari Widtsoe Koplin Robinson are Dunford descendants.

55. Cracroft, "Susa Young Gates," ii.

56. The following quotes from Susa and summary of her divorce come from this letter, which, as of this writing, is scanned and available online through the CHL. See Young to Williams.

my face wet with tears, and shaking from terror. ... Also of the numbers of times when Alma was what he termed tight (not *drunk!*) [emphasis in original] ... and so on till the afternoon when, with my six month's old girl I came to your mother and begged her to let me stay with her as Alma had first abused me, then sternly ordered me from his roof telling me never to return. ... My sorrow, and finally my returning to take up my cross, and seek to be ever more kind more forgiving. Call to your memory the times I have told you how full of anguish my life often was.

Susa explained that the move to St. George in 1876 was an attempt to allow Alma to break loose from unhealthy associations "and bring to both our hearts that peace and love which never had been with us since the first few weeks of wedded life, and which I had almost completely despaired of."[57] But this did not resolve their problems since "our unhappiness was constantly increasing and finally God sent his servant [Brigham Young] to call him [Alma] on his mission. ... If ever he would have a chance to reform it would be on his mission." This may have explained her loving letters to Alma while he was in England; Susa probably wanted to be encouraging in the hope that things would finally turn around. However, absence did not make the heart grow fonder, and when Susa returned to Salt Lake City after spending the summer of 1877 with Alma's family in Idaho, she found that "the longer Alma and I were seperated the less like ever seeing him I felt."

Susa claimed to Zina that she confronted this issue in a letter to Alma but received no answer for several weeks. When he finally responded, he said,

Now wife, as far as my drinking, you know well enough how I talked to you before I left Dixie. ... And as for proving myself, I can do that home as well as I can here. You can believe it or not, it is the honest truth, I never started out with the intention of getting drunk in my life. ... You say if I come home with that terrible appetite still clinging to me you are afraid I will find neither wife nor home. ... I can make money and enjoy myself, and I am not going to throw myself away for nobody; just write & let me know how you feel long about the time you think I will get released from my mission, cause if I cant find wife nor home, I shall stay in this country for a while for I can do *very* well in this country [emphasis in original].

57. Susa sharply, as I read it, underlined this sentence in her original letter.

Susa found this answer unpalatable and remarked to Zina, "This cool indifference, and slurring reply to only a request to leave off that beastly habit, just settled itself down in my mind as the key which firmly locked the door to all further intimacy between A. B. Dunford and myself." She tried desperately to do the right thing, and she took her sealing to Alma seriously. "Each morning and night, I prayed God to show me which was the right way to take. I knew how sympathy would run, for I had proudly and silently kept the door locked on the hideous skeleton, who had been my companion for years."

The divorce and aftermath were extraordinarily acrimonious, and there is little evidence that during her lifetime Susa ever regretted any of her actions with regard to Alma. Numerous biographical entries over the rest of her life make no mention of him.[58] As Susa went on to become one of the most well-known women in Mormondom, Alma B. Dunford did not register in her reckoning.

Dunford did become a successful dentist. In 1882 he married Lovinia Clayton, daughter of William Clayton, author of the famous Mormon hymn, "Come, Come Ye Saints." They had eight children. According to one of their granddaughters,[59] Dunford continued to struggle with alcohol and gambling until shortly before his death in 1919.

One final theory on the divorce suggested that Susa made a deathbed confession, saying, "May the Lord forgive me for any wrong I may have done Dr. Dunford—unknowing."[60] This purported admission, first mentioned without attribution, has no evidence. Unfortunately this so-called "confession" has been perpetuated in later publications.[61] Lurene Gates Wilkinson, the granddaughter who served as Susa's amanuensis during the last year of Susa's life, and spent three to four afternoons a week working with her, insists that Dunford's name never once crossed Susa's lips the last year of her life, at least in Lurene's presence, and no mention was ever made of their marriage.[62]

---

58. See, for example, a *Deseret News* article naming her Utah's Mother of the Century. *Deseret News*, Sep. 6, 1975, W1.

59. Personal communication, Nov. 2010.

60. Cracroft, "Susa Young Gates," 38.

61. See, for example, Cornwall, "Susa Young Gates," 69; Harold Schindler, "Utah War Broke Hold," *Salt Lake Tribune*, July 23, 1995, J1, 4.

62. Lurene Gates Wilkinson, personal communication with the author, Feb. 2009.

6

Brigham Young Academy, the Sandwich Islands, and Jacob Gates

Susa's decision to divorce Alma Dunford and its troubling aftermath rippled through the two families and their communities. It would saddle Susa with financial obligations that she could not manage, and her separation from her daughter devastated her. But her newly single status would also open up possibilities for her future—possibilities she likely could not have imagined as a young married mother of two children.

At least some members of the Dunford family were upset that Susa sought a divorce while Alma was in England on a mission. He was teaching the gospel and, at least to their minds, overcoming the weaknesses that led Susa to leave him. Susa's half-sister Zina Young Williams responded to Susa's lengthy letter with one of her own and admitted that "public feeling has been against you," but reassured her that "your friends have been with you in your sorrow."[1] Zina, ever faithful sister, commiserated with Susa: "Is it possible one of my own dearest sisters should have to pass through all this? My blood boiled, my tears flowed, my heart ached." Zina shared a "sweet peace" that stole over her, and tried to comfort Susa with the words she felt God whispered inside her: "I am God, she is one of my children, if she wears a crown she must earn it." This was, according to Zina, a trial Susa would have to pass through, and when she came out on the

---

1. Zina Young Williams to Susa A. Young, May 29, 1878, box 3, fd. 14.

other side, though it would "take time," she would be "a wiser and a better woman (now) you were good as gold before."[2]

One friend from Bloomington, Idaho, who knew Alma's parents, offered to speak to them on Susa's behalf and plead her case. The Dunford family remained convinced that Susa had no cause to divorce Alma. In the absence of what they felt was a reasonable justification for such a rash act, one wonders what, if any, *mala fides* they might have ascribed to Susa. Aware that the Dunford family did not think Susa was "justified in taking the steps you have," her Bloomington friend, L. M. Hart, suggested that she could confide to Alma's mother and "tell her some things you have told me." Whether or not such a conversation took place is unknown, but it seems unlikely that Alma's parents would have been easily persuaded to see things from Susa's point of view.

After her divorce, Susa conferred with John Taylor, who had been sustained as president of the Quorum of the Twelve Apostles two months after Brigham Young's death. She expressed interest in returning to school. She told Taylor she had quit school at fourteen, although records show that in 1872, when she was sixteen, she was attending Richard Horne's school in St. George. Taylor offered Susa a "Normal scholarship in the University of Deseret," and help with books and supplies.[3] However, Apostle Erastus Snow, a close friend of the Young family in St. George, advised Susa, "If you want to go to school, I'll tell you the place to go, a school which has been founded and endowed by your own father and where you will not only be taught the different branches of education, but a place where the spirit of God burns in every line and word spoken and written by its preceptor."[4] Snow wanted Susa to go to the Brigham Young Academy (BYA) in Provo.

The next day Susa took the train from Salt Lake City to Provo, where she met Karl G. Maeser, the Dresden-born president of BYA, and one of her old teachers at the schoolroom near the Beehive House. Susa came to regard Maeser as the greatest educator in Mormon

---

2. Williams to Young.

3. Susa Young Gates, "The Original Music Department," *Young Woman's Journal*, May 1892, 337.

4. "Original Music Department."

history, a man for whom she developed a "reverent filial love," which was second only to what she felt for her father.[5] Shortly thereafter, Susa enrolled for the fourth academic year of the institution.

Susa, a twenty-two-year-old divorcee, was something of an anomaly at the school, but she was a motivated and dedicated student. She knew she could learn "in schools and colleges of the various cities in the Territory," but BYA's combination of "religious training with other first-class advantages" was what caused her to enter "my name as a student." She hoped to "discipline my mind, and establish those habits of method and order, which form so valuable an adjunct, to the usual school duties. ... My intentions are strictly honorable, and highly proper."[6]

The school year of 1878–79 was a seminal event for Susa. She reveled in a world of freedom, discovery, and intellect. She enjoyed the Polysophical Society,[7] and through her association with Maeser, she "imbibed a love for the application of the gospel to every study and every pursuit."[8] He encouraged her to pursue a literary career and taught her critical thinking, how to "think out the answer of my problems."

Several weeks after school began, Susa's mother intervened with Maeser and asked that Susa be allowed to teach music lessons at the academy. This would allow Susa to provide, at least, in part, for herself. When he asked if Susa was qualified, Lucy responded that Susa had been giving music lessons since she was fourteen years old. Within a few days plans were underway for the creation of a music department under Susa's direction. Susa bought a piano and contributed it to the academy. Teaching kept her busy with forty-four thirty-minute lessons twice a week for twenty-two piano students, five half-hour vocal lessons, regular two-hour choir practices, and lesson preparation—all in addition to her own classwork.

---

5. "Original Music Department," 339.

6. Susa Young Gates, autobiographical notes, box 1, fd. 2, SYGP (USDH).

7. The first Polysophical Society in Utah was founded in 1854 by Eliza R. Snow and her brother Lorenzo, and meetings were held in his home in Salt Lake City. It functioned as a cultural and intellectual club, and attendees heard readings, poetry, music, and watched dramatic performances. The society was shut down in 1856 at the height of the Mormon Reformation, but by the 1880s various wards and communities had begun to sponsor them. See McKenzi Christensen, "The Polysophical Society," *Intermountain Histories*, www.intermountainhistories.org, accessed Mar. 27, 2020; Davidson and Derr, *Eliza*, 88.

8. Gates, "Original Music Department," 339.

Despite this busy schedule there was a plethora of extracurricular activities for Susa to join in. After an unhappy marriage, Susa was attending parties, weddings, receptions, concerts, and picnics. She was going on hikes in the canyons, swimming in the Provo River, riding astride a mule, sitting around campfires, attending overnighters, and jumping into late-night bull sessions with fellow students.

Susa was stimulated by her contact with the other students. Zina, whom Susa had poured her heart out to after her separation, was with her in Provo. Among the other students was a veritable who's who of future luminaries: Samuel Thurman, Chief Justice of the Utah State Supreme Court; Benjamin Cluff, president of Brigham Young University; William King, US senator; James E. Talmage, apostle; Reed Smoot, apostle and US Senator; Joseph Keeler, dean of the BYU Business College; and Stephen Chipman, president of the Salt Lake temple. In 1879 George Sutherland, future US senator, president of the American Bar Association, and US Supreme Court Justice, began his studies at BYA.

In addition to her associations with other students, Susa was earning her own money. Because she was a teacher, the school board paid her $50 a term (ten weeks) with a promise of much more "next term" and got her "a carpet for my floor." With the money she earned and the purchases from the board, her living arrangements were comfortable. "My room looks quite nice now, it is white washed, carpeted, with a lovely carpet, blinds, curtains, nice walnut table, new chairs & I have also my piano here."[9]

While all of this was exciting for Susa, her first year at school also brought a surfeit of problems, the most painful of which were the aftershocks of her divorce. Alma had been awarded full custody of their daughter, Leah, and over the next several years Susa would see her infrequently. Following the split in May 1878, Leah first lived with her father in Parowan in southern Utah while he practiced itinerant dentistry. But after September of that year, Leah went to live with Alma's parents in Bear Lake.[10] She stayed in Bear Lake until 1882, continuing to live with her grandmother after her grandfather, Isaac Dunford, died in October 1879. But in February 1882, Alma

9. Susa Young to Dora L. Young, Feb. 2, 1879, box 1, fd. 4.
10. Alma Dunford to William Dunford, Sep. 10, 1878, in Dunford, "Letters."

married Lovinia Tricilla Clayton, three days after Leah turned eight. Lovinia was the daughter of William Clayton, Joseph Smith's scribe in Nauvoo. Thereafter, Leah lived with her father and his new wife in Salt Lake City.

Susa had been awarded custody of her son, Bailey. It is not always clear where Bailey was living over the next few years. He was with his mother at least part of the time, and for several weeks in March and April 1879 Susa missed classes after Bailey got sick. She cared for him, and as word spread to her friends of the illness, letters came with advice. One suggested she "take a weak solution of blue vitrol ... and swab out his throat."[11] James Bleak, a close friend in St. George, kept his medical advice to himself and offered that he was "thankful that you were privileged to be near your little boy in the time of danger; and fervently pray that you and he too may be preserved from the contagion."[12]

But while Susa had Bailey with her during this time, at least one report says he lived with his father's parents in Bear Lake at some point. Given that Susa was busy teaching and doing her own schoolwork, it is likely that Bailey spent time in other homes, though not his maternal grandmother's. Susa's mother, Lucy, was still in St. George and unable to spend time with her family, and she was miserable for it. She lamented to Susa, "*My Dear Daughter* why is it that we are so scattered. Dora and Dear little [Georgie] out in the cold world. Darling Leah in Idaho. You and Dear little Baby in Provo, and our Dear Br. W.[13] we know not where, and Rhoda [Mabel] and Johnny and [illegible] and I here in St. George" [emphasis in original].[14]

Susa, perhaps shaken by Bailey's illness, grew desperate to see her daughter. She wrote to LDS President John Taylor and asked him to intervene with her ex-husband on her behalf. Although that letter is now lost or unavailable, Taylor's reply indicates that Susa had made a proposal and was using the church president as an intermediary. He told Susa that he had "no objection to the plan you suggest with regard to your children," but that he could not promise that

---

11. [William V. Price] to Susa Young, Mar. 20, 1879, box 1, fd. 4.
12. James Bleak to Susa Young, Apr. 4, 1879, box 1, fd. 5.
13. "Bro. W" may well be Wilford Woodruff, whom Dora had recently divorced.
14. Lucy Young to Susa Young, Mar. 14, 1879, box 1, fd. 1.

Alma "will be disposed to listen to my suggestions." Taylor asked for Dunford's address, but regardless of whether or not he passed on Susa's suggestion, nothing happened and Leah remained in Bear Lake with her grandparents.[15]

While Susa juggled teaching, schoolwork, and worries over her children, her mother was unhappy and her sister's life was unraveling. Lucy struggled with the unhappy marriages of all three of her daughters; Dora and Mabel ("Rhoda") were each married three times and Susa had just gone through a divorce. Susa asked Dora, living in Salt Lake, "My girl why can you not go south just a little while this winter." She brought her many literary talents to bear to guilt her sister into action. "Think of that dear old gray haired mother weeping, praying, and longing for her beautiful first born. ... Oh could you not sacrifice a few months out of your young life to comfort the weary heavy heart of your old mother?"[16] Dora's abrupt response six days later made it clear she did not appreciate her sister's clumsy attempt to strike at the pangs of her conscience. "In the first place I think it would be foolish to start on such a long journey in the midst of winter, even if I had the chance to go, which I have not. And again I do not want to go. I have made up my mind to spend this winter here in Salt Lake and I consider I have a perfect right."[17]

Dora's refusal to visit her mother was nothing compared to the rumors that she was collaborating with US marshals, presumably in anti-polygamy pursuits. At least someone claimed to have spotted her "riding out with the officers of the Court and other strangers & walking with U.S. Marshall." The rumors reached Lucy who "feels terrible bad," and it was under this guise that John McAllister wrote to Susa from St. George to ask her if she knew anything. He acknowledged that he "cannot judge" the truth of the rumors, but that, in addition to being seen with the marshals, there was worry that she had sworn out an affidavit against someone, likely her ex-husband, Wilford Woodruff.[18] Susa took the rumors seriously enough to ask her sister, who vehemently denied the charges. That she had to

---

15. John Taylor to Susa Young, May 9, 1879, box 1, fd. 5.
16. Susa Young to Dora L. Young, Feb. 2, 1879, box 1, fd. 4.
17. Dora L. Young to Susa Young, Feb. 8, 1879, box 1, fd. 4.
18. McAllister to Susa Young, Mar. 10, 1879, box 1, fd. 4.

answer at all made her "indignant," as she would rather "die before I turned traitor or informant."[19]

While she worried about her family and her schooling, Susa also had to solve multiple property problems. She had been awarded the St. George house in her divorce, while Alma had received the Salt Lake City property—the exact reverse of what Susa had asked for during the trial. Not only had the Salt Lake City property been her father's and she had promised never to sell it, the house in St. George was unfinished and uninhabitable, and debts were outstanding. Sometime early in 1878 David Cannon had filed a lien on the Dunford home while Alma was still in England. Susa had sold the family furniture to pay the debt, and her efforts to help only became another source of contention during the divorce proceedings.[20]

Five months after the divorce, Susa learned that Isaac Hunt and David Rogers, both of St. George, had filed liens on the Dunford home for $293.65 and $92.36, respectively. Alma refused to pay the debts since Susa had been awarded the property. If she did not pay, the property would "probably be sold to pay the debts."[21] James Bleak had counseled Susa to sell the St. George home, since she did not intend to live in it anyway. He thought she could exchange the house for a Salt Lake City property, which would be easier to sell. "I think you had better pay what 'Alma house' debts you can, in Winsor [Windsor stocks, bequeathed by her father] at par." If she did so quickly, Bleak thought she could "pay most of the building debts."[22] But Susa had not acted fast enough, and Bleak, who had agreed to help her repair the property, grew "very much annoyed by the water rising in the cellar" of the house. Despite attempts to fix a stopped drain and repair a pump, water continued to accumulate, probably because of gopher holes. In addition, Lucy's mental and physical health continued to suffer. Bleak told Susa that her mother "needs our faith, prayers, comforting words written and spoken, and our

19. Dora Young to Susa Young, Apr. 24, 1879, box 1, fd. 5.
20. Whitehead, "Sketch of Whitehead," 3.
21. Whitehead, 28. Adolphus Whitehead, the same clerk who oversaw Susa's divorce, informed her on October 22, 1878, of the liens.
22. Bleak to Susa Young, Aug. 17, 1878, box 1, fd. 3.

kind acts. She feels comforted in hearing from you, and from your certainly good sister Zina."[23]

Susa was fortunate to have a job teaching music at BYA, but she faced additional financial problems. She received no alimony or child support from Alma, and she worried frequently about how to earn enough to support herself and Bailey. She had inherited a large sum from her father, valued at $18,000—surely enough to let anyone live handsomely in 1879.[24] But the Brigham Young estate, intertwined with church and territorial finances, was embroiled in controversy and lawsuits for several years, and Susa likely had difficulty getting cash from her assets.[25] In fact, her sister Dora was one of seven Young children who contested Brigham's will.[26] Getting her inheritance was on Susa's mind, at least, partially, because Zina continued to investigate on her behalf: "The estate affairs are still agitated, the Lord only knows how things will end, but we will hope for the best."[27]

It had been a whirlwind of an academic year for Susa, "crowded full of experiences, and the many and valuable lessons I learned during that period have been of incalculable worth to me." She learned a great deal and felt that "the friendships and acquaintances formed in this beloved institution will go with me through all time and I hope through all eternity."[28] But, as it would transpire, her first year at the Brigham Young Academy was also her last. Susa was about to embark on a sea voyage that would lead to another unexpected turn in her life.

Shortly before his death, Brigham Young had an idea to combat the public outrage towards polygamy. Americans who read dime novels and newspapers, or attended lectures on polygamy across the country, were told, seemingly ad nauseam, that LDS women were oppressed, bullied, and even trapped or kidnapped by wily Mormon missionaries and forced into ruinous plural marriages. What better

---

23. Bleak to Susa Young, Apr. 4, 1879, box 1, fd. 5.

24. Approximately $350,000 in 2022 US dollars.

25. Inventory of Susa A. Young estate, box 3, fd. 13, SYGP (CHL).

26. The others were Emeline A. Young, Vilate Y. Decker, Elizabeth Y. Ellsworth, Ernest I. Young, Louisa Y. W. Ferguson, and Marinda H. Y. Conrad. See Arrington, *Brigham Young*, 429.

27. Zina Williams to Susa Young, July 1879, box 1, fd. 5.

28. Gates, "Original Music Department," 339.

way, Young thought, to combat such notions than to send prominent Mormon women throughout the country to speak on the status of women in Utah and in LDS households? He proposed six women, including two of his best-known wives, Eliza R. Snow, who was serving at the time as general president of the Relief Society, and Zina D. Huntington Young, who would succeed Eliza as the general president of the Relief Society in 1888. Young also envisioned his daughter Susa and her half-sister Zina as members of the committee. Eliza went to talk more with Brigham about his plans, but he responded, "It is an experiment I would like to see tried. You go lightly along Eliza, but I am tired, and I shall now go and take my rest."[29] That same night he lapsed into a coma and died, but plans went forward to carry out his idea.

Almost two years later, Zina D. Huntington Young departed for the Sandwich (Hawai'ian) Islands.[30] Susa had always been close to "Aunt Zina," as Zina was universally called. At the end of her first school year at BYA, Susa wanted to go to London to study. But she had listened to two church leaders who told her to go to the academy, and now she listened to another—Joseph F. Smith—who recommended she accompany Aunt Zina to Hawai'i.[31] Susa agreed to go, and they departed in early July 1879. The *Deseret Evening News* wished them "a happy voyage, a pleasant visit, and a safe return."[32]

With the benefit of hindsight, it is tempting to think Susa's decision was influenced by the presence on the islands of an old friend from St. George, Jacob F. Gates. She had written to him months before her journey, and he had answered back in a letter from Wailuku, Maui, certain it was her "on seeing the postmark" because he had "no friend in that vicinity unless it was Susie Young." He wrote that he

---

29. Susa Young Gates, "Thoughts about Death," box 1, fd. 5, SYGP (USDH).

30. The name Sandwich came from James Cook, a European explorer who sailed to the islands in 1778. The islands, occupied by "up to one million Polynesians whose ancestors had been in residence for at least a thousand years," were not seen as one place by locals, but several. The islands had separate names and meanings, but sometime in the nineteenth century the name Hawai'i, itself a "colonial by-product," gained prominence as the name for all the islands. Because the LDS missionaries called it the Sandwich Island mission, I use that name as well as Hawai'i, aware of the complicated history of western colonists imposing European names on native peoples. Herman, "Aloha State," 76.

31. Jenson, "Susa Young Gates," 137.

32. "To the Islands," *Deseret Evening News*, July 3, 1879, 3.

"should like to see you" because he had a "great deal to talk about" with an "old friend."[33] Susa's letters to Jacob during this time have not survived, but he expressed delight at the correspondence, and, upon learning that she was coming to the islands, the hope that he would have the "extreme pleasure" of her company. "If per chance we meet, which we might do, we will try and have a good time." Still, he held back somewhat. "I never commit much to paper Su, or I might say a little to you on a certain subject that you may be sure springs up in this mind occasionally. But I will postpone it till we meet."[34]

By 1879, travel to the Sandwich Islands was more reliable than it had been when the first LDS missionaries arrived on the islands in 1850. Steamships made regular journeys with mail and cargo, and Mark Twain had helped popularize the islands when he visited in 1866, stayed for four months, then afterward lectured and wrote about his experiences.[35] But although Susa and Zina likely traveled in relative comfort, safe passage was not guaranteed, nor was the safety of the islands. James Bleak offered a wry look at Susa's personality when he wrote to her that "it seems such an odd break for even your eccentric self to make an excursion to what, but a few years ago, were called the 'Cannibal Islands!'"[36] Bleak's hyperbole aside, while Susa was in no danger from cannibals, disease and other hazards were distinct possibilities. Indeed, Zina was sick most of the two-week journey, while Susa enjoyed the crossing.[37]

Jacob Gates wrote to his parents that "Sis. Zina D. Young and Susie" arrived safely on July 18 and were "enjoying themselves very much."[38] Susa and Jacob spent a great deal of time together during her six-week stay.[39] Susa and Zina remained busy during their visit—meetings of the Relief Society every other day with the natives, sleeping in "native houses," purchase of an organ for the branch of the church, donations of $50 each "for the good of the natives,"

---

33. Jacob Gates to Susa Young, Jan. 8, 1879, box 6, fd. 2.

34. Gates to Young, Mar. 18, 1879, box 1, fd. 5.

35. Mak, "Paradise in the Pacific," 5.

36. Bleak to Susa Young, July 17, 1879, box 1, fd. 5.

37. Cornwall, "Susa Young Gates," 70.

38. Gates to Parents, July 28, 1879, box 4, fd. 10.

39. Proscriptions against dating while on a mission apparently did not exist in 1879, as they do today.

outings hunting for ferns, and mule rides.[40] Jacob was an indispens-
able part of the Relief Society meetings, ostensibly for the purpose
of translating from Hawai'ian, in which language he was fluent.

Jacob Forsberry Gates was named after both his parents, Jacob
and Emma Forsberry Gates.[41] The two were stalwarts in the fledgling LDS Church. The elder Jacob was born on May 9, 1811, in St.
Johnsbury, Vermont, to Thomas and Patty (or Lucy) Plumley. He
worked as a farmer with his father and also did work as a carpenter and joiner. He was baptized alongside his father and brother by
Orson Pratt on June 18, 1833. Jacob Gates weaved through prominent church history events. He worked on the construction of the
Kirtland (Ohio) House of the Lord (also temple), participated in the
Army of Israel, also called Zion's Camp, moved to Missouri when
the Saints left Ohio, was imprisoned for three weeks there, and finally made his way to Quincy, Illinois.

Jacob wed Mary Minerva Snow on March 16, 1833. Mary was
one of only ten women in the Army of Israel. In December 1838,
during the turmoil in Missouri, Jacob was ordained a Seventy by
Joseph Smith and his first counselor, Sidney Rigdon.[42] Jacob served
several missions to Ohio, Missouri, and Indiana, before leaving for
New England in June 1843. After Joseph Smith and his brother
Hyrum were killed a year later, Jacob and Mary prepared to leave
with other Saints to the West.[43] Because of Mary's inability to have
children, she encouraged Jacob to enter into a plural marriage with
Caroline Hutchins. The two were married in the unfinished Nauvoo
temple on January 21, 1846. Caroline later died in childbirth; the
baby girl also did not survive, and both were buried on the west side
of the Missouri River.[44]

Jacob and Mary arrived in the Great Salt Lake Valley on October 4,
1847, and settled into the new home of the Saints. He was called on a
mission to England two years later. On his way east to sail to Liverpool,
he stopped in Richmond, Missouri, to meet with an old acquaintance:
Oliver Cowdery. Cowdery had been one of Joseph Smith's earliest

40. Zina D. H. Young, Diary, qtd. in Cornwall, "Susa Young Gates," 70.
41. For clarity, I refer to the father as Jacob and to his son as Jacob F.
42. Jenson, *LDS Biographical Encyclopedia*, 1:197.
43. Jenson, 1:198.
44. Jacob F. Gates, "My History," box 5, fd. 12, SYGP (CHL).

confidants and was one of the Three Witnesses of the Book of Mormon, but he subsequently became disaffected with Smith. Jacob would later recount that Cowdery testified to him that the "Book of Mormon was translated by the gift and power of God," and that after he left the church he "felt wicked."[45] Jacob Gates's story about Cowdery, which purported to recount specific dialogue between the two men decades after they spoke, became an important part of the way Latter-day Saints remembered an increasingly mythologized past.[46]

Jacob's first British mission lasted three years (1850–53), during which he presided over several conferences and, upon his return home, oversaw a company of British converts emigrating to Utah Territory. One of the members of the pioneer company was Jacob F.'s mother, a young twenty-three year old named Emma Forsberry. She and Gates married on October 23, 1853, less than a month after their arrival together in the Salt Lake Valley.

Emma was born on July 27, 1830, in Leicester, Leicestershire, England, to William and Sarah Forsberry, a middle-class working family. When she was about sixteen years old, Emma was first taken to an LDS service by a friend named Betsey. Attracted by the singing of their hymns, Emma soon converted against the wishes of her well-intentioned parents. She became interested in "gathering with the Saints in Zion," and she and Betsey began to save their money for passage to America. When the time came, she and Betsey secretly gathered their belongings and stole away to Liverpool, there to board the sailing ship *Ellen Maria*, bound for New Orleans, with other Mormon immigrants. Emma was missed immediately, and her father, accompanied by a police officer, followed her to Liverpool, where he found her already on board the ship. Emma would recall that a tearful encounter ensued, and she finally persuaded her father to let her go. When he gave his assent, the two of them each cut a lock of hair for the other, and Emma never saw her father or her mother again.[47]

---

45. Jacob Gates, "Testimony of Jacob Gates," box 5, fd. 12, SYGP (CHL), later printed in the *Improvement Era*, Mar. 1912, 418–19.

46. See, for example, Flake, *Politics of American Religious Identity*.

47. Jacob Gates, "My History," typescript, in Autobiographies, box 5, fd. 12, SYGP (CHL). Fifty years later Emma returned to England with her daughter-in-law Susa, her step-granddaughter Leah Dunford Widtsoe, and Leah's husband, John A. Widtsoe. Although her parents were deceased, Emma was reunited with her younger sister Sarah.

Emma's trans-Atlantic voyage lasted nine weeks before she disembarked in New Orleans. Many Saints who immigrated to Utah
had to stop along the way and find work to pay for the remainder
of their passage, and Emma was no exception. She worked briefly in
New Orleans, made her way to St. Louis, and then to Keokuk, Iowa,
where she met Jacob Gates for the first time. Nine months and one
week after they were wed, Jacob F. Gates was born. Jacob Gates was
forty-three years old; Jacob F. was his first child to survive infancy.
He and Emma had five more children; he and another plural wife,
Mary Ware, would have five sons and two daughters. Jacob continued to serve in the church, including another mission to England,
outfitting companies to cross the plains, and finally as a president
of the Seventy for thirty years. He died April 14, 1892, in Provo;
Emma lived for another fifteen years, dying on October 12, 1907.

Jacob F. Gates's earliest recollection was in 1858 when the Saints
in the Salt Lake Valley, fearing destruction by the invading United
States army, fled south. The Gateses settled on the banks of the Provo
River where young Jacob recalls falling into a big spring of water from
which he had to be rescued. The move was temporary and the family
returned to Salt Lake City. In 1861 Jacob F's father was called to settle
the southern part of Utah Territory in St. George. Jacob F. was seven
years old and became a hero among his young friends in Salt Lake
City because of the impending move. The family, consisting of Father
Jacob; two of his wives, Emma and Sarah; and his and Emma's three
sons (Jacob F., Franklin, and Jedediah) lived in a tent all winter. The
school Jacob F. and the other children attended was likewise held in
a large tent. Life was difficult—the hot weather was miserable; brush
was used to construct fences because of lack of wood; the land was
"sandy and poor"; and the alkaline water was not fit to drink. The
boys traded with the indigenous peoples for arrows, which they used
to hunt rabbits. The Navajos came to trade blankets for horses, some
of which were "desert wild horses," tamed by the settlers, including
Jacob and his sons. Amusements consisted of simple games, such as
"town ball" (similar to baseball), "pomp pomp pullaway," "steal sticks,"
"hopscotch," and "root the pig." The elder Jacob soon built his family a
comfortable home, one of the finest in the new city.[48]

---

48. Gates, "My History."

But the harsh landscape was punishing. Jacob F.'s "Aunt Sarah," one of his father's wives, died of typhoid fever, the first known death in the colony. After his mother, Emma, gave birth in 1862 to her only daughter, she was easily fatigued for the rest of her life. Perhaps that was why, when his father continued to be a prominent leader, including as a member of the Territorial House of Representatives, Jacob F. went to Salt Lake City at least twice to live with his father's first wife, Aunt Mary Snow Gates, who had remained behind. He stayed with her from 1864 to 1865, and again during the 1866–67 school year.[49]

In September 1875 Jacob F. went north once more from St. George, this time as a twenty-one-year-old student at the University of Deseret. A year later he received a mission call to sail to the Sandwich Islands. He departed on January 30, 1877, and arrived to the Islands in February. He performed missionary labors among the natives and oversaw the field work on the church-owned Laie Sugar Plantation. He became skilled in the native language and twenty-five years later would complete a second translation of the Book of Mormon into the Hawai'ian language. A little over two years later, he was reunited with his St. George friend, Susa Young.

After their time together, Jacob F. hoped he would be able to return home with Susa. But his mission release did not come in time and instead he escorted her and Aunt Zina to their steamship.[50] Susa's departure, if anything, only increased Jacob F.'s ardor. He wrote to her a week after she left, calling himself "Jake," and her "my love, my darling, her in whom all my hopes of future happiness have centered." In a few months' time, Jacob F. Gates had gone from "never commit[ting] much to paper" to openly declaring his love for Susa in a letter. Their time together on the islands must have been idyllic, at least, to him. No amount of rapturous affection was enough: "O how my heart yearned for you and how I longed to reach out my arms to the fast receeding vessel that was carrying you away, and snatch you from among that crowd ... and bring you back to that busom (upon which you so loved to rest)."[51] Jacob F's long-awaited

49. Gates.

50. Jacob F. Gates to Parents, Sep. 1, 1879, box 4, fd. 10.

51. Jacob F. Gates to Susa Young, Sep. 7, 1879, box 6, fd. 2.

release came sometime in September, and he arrived in San Francisco on October 8. He wrote to Susa of his joy at seeing "family, friends—and what is dearer than all—my Sue."[52]

Perhaps given the intensity of his letters to Susa, some writers have wondered if Jacob Gates was a cause of Susa and Alma Dunford's divorce.[53] It seems unlikely, given the chronology of events. Susa and Jacob had known each other at least since 1870, and Jacob later recorded that he was impressed when he saw Susa dance in the Salt Lake Theater in 1867. But this recollection only came after their marriage. Jacob had been in Hawaii since February 1877, and there is no evidence of romantic inclinations prior to their time together in Hawai'i. Jacob's first extant letter, dated January 8, 1879, is friendly but platonic. Whatever happened before in their pasts, Jacob was now madly in love with Susa, and she apparently reciprocated his feelings. On January 5, 1880, less than three months after Jacob returned to the United States, the young couple married in the St. George temple.

---

52. Jacob F. Gates to Susa Young, Oct. 8, 1879, box 6, fd. 2.
53. See, for example, Petersen, *William Snow*, 151; and Macfarlane, *Yours Sincerely*, 175.

Family Life

Susa and Jacob spent the first three years of their married life in St. George. It was a busy time for them; Susa gave birth to four children between their marriage in 1880 and their departure to the Sandwich Islands for a four-year mission in 1885. Susa was occupied with childbirth, homemaking, writing, and acting, while Jacob engaged in several professional endeavors and spent much of his time traveling to support the family.

Throughout their lives, during their frequent, often extended, absences from one another, Susa and Jacob usually corresponded on a daily basis, sometimes every other day, and rarely at longer intervals. On Susa's way home to St. George from Milford and Minersville, in company with Bailey, she wrote to Jacob, "Oh I am so passionately anxious to see you my king *my own*" (emphasis in original).[1] She and Jacob were both hopeless romantics in their letters; they seemed delighted to be married to each other. No detail was too mundane. Susa described household cleaning chores at great length: "I shall write the little home chronicles like these for it is my life, dear."[2] Susa's son through her first marriage, Bailey, must have liked Jacob, since he elected to travel with him on some of his work excursions.

Ten months to the day after they were married, Susa and Jacob's first child, a daughter named Emma Lucy, was born on November 5, 1880, in St. George. Susa's mother was absent in the East at the time

---

1. Susa Gates to Jacob Gates, July 22, 1880, box 9, fd. 4.
2. Gates to Gates, Oct. 13, 1880, box 9, fd. 4.

of the birth of Emma Lucy, who was called "Lule" in her early life.[3] Lucy had become intensely involved in temple work after the 1877 dedication of the St. George temple, and because of the Mormon emphasis on work for the dead,[4] she had carried on considerable correspondence with cousins to obtain family history records. A Bigelow family reunion was scheduled for the summer of 1880, and Lucy braved the journey alone across the country to the gathering in New York. The railroad had come a long way, making what once must have seemed to be an unthinkable journey into a possibility, but it was still an arduous trip for Lucy. The Utah Southern Railroad terminated several hundred miles north of St. George, and Lucy needed to make the overland journey to the nearest station.

This was Lucy's first trip outside of Utah Territory since she had crossed the plains in 1848. Susa missed her mother, but was cheered by visits from her father's widows, Aunt Eliza Snow and Aunt Zina Young, who were "holding meetings with the sisters."[5] When Lule was six weeks old, Susa wrote her mother, "I have not been very well; had several 'back sets,' and am only now beginning to feel at all like myself. ... You will of course want to know about 'our baby.' Need I say, she is the sweetest baby ever born."[6] Lucy made the return journey home from New York and arrived in St. George in late 1880. She stopped in Salt Lake City for a time to attend to outstanding Brigham Young estate financial matters.

Susa had a new husband, a new baby, and her mother was back in town. Perhaps she recalled the loneliness of her first marriage, ensconced in the Beehive House after Alma left for England, but she jumped at the chance to spend time with people. Susa reveled in the celebration of milestones, births, anniversaries, and commemorations. Her busy life could seem like a never-ending parade of such events, and so in December 1880 she sent family and friends

---

3. Throughout her life, Emma Lucy was called by multiple names—Emma Lucy, Lu, Lulu, Lule, and, finally, professionally, at least, Lucy

4. Joseph Smith taught in Nauvoo, Illinois, that proxy work for the dead could be completed to ensure baptism and other sacred rites were available to all the human family. Such work is carried out in temples, and it is why Saints such as Susa are interested in genealogy.

5. Gates, "Lucy Bigelow Young," 98.

6. Susa Gates to Lucy Young, Dec. 1880, box 30, fd. 3.

an invitation. "Bro. & Sist. J. F. Gates will be pleased to see you at their house on the First Anniversary of their Marriage, Jan. 5th, 1881, at 6 o'clock p.m."[7] A month after Susa and Jacob's anniversary, the two performed together in a play for the St. George Dramatic Association, which presented "the Beautiful Domestic Irish Drama, Kathleen Mavourneen," starring "Mrs. S. Y. Gates" in the title role of Kathleen O'Connor. "Mr. J. F. Gates" played the role of Capt. Clearfield.[8] It was a happy time for the family.

In 1881 Jacob was ordained a Seventy by Wilford Woodruff,[9] a significant occurrence in view of the responsibility for missionary work shouldered by the Seventies and the fact that Jacob would serve an additional three missions, again in Hawai'i (1885–89), in New York City (1902–03), and in Germany (1913–14).

Jacob continued to work and travel. The exact source of his income is unclear, but he dabbled in several fields to support his family. In addition to farming, he studied law with S. R. Thurman, a prominent early Utah attorney; he received an appointment as a notary public; he joined in unspecified business ventures with John W. Young, Susa's half-brother, who made and lost millions of dollars.[10] Jacob also dabbled in real estate, and by 1885 he was selling fire insurance in Provo through the office of Halliday & Keeler for Fireman's Fund Insurance Co. In August 1885, Jacob was working for Aetna insurance, and told his wife they "raised our commission … to the *highest rate* paid any agents" (emphasis in original).[11] Before he and Susa would depart on a mission together, he made a trip to New Mexico to help Susa's sister Rhoda Mabel and her estranged husband Daniel McAllister with their business activities, and may have been paid for that work. He also owned shares in the Silver King Mining Company.[12]

Letters from Jacob to Susa in the spring and summer 1881 came

---

7. Invitation, box 3, fd. 11, SYGP (CHL).

8. St. George Play Program, box 3, fd. 10, SYGP (CHL).

9. Jacob was ordained on March 20, 1881.

10. John W. Young died penniless in New York City in 1924 while working as an elevator operator. See Jessee, *Letters of Brigham Young*, 91.

11. Jacob Gates to Susa Gates, Aug. 23, 1885, box 6, fd. 6.

12. The references to Jacob's many business ventures are in the Jacob Gates papers portion of the SYGP (CHL). See correspondence and business documents in box 4, fd. 14, box 5, fd. 2, and box 5, fds. 5–6.

from throughout the territory: Milford, Minersville, Provo, Salt Lake City, and Beaver. The intensity of their romance continued beyond their first year of marriage, and Jacob wrote to Susa, "I knew not how much I loved you until this separation, I never missed your society so much since you were mine, never felt this almost consuming passion of the *heart* to such an extent. O Su, if any wife ever had the whole & undivided heart of her husband you have" (emphasis in original).[13] The family grew as three sons followed in quick succession after Emma Lucy's birth. Jacob Young was born eighteen months after his sister on May 11, 1882; Karl Nahum was born in Provo just fourteen months after Jacob; and Simpson Mark (who went by his middle name) followed another eighteen months after that on January 20, 1885, also in Provo.

Susa remained piqued at her treatment during her divorce from Alma Dunford. With Jacob on her side, she enlisted him to write to another church leader on her behalf after her entreaties to John Taylor did not resolve anything. Jacob wrote to George Q. Cannon in Washington, DC. Cannon was serving simultaneously as First Counselor in the First Presidency and as Utah's territorial delegate to the US House of Representatives. Jacob's letter does not survive, but Cannon's reply on April 4, 1882, reflects the prejudice of church leaders against trusting civil courts and church members airing their conflicts publicly. Cannon cautiously acknowledged that he did not know "all the particulars of the divorce case and the transfer of your wife's lot to A. B. Dunford," but after reading Jacob's account, he "sympathized very much with her side of the case." Cannon knew that he had read only one side of the account from a hardly disinterested party, so he wrote "with some degree of caution, because of my ignorance of all that happened," but felt that Susa "was treated badly." Cannon encouraged Jacob and Susa to avoid civil courts and instead to turn to the church:

> I do not think it would be a wise thing for you under present circumstances to have recourse to courts of law, nor to the aid of outside attorneys to correct any wrong that may exist. ... [But] I do not think that you are required to sit down quietly and bear it. There is a way

---

13. Jacob Gates to Susa Gates, June 11, 1881, box 5, fd. 8.

provided in the Church for the ratification of wrongs of this kind ... will it not be practicable for you to have the matter brought up before the High Council at St. George—or if A. B. Dunford is not there, at Salt Lake City, and endeavor to get the matter righted in the Church, as I suppose he is a member of the Church in regular standing at the present time? With my feelings, I would rather submit to a wrong and leave it to be settled in eternity than to go to a court of law with one of my brethren, even if I knew that I would get my wrongs righted. ... It is evident that it is not the Lords will that we should go to law with our brethren.[14]

Just as nothing happened with Susa's pleas with Taylor, Jacob's plea to Cannon went nowhere.

Susa became politically active in St. George. She first voted as a young wife in 1872, and may have voted in 1870. On February 14, 1870, Utah became the second territory[15] in the nation to grant women the right to vote, provided they were married. Enfranchising women served two purposes: it blunted criticism that Mormon women were oppressed victims, ground under the thumb of polygamy, and it doubled the number of Latter-day Saints who could vote, ensuring church control over local elections even if men who practiced polygamy were stripped of the right to vote by federal legislation.[16] Susa would become an outspoken proponent of women's suffrage.

She first organized "Civil Government classes" in St. George in 1880, as part of her ongoing interest in politics.[17] Now, in September 1882, "Susie Y. Gates" was elected as an alternate delegate of the Washington "County Convention of the Peoples Party" to the territorial convention scheduled in Salt Lake City on October 9.[18] The People's Party was the party of the LDS Church and it was heavily promoted by the church-owned *Deseret News*. It emerged in the 1870s as a response to the Liberal Party, the first serious challenge by non-Mormons (and some alienated Mormons) to LDS control of Utah Territory. Both parties were dissolved in the 1890s as Utah

---

14. George Q. Cannon to Jacob Gates, April 4, 1882, box 4, fd. 12.

15. Wyoming was first, but Utah held elections before Wyoming, so women in Utah were the first in the nation to cast ballots.

16. For more on women's suffrage in Utah, see Madsen, *Battle for the Ballot*, and Ulrich, *House Full of Females*.

17. "Political Activity of Susa Young Gates," box 3, fd. 35, SYGP (CHL).

18. Box 1, fd. 3, SYGP (CHL).

moved toward statehood by embracing the national Democratic and Republican Parties.[19] Susa was unable to attend the convention, but her nomination demonstrated her prominence and her commitment to political activism.

It was that same prominence—and her outspokenness—that ensured Susa would be a topic of discussion in the community and, occasionally, a lightning rod of controversy. The daughter of the prophet, divorced from her first husband, enrolled for a year in school, and now politically active, starring in plays and writing history while juggling a family, was a juicy topic of "gossip." This gossip came to Susa second- or third-hand, so it ought to be taken with a grain of salt, but it reflects the ongoing interest people had in Susa. In one instance, her half-sister Zina had attended a dinner where talk turned to Susa and Jacob. Zina was asked how the couple were doing, and she benignly replied that they were fine. A friend of Susa's named Cad quickly jumped in and opined that Susa's "first baby it was decidedly homely." Cad also said that Susa makes "a pretty good wife; but, that naturally she liked literary pursuits better than she did household duties." She went on to hint that much of Susa's success was due to Jacob's being available to take care of her financially. That such nakedly candid chatter reached the Gateses' ears suggests it was not the first, nor the last, time such gossip took place.

When Jacob wrote to Susa, he left an underlined blank space in his letter to substitute for whatever profanity he envisioned to describe Cad. "O Su, it makes me so indignant that I can hardly control myself." Zina came to their defense, coolly responding that those "who proffessed to be Su's friends to let her affairs alone & not talk about them." More was said, but Jacob, sparing Susa's feelings, did not record them in his letters. But reflecting the unsteady and unreliable nature of such personal gossip, Jacob got a few details wrong. Somewhere in Zina's account to him of what had happened, Jacob had misunderstood and he quickly followed up with another letter to Susa explaining that Cad had not insulted the physical appearance of their children. Still, Jacob was not inclined to let this matter drop and ignore it. "I will not fellowship those who vilify

---

19. For more on the history of Utah's political parties, see Walker, *Wayward Saints*, and Lyman, *Finally Statehood!*

& scandalize, her whom I love better than my life." But if Jacob or Susa sought out Cad or other gossipmongers, there was no apparent satisfaction regarding the scurrilous comments.[20]

Jacob was understandably incensed at the news. It could not have helped when he learned that he was accused of whipping Bailey "all the time" and that both Susa and Jacob's treatment of her first son was "scandlous," and that the boy would be better off in Alma's care. Jacob, who took Bailey with him on business trips, must have been deeply hurt at such news

Even as her family grew, Susa's political activism increased, and, her responsibilities enlarged, she continued to write. In 1883 her first book was published. It was a short biography of Lydia Knight, an early LDS convert who had been born in Massachusetts and joined the church in 1833. Lydia's story was inspiring; she was the only member of her family to align herself with Joseph Smith's new faith. She moved to Kirtland in 1835 and married Newel Knight after her first marriage to Calvin Bailey failed. Susa's description of Lydia's first husband might have been autobiographical; Calvin Bailey, like Alma Dunford, was alcoholic, and abusive and, like Susa, Lydia married her first husband when she was just sixteen years old:

> Shall I attempt to picture her sufferings? The long, lonely hours of wait-ing, the longing dread to hear the stumbling footsteps, the tortures of fear, the vile abuse, the bitter cursings heaped upon her head, the vain regrets, the puny hopes of a better life born but to be strangled by the next night's waiting agony, the gradual benumbing, crushed feeling that life was made ... for suffering—shall I tell of this? No! for those who are waiting and watching for the unsteady step know all I can tell, and they who have never borne the dreadful burden would not understand me.[21]

Lydia's second husband, Newel, died during the trek west in early 1847, leaving Lydia with seven fatherless children. She gave birth to an eighth child, arrived in Salt Lake in 1850, married again in 1852, divorced again, and finally married James McClellan in 1864. He died in 1880, and Lydia moved to St. George two years later, where she met Susa.

---

20. Jacob Gates to Susa Gates, Oct. 11, 1882, box 6, fd. 5. The identity of Cad is unknown.

21. Gates, *Lydia Knight's History*, 11.

Susa wrote Lydia's story under the nom-de-plume "Homespun." It became her most-commonly used alias, but not her only one. It was not uncommon in the nineteenth century to write under a pseudonym and the identities of such authors were often open secrets. The book was published under the aegis of the *Juvenile Instructor*, which was owned by George Q. Cannon and sons. It was "The First Book of the Noble Women Lives," which was planned as a series but stopped after only two volumes, *Lydia Knight's History* and *Heroines of Mormondom* the following year. Susa had also contributed a short biography to *Heroines*.[22]

After years of living on and off in St. George, Susa in 1883 moved with Jacob to Provo. Like most family moves, it was probably undertaken for a variety of reasons. First and foremost was Jacob's employment; there were more opportunities, and it helped that Provo was a relatively short train ride away from Salt Lake City.[23] There was also the possibility that Susa could teach at Brigham Young Academy, especially since she had taught there before.[24] Finally, Jacob's father lived in Provo, and the chance to be closer to him probably influenced the decision to relocate.

Living farther north brought other benefits for the family. Susa, who had acted as scribe for the dedicatory services at the St. George temple in 1877, was asked by church president John Taylor to serve as assistant secretary and reporter at the May 1884 dedication of the Logan temple, the second temple completed in Utah Territory. President John D. T. McAllister of the St. George temple, because of his experience, had been asked to oversee the initial operation of the Logan temple and to train its personnel. McAllister asked Lucy Bigelow Young, who herself had extensive experience in working in the temple, to help train the female workers. So it was that Susa's mother and her sister Mabel traveled to Logan where they met with Susa for the temple dedication. Both Lucy and Mabel would stay in Logan for six weeks.

Mabel had divorced her first husband, John D. T. McAllister's son

---

22. *Heroines of Mormondom* had short biographies of three Mormon pioneers: Mary Fielding Smith, by her son Joseph F. Smith; Mary Chittenden, by "Homespun" (Susa Young Gates); and Amanda Smith, by Emmeline B. Wells.

23. Susa Gates to Jacob Gates, Sep. 5, 1882, box 9, fd. 6.

24. Susa would become intimately involved at Brigham Young Academy, later BYU, and serve on its board of regents for many years.

Daniel, and she and her sister Dora continued to cause their mother consternation. Dora, who had two sons from her first marriage to Moreland Dunford, had married and divorced Wilford Woodruff, then married Albert Hagan, a prominent Catholic lawyer. They settled initially in Denver before moving to Chicago. The couple had four children, two sons and two daughters, only two of who lived into adulthood. When Dora died thirty years later in 1921, it was as a member of the Catholic Church. Susa later wrote that her sister "was a constantly increasing problem to Mother. For she finally left Utah and denied the religion she had so faithfully followed till her maturity, leaving all for the love and lure of the world."[25]

Her mother's heartache can appear puzzling. To nearly anyone else, a long marriage to a successful attorney, living in one of the largest cities in the country, might seem like a dream outcome. Dora's first marriage ended because her husband was an abusive alcoholic, hardly her fault, though her rush to get married had devastated both her mother and her father. Her second marriage, albeit to a prominent LDS apostle, saw her wedded to a man in his seventies when she was still young, and she was numbered among many wives and likely got little attention from her new husband. Now, married to Albert Hagan, Dora converted to Catholicism, her husband's religion, and seemed to be more at peace. But Susa's words that Dora abandoned her religion "for the love and lure of the world" implied that her mother was less concerned with her daughters' temporal comfort than with their spiritual well-being. Lucy had known nothing but the LDS Church since she was a child. She had been the wife of the most famous polygamist in the world, and she could apparently not look past Dora's apparent loss of faith, even as her daughter gained a family.

Susa's younger sister, Mabel, fared no better at marriage. Mabel, like Susa, had married at age sixteen. Her father-in-law, McAllister, was a close friend of the Young family. But regardless of the prominence of her husband's family, Mabel and Daniel McAllister's marriage did not last. They had one son, Daniel Jr., before divorcing. Mabel had another son, Brigham Winfred Witt, with her second husband, Daniel

---

25. Gates, "Lucy Bigelow Young," 100.

Witt. Her third and final marriage, like that of her sister Dora, was to a non-Mormon, Joseph Abbott Sanborn. He was described as kind and gentle, and considerate of Mabel and her mother. He and Mabel had two sons and a daughter. Joseph Sanborn never joined the LDS Church, but Mabel did not leave the church as Dora had.

Jacob Gates was soon dragged into the worries over Dora and Mabel. When Mabel went to visit Dora in Chicago in fall 1883, she took her son, Danny, along. By then her marriage to Daniel McAllister may have been rocky, but she had not yet divorced him. Her continued association with her sister outraged her father-in-law, however. John McAllister wrote to Jacob and called Dora "a comon woman," an offensive insult in that era that called her an adulterer of loose morals. McAllister believed that Dora would "do all she can to pull Rhoda [Mabel] down with her."[26] Daniel McAllister was traveling in New Mexico at the time, where he was involved in a trial. He wrote to Jacob that he does not "consent to him [Daniel Jr.] being brought under the influence of Dora."[27] In May 1885 Jacob traveled to New Mexico to handle ongoing business for Mabel and Daniel, who by this time had separated. Jacob grew frustrated with Mabel and declared that she "has not good sense." He concluded harshly to Susa, "I sometimes feel that it is not much of an honor to be sister to them [Dora and Mabel]."[28]

In the midst of this family drama and the challenge of attending to her mother, maintaining relationships with her sisters, and supporting her husband, Susa lost a child for the first time. Mark, her third son with Jacob, died when he was three months old. Susa had taken Mark with her to Logan in March 1885 and visited her half-sister Zina. When she returned to Provo, Mark died on April 21. It was not the last child Susa and Jacob would watch die; tremendous loss lay ahead for the young couple.

Lucy rushed from St. George to Provo to help Susa for several months after Mark's death. Susa's loss was unbearable, and her mother worried terribly for her. She wrote to her own mother, Mary Bigelow, then seventy-five years old, that "our Darling Susa is far

26. John D. T. McAllister to Jacob Gates, Apr. 1884, box 4, fd. 13.
27. Daniel McAllister to Jacob Gates, box 4, fd. 12.
28. Jacob Gates to Susa Young Gates, June 1, 1885, box 6, fd. 6.

from it [well]. She is in a delicate situation, and what makes it so much worse, she is in a very low state of nervous prostration, and has been very sick since her darling Mark was taken away."[29]

By the fall, Susa was feeling better, at least well enough that Lucy decided she could leave to attend to another daughter. Lucy attended general conference in Salt Lake City in October, then made plans to take Mabel on an extravagant trip. Mabel had been teaching music at the Brigham Young Academy in Provo but had "become worn out with overwork."[30] Lucy had recently sold some property, and with the extra money decided she and Mabel needed a long vacation, perhaps around the world. After the end of general conference, they started west, stopping in San Francisco for several days. While there startling news reached them from Susa. "Yesterday afternoon Jacob got a letter from Pres. Taylor that he is called on a mission to the Sandwich Islands, to be in San Francisco to sail on the 1st of Nov."[31] Missionaries in this era were often married, and while they usually left their families behind, they sometimes were allowed to take family members with them. Susa indicated that nothing definite had been said about whether she and the children would accompany Jacob, although she did not think it was likely that they would. Instead, she let her mother know that if she was still in San Francisco when Jacob "gets there[,] he and you will sail together."[32]

It was a precarious time for the church. Jacob's missionary call of October 28, 1885, was signed by only two of the three members of the First Presidency.[33] President John Taylor and his counselor George Q. Cannon had signed, but Joseph F. Smith's signature was absent. Smith was himself in the Sandwich Islands, hiding from federal officials hunting polygamists. Taylor and Cannon also were often in hiding, trying to avoid arrest. In 1882, the Edmunds Act, the harshest anti-polygamy legislation to date, had passed the US Congress and was signed into law by President Chester A. Arthur. Lorenzo

---

29. Lucy Bigelow Young to Mary Bigelow, July 1885, qtd. in Gates, "Lucy Bigelow Young," 103.

30. Gates, "Lucy Bigelow Young," 104.

31. Susa Gates to Lucy Bigelow Young, Oct. 12, 1885, qtd. in Gates, "Lucy Bigelow Young," 107.

32. Gates to Young.

33. Jacob Gates Mission Certificate, box 5, fd. 13, SYGP (CHL).

Snow, a prominent apostle who would later become president of the church, would be arrested in November 1885 and imprisoned under the terms of the law. George Q. Cannon wrote, "I felt worse about this arrest than I have about any that has taken place; and I felt that if I could go to prison for him, and relieve him, and if it should be wise to do so, I would be willing to go."[34] But Cannon would get his own chance at prison; he was arrested in 1888. Other apostles and prominent leaders would also be sent to the Utah Territorial Penitentiary.[35]

George Reynolds, secretary to the First Presidency, wrote to Jacob to reassure him that taking Susa and the children on his mission was an option. Some of the brethren called already to the Sandwich Islands intended to take their wives with them. "There is no doubt but that faithful, honorable women can do an excellent amount of missionary labor on the Islands," Reynolds wrote, "therefore, especially where they have means to pay their own way, there can be no objection to their going, if they are women of the right disposition. But as to the accommodation they will have after they reach there, we are not in a position to say."[36] George Q. Cannon followed up on Reynolds's letter to let Jacob know that "as a rule, I think a man (as the Mission on the Sandwich Islands is now situated) is better off to take a wife with him, if she is a prudent, industrious, faithful woman, as a woman can do much good there if she is so disposed." Cannon knew that Jacob had already served on the islands and that shelters "are easily built and without much sod, and it would not be much trouble for a man to make his wife comfortable." He concluded that there was no "objection to your taking your wife with you."[37] Reynolds's and Cannon's letters suggest the matter was of concern to Jacob, who must have made his desire to take his family with him clear.

Less than a week later, Susa, Jacob, and their children were on their way to Salt Lake City, and from there they would go to San Francisco, ready to depart for the Sandwich Islands. Susa was five months pregnant. But when they stepped off the Utah Central Railroad in Salt Lake, a disturbing sight was waiting for them: Alma

34. Cannon, Journal, Nov. 20, 1885.
35. Lyman, *Finally Statehood!*, 110–32; Bitton, *George Q. Cannon*, 268–78; Gordon, *Mormon Question*.
36. George Reynolds to Jacob F. Gates, Oct. 20, 1885, copy in author's possession.
37. George Q. Cannon to Jacob Gates, Oct. 1885, copy in author's possession.

Dunford, armed with a court order. Shortly after Jacob had received his mission call to the islands, he had written to Alma that Susa "desired to take [Bailey] with them if there was no objection." Alma apparently did object, but instead of replying to Jacob's letter, he obtained the court order granting him custody of Bailey and, for good measure, publicized the conflict in the press. While the divorce decree initially gave Susa custody of Bailey, it stipulated "in rather conflicting terms at the same time that *guardianship of the boy should be with the father*," and then after age eleven Bailey should choose where he wanted to live permanently (emphasis in original). Bailey had spent most of his time with his mother and stepfather, and Alma complained to a *Salt Lake Herald* reporter that "he had only been able to secure five visits from him in the seven years." Alma also repeated the rumors that Bailey was mistreated by Jacob. Susa quickly sought legal counsel from Williams & Young, who delivered the devastating news that "the decree giving the father guardianship, also included custody, and it would be useless to appeal to the law."[38]

Confronted by Alma and his court order, Susa consented for Bailey to spend the night with his father. But Alma refused to allow ten-year-old Bailey to leave for the islands. The next evening Dunford brought Bailey to the depot, accompanied by a sheriff's deputy, to say goodbye to his mother. "Considerable attention was attracted to the group by the affecting scene which ensued. The boy wept loud and bitterly at the parting, and seemed very eager to go to his mother." Susa insisted that the boy had been well taken care of and that "Dunford has been deceived when he has been told anything to the contrary." Susa was "nearly heartbroken at having to separate from her child." But no one could intervene legally. Bailey passed into the custody of his father, and Susa lost another child, six months after her little Mark had died.[39] The family's mission was off to an excruciating start.

38. "Mother and Father, *Salt Lake Herald*, Oct. 29, 1885, 8.
39. "Mother and Father." Efforts by Susa and Jacob to have Bailey visit them in the Sandwich Islands were rebuffed by Alma Dunford.

Hawai'i

Susa, Jacob, and the three surviving children they had together—Emma Lucy, Jay, and Karl—all arrived in San Francisco, safe but hardly sound. When they set out from Provo, they were six; now, with Bailey in the permanent custody of his father, they were five. So abrupt was the separation that when the *Deseret News* reported on the missionaries bound for the Sandwich Islands, it wrote that Susa and her "four children" were part of the traveling party. They were part of a larger missionary group that set out for the Sandwich Islands on the steamer *Mariposa,* and after an uneventful seven-day voyage, arrived in Honolulu on November 10, 1885. Susa spent most of the journey sick and Jacob "felt a little anxious for her."[1] The group also included three newlywed couples, all from Salt Lake City, and Enoch Farr Jr., son of the current mission president on the islands, was also part of the group. They were accompanied by Susa's mother, Lucy Bigelow Young, and her youngest daughter, Rhoda Mabel Young McAllister, who were already in San Francisco, waiting for the rest of the travel group to arrive.[2] The presence of her mother and her sister may have helped to soften Susa's distress at leaving her son behind.

In 1865 the church had purchased a 6,000-acre plantation on the north shore of Oahu at a remote place called Lā'ie. Today the site

---

1. Jacob Gates to Father [Jacob Gates Sr.], Nov. 12, 1885, box 4, fd. 11.
2. Gates, "Lucy Bigelow Young, 108; "Off for the Sandwich Islands," *Deseret News,* Nov. 4, 1885.

is the home of the first LDS temple outside the continental United States; the Church College of Hawai'i, founded in 1955, but since 1974 called Brigham Young University—Hawai'i; and the Polynesian Cultural Center, established in 1963 and now a top tourist attraction in Hawai'i.

In 1885, by contrast, Lā'ie was a large sugar plantation, and when the Gateses arrived it bore little resemblance to how it looks today. Living conditions were basic. The few missionary families living there were housed in huts without electricity or running water. The summers were hot and the rainy season was wet and cold. Jacob would serve as sugar boiler superintendent of the plantation.

Susa spent much of their first days crying over the loss of Bailey. The house they were to live in had vermin, so Jacob built a "small tight room" to keep them out.[3] Mosquitoes were a ubiquitous problem. Lā'ie was thirty-two miles by horse or buggy from Honolulu "over the roughest possible trail," requiring a ride of several hours.[4] Mail arrived by ship every two weeks in Honolulu and then had to be brought to Lā'ie. There was a small store from which resident missionary families could draw some supplies.

Work at the sugar factory was hard, and the wives of the missionaries also endured backbreaking work in their homes. Susa describes sewing, mending, cooking, baking, soaking and washing clothes after heating water, ironing, churning butter, cleaning house and yard, scrubbing, making preserves and soap, whitewashing, painting—all amidst giving birth to three more children. The family raised chickens and had cows that yielded a good quantity of milk. Yet Susa found time to write in what scant spare time she was able to garner, all in addition to taking an active part in missionary and other church activities in the settlement.

Life in Lā'ie was punctuated by diversions, including frequent trips to the beach, often to bathe; picnics and other outings; church socials; "native feasts"[5]; communal celebrations of holidays; trips to Honolulu and the volcanoes of the Big Island; and excursions to pick bananas, oranges, mangoes, and guavas. Susa had access to a sewing machine

---

3. Gates to Father.
4. Gates, "Lucy Bigelow Young," 111.
5. Gates, 113.

two days a week that was shared among the women. She was an ex-cellent seamstress and made nearly all of the clothes for her family, often trading her sewing skills for assistance with what she considered more mundane household chores, such as ironing. Susa lamented that dress standards in Lāʻie were higher than she had anticipated. She lambasted corsets as "abominable" and "cursed instruments of torture." She had expected that they would "live and dress plainer than at home here on a mission. But it has not been so."[6]

Susa's time in the islands represented one of the few times in her life when she kept a journal on a regular basis for a significant period of time, eighteen months between January 8, 1888, and July 18, 1889. She often wrote daily and never went more than two weeks without a new entry. She wrote early in her journal, "Another weary, hard working day." After toiling for hours, she made her family din-ner, which Jacob observed was "not fit for a dog to eat"—she had put potatoes in with the poi. Jacob later apologized, and Susa quickly forgave him. "I cannot ever hold a cross feeling against him even if I should wish." She threw herself into her labors and learned to glory in the hard work: "Verily, this mission has been a blessing to me, for I have learned as I never knew before, the beauty and grace of work." In fact, "what an unsatisfied and miserable feeling comes over me when I might work or spend any time in idleness." Another entry mentions that "it always gives me the blues to spend time in anything but work."[7]

More details about the family's life on the islands may be gleaned from a curious story Susa wrote in 1889 under her favorite pseud-onym, "Homespun." The ostensibly fictional "Little Missionary" is a thinly disguised autobiography published in twenty-three in-stallments in the *Juvenile Instructor*.[8] Each new entry was titled as a chapter of the story and, if assembled together, would have been the length of a small book. It is unclear why Susa chose to publish her story as the wife of a missionary in the Sandwich Islands as a fictional

6. Gates, Journal, Mar. 24, 1888, box 105, fd. 2, SYGP (CHL). Susa's journal is in two folders in box 105 of her papers at the CHL. Hereafter cited as Gates, Journal.

7. Gates, Journal, Jan. 17–20, Sep. 20, 1888.

8. Homespun [Susa Young Gates], "The Little Missionary," *Juvenile Instructor*, Jan.–Dec. 1899. "The Little Missionary" was published in all but one of semi-monthly issues of the *Juvenile Instructor* that year. Hereafter, "Little Missionary."

account; she did not even bother to change all of the names. Perhaps she felt it would give her the freedom she needed to express herself, but whatever her reasoning, the story offers a valuable glimpse into how Susa perceived the mission a decade after the family returned home. Because it is fiction, some of the specific details not present in contemporary accounts need to be weighed carefully, such as the story of the oldest daughter proselytizing a "Major Goldthwaite," a soldier in the British army.[9] But Susa's writing gives a flavor to life in the islands that is absent in other records of the family's mission.

"The Little Missionary" is the story the Argyle family, and the parallels with the Gates family are easily discerned. There are father and mother Thomas and Jane (Jacob and Susa) and their three children, Mary, Allan, and Thomas (Emma Lucy, Karl, and Jay). The children's Grandmother Howe (Lucy Bigelow Young) and their aunt Maidie (Mabel) accompany them to the islands and remain for about six months. Two unnamed children (Leah and Bailey) are left at home. The "little missionary" of the story is Mary, who is later called by Grandmother Howe the best missionary of the family and "the noble, unselfish lessons she has taught to us all are worthiest of praise."[10]

Jane Argyle was Susa rendered in print, and the character showed Susa's genius for controlling the public's perception of her. Jane, like Susa, ate meat only sparingly, as part of her commitment to strictly keep the Word of Wisdom, something she and her husband agreed to do after they wed.[11] Jane loves to sightsee and travel, and she has an abiding conviction that no fatal disease could attack her children. Like Susa, Jane complains of gossip about her. She is suspicious of modern educators who are too gentle with children, who Jane believes need to be challenged and disciplined. Finally, Jane talks often of death; indeed, death is a persistent theme in the story. The two Argyle boys ask their mother to tell them about their deceased

---

9. Goldthwaite responds to the little girl that Mormonism is "a queer religion that, which insists upon purity in men and brains in women and children! Very queer!" "Little Missionary," 45.

10. "Little Missionary," 781.

11. The Word of Wisdom went through periods of greater emphasis after Joseph Smith revealed it in 1833. It was not until the early twentieth century when it was finally rendered the commandment Latter-day Saints today consider it to be. See Dirkmaat et al., *Documents, Volume 3*, 11–20, and Peterson, "Historical Analysis of the Word of Wisdom."

brother, resting in peace in a grave at home.[12] It is not difficult to imagine Susa's surviving boys, Jay and Karl, asking about their baby brother, Mark, and Susa telling her children about the boy's short life. They would soon have another brother to tend to.

On February 22, 1886, only a few months after they arrived, Susa gave birth to a son named Joseph Sterling, attended by midwife Julina Lambson Smith. Julina was living in Lā'ie with her husband, Joseph F. Smith, second counselor to church president John Taylor. Smith was living on the "Underground" in the islands to avoid prosecution for polygamy. Susa and Jacob named their son in honor of Smith.[13] Susa was fortunate to still have her mother and sister with her; the pair would not leave the islands for Utah until April. Lucy would travel three times to the islands while the Gates family lived there.

A year after Joseph was born, his brother Jay began to complain about a sore throat. His condition quickly worsened, and Jay asked Susa to bless him with consecrated oil, which she did. Jacob Sr. rushed home from a conference in Honolulu, and he also gave blessings to the boy, as did other local members. Susa was three months pregnant, and Jacob finally persuaded her to get some rest at a neighbor's home. Jay was cared for that night by his father, and the next day, February 23, 1887, he slipped away. "Oh how brave, how patient, how manly our darling was," Susa wrote to her mother. "He never complained. His was one of the noblest choicest spirits ever sent to this sad earth. Mother, mother, I can't write any more it just kills me pretty near."[14]

Jay died of diphtheria, a terrible disease that had a high mortality rate in young children. Today there is a vaccine; in 1887 there was no treatment but to keep those afflicted comfortable and hope they would recover. Susa and Jacob did not believe in contemporary medical treatments, and a neighbor complained that "they are doing very little" for Jay.[15] Even two years later, when new baby Harvey had whooping cough and Jacob brought home some cough medicine, Susa, ever stubborn, declared, "I have no faith whatever in any

---

12. "Little Missionary," 115.
13. Gates, "Lucy Bigelow Young," 113.
14. Susa Young Gates to Lucy Bigelow Young, Mar. 6, 1887, box 4, fd. 11.
15. Elizabeth L. Noall, Journal, Feb. 23, 1887, box 14, journal 2, in Noall, Papers.

medicine, but hygienic simple aids such as warm baths and water, and above all consecrated oil and the blessing of God through the Priesthood" (emphasis in original).[16] Given the severity of the disease and the medical care available at the time, it is unlikely that any intervention could have saved Jay. He was buried in a grave that Susa later noted was too wide for him.[17]

Diphtheria is an infectious disease, and three days after Jay died, his three-and-a-half-year-old brother, Karl, became ill. Despite the priesthood blessings, the prayers, and the great faith summoned by the missionary families in Lā'ie, Karl—called Karlie by his mother and father—died on March 2, a week after his brother. Jay's too-wide grave would now accommodate Karl as well. A neighbor observed that Joseph F. Smith had "a dream before the first died [and] saw the grave made for two."[18] Susa later remembered this in the "Little Missionary" story and added that she felt inspired to take the family to Honolulu to get their portraits taken shortly before the children died. One photograph shows the family just before the tragedy, Susa seated with baby Joseph in her lap, Jay on her right, Karl and Emma Lucy on her left in a chair, and Jacob standing behind them.[19] Joseph F. Smith (rendered as "Brother Hale" in the "Little Missionary" story) only briefly dedicated the grave, since both children would be disinterred and reburied in Provo at the conclusion of the mission.[20]

During this trial the Gates family received substantial spiritual comfort and guidance from Joseph F. and Julina Smith, which cemented their lifetime friendship. Susa noted, "That Bro. S[mith], angel in human form that he is, never deserted us for one moment during our greatest need. He closed both our darling's eyes." Julina had bathed and clothed the boys for burial.[21] Susa had endured many tragedies in her life, and she would encounter many more. Her resilience is noteworthy; she never gave up, and she always bounced back. She relied on her faith: "Still with all this we know that God rules

16. Gates, Journal, Feb. 8, 1889.

17. "Little Missionary," 654.

18. Matthew Noall, Journal, Mar. 9, 1887, box 14, in Noall, Papers.

19. The picture is in Joseph F. Smith Personal Photographs, ca. 1860–1918, PH 2016.

20. "Little Missionary," 654.

21. Susa Young Gates to Lucy Bigelow Young, Mar. 6, 1887, box 4, fd. 11.

in the Heavens. The Lord giveth, and the Lord taketh away, blessed be the name of the Lord!"[22] One of the virtues of Susa's life was the ability to rise triumphant from the ashes of tragedy and persist.

Even with her faith and the loving support of close friends, the deaths of their sons was a severe trial for Susa and Jacob. Susa wrote that "I didn't dream people could die while on missions."[23] Like Jane Argyle, Susa had always believed that keeping the Word of Wisdom would avert life-threatening illness. They also were not free of fear yet. Emma Lucy "Lule" and Joseph still had "swollen tonsils and at time inflamed throats," which terrified their parents. Susa wrote that "our house has been aired, fumigated, whitewashed and everything stands in all the abject confusion of desolation and death. We shun it as much as we can." Jacob was no less devastated than Susa. He was "stricken with this sad heavy blow. ... He takes it very hard. But oh if I could only weep as he does, and relieve my heart ... I would be glad."[24] As the months passed, neither stopped thinking about their sons. Jacob wondered if "the time [will] ever come when I can think of this bereavement with a degree of resignation."[25] Susa wished she had written down some memories, a record "of the little sayings and doings of my two angel boys. Oh my noble Jay, and my sweet Karlie, how my heart longs for a sight of your sweet faces. Every day, a hundred incidents brings back the lost joys, the present pains."[26] She visited their graves often, and shortly after one visit wrote, "Oh my darlings, my darlings, how my heart aches in thinking of you. How I loved you, and how I have missed you, only One knows."[27]

The preoccupation with death in Susa's story, "The Little Missionary," comes painfully into focus, as does its elevation of little Mary (Emma Lucy) as the center of the tale. Lule, as the family called Emma Lucy, was barely six years old when her brothers died. She helped her mother with chores, she watched over her baby brother, Joseph, and she was there with her mother even as Jacob had to continue to travel around the islands as part of his missionary

---

22. Gates to Young, Mar. 6, 1887.
23. Gates, Journal, Feb. 23, 1888.
24. Gates to Young, Mar. 6, 1887.
25. Jacob Gates to Susa Young Gates, Dec. 1887, box 6, fd. 7.
26. Gates, Journal, Jan. 15, 1888.
27. Gates, Journal, Feb. 24, Apr. 5, 1888.

responsibilities. She was, her mother would later write, "a little missionary from heaven" and "a missionary of light and sunshine in our house every day."[28] True, Susa wrote these things about a fictional daughter, Mary. But it is not hard to imagine the gratitude Susa felt every time Lule held little Joseph, or swept the floor, or sat with her mother, resting her head on her shoulder. If what Susa wrote in "The Little Missionary" was even partially factual, then Lule was a tremendous comfort to her during their three-and-a-half years on the Sandwich Islands, both before and after the deaths of Jay and Karl.

Susa wrote later in her life that "Death, a glorious, honorable, death, is far more to be preferred than an ignoble, impure, pusillanimous life."[29] As time marched on and more and more death and loss would surround her into her adult years, these became words to live by for Susa. She wrote less frequently about the loss of her children, and instead, seemed to bear through the pain, never looking back.

In the wake of the tragedy, and with yet another child on the way, Susa implored her mother to return to the islands again for her expected delivery in August. Lucy sailed in June of that year with Lucy White King, plural wife of the newly appointed president of the mission, William King. Having been taught midwifery the previous year by Julina Smith, who had since returned to Utah, Lucy Young acted as midwife for the birth of Susa and Jacob's son, Brigham Cecil, on August 17, 1887. Lucy returned to Utah in early fall, having taken an active part in all aspects of community life during her stay. She tried to learn to swim, she made frequent trips to the beach, she took long horse rides, and she visited the volcanoes on the Big Island.

The next year, in June 1888, Jacob took Susa on a ten-day trip to Honolulu and to the Big Island to see the volcanoes herself. On their way back to Lāʻie, they stopped at the mission office in Honolulu. By now the family had been gone for two-and-a-half years, and while missionaries were not called for a set period of time, Susa could have reasonably expected that by the end of the year Jacob would be released, allowing the family to return home. Susa was disappointed to instead learn that the mission president had received instructions from Salt Lake City that if missionaries had brought their families

---

28. "Little Missionary," 42, 116.
29. Gates, "The Church Militant," *Relief Society Magazine*, Nov. 1916, 649.

with them, he was authorized to lengthen their missions. Susa complained, "I dont know when I have felt more tried than over that! ... Another year here seems such an everlasting time. ... Few comforts or conveniences, and lots of hard work." Within a few days she realized the need "to overcome this weakness. For I am blest! Husband, children, a peaceful quiet home and above all the unlimited blessing of the gosple. Father, forgive me my heart-wanderings, and let me come near Thy throne even to Thy tender bosom!"[30]

In the midst of their personal tragedies and family challenges, there was still a mission to perform. In the nearly three-and-a-half years the family lived in the Sandwich Islands, Jacob's assignments took him to Honolulu, Maui, and Kaua'i, usually in the off season when the sugar mill at Lā'ie was dormant. He "was elected president of the Mutual improvement association & Sunday School on the Hawaiian Islands," with Matthew Noall and Robert B. T. Taylor as his counselors.[31] Jacob visited other sugar mills in Maui (Paia) and Kaua'i (Kealia and Koloa) to learn how the church might improve production techniques at Lā'ie. He spent three weeks in Maui in July and August 1886, and almost two months in Kaua'i from October to December 1887. In March 1888 he spent several weeks in Honolulu, helping to finish the meetinghouse there. His lengthy trip to Kaua'i was especially difficult for Susa, and she was uncertain that Jacob would be back in time for Christmas. Before he returned home (he did make it in time for the holidays), he wrote to Susa to reassure her not to fear "that I'll forget thee. The mother of my children ... the best and dearest part of self. Who could forget that fountain from whom his little ones derive their life & joy."[32]

In April 1888, the missionaries were overjoyed by a surprise visit from Queen Lili'uokalani, who in three years would succeed her brother, David Kalākaua, as sovereign of the islands. The missionaries and natives prepared a dinner of roast chicken and cake for the queen and her party of ten. Lili'uokalani, blessed with a remarkable memory, said she remembered meeting Jacob years earlier during his first mission to Hawai'i. She had also been told who Susa was—the

---

30. Gates, Journal, July 1, 1888.
31. Matthew Noall, Journal, Apr. 1, 1886, box 14, journal 1, in Noall, Papers.
32. Jacob Gates to Susa Young Gates, Dec. 2, 1887, box 6, fd. 7.

daughter of Brigham Young—and the queen was delighted to meet her. Lule, who played the ukulele, sang for the royal party. The preparations had been hectic, but it was a welcome celebration.

Fleeting and oblique references to living the United Order—the LDS cooperative movement—in Lāʻie, or attempting to do so, are found in both the Gates and Matthew Noall papers. In 1831 Joseph Smith had a series of revelations that established the law of consecration and created a bishop's storehouse so that community members might share common goods. Church members would "consecrate" at least a portion of their property to the church for the use of the whole community. In Utah Territory, Brigham Young took this a step further and made different attempts to establish the United Order of Enoch, a true communitarian system of living where goods and services were shared equally among the Saints. These efforts at a utopian-style community fared better in some towns than in others, but nearly all fell short of Young's lofty goals, and they eventually floundered and failed. In Salt Lake City and other large cities, Young settled for a cooperative system that privileged LDS-owned businesses over those operated by non-Mormons or "outsiders," as Young labeled them. This was the start of what became the church-owned ZCMI department store.[33]

The small community at Lāʻie mirrored those of LDS communities in Utah. While attempts were made to share and live as a cooperative society, economic realities and human nature made a true practice of the United Order impossible. Susa recorded at least one instance when she and Jacob disagreed over the "righteous" amount of their property they ought to share. Jacob brought home a lot of guavas, and he did not want to divide them evenly with other missionary families. "It bothers me," Susa wrote, that "while we are trying to live in the U. O. [United Order] we ought to do our part. Of course he took some [of the guavas] over [to other families], but not a righteous part." Apparently Susa won out because she recorded that Jacob "will fix it up tomorrow."[34]

---

33. For more on the United Order, see L. Dwight Israelson, "United Orders," in Ludlow, *Encyclopedia of Mormonism*, 4:1493–94; Arrington, Fox, and May, *Building the City of God*; Anderson, *Salt Lake School of the Prophets*.

34. Gates, Journal, Jan. 27, 1888.

When Jacob was not traveling and the family was able to spend time in the evenings together, the couple often reading together, including *Julius Caesar, Othello,* and Plutarch's *Marcus Brutus.* They subscribed to several magazines, notably *Godey's Lady's Book* and *Century*, and arrival of the magazines via the infrequent mail deliveries was an occasion for rejoicing. Susa carved out time in the evenings after the children were in bed to write, primarily for the *Juvenile Instructor* and the *Woman's Exponent.* "The birdies are folded away to sleep," she recorded in her journal one night, "and mama is at her quiet writing."[35] In other entries she mused over her longing to write.

The *Juvenile Instructor* for children was edited by George Q. Cannon, and the *Woman's Exponent* for women by Emmeline B. Wells. During these mission years Susa published seventeen articles in the *Juvenile Instructor*, most of them on island life. "How Two Little Children Spent Christmas in the Tropics," "Sandwich Island Women," "Karl and Ina at Waikiki," and "What the Sandwich Island Children Are Doing" are a few titles. She wrote eleven articles for the *Exponent*, mostly brief letters or dispatches about life on the Islands. All were published under Susa's pseudonym "Homespun." She also wrote letters to the editor of the *Deseret News.* She was a fast writer; in one evening alone she wrote a 2,000-word story. Was it during these quiet evening writing sessions that she realized there was a gap to fill? There was a magazine for children and a magazine for women; could there be a magazine for the young women of the church? During the late summer and early fall of 1888, Susa was busy with correspondence filled with details about starting such a magazine.

Susa also had her first national article published while she was on the islands. "Tropical Dresses" was published in the July 1887 issue of *Godey's Lady's Book*, the most fashionable and popular magazine of its day. Susa took great pride in her piece about native Hawai'ian dress for women, which she characterized as "simple" and "primitive" and on which observers would "gaze with delight."[36] She carried on a regular correspondence with one of the magazine's editors and exulted in the $3 check she received for her work. Susa exclaimed, "Of course I was quite excited & pleased. It is really the first money I ever

---

35. Gates, Journal, Jan. 18, 1888.
36. Susa Young Gates, "Tropical Dresses," *Godey's Lady's Book*, July 1887, 62.

earned by my pen." She had won $10 as a prize for a Christmas story she published in the *Contributor*, the magazine directed at young LDS, but payment for an article published in a national magazine seemed something else entirely.[37] Encouraged, she submitted an article on "Poi," but it was rejected by *Godey's* and instead published in the *Exponent* in April 1888.

Susa was anxious to learn and improve. She submitted a sample to the "Writer's Bureau" and received an assessment that she summarized in her journal: "the story: pretty good. I have a very fair talent which may be improved by self-training and care. Which let me say candidly and truthfully is exactly my own opinion." She had some "errors in syntax," which was understandable since, like most writers, she learned not through formal training but by "ear and intuition."[38]

Susa had not forgotten about her two older children in Utah, Leah and Bailey. Her worry could have only deepened and the separation grown more acute after the loss of Jay and Karl. Two years into her mission "a longing came over me to see Bailey and take him to my heart. My darling boy." Susa always hoped that Bailey would visit Hawai'i with Lucy, but Alma never allowed it. "Bailey is still anxious to come and live with me on my return. Oh if it is Thy Will and for the best, let him come back to me my dear Father in Heaven."[39] For now she had to settle for letters from her children. Leah's letters were generally cordial, although Susa thought that "Leah has grown away from me and my interests so much and it seems all her thoughts are with others."[40] Leah was thirteen and living with her father and stepmother in Salt Lake City, so it is not surprising that her mind wandered from her mother, whom she had seen but little in the last nine years.

Bailey, living with his father for the past three years, had changed "from the dear boy that I have known." In a note to Susa he signed his name three times as "Alma B. Dunford Jr.," and wrote that "boys are boys. And I am a boy. Boys can write to their father and find plenty to say, but when it comes to the mother business, I ain't in it." Susa, stung

---

37. Gates, Journal, July 1887.
38. Gates, Journal, May 5, 1888.
39. Gates, Journal, Apr. 22 and June 15, 1888.
40. Susa Young Gates to Lucy Bigelow Young, Apr. 6, 1887, box 4, fd. 11.

by Bailey's newfound devotion to his father, deviated from her rule of never discussing her first marriage. She confided to her journal, "Why is it I have to suffer not only the five drawn out years of torture which I endured as the wife of a bad, vile, man, but now after all these years, every time my dear children speak or write the hand they hold out to caress me with holds a double-edged dagger!"[41]

Susa also worried about the relationship between her husband and her mother. Although Jacob and Lucy appear to have gotten along well later, in the early days of the marriage there were some challenges. After Lucy returned to the islands for the third and last time in November 1888 to help with the birth of Harvey in January 1889, Susa wished "she [Lucy] had a little more affection and patience with my beloved husband ... how badly I feel sometimes between Ma and Jacob. ... They always are on contrary sides. No open rupture only the constant friction." Nevertheless, Susa felt blessed to have "so lovely and dear a mother and so wise and good a husband. I just try to leave it with God and ask Him to turn their hearts to each other."[42]

Life on a remote Pacific Island with forty white people and an unknown number of Hawai'ian natives did not always function smoothly. There were frequent misunderstandings, and Susa often found herself in the middle of them. She was the daughter of a church president, intelligent, well-spoken, accomplished, and opinionated. She was connected to virtually everyone of standing in Salt Lake City. She was older than most of the women at Lā'ie, and she could be imperious and intimidating. Jacob, ever a calming influence in Susa's life, helped guide her through these difficulties. When the storekeeper of the plantation complained to Susa that the Gates family used more stamps, and therefore cost more money, to mail correspondence, Susa retorted that "writing to friends and receiving letters is the only luxury we enjoy down here."[43] Writing, not only to friends and family, but also her articles and manuscripts that she then mailed to the mainland, was one of Susa's few respites from work and responsibility. Jacob reassured Susa, "I do expect that we do cost the plantation about as much as all the balance of the

---

41. Gates, Journal, Jan. 16, 1889.
42. Gates, Journal, Mar. 11, 1889.
43. Susa Young Gates to Jacob Gates, Nov. 1, 1887, box 9, fd. 7.

mission in this respect [of using stamps]. Don't show resentment at trifles." Susa's frustration may have continued because later in the month he told her, "No one is going to think the less of us because we spend a dollar or two more than someone else does."[44]

Susa had one correspondent who has since spawned a great deal of folklore and historical analysis. While living in Lā'ie, Susa read the account of American journalist George Kennan's interview with Count Leo Tolstoy, conducted at the Tolstoy summer home in Yasnaya Polyana.[45] Kennan's wide-ranging interview covered many topics, including Tolstoy's immutable aversion to "violent resistance to evil ... under any circumstances." Tolstoy told Kennan that "I receive many letters ... from people in America." He pulled one from a drawer about a man who started a church after reading Tolstoy's "My Religion." Tolstoy, who eschewed organized religion, said, "You see he doesn't understand; he thinks that he cannot have religion without a church. I wrote him that he didn't need a church in order to live rightly."[46]

But despite his views on religion, Tolstoy defended the LDS Church. He lamented that America had "proved false to her traditions" by "the persecution of the Chinese and the Mormons." He referred to the recently passed Edmunds–Tucker Act that disenfranchised church members and seized church property. "You are crushing the Mormons by oppressive legislation, and you have forbidden Chinese immigration." Kennan, surprised by the count's views, tried to persuade him against the Chinese but "abandoned the discussion" of Mormonism.[47] Susa picked up where Kennan left off.

She wrote to Tolstoy an uncharacteristically deferential letter. She had "wished to write ... and yet have hesitated and allowed my fear to overcome my desire." Susa, so normally willing to share her opinion on those topics she knew about, confessed that "I shrink from intruding that upon you which might be entirely unwelcome." She offered to send a Book of Mormon and to "give you a 'mormon's' view of the

---

44. Jacob Gates to Susa Young Gates, Nov. 1887, box 6, fd. 7.

45. The interview, "A Visit to Count Tolstoi," was in the June 1887 issue of *The Century* magazine. Kennan was the father of American diplomat, George F. Kennan.

46. Kennan, "Visit to Count Tolstoi," 261.

47. Kennan, 263.

Mormon question." She explained that she was on a mission away from Utah, "but, I love my home, my people, and my religion."[48]

Susa's letter was answered by Tatiana, Count Tolstoy's oldest daughter, who wrote that her father "thanks you very much for your letter and your kind offer to send him 'The Book of Mormon.'" She continued that the count "has indeed heard a great deal about the Mormons." Tolstoy had apparently met two LDS missionaries in Bern and Geneva, Switzerland, in 1857 when he was twenty-eight years old.[49] Susa must have been delighted at the request for more information and continued correspondence: "You will very much oblige my father by giving him knowledge about your people."[50] In September 1888, two of Tolstoy's books arrived on the island for Susa. She read enthusiastically and thought, "A strange writer. How vivid!"[51]

Susa replied to Tatiana in October 1888[52] and gushed, "Now let me thank your father for this priviledge he has granted me. I feel honored in presenting such books to such a man." Susa explained that she would have her publisher in Salt Lake City send Tolstoy a Book of Mormon and the *Life of Joseph Smith* by George Q. Cannon.[53] Tolstoy seems to have genuinely enjoyed his correspondence with Susa, and he wrote in his diary that he received "a beautiful letter from an American woman."[54] But he read the books Susa arranged to have sent and "was horrified. Yes, religion, religion proper, is the product of deception, lies for a good purpose. An illustration of this is obvious, extreme in the deception: The Life of Smith; but also other *religions*, religions proper, only in differing degrees."[55]

Susa's last letters with Tolstoy came after she was back in Utah,

48. Susa Young Gates to Leo Tolstoy, July 8, 1888. Susa and Tolstoy's correspondence is reprinted in full in Fetzer, "Tolstoy and Mormonism."
49. Fetzer, "Tolstoy and Mormonism," 16.
50. Tatiana Tolstoy to Susa Young Gates, undated, box 49, fd. 6.
51. Gates, Journal, Sep. 10, 1888. The books were *Sebastopol* and *The Two Generations*.
52. Susa made her own copy of this letter for herself, but while the overall content is similar, it differs significantly in specific wording. It was very uncharacteristic of Susa at this point, before her use of a typewriter and carbon paper, to keep copies of outgoing correspondence, but she obviously treasured her correspondence with Tolstoy. See "Precious Tolstoy Letters" in box 49, fd. 6, SYGP (CHL). Leland Fetzer found Susa's original letter in Tolstoy's papers in Moscow and reprinted it in his article, "Tolstoy and Mormonism."
53. Fetzer, "Tolstoy and Mormonism," 19–20.
54. Tolstoy, Diary, Jan. 1, 1889, qtd. in Fetzer, 20.
55. Tolstoy, Diary, Jan. 23, 1889, qtd. in Fetzer, 21.

and she wrote to confirm that the books had been received. Tatiana replied that her father had received the books and he read them "with very much interest."[56] This brief—but thrilling for Susa—correspondence with Count Leo Tolstoy has since spawned rumors that Tolstoy greatly admired Mormonism. Such folklore is common among the Saints when a famous person comes into contact with the church or its missionaries.[57] But Tolstoy's purported attraction to Mormonism has likely been exaggerated, especially in light of his "horrified" reaction to the books Susa sent him. He did seem charmed by Susa, and he did take her correspondence and the books she offered him seriously.[58]

If her letters to Tolstoy and others, and their requisite need for stamps, irked the plantation storekeeper, other islanders were unhappy with Susa's penchant for gossip. Susa clashed with the wife of Jacob's counselor, Elizabeth Noall, who Susa thought was "one of the strangest woman I ever knew." Susa vowed to pray for the sister rather than blame her since "her unfortunate disposition seems to have made her a lot more trouble."[59] Noall, for her part, may have been intimidated by Susa and her influence. She resented that Susa was "a busybody in everybodis affairs" and that "what Sister Gates had said … had kept me awake most of the night." She apparently felt that she could not stand up to Susa or respond in kind (what exactly was said was never recorded) because Susa "carries such an influence where she goes."[60]

Susa knew of her sharp tongue and occasional tendency to gossip. But that part of her personality that kept Elizabeth Noall up most of the night troubled Susa only a little. "Ah me, I gossiped again," she wrote in her journal. "What a tongue is mine. Father, help me to master it!" Even as she acknowledged that the missionary families "tattled and chattered about each other," she seemed to think this something they all could easily "forgive and forget."[61] They would

---

56. Gates and Tolstoy correspondence, box 49, fd. 6.

57. See, for example, rumors that Elvis Presley read the Book of Mormon and considered joining the LDS Church, in Erekson, "Elvis Has Left the Library."

58. Fetzer, "Tolstoy and Mormonism," 24.

59. Gates, Journal, Aug. 13, Sep. 27, 1888.

60. Elizabeth L. Noall, Journal, Feb. 11, 1887, box 14, Journal 2, in Noall, Papers.

61. Gates, Journal, Feb. 1, 22, 1888.

have to; some months after the conflict with Noall, she and Susa were called to serve as counselors to Lucy M. King in the Relief Society presidency.[62] Despite the challenges of living close together in an isolated Pacific island, life in the small colony was by and large congenial and uneventful, except for the tragic deaths of young children, which was not limited to the Gates family.

While living in Hawai'i (and likely before), Susa and Jacob confronted a question that, at one time or another, faced nearly all prominent Mormon couples: Should Jacob take another wife? Susa was, after all, a great proponent of polygamy—at least, in theory. Throughout her life she would write affectionately, even idyllically, of her childhood as a daughter of polygamy. Shortly after arriving home from the islands, she would write, "I adore my mother, reverence and idolize my father, love all my father's wives, and am devotedly attached to every one of my numerous brothers and sisters." Polygamy, she said, "makes men humble, obliges them to go to God for wisdom to lead his family into the haven of peace and righteousness, and it makes women forget themselves and their selfish want in the desire to help others to be happy and contented." This defense of polygamy was not confined to her journal or in a letter to a friend; it was an editorial published in the *New York Sun*.[63] Another rhapsodic treatment of polygamy followed a few months later in the *North American Review*.[64]

If Susa were such a devoted member of the church—and she certainly was—and if she were so smitten with polygamy, why then did she not encourage Jacob to take another wife? A partial answer may be in a letter Susa wrote to Jacob shortly after the deaths of Jay and Karl. It was Susa's thirty-first birthday, and she gloomily expressed that her "own earthly end is very near," perhaps a sign of how down she felt over the loss of her children. She explained to Jacob that when she died, none of her personal property was to be given to any other wives he took. "No matter how dear to you, your other wives may be, it would be not right to install them as mistress over that which was mine. Is that selfish? Forgive me." After listing some

---

62. "Sandwich Island Letter," *Woman's Exponent*, Jun. 15, 1889, 16.

63. Susa Young Gates, letter to the editor, *New York Sun*, Aug. 11, 1889.

64. Gates, "Family Life Among the Mormons."

furniture, clothing, books, and some of her father's things, she told him, "Dont let your other wives near my jewelry or use my own private things."[65] It seems likely that Susa, for whatever reason, could not share Jacob with another woman. She was not alone in this apparent hypocrisy. Other Mormon women might be the products of polygamy, or defend it and support their leaders, but such beliefs did not always extend to their own husbands.[66]

The question of other wives in the Gateses' marriage may have been real, and not just theoretical. The details are scant, but evidence suggests Susa and Jacob confronted the question while in Hawai'i, where US anti-polygamy laws were not in effect. A letter from Joseph F. Smith, responding to a now-lost letter from Susa and Jacob, hints that the couple may have come close to entering into polygamy—and they may have even had a particular second wife in mind. Smith wrote that he could "find no objection to your intended proposition to [mission president] King, and I will do what I can to get him a dispensation [permission] to unite the bond, Susa consenting! But Susa must not lay any of the responsibility on me, for your doing a simple duty. I think it is a good plan nevertheless. It would exempt you from the polygamy act entirely. Now is your chance. The Brethren do not dissent."[67]

Smith's mention of uniting "the bond" and "Susa consenting" has all the hallmarks of approving of a polygamous union, since first wives were supposed to give permission for their husbands to take additional wives. When Smith speaks of exemption from the "polygamy act," he almost certainly means the recent Edmunds–Tucker Act disenfranchising Mormons and further punishing those who

---

65. Susa Young Gates to Jacob Gates, Mar. 18, 1887, box 9, fd. 7.

66. Numerous examples abound. Sanie Lund, wife of future apostle Anthon H. Lund, agreed to marry him only after he promised her he would never take a second wife. Lund, "Out of the Swan's Nest," 84. Alice A. Richards, wife of Apostle George F. Richards, reportedly promised her husband that she would bear as many children as he wanted if he would not marry a second wife. They had fifteen children. (Paul Richards, personal communication, May 2015). George's half-brother, Franklin S. Richards (1849–1934), long-term general counsel for the church, likewise chose monogamy. His wife, Emily S. Tanner Richards, was one of the founders of the Utah Women's Suffrage Association. A similar choice by Reed Smoot (1862–1941), US senator (1903–33) and apostle, was the major factor which allowed him to be seated in the senate after his election. Two years after the death of his first wife, Alpha (Allie) Eldredge Smoot, in 1928, he married Alice Sheets.

67. Joseph F. Smith to Susa Young and Jacob Gates, Nov. 17, 1887, box 46, fd. 30.

enter plural marriage. Since Susa and Jacob were living in Hawai'i, then not a part of the United States, they were excepted from anti-polygamy legislation. After the 1890 Woodruff Manifesto, plural marriages continued to be solemnized under the rationale that if such unions took place outside of the country, no laws were broken. Marriages were approved and conducted in Canada, Mexico, and in other jurisdictions.[68] Nothing seems to have come of Smith's letter, but whatever Jacob and Susa might have been contemplating, Jacob remained a monogamist, likely because of Susa's apprehensions.

Susa had one more child to birth before she left the islands. Her account of the day, January 19, 1889, is vintage Susa. She "molded bread," embroidered, made eight pies, cooked dinner, made a quart of guava preserves, attended two and a half hours of meetings sitting on a hard bench, "preached a little, made a cupful of jelly, made a big pot of yeast, washed dirty dishes, made buttonholes in Josie's garments, and am now writing." It was 8:00 p.m. An hour later, she gave birth to her third and final son born on the islands, Harvey Harris, with mother Lucy Young acting as nurse and midwife. She had been in "labor all day," but it did not stop her from any of her usual work.[69]

At last, six months after Susa had hoped it would come, the release from missionary service in Hawai'i was granted to the family. They had decided after Jay and Karl's deaths to bring their bodies back to Utah for reburial in Provo. Jacob found a tinsmith in Honolulu to make lead coffins for $20 each, while Jacob would make his own "outer cases."[70] Jacob disinterred his children's bodies himself, "taking up all that is earthly of our darlings and boxing them up ready for sending them on the vessel."[71]

Even though the bodies were "hermetically sealed in metallic coffins,"[72] the personnel on board the steamer *Maricopa* refused to transport the coffins, and alternate plans had to be made. The Noalls and two other missionary couples left Honolulu on this vessel one week before the Gateses. Jacob and Susa found that "their old friend Capt. [J. C.] Wilding" was in port with the *Forrest Queen,* and he

68. Quinn, "LDS Church Authority," and Hardy, *Solemn Covenant.*
69. Gates, Journal, Jan. 19, 1889.
70. Jacob Gates to Susa Young Gates, Mar. 6, 1889, box 6, fd. 7.
71. Gates, Journal, Mar. 16, 1889.
72. Gates, "Lucy Bigelow Young," 134.

agreed to take the bodies as freight with the stipulation that "full passenger price be paid for the two coffins" and that his "superstitious sailors" not be told the nature of that "freight."[73]

On April 14, 1889, after three and a half years on the Hawai'ian Islands, the Gates family departed. There were Jacob and Susa and their four children; Lucy Bigelow Young; Christine Young, a cousin; and sixteen native Hawai'ians, who would settle in Iosepa, a Polynesian enclave started in 1889 about seventy-five miles southwest of Salt Lake City.[74] Susa was poised to begin what would become the busiest decade in her eventful life.

---

73. Gates. Wilding expected the ship to land in San Francisco around May 10.

74. "Departures" and "Local and General News," *Daily Bulletin (Honolulu)*, Apr. 15, 1889. Iosepa, settled by Hawai'ians who wanted to gather to Zion with the rest of the Saints, eventually totaled about 200 citizens but was abandoned in 1917 and is now a ghost town.

Influence

The 1890s were the coming of age for Susa Young Gates. In the next ten years she became a substantial person of influence, not just within the LDS community, but also nationally, and, to a limited degree, internationally. In January 1890, Susa was a thirty-three-year-old mother living in Provo, Utah. By December 1899, she had published nationally, founded the *Young Woman's Journal*, attended Harvard University, hosted eminent American and British women, and worked with top church leaders. This decade was "life's most crowded years for me."[1] Susa traveled widely, including to Europe, organized or otherwise became involved in multiple women's organizations, gave birth to four children, and suffered more loss.

She cofounded the Utah Women's Press Club, organized the Sons and Daughters of the Utah Pioneers, and founded the Utah chapter of the Daughters of the Revolution. She helped to organize the National Household Economic Association. She was a board member of Brigham Young University, and there she created the home economics department and taught a physiology class, where her frankness caused a small scandal. She attended summer school at Harvard, where she met her future son-in-law, John A. Widtsoe. She was a member of the general board of the LDS Young Ladies' Mutual Improvement Association, and there she developed the concept of standardized lessons and wrote the first two guidebooks. She taught a weekly Sunday school class for young women in her home ward in

---

1. Susa Young Gates, "Hail and Farewell," *Young Woman's Journal*, Oct. 1929, 676.

Provo. She entertained three presidents of the LDS Church, as well as multiple apostles and members of the Seventy.

The list of people she met reads like a Who's Who in American Women and includes Susan B. Anthony, May Wright Sewall, Dr. Anna Howard Shaw, Charlotte Perkins Gilman, Kate Waller Barrett, prominent members of the Women's Christian Temperance Union, Dr. Mary E. Green, Dr. Susanna W. Dodds, Miss Sadie American, and Lydia Mountford.[2] Susa joined the National Council of Women and served as chair of its press committee. She joined the International Council of Women and spoke at meetings of both organizations. She wrote and edited the *Young Woman's Journal* and wrote for the *Juvenile Instructor* and other magazines.

In her family life, she reconnected with her two oldest children from her first marriage, Leah and Bailey. She was influential in Leah's selection of a husband and tried to intervene in Bailey's increasingly wayward life. She did much of this while pregnant and giving birth to four children as she maintained a busy household in Provo, aided by a mostly indulgent husband. In managing her busy life, Susa frequently made to-do lists, and they offer a glimpse into her daily schedule:

Notes for the Day's Work: Provo, Utah, August 19, 1895

Go down cellar with Emma Lucy and show her how to clean it.
Go to Aunt Corneel's and take her to Eikens and get hers and my fruit.
Darn Dan's stockings.
Boil over the bottle of spoiled fruit.
Clean my office.
Answer Leah's, Sterling's, Sis. Taylor's, and Mrs. Grey's letters, and Carlos's.
Prepare talk on "Women and Literature" and go to the [Brigham Young] Academy's opening exercises at 10 o'clock.

---

2. Gates. These women were all prominent social reformers, dedicated to women's suffrage, education, improvements in medicine, and temperance. Lydia Mamreoff von Finkelstein Mountford was an author and a lecturer on the Holy Land, and became friends with Wilford Woodruff. Some scholars have speculated that Woodruff married Mountford as a plural wife aboard a ship off the coast of San Francisco after he issued the 1890 Manifesto. Woodruff's biographer, Thomas Alexander, doubts that this happened. See Alexander, *Things in Heaven and Earth*, 324–28.

Talk to Aretta Young about her story.

Write to Pres. Joseph F. Smith, Pres. George G. Cannon, Apostle Franklin D. Richards, and Elder B. H. Roberts about writing for *Young Woman's Journal*.

Also write Mrs. M.E. Potter and Marie D.

Write and thank Carol for her lovely gift.

Get the cloth for Dan's pants and boys' clothes and send them to the tailor.

Finish the last chapter of 'John Stevens' Courtship' for *The Contributor*.

Sketch out editorials for *Young Woman's Journal*.

Wash my head.

Get the kitchen carpet and have the girl and Dan put it down.

Get cot and crib from store.

Also washstand and glass and wardrobe.

Get vegetables and fruit for dinner.

Take my bicycle dress over to Polly and have it fixed.

Take clothes to the Relief Society.

Get consecrated oil.

Bless Cecil to do his chores well.

Administer to baby Franklin.[3]

Susa, like many of her contemporaries, saw idleness in an increasingly urbanized, entertainment-filled world as sinful, even dangerous. Her action lists were not only an attempt to remain organized, but were part of what she saw as a righteous lifestyle. As always, her faith and beliefs guided her work and her home life throughout the 1890s.

Susa began the decade with the publication of her article, "Family Life Among the Mormons: By a Daughter of Brigham Young," in the March issue of *North American Review*.[4] The *Review*, founded in 1815, was the first literary magazine in the United States. It became one of America's "longest-lived magazines" and had "brilliant contributors, the cream of New England intellectuals." It was considered "a remarkable repository, unmatched by that of any other magazine of American thought."[5]

It was Susa's first article in a major American publication. She had

---

3. Susa Young Gates, "Notes for the Day's Work: Provo, Utah, August 19, 1895," qtd. in Arrington, "Women as a Force," 5–6. I have added minor punctuation for clarity.

4. Gates, "Family Life Among the Mormons."

5. Tebbel and Zuckerman, *Magazine in America*, 12.

often dreamed of becoming a mainstream author, but throughout most of her life, Susa's writings would be directed largely toward Mormon audiences. The article was published six months before the First Presidency issued the Manifesto, which ostensibly forbade further plural marriages as Utah pursued statehood.[6] Susa's article is an apologia for polygamy, and she wasted no time in making her point: "The common statement that plural marriage debases husbands, degrades wives, and brutalizes offspring, is false." She described and lauded the health and intelligence of her father's fifty-six children, the happiness of the family's home life, the remarkable educational opportunities afforded the Young children, the rather strict religious tone of the home with daily prayers, the healthy and extensive recreational activities of the children, the directive influence of their father in the selection of friends, and the impressive accomplishments of Brigham's progeny. "The polygamous women of Utah know the value of the experience they have gained, and, to a woman, would refuse to exchange places with any other," and she suggests the readers talk to these women "rather than [reply] on the hearing of second-hand, fabulous stories."[7]

Most of Susa's writing the first year back from Hawai'i was for an LDS audience. She wrote a twenty-one part serial, "Up From Tribulation," for the *Juvenile Instructor* in 1890 as Homespun, based on the trials of a young Virginian convert named Willard Gibbs.[8] She also wrote a "historical cantata" on "The Life of Brigham Young," with music composed by Professor H. E. Giles of the Brigham Young Academy, which was presented at the Provo Opera House on June 4, 1890, as part of a "Celebration of Brigham Young Birthday Primary Association Entertainment."

Susa discontinued keeping her journal, but she and Jacob wrote to each other often, since both were traveling frequently. On rare occasions they would write to each other twice a day; usually, they

6. Plural marriages continued after the 1890 Manifesto, usually outside of the United States and often approved by members of the First Presidency and performed by high-ranking church leaders. Joseph F. Smith would issue a second manifesto in 1904. Thereafter, church members who entered into plural marriage were subject to church discipline. See Quinn, "LDS Authority"; Hardy, *Solemn Covenant*; Flake, *Politics of American Religious Identity*.

7. Gates, "Family Life."

8. Homespun, "Up from Tribulation," *Juvenile Instructor*, various issues, 1890.

would correspond every day or two; infrequently, communications would occur at intervals of three days or longer. Both Jacob and Susa would bitterly lament if the other went longer than a day or two without writing. Often the letters arrived in bunches because of the distances involved. But despite this flurry of correspondence, large gaps exist in Susa's personal papers; neither she nor Jacob saved every letter, and she rarely used a typewriter or carbon paper to make copies. Entire years of her correspondence to Jacob are no longer extant, and, as will be seen, she also occasionally asked Jacob to destroy her letters.

Susa traveled to Logan in northern Utah in June 1890 for a month. She was the founder and editor of the *Young Woman's Journal*, and it kept her busier than most other responsibilities.[9] The *Journal*, barely eight months old, was hemorrhaging cash. Susa had enlisted her mother to help, and Lucy canvassed the southern parts of Utah for several months in her horse and buggy trying to garner subscriptions while Susa went north to shore up support. By mid-July, Jacob had not heard from Susa for a few days and wrote tenderly, "My darling, I feel as if I could not stand your absence much longer." But four days later, having gone at least a week without a letter, his anger bled through the page: "I feel anything but pleased at the treatment I have received in this matter, and shall cease to write till some explanation is made."[10] Susa's letters resumed.

Lucy convinced Susa to attend the Bigelow Family reunion with her in Worcester, Massachusetts, on September 10, 1890. Lucy had been east before to visit family and perform genealogical research. Susa, financially stretched, could not afford to go, so Lucy paid all of her daughter's expenses. It would be Susa's first foray into genealogical research, and it would spark a lifelong interest. It was also the farthest she had ever been away from her husband and children.

The cars pulled slowly out of the station and gathered speed, but only a few miles from Ogden, Utah, the train derailed. As the train slid off the tracks, Susa jumped up to grab her mother, but was thrown against the roof of the car. She was knocked unconscious for eight hours, had lacerations on her body, and a fractured

---

9. The creation of the *Young Woman's Journal* is detailed in chapter ten.
10. Jacob Gates to Susa Young Gates, July 14 and July 18, 1890, box 6, fd. 9.

hand. Lucy was bruised and shaken but relatively unhurt. Lucy "got out her little bottle of [consecrated olive] oil and annointed the hand" before the splints and bandages were placed on Susa's arm, and prayed mightily.[11]

Lucy was determined to continue to the reunion, despite Susa's injuries, a decision that Susa later applauded. She was confined to a bed until the train reached Chicago, where she transferred by wheelchair to a connecting train to Boston.

Both mother and daughter delighted in the trip and thought it a great success. Susa took pride in her Bigelow lineage, and she always considered the family one of New England's most prominent and outstanding. Lucy and Susa spent a week in Northborough, Massachusetts, at the home of Gilman Bigelow Howe, secretary of the family organization and compiler of the book on Bigelow genealogy to which Lucy had contributed. They made a trip to Boston and spent a day visiting the New England Genealogical Library, then made their way south to New York City. When they arrived in the city, the Statue of Liberty had stood for three years, and the Brooklyn Bridge was still taller than any building. While there, they visited Jeannette Young Easton, a half-sister of Susa, who was married to Robert Easton, an aspiring professional singer. At Lucy's insistence, they stopped in St. Louis, Missouri, on their way back to Utah to visit the St. Louis Hygienic College. Susa met the college director, Dr. Susannah W. Dodds, with whom she had corresponded regarding current principles of hygienic living, particularly with regard to food and drink.[12]

When Susa arrived back home, she was still injured from the train derailment, and it took her several months to fully heal. Family member and attorney LeGrand Young helped Lucy obtain $250 from the railroad for her injuries; Susa received $2,000, also from the railroad, for her pain and suffering.[13]

Susa helped to broker the transfer of Brigham Young Academy from the heirs of Brigham Young to the school's board of trustees. "All the property mentioned in Brigham Young's original deeds of

---

11. Gates, "Lucy Bigelow Young," 144.
12. Gates, 145.
13. Gates, 145.

1875 and 1877" was transferred to the board, empowered to establish the by-laws of the school, provide adequate accommodations for the school, fill board vacancies by a majority vote, and create a corporation under Utah law.[14] Susa herself obtained "the signatures of eighty-three heirs" to effect the transfer of the academy to the church.[15] Other stipulations added that the name of the school would never be changed (although it later became Brigham Young University) and that there would always be at least three heirs of Brigham Young serving on the board. (This is no longer the case.) Susa was named to the board of trustees, a position she held until 1932, making her the longest-serving trustee of the university in its history.

On June 16, 1891, the *Provo Daily Enquirer* carried an abrupt notice: "Joseph Gates, son of Jacob F. Gates, died this morning. The funeral will be held at the residence of Grandma Gates, at 2 o'clock to morrow."[16] There was no mention of the boy's mother, and no cause of death was given. The family always attributed Joseph's death to a candy wrapper inadvertently tainted with poisonous materials. Joseph had been born in Hawai'i and, following a grim pattern of Susa and Jacob's deceased children, was only five years old. Susa, who had written of her agony after the excruciating deaths of Jay and Karl in Hawai'i, wrote almost nothing about Joseph's death. She was so prolific when she wrote about her family's history, but she evidently could not bring herself to write much more about her lost children, even in letters to Jacob or to other family members.

Five days after Joseph's death, daughter Sarah Beulah was born. Beulah, as she was called, became a great comfort to Jacob during Susa's frequent absences from home. He wrote that "Beulah is the sweetest spirited child that we ever had or will have perhaps." And Emma Lucy—now variously called Lucy, Lu, Lule, or Lulu—was often tasked with caring for her father and siblings during her mother's longer absences, which could last for weeks or months. Lule, her father reported, does not "complain in the least."[17] Susa, "twice a month, or oftener," traveled to Salt Lake City, for *Young Woman's*

---

14. Wilkinson and Skousen, *Brigham Young University*, 95.
15. "Brigham Young Academy," box 16, fd. 7, SYGP (USDH).
16. See p. 2 of the *Daily Enquirer*, under date.
17. Jacob Gates to Susa Young Gates, Feb. 25, 1895, box 6 fd. 12.

Journal business, "sometimes with my nursing baby and little Lulu as day nurse."[18] Jacob later wrote to his wife that the family adjusted well to Susa's frequent absences: "The children keep remarkably well. Lulu does a great deal of the house work every day, but does not complain. ... If it wasn't for her you couldn't leave home as you do."[19]

Susa came to work with many venerable women in Utah as her responsibilities expanded. In October 1891 she partnered with Emmeline B. Wells, editor of the *Woman's Exponent*, and Wells's predecessor as editor, Louisa Lula Greene Richards, to organize the Utah Woman's Press Club, patterned after the Woman's Press Club of New York, founded two years earlier.[20] It was established "for the benefit of women engaged in active journalistic or newspaper work in Utah Territory," with membership limited to women with a history of published writings.[21] Susa served for two terms as first vice-president of the group, an experience that helped to prepare her for her work as chair of the Press Committee of the National Council of Women.

In the summer of 1892 Susa traveled to Cambridge, Massachusetts, to attend classes at Harvard University. There she met two people who would become lifelong presences in her life: her future son-in-law, John A. Widtsoe, and her close friend, Maud May Babcock. Susa took courses in literature to hone her writing skills. Always interested in diet and exercise, she also took a course in physical education taught by Babcock, who had previously joined the "Harvard Summer School for Physical Training, a proprietary school organized by Dudley Allen Sargent."[22]

While in Cambridge, Susa persuaded Babcock to come to Utah and made arrangements for her to teach at the University of Utah and the Brigham Young Academy. Babcock lived with the Gates family in Provo during the two days a week she was teaching there. Four months later, she joined the LDS Church, much to the chagrin of her parents. Susa later wrote that she "helped in [Babcock's] conversion and claim her as my spiritual daughter in answer to my

18. Gates, "Hail and Farewell," 678.
19. Gates to Gates, Feb. 25, 1895.
20. Derr, "Strength in Our Union," 182.
21. Mary F. Kelly Pye, "Utah Women's Press Club History," qtd. in Derr, 205.
22. Ulrich, "Give Us an Expanding Faith," 2.

prayers."[23] Babcock settled in Salt Lake City, where she founded both the Department of Physical Education and the Department of Speech at the University of Utah. She taught at the university for forty-six years, serving also many years on the General Board of the Young Ladies' Mutual Improvement Association. She was named the "first lady of Utah drama," by the university newspaper, the *Daily Utah Chronicle* and vied with Susa herself as the mother of physical education in Utah.[24]

The beginning of Susa's friendship with John A. Widtsoe was rather more rocky. Although she was a prolific writer, Susa exercised tight control over her public image and went to pains to ensure that episodes she found embarrassing might not come to light. She had done this with her marriage and divorce to Alma Dunford, and she would do the same with her time in Cambridge. When she was first at Harvard, she told Jacob that she wanted all her letters kept for "future reference," although she admitted they could prove embarrassing.[25] Some thirty months later, she asked Jacob to destroy the letters. Jacob complied and burned all the letters she had written while at Harvard.[26] Some inferences about Susa's life in Massachusetts may be made from her time spent with Babcock and Widtsoe. Indeed, it is possible Susa wanted her correspondence destroyed because she was smitten with young John Widtsoe, and likely decided very early that he was the right man to marry her daughter Leah. Widtsoe later wrote of that summer that he and Susa "became good friends and spent much time together."[27]

Widtsoe, future LDS apostle and respected scientist, was born in 1872 on Froya Island, Norway, and immigrated to Utah in 1883 with his widowed mother, Anna, and his brother, Osborne, after Anna had converted in 1881. The Widtsoes settled in Logan, Utah, where in the fall of 1889 John enrolled at Brigham Young College (BYC), which had begun operation eleven years earlier. John was significantly influenced by a Karl Maeser protégé, Joseph Marion Tanner, who had been appointed as the third principal of the college

23. Gates, "Hail and Farewell," 676.
24. Ulrich, "Give Us an Expanding Faith," 1.
25. Susa Young Gates to Jacob Gates, Aug. 10, 1892, box 9, fd. 7.
26. Jacob Gates to Susa Young Gates, Mar. 21, 1895, box 6, fd. 12.
27. Widtsoe, *Sunlit Land*, 38.

in Logan. In 1891 Tanner decided to relocate to Massachusetts to study at Harvard, taking with him several of his most outstanding students, among them Widtsoe.[28]

Susa aggressively lobbied for Widtsoe as a suitor to her daughter, Leah, both in person and by letter. Susa wrote to him after she returned to Utah, and in one letter sent a picture of Leah, with an inscription on the back: "To John A. Widtsoe from Leah and her mother. Leah age 18, Cambridge, Mass, Aug. 15, 1892." John, under stress to finish school, pay off debts, and support his mother, attempted to curtail his friendship with Susa, which shows how little he knew of her intensity. Susa took umbrage and asked "that John return her letters and photographs." Her words to him—"May God bless you in all your walks and works, and raise up friends to you who will be deserving of your confidence and esteem"—are a glimpse into how biting Susa could be and how skilled a writer she was to be able to provoke guilt.[29]

Fortunately, their letters resumed, despite John's initial diffidence. In the summer of 1893, Babcock, now living in Utah, returned to Harvard to teach physical education, and she brought four young women from Utah, including Leah Dunford, no doubt at Susa's urging.[30] Susa, now a member of the general board of the Young Ladies' Mutual Improvement Association, often thought about the roles of children in public and family life. Months earlier, she had spoken to the quarterly conference of the Salt Lake Stake of the YLMIA on the "Duties of Children to Parents." She told her listeners that "we must impress upon our children what they owe their spiritual parents," and she "urged the young ladies to pray for their parents and sustain them by their love and kindness as well."[31] In 1892 Susa had recommended that a guide with specific lessons to be taught should be developed by the Young Ladies' Mutual Improvement Association. Susa reported, "The first Guide was published in 1893 and was an instant and unqualified success; two years later a second one followed, with more difficult lessons."[32]

---

28. Parrish, *John A. Widtsoe*, 54–55.
29. Parrish, 67–68.
30. Parrish.
31. Gates, "Duties of Children to Parents," *Young Woman's Journal*, Dec. 1892, 140.
32. Gates, *History of YLMIA*, 181–82.

The young Utah girls raised quite a stir in Cambridge. Leah wrote her mother, "You would die if you see the reaction to finding we are Mormon." She expressed anxiety at meeting Widtsoe, but after the two met, they spent a fair amount of time together that summer. Leah wrote, "I cannot even talk with John Widtsoe on anything or subject but you." Susa was such a forceful personality that even some 2,000 miles away she still dominated the conversation. Widtsoe was sensitive that he had hurt Susa's feelings, and Leah said that "he sends his kindness and best regards to you, but will not believe but that you are angry with him." Leah quickly grew infatuated with Widtsoe and told her mother that she was "never so attracted to anyone in my life." However, John and Leah's courtship moved slowly—too slowly for Susa's taste.[33] On the way home to Utah, Leah and her friends stopped at the Chicago's World's Fair. Leah considered the Fair "too grand to describe." The fair was illuminated by great electric spotlights and lamps, and was dominated by a massive Ferris wheel. Leah may also have seen Thomas Edison's kinetoscope, one of the earliest ways to watch motion pictures. She also visited her mother's younger sister, Aunt Mabel,[34] in Chicago.

In April 1893, Susa kept the "official minutes for the forty-one [actually thirty-one] dedicatory services held in the Salt Lake temple," between April 6 and April 24.[35] Construction of the temple had taken forty years, off and on, from the original groundbreaking in 1853 and represented great sacrifice on the part of the Saints, particularly in view of the embarrassed state of finances of the church due to escheatment of properties resulting from anti-polygamy legislation. Susa, an expert in shorthand, had performed this same task at the dedications of the St. George and Logan temples in 1877 and 1884, respectively, and she likely would have kept the minutes of the Manti temple dedication in 1888 had she not been in Hawai'i. Susa not only kept the minutes of the multiple lengthy dedicatory services, she did so while pregnant with Franklin Young, born three weeks after the dedications were complete, on May 17, 1893.

---

33. The couple would not marry until 1898.

34. Leah Dunford to Susa Young Gates, various letters, July-Aug. 1893, box 12, fd. 6.

35. Susa Young Gates, Autobiographical Sketches, box 3, fd. 35. See also Stuy, "Come, Let Us Go Up," 109.

While Susa was in Salt Lake City, Jacob was overseeing construction on their home in Provo. He was vexed and impatient that Susa did not answer his telegram regarding questions he had. "Why could you not come down in the evening and go back in the morning, if it is so necessary that you be there all the time."[36] Jacob may have been under terrible financial strain with the Panic of 1893, and in letters to Susa that summer, he detailed the economic turmoil roiling the community. He found that businessmen were "blue" and that "things here are in an awful condition" and that soon people would not have enough money for groceries.[37]

Until it was eclipsed by a more severe economic collapse in 1929, the Panic of 1893 was called the Great Depression. It highlighted how economies had intertwined across the globe; the panic had causes as varied as Argentinian crop failures and European credit speculation. After years of struggle, in May 1893 the New York Stock Exchange collapsed. There was a run on banks and over 350 failed.[38] For the next several years, the depression would impact families across the country, including the Gateses.

Chicago felt the strain of the panic later than most cities because of the World's Fair. Latter-day Saints saw an opportunity to visit the city and proselytize. The Mormons had been vilified for decades over the practice of polygamy, and the World's Fair, less than three years after the Woodruff Manifesto, offered a chance at what historian Reid Neilson called the rehabilitation of the church's public image. The fair "marked the dramatic reengagement of the church with the non-Mormon world," wrote Neilson.[39] The Mormon Tabernacle Choir performed at the fair as many Saints traveled as tourists, while others, like Susa, were part of national reform or education movements. Susa "joined in organizing the National Household Economic Association there, in connection with Mrs. Linda Hull Larned and Dr. Mary E. Green."[40] No matter how vitriolic the non-Mormon women could be regarding Mormons and polygamy, they were almost universally charmed by the women the church sent to represent it. Susa wrote to her husband,

36. Jacob Gates to Susa Young Gates, Apr. 15, 1893, box 6, fd. 11.
37. Gates to Gates, June-July 1893, box 6, fd. 11.
38. White, *Republic for Which It Stands*, 765–73.
39. Neilson, *Exhibiting Mormonism*, 7.
40. Gates, "Hail and Farewell," 676.

"Jacob there is certainly a different spirit abroad in the land in regard to our people." Indeed, Mormon women were successful in ways men were not, and it was due to their efforts that a thawing in public sentiment against the LDS Church occurred.[41]

Lucy Young was in Provo to help take care of the children. Susa lamented to Jacob, "The sight of [Franklin's] poor yet sweet little face is continually before me," but of the fair she effused, "oh the beauty and glory of it all … the beautiful things mine eyes have rested upon today."[42] Echoing this sentiment, her surviving letters contain five themes almost universally present: homesickness, the difficulty of the work, her missionary zeal, her love and devotion to Jacob, and delays in her return home. She missed her family, and she was tired, but she was happy to be doing missionary work. "Two of the elderly ladies here began asking me questions about Mormonism. They were really interested & I felt it my duty to lay the Gospel before them as plainly as I could." Despite her homesickness, she felt like she had more to see, writing to Jacob, "Would you or Mother object if I stayed a few days longer? … There is so much to see & I do not want to give a hurried look at everything."[43] Susa's travel companion was Teenie Smoot Taylor, a longtime friend dating back to student days at Brigham Young Academy. Taylor's slower pace was a regular irritant to Susa, who wanted to see everything.

While in Chicago, the friends stayed where her Susa's sister Mabel was living, but if Susa said anything about Mabel to Jacob or other correspondents, it has not survived. Nor did she write anything about her older sister, Dora, who by now was Mrs. Albert Hagan, also living in Chicago. In fact, only one letter survives between Susa and Jacob for all of 1894, a report from Jacob about the construction of what was most likely Lucy's new home in Salt Lake City. The lack of correspondence suggests Susa stayed close to home that year. She organized and "taught for one year the first Home Economic department in Church schools." In her home ward, the Provo Fourth, she organized a Sunday School class for young women, which she taught for the next seven years, developing her own lessons, since

41. See Radke-Moss, "Mormon Women, Suffrage, and Citizenship."
42. Susa Young Gates to Jacob Gates, Sep. 24 and 29, 1893, box 9, fd. 8.
43. Gates to Gates.

there was no organized study guide.[44] She was also pregnant with her twelfth child and ninth son, Heber.

Susa delivered on November 22, 1894, but Heber was either still-born or died shortly after birth. She wrote to her oldest son, Bailey, who was then living in Butte, Montana, "I lost my dear babe at birth. So you see we have rather a sad house."[45]

Since he had been wrenched from his mother's arms when he was ten years old,[46] Bailey had had a troubled life. After he went to live with his father and stepmother, Lovinia "Vinnie" Clayton Dun-ford, he did not get along well with his father, and his stepmother disapproved of some of his behavior. He wrote to Susa shortly before she returned from Hawai'i that he was doing well in his classes, in either the highest or second highest level in every subject.[47] Nine months later he lamented, "My heart is a beating to have a kiss from your dear old lips ... I cant stay here papa is too cross to me. I cant stand it, and I don't know what to do about it. ... I cant help but cry when I think about you and the children."[48] He asked Susa not to mention his letter to Leah, since she would tell their father about it, and Alma would get angry. But Bailey himself went to Leah, who wrote to Susa, "What do you think is the best thing for Bailey to do? He seems to want to live with you. Do you want him? Tell me truly."[49] One source of contention may have been that Bailey did not want to follow his father into dentistry.

By January 1890 Bailey was no longer in school; he asked Susa to send him money to come down to Provo. There is no evidence that he spent much time with the Gateses in Provo. He signed multiple letters, "From your loving Boy," "From your Dear Child," "Your dar-ling boy," and "Your Loving Son." In September 1890, Bailey and a friend were playing in an alley in Salt Lake City near the Social Hall building. They peeked over the fence into a neighboring yard and spotted a bundle. They climbed the fence and found, wrapped in an undershirt, a dead baby girl. The baby had apparently been born

44. Gates, "Hail and Farewell," 676.
45. Susa Young Gates to Bailey Dunford, Dec. 18, 1894, box 14, fd. 9.
46. See chapter seven, herein.
47. Bailey Gates to Susa Young Gates, Dec. 17, 1888, box 14, fd. 8.
48. Gates to Gates, Aug. 6, 1889.
49. Leah Dunford to Susa Young Gates, Apr. 13, 1890, box 12, fd. 3.

healthy, then strangled to death.[50] Bailey, barely fifteen years old, may have been somewhat traumatized by the discovery. At some point, he ran away from home and lived for some three months with a family named Langstroff. Isabell Langstroff begged him to return home, apparently without success. Alma could not understand why Bailey should want to run away.

Bailey fell in with "a bad crowd of boys" and did not write to his mother for nearly two years.[51] At some point Susa's mother became involved. Lucy wrote to her daughter in January 1893 that she went to look for Bailey to get him away from these bad influences. She asked Susa to come to Salt Lake City and see Bailey, but Susa's response is no longer extant.[52] Susa was five months pregnant at the time and may not have been able to travel easily. Leah passed on to Susa that she had heard Bailey had come home drunk "the other night."[53] At some point, Bailey must have made his way to the northwest, because several months later Susa's sister Mabel wrote that the family had heard that Bailey was "still in Spokane."[54]

Bailey finally wrote to his mother, from Benicia, California, northeast of San Francisco. He said that he " had some pretty hard times & some good times too." He had traveled to Omaha, "Ogden, Cheyenne, Denver, Virginia City, Carson City, Sacramento, Oakland, and San Francisco."[55] He had become "a veritable tramp riding on the cars."[56] He worked here and there to buy clothes and railroad fare. He asked Susa for "$5 or $10 at present," which Susa sent.[57] Life was hard; he wrote to his half-sister Lule, "I know what it is to have a good home and when I get there again I will have sense enough to stay there." He hoped to earn enough money in California "to set himself up in business at home."[58] He received a money order from Susa, but had not been able to cash it.

50. "A Horrifying Discovery," *Utah Enquirer*, Sep. 9, 1890; "An Infant Murdered," *Deseret Evening News*, Sep. 8, 1890.
51. Dunford to Gates, Mar. 26, 1893, box 12, fd. 5.
52. Lucy Bigelow Young to Susa Young Gates, Jan. 20, 1893, box 30, fd. 8.
53. Dunford to Gates, Mar. 26, 1893.
54. Mabel Young to Susa and Jacob Gates, June 22, 1893, box 6, fd. 11.
55. Bailey Dunford to Susa Young Gates, July 23, 1893, box 14, fd. 9.
56. Bailey Dunford to Lule Gates, Oct. 16, 1893, box 14, fd. 9.
57. Bailey Dunford to Susa Young Gates, July 23, 1893.
58. Bailey Dunford to Lule Gates, Oct. 16, 1893.

Bailey worked in Benicia and nearby Cordelia, working at a fruit stand for room and board, in a sugar mill, and on a ranch milking cows and haying. He bought half-interest in a boat, which was used for clamming. Susa, ever concerned about his spiritual well-being, must have asked pointed questions, for Bailey tried to reassure her, "I am trying awful hard [to] overcome it [alcohol] and I don't think there is anything I can be held accountable for taking since I have been out here." A month later he wrote, "No Dearest Mamma I have not forgotten *my* religion" (emphasis in original).[59]

Several months later Bailey was in Salt Lake City, but he slipped out of town without saying goodbye to his grandmother because he owed her money. If Susa saw her son during this trip to Utah, no record of it survives. She wrote him at his latest location in Butte, Montana, and chastised him for leaving without saying goodbye to his grandmother because of the unpaid debt. "I know your heart is true and honest ... you would not fail to give every one every dollar you owed. But you must learn, my darling son, that the world does not judge by our intentions, but our actions. Men are led on from one weakness to another, and you must guard against your dislike to say agreeable things or to listen to reproof. So, pay the money you owe her, and we will see you in the spring."[60] Four days later Bailey responded that he would send his grandmother the money, all of it, as soon as he was able. He said he was sorry that he did not have money to send Christmas presents.

On January 16, 1895, Bailey was at a social hall with an ice skating rink in Butte with a friend. There was an explosion followed by a fire. Bailey joined the volunteer firefighters and offered to help hold one of the hoses. As they fought the flames, there was a second explosion. Bailey was thrown and killed almost immediately. The coroner found only one item on Bailey's body: Susa's last letter to him. He was nineteen years old.

Newspaper accounts of Bailey's death barely mentioned Susa, if at all. Instead he was "the son of Dr. A. B. Dunford," and it was Alma and Leah who traveled to Butte to retrieve Bailey's body.[61]

59. Bailey Dunford to Susa Young Gates, Mar. 5 and Apr. 9, 1894, box 14, fd. 9.

60. Susa Young Gates to Bailey Dunford, Dec. 18, 1894, box 14, fd. 9.

61. See "Salt Lake Boy Killed," *Salt Lake Herald-Republican*, Jan. 17, 1895; "Territorial News," *Ogden Daily Standard*, Jan. 17, 1895; "Alma Bailey Dunford," *Provo Daily*

His funeral was held a week after he died, near the border of Utah and Idaho, where Alma's parents lived. Susa was still bedridden after giving birth to Heber, and she did not attend. Susa, worried about Bailey's soul, asked Isabell Langstroff if Bailey had been "pure in regards to women." Langstroff's reply tried to reassure Susa: "I do not think he cared for women's company. I think Bailey was a good boy in everything he had grown to be so sensible and manly."[62] Twenty-five years after his death, Susa wrote to Logan temple workers about Bailey's temple work. Frederick Scholes, the recorder for the temple, responded that the work was "attended to" on September 12, 1900.[63] Once again, within a short amount of time, Susa had lost two sons.

Susa's relationship with Leah had also been strained, and now, as Leah turned twenty-one, things were gradually improving. Jacob had apparently also been troubled by Leah, for Susa wrote to him that "it just makes me thrill and think that the old annoyance is wearing off and that you can bear to have her around."[64] At least part of the tension came from Leah's positive relationship with her father. In one letter to her mother, full of apologies for unkind things she had said previously, she wrote, "But you know my feelings and I cannot help sharing. I love my mother dearer than tongue can tell, but I also love my father."[65]

Many children have complicated relationships with their parents, and it is impossible to guess how Susa's divorce from Alma affected her bond with Leah and Bailey, but it could not have been easy. Two-and-a-half decades later, Leah, with the benefit of hindsight and some of the wisdom adulthood bestows, wrote to her mother to explain: "I never knew you, Mother, till I was fifteen years old." Until then, Susa was nothing more than "a Beautiful Lady who sent me occasional shell trimmed cards ... with sweet verses and a few lovely, dear, letters." Like Bailey, Leah did not get along with her stepmother, whom she "feared and dreaded." She believed that Vinnie Dunford "did not love me," and she could never "approach my

Enquirer, Jan. 18, 1895; "Two More Victims," *Salt Lake Herald–Republican*, Jan. 18, 1895; "Terrible Explosions at Butte," *Deseret Weekly*, Jan. 26, 1895.

62. Isabell Langstroff to Susa Young Gates, Jan. 27, 1895, box 14, fd. 10.
63. Frederick Scholes to Susa Young Gates, Nov. 23, 1920, box 14, fd. 12.
64. Susa Young Gates to Jacob Gates, Mar. 1895, box 9, fd. 10.
65. Leah Dunford to Susa Young Gates, Mar. 24, 1893, box 12, fd. 5.

Stepmother—I was just a disagreeable child to her—& I must have been a great cross to her—who lived a hard life." She found refuge in her father, who she "knew loved me," and "most of the sunshine of my child life came thru him. But he didn't dare show it." Fortunately, in the intervening years, Leah and Jacob developed a close relationship, and Susa, Leah wrote, "richly ... made up to me for the loneliness of my childhood."[66]

The first meeting of the National Council of Women (NCW) was held in Washington, DC, on March 25, 1888, forty years after the first Women's Rights convention in Seneca Falls, New York. The first officers were Frances E. Willard, president; Susan B. Anthony, vice-president; Mary Eastman, recording secretary; and Louise Thomas, Treasurer. They adopted a preamble to their constitution:

> We, women of the United States, sincerely believing that the best good of our homes and national will be advanced by our own greater unity of thought, sympathy and purpose, and that an organized movement of women will best conserve the highest good of the family and the state, do hereby unite ourselves in a confederation of workers, committed to the overthrow of all forms of ignorance and injustice, and to the application of the Golden Rule to society, custom and law.[67]

The convention invited all three organizations of women in the LDS Church—the Relief Society, Primary, and Young Ladies' Mutual Improvement Association—to send representatives to the founding meeting in Washington. Representatives from the church were sent, and Susa attended her first meeting of the NCW in February 1895.

Susa was finally able to travel on February 9, and left by train with: Elmina S. Taylor, president of the YLMIA and one of the founding members of the NCW; Dr. Ellis Shipp, one of the first female doctors in the American west, the Relief Society delegate; and Minnie J. Snow, the YLMIA representative.[68] Three other women— Emmeline B. Wells for the Relief Society, Aurelia Rogers for the

---

66. Leah Dunford Widtsoe to Susa Young Gates, Oct. 26, 1929, box 8, fd. 6, Widtsoe Family Papers. See also Parrish, *John A. Widtsoe*, 98–99.

67. Gates, "History," 200.

68. Taylor was the first president of the LDS young women's organization. Ellis Shipp studied in both Philadelphia and Michigan. Minnie J. Snow was the favorite wife of apostle and future church president Lorenzo Snow.

Primary, and Marilla Daniels of Provo—were already in the capital.[69] Susa was pleased to inform Jacob that Elmina Taylor wanted Susa's expenses for the Washington portion of her trip to be paid for by the YLMIA board. Susa would pay her own expenses for a trip to Boston to research family genealogy. In Washington, Susa stayed in the home of Belva Lockwood, prominent attorney and suffragist, whom she found unexpectedly to be "unassuming ... anything but critical of other people ... kind without ostentation."[70]

The Utah delegation was invited to a birthday party for Susan B. Anthony the night before the convention began. Susa commented on the "shabby" condition of many of the homes she encountered, which were not as nice as her own in Provo, and on "the magnificence of the Capitol."[71] Susa was kept very busy by the whirlwind of meetings, so much so that one night she was too tired to stand in line to meet President Grover Cleveland.

Her letters from Washington were full of love for her family. She still gushed over Jacob and missed him intensely: "Oh my darling, my heart is so entirely yours that I long constantly for your voice and presence. Every time I go away from you I think I will never do it again. My baby!" Even as she grew in prominence, she still felt the pressures of social expectations for women, and she worried about the impression she gave other people because of her frequent travel and long absences from home. Apparently she had heard gossip that "people think I impose on Lulu. It hurts me a little. But I ought to know folks will talk about me."[72] Jacob reassured her that Lulu "feels proud she is able to take some of the worry and cares off your shoulders" and wished that someday they could "travel together." He seemed to take pride in supporting Susa and was "willing to grant my wife all the freedoms in opinion and action consistent with her duties to me and my family."[73] He was also gaining prominence and had recently been elected a director of the new Provo Chamber of Commerce.

Susa reported that she was a "member" of the NCW and not a

---

69. Susa Young Gates, "Utah Women at the National Council of Women," *Young Woman's Journal*, June 1895, 391.

70. Gates.

71. Susa Young Gates to Jacob Gates, Mar. 1895, box 9, fd. 10.

72. Gates to Gates, various letters, Feb. 1895, box 9, fd. 9.

73. Jacob Gates to Susa Young Gates, various letters, Feb.-Mar. 1895, box 6, fd. 12.

"delegate," so she had to sit "downstairs." Nonetheless, Taylor obtained for her a press badge, and Susa spoke later at the Press Club. She and Emmeline B. Wells had dinner with "General Pickett" of the Civil War and his wife.[74] Susa also had lunch with Nellie Powell Thompson, sister of the famous southwestern US explorer John Wesley Powell.[75]

Susa "stirred up a hornet's nest" when she delivered a paper at the convention that she felt was misinterpreted as a protest against "women's education and refinement."[76] Her paper, "What Is Modern Education Doing for the American Girl?" worried about current teaching techniques and said that "modern education" was physically and emotionally taxing to young women. She pushed for a dual role of spirituality and intellectuality, which "in our modern world [have] been deemed incompatible." Susa did plead for "the necessity of equal suffrage and equal privileges for the sexes," but it is not surprising that her words, which seemed to suggest girls were too delicate and fragile without the "spiritual ideal ... firmly embedded" in their hearts, were not well received at the convention.[77] She told Jacob that the "day was a severe trial" and that the listeners "can like it or lump it."[78]

Susa traveled by rail to New York City, spent a couple of days there, then went on to Boston, where she began genealogical research on March 6, 1895. Jacob had urged Susa to "stay till you get through with what you have to do."[79] With that reassurance in hand, nine days later she wrote to Jacob, "I may have to be here a month longer."[80] But after Susa mentioned perhaps staying up to six months longer, Jacob retorted, "If the [Young] family want that amount of labor done they will have to hire someone else, for I want my wife home at once too." He felt that he had reached his limit. "I have endured your absence just as long as I care to and I want you

---

74. It is unclear whom Susa referred to, since General George Pickett, of Pickett's Charge at Gettysburg fame, died in 1875.

75. Susa Young Gates to Jacob Gates, various letters, Feb.–Mar. 1895, box 9, fds. 9–10.

76. Gates to Gates.

77. Gates, "Utah Women at the NCW," 410–15.

78. Gates to Gates.

79. Jacob Gates to Susa Young Gates, Feb. 1895, box 6, fd. 12.

80. Susa Young Gates to Jacob Gates, Mar. 15, 1895, box 9, fd. 10.

home. I dont think I am unreasonable in my demands." Susa's birthday, March 18, was the first birthday since their marriage that they had not spent together.[81] Susa wrote that she wished "that I could be in your dear arms tonight, and be awakened by your lips on my own kissing me a happy birthday. Dearer than life, than everything but God and our religion."[82]

Susa was torn between her love of genealogy work and her love of her family. She wrote that the "thought of going home is simply glorious—but oh, I should have felt so much more satisfied if I could have finished up this work here." She understood Jacob's feelings but, as she worked, she felt the "sad undertone of your displeasure and it is very hard to bear." Finally, she returned home to Provo after a two-month absence.

About this time Susa had a great spiritual awakening. Years before, Brigham Young had shared his testimony of the LDS Church and its teachings with her in the Lion House. Susa wanted to know how she could obtain the same conviction that her father and mother had. Young replied that this knowledge came only with specific, fervent daily prayers. Susa later wrote, "During one year, when I was nearly 40 years old, I disciplined my taste, my desires and my impulses—severely disciplining my appetite, my tongue, my acts, for one whole year, and how I prayed!" One day, while sweeping, she heard "a voice within my soul—that ... spoke to my spirit these simple words: 'You know it is true! Never doubt it again.' I never have! All other truths ... I measure by one standard only: Does this or that idea ... agree ... with the truths of the Gospel. ... If it agrees, it is mine! If it does not, I cast it out."[83]

Susa and Jacob bought land in Rock Canyon, what is now Brighton in Big Cottonwood Canyon east of Salt Lake City, and Susa spent part of the summer of 1895 there. She and the children enjoyed the cooler summer weather, especially compared to their home in Provo. Her annual retreat to the mountains would become one of her favorite respites in a hectic, whirlwind life. Living at first in

---

81. Jacob Gates to Susa Young Gates, various letters, Mar. 1895, box 6, fd. 12.
82. Susa Young Gates to Jacob Gates, Mar. 17, 1895, box 9, fd. 10.
83. Gates, *Why I Believe the Gospel*, 27.

tents, the family had decided by 1897 to build a summer home there. Jacob could commute fairly easily to and from Provo.[84]

Susa spent most of 1896 at home in Provo, largely because she gave birth to her thirteenth and last child, her tenth son, Brigham Young Gates, on April 19, 1896. She was forty years old. One month later, she spent a week in Salt Lake City at the general conference of the Young Men and Young Ladies Mutual Improvement Association. During her absence Jacob wrote several letters, calmly indicating that Frank (age three) had tried to set the barn on fire again and that the family had gone to the graves of Karl and Jay on Memorial Day to place wild flowers that Lulu had picked.[85]

At the end of May, Susa delivered an address alongside Brigham H. Roberts, a general authority Seventy, respected Mormon historian, and famous politician. Less than a year later, Roberts would find himself in New York City at the same time Leah was there to study at the Pratt Institute, and the two grew close.[86] Leah roomed in the city with Donnette "Donnie" Smith, daughter of Joseph F. Smith. Ever the successful student, Leah took full advantage of her educational opportunities, preparing herself for her future career as a leading nutritionist, and she drew praise from her instructors. She worked to save money, eating only two meals a day. She asked for a monthly allowance of $25.00 from Susa and Jacob. She wrote to her mother and her stepfather of her gratitude (apparently her biological father did not support her).[87]

Despite her busy studies, Leah found time to socialize with Roberts, who quickly became infatuated with Leah, telling her often how much he enjoyed spending time with her, holding her hand, and rhapsodizing about her beauty. They visited the Statue of Liberty, St. Patrick's Cathedral, and art galleries with other Latter-day Saints in New York. Roberts was already married to three women, and he had spent time in the Utah Penitentiary for cohabitation. It is likely that he married his third wife, Maggie Shipp, after the Woodruff Manifesto, and so he perhaps thought he could take Leah

---

84. Susa Young Gates to Jacob Gates, June 19, 1897, box 9, fd. 11.

85. Jacob Gates to Susa Young Gates, various letters, May 1896, box 6, fd. 14.

86. The Pratt Institute was founded by oil tycoon Charles Pratt, and Leah was studying domestic sciences.

87. Leah Dunford to Susa and Jacob Gates, various letters, 1897, box 13, fds. 1–4.

as a fourth wife in secret. Susa at one point entertained such a union and counseled her daughter

> to think seriously before you decide to give BH [Roberts] the cold shoulder. He has evidently said all to you he could say—& make it a subject of fasting and prayer as to what you reply. Your whole soul would be satisfied in time & eternity with such a man for a leader and companion. How about the other? I fear, and so does Uncle J[acob], that you would grow away from J[ohn] A W[idtsoe], narrow minds will dwarf you: and think darling of the children who come from a union with BH. Oh Well! I would not influence you one way or the other. Only I want you to think long & seriously dear. These "happenings" are the vital turning points of your life. Try and realize that![88]

Roberts himself wrote to Susa, and while he couched much of his affection for Leah in the language of friendship, he also asked, "Who can view the upturned nose and not admire? Or, curiously behold the smoothness of the skin, of beauty's cheek?" Susa forwarded this letter to Leah and wrote, "How superior to John's [John A. Widtsoe]! Talk of poetry and passion. Yet how manly, dignified and controlled. You are a fortunate girl, Leah."[89]

But after a month of this whirlwind romance, Leah wrote to her mother, "What would be the good of wasting my love and pining away for a man who can never be mine this side of eternity?" She knew that she and Roberts could not marry even "if we both wanted to ever so much."[90] Being a plural wife was never easy, but entering into a polygamous marriage after the Manifesto meant secrecy and only the rarest chances to see one's husband.

Leah had not entirely abandoned thoughts of Widtsoe, but she was clearly torn. She wrote her mother to ask if Widtsoe was becoming indifferent to her, and when she wrote directly to him, she would call him her "true love" but then, in the same letter, refer to him as a "dear friend." After Roberts left New York, Leah and he continued to correspond, but over a period of weeks the passion dissipated, and while Roberts, Susa, and Leah would write to each

---

88. Susa Young Gates to Leah Dunford, undated, box 12, fd. 1.
89. Gates to Dunford, Mar. 22, 1897, box 8, fd. 6, Widtsoe Family Papers.
90. Leah Dunford to Susa Young Gates, Mar. 7, 1897, box 13, fd. 6.

other and interact over the years, it was always as cordial friends and acquaintances.[91]

Susa was named chair of the US National Council of Women Press Committee. The same year, under the direction of BYA President Benjamin Cluff, she began a public lecture course at the academy in "Domestic Economy," with what appears to be the intention of bringing Leah the next year to the academy to work with her. The lecture series included such luminaries as George Q. Cannon and Joseph F. Smith of the First Presidency, as well as Karl Maeser and George Reynolds, secretary to the First Presidency.

At the end of 1896, the First Presidency wrote to Jacob to ask if he could be the president of the Eastern States Mission in New York City. Susa had enjoyed her time on the East Coast and it seems probable she would have liked to relocate the family there. But Susa noted at the bottom of the letter from First Presidency secretary George Reynolds that Jacob "refused" the appointment because of "debts."[92]

The couple struggled financially as the Panic of 1893 continued to impact the world. They had supported Leah with tuition during her last year of college at the University of Utah, before she went to the Pratt Institute in Brooklyn. As an honors graduate in 1896, Leah was invited to be a commencement speaker. Once Leah was at the Pratt Institute, Susa and Jacob were responsible for most of her expenses. Alma Dunford, despite being a respected dentist by this time, did not provide her with any financial support except for a railroad ticket to New York City. He probably could not afford more, stemming from his large second family of seven children, heavy drinking, and possibly gambling.

As Leah's return home approached, many of her letters focused on her plans for the 1897–98 academic year. She wanted to teach, but there were no opportunities at the University of Utah. She asked her mother about the domestic science department at Logan, where Susa had recently visited and where John Widtsoe had started teaching at $1,500 per year with no prior experience. She emphasized that

91. For a detailed look at Leah's relationship with Roberts, see Sillito, *B. H. Roberts*, 282-89.

92. George Reynolds to Jacob Gates, Nov. 11, 1896, box 4, fd. 1.

182

President Cluff of BYA in Provo would have to "engage me as he would any other teacher," and she beseeched Susa not to go to Cluff to "coax him with a long story about my superior qualities and beg him to offer me the position." Eventually, at the end of May, Cluff came through with a "definite engagement," although Leah knew that the girls at the academy would be disappointed at Leah's replacing Susa. Susa had begun the domestic science department at BYA in October 1896, and it appears that she considered herself largely a placeholder until Leah finished her education. Susa, however, did continue as a lecturer.[93]

She also continued traveling on church assignments. She and half-sister Zina, now remarried to Charles Ora Card, traveled to Springville, Spanish Fork, and Payson in one week in February 1897. By the time Leah arrived home from New York at the end of June 1897, Susa was on a three-week trip to northern Utah with Estelle Neff, who had taken over "the heavy burdens of finances, circulation and printing" of the *Young Woman's Journal* after the death of Apostle Abraham H. Cannon. They traveled first to Logan, where they attended the Brigham Young College commencement exercises.[94]

Susa was chagrined to learn that the citizens of Logan had contributed $35,000 for a new building at the educational facility there. Worried that the Logan school would surpass the Provo campus, she complained to George Q. Cannon, who was also in Logan for the commencement. Cannon said "he wanted the Provo Academy to be the 'banner school' of them all," and to be "the Church university," despite whatever flaws Cluff, whom Cannon found to have an "indomitable spirit," might have. Susa and Estelle then traveled around the southern part of Cache County, holding up to four meetings per day, championing the *Journal,* and trying to sell back issues to retire the debt of the magazine. In addition, Susa declared, "Stella and I preach Academy wherever we go." Besides Logan, they visited Brigham City, Hyrum, Mantua, Willard, Ogden, Huntsville, and Riverdale.

She reported "doing very successful work," but complained to Jacob, "My darling, this absence of mine cannot be half the trial to

93. Leah Dunford to Susa Young Gates, various letters, box 13, fds. 5–7.
94. Gates, "Hail and Farewell," 675.

you it is to me." She conveyed "love unspeakable to every one of you dear ones. Noble Cecil, bright Hal, good Dan, loving Winfred, sweet Beulah, blessed Franklin ... and to our dear kind Lucinda."[95] Dan was Daniel McAllister, seventeen-year-old son of Susa's sister Mabel and her first husband, Daniel McAllister, who had died at age thirty-six in 1893; Winfred, who went by Witt, was the nine-year old son of Mabel and her second husband, Brigham Winfred Witt. Mabel was at this time twice divorced, working hard to eke out a living. For several years Dan and Witt lived with the Gates family, to whom Mabel paid a small stipend for their room and board. Lucinda was hired to help around the house.

While Susa was gone, Jacob sent her a teasing note, addressed to "Dear Madam, Do you expect to be in Provo this season or will you sojourn in the South." He had not heard from her, he claimed, for "about a month." He received three letters the next day and, mollified, wrote to her, that the letters "drove away my harbored ill will on account of your not writing oftener." Soon enough he was back to his usual effusive praise, even comparing Susa to the Garden of Eden.[96]

At the end of August, Susa left Provo again for almost a month, this time headed to southern Idaho, where she visited Pocatello, Oxford, Mink Creek, Mound Valley, Thatcher, Preston, Blackfoot, Ammon, Idaho Falls, Rexburg, Cassia, Chesterfield, Dempsey, McCammon, and Albion. She longed "to get all these business matters straightened out and get the poor Journal out of debt, and then settle down for the winter."[97] It was a grueling trip; once again she often held multiple meetings each day, she slept on hay at least once, and often she got only one to two hours sleep at night. But her trip accomplished its purpose: in the eighth year of the *Young Woman's Journal's* existence, its debt was finally retired.

Meanwhile, Jacob commented that he was not getting much work out of Susa's nephew Dan. She asked Jacob to "be patient. Let him be like our own son. I feel as if I were in some way atoning for Bailey when I am doing for Dan." She felt that, unlike she was able to do for Bailey, "God will help us and we can be instrumental in

---

95. Susa Young Gates to Jacob Gates, various letters, June-July 1897, box 9, fd. 11.

96. Jacob Gates to Susa Young Gates, various letters, June-Aug. 1897, box 6, fds. 15–16.

97. Susa Young Gates to Jacob Gates, box 9, fd. 11.

his hands of saving their souls." Jacob wanted at least to charge him board, but Susa persisted, "Never mind, dear, about his board. Think of your coal mine! You'll be rich someday."[98]

Jacob was working to acquire a coal mine with Bishop Joseph Keeler, to whom he served as counselor. He informed Susa, "I dont think I should consent for you to go on these extended trips and so far away if it were not apparently absolutely necessary." Five days later he reiterated his feelings, "It is quite a sacrifice I am making I can tell you—I dont know who else would do it graciously."[99]

Of greater concern to Susa than Daniel McAllister was a young professor in Logan by the name of John A. Widtsoe. The slow pace of their courtship, coupled with the recent attentions B. H. Roberts had given Leah, may have led Susa to feel that John underappreciated her daughter. She was unhappy enough to turn to xenophobia and complain to Jacob that "it hurts me to see her think of marrying a man who will want to take her a hundred miles away from us [to Logan], and who is of another race and nation [Norway] from us."[100] What Susa did not know was that several days previously Leah had received a marriage proposal from John. Three weeks later Leah, who had learned of Susa's comments, expressed her displeasure to Susa. These circumstances are certainly ironic, since Susa was clearly infatuated with Widtsoe from the beginning, and they enjoyed a close, loving, respectful relationship throughout the rest of Susa's life.

In 1897 Susa founded both the "State Chapter of the Daughters of the Revolution and was Regent and state organizer for some years, wrote their by-laws and constitution"[101] and the Sons and Daughters of the Utah Pioneers. She organized the latter with Reed Smoot, future apostle and US senator, with the help of Richard W. Young, who wrote the constitution and by-laws. The fledgling organization would founder in the wake of Susa's health issues and Smoot's election to the US Senate, and its place was taken by the Daughters of the Utah Pioneers, founded in 1901.

98. Gates to Gates, box 9, fd. 12.
99. Jacob Gates to Susa Young Gates, various letters, box 6, fd. 16.
100. Susa Young Gates to Jacob Gates, Sep. 10, 1897, box 9, fd. 12.
101. Gates, "Hail and Farewell," 676.

Susa always spoke directly, in clear and unmistakable terms, and at the end of 1897 it caused a small scandal at Brigham Young Academy. President Cluff wrote and said that he learned Susa "had been speaking quite plainly ... in relation to the sexes and their connection with propagation. In fact, so plain ... that should it continue, you would do the school a great injury." He asked her "not speak so directly upon certain subjects," but made it clear he did "not design that you cease your lectures, not by any means, but that you would restrict your subject to such as will not be considered new and radical."[102] Cluff did not specify what he found so objectionable in Susa's comments, but he clearly felt that she had crossed some line of decorum. Susa, it seemed, was too conservative in her thoughts on education for the National Council of Women but not conservative enough for the Brigham Young Academy.

On June 1, 1898, Brigham Young's birthday, his granddaughter Leah was finally married in the Salt Lake temple to John Widtsoe. Susa was home after more traveling, this time to Vernal and Price, Utah. The wedding was reported at length in the *Young Woman's Journal*. Both Leah and John had written for the *Journal* and would continue to do so, she on the "lofty ideals of 'The Home,'" and he on the "advanced theories of 'Foods.'"[103] After a post-wedding luncheon in Salt Lake City, there was a dinner reception prepared and served by the students in the domestic science department at the Brigham Young Academy in Provo. It was the beginning of a fifty-four-year union of a giddy young couple. Widtsoe's biographer Alan K. Parrish wrote that "Leah's charm, wit, and spirit were the perfect complement to John's studious, practical nature."[104] John wrote to Susa that, after they arrived in Logan, the locals "did nothing after our arrival ... except to grin at me and stare at Leah." Leah wrote later that "Mama Widtsoe is spoiling me," and asked Susa to allow Lule, then age seventeen, to "come to us in Germany," where John was planning to begin graduate studies that fall.[105]

---

102. Benjamin Cluff to Susa Young Gates, Dec. 6, 1897, box 6, fd. 16.

103. Susa Young Gates, "A Union of Art and Science," *Young Woman's Journal*, July 1898, 332.

104. Parrish, *John A. Widtsoe*, 109.

105. John Widtsoe and Leah Widtsoe to Susa Young Gates, various letters, box 13, fd. 12.

A few weeks after the wedding Susa attended the Biennial Federation of Women's Clubs in Denver with Emmeline B. Wells and Minnie J. Snow, as well as Susa's close friend Augusta Grant, wife of apostle and future church president Heber J. Grant. While in Denver, Susa spoke with Dr. Mary E. Green, president of the National Household Economic Association, who asked her to speak at the association's annual meeting in Omaha in October. In a letter home Susa asked Jacob, "I dare say that if I told you I was homesick and longing for you and home—you would say 'Well what did you leave me for?'"[106]

Apostle John W. Taylor was in Denver at the same time as Susa, and he asked her to stay one more week to visit and fellowship church members in the area. Susa, ever obedient to priesthood authority, complied and returned home in early July after making numerous visits, including to some distant members of the church in Colorado. Jacob's feelings at her lengthened stay were typical: "I do miss my wife and feel at times that I do sacrifice too much of her time."[107]

On July 22, 1898, a couple of weeks after Susa arrived back home, seven-year-old Beulah was killed in a freak accident. The Gates children "were putting on a little homemade drama" on the front porch of the Gates home in Provo. The play involved a "soap bullet," which was felt to be harmless, "and one of the brothers shot his little sister" with the piece of soap fired from a gun. Granddaughter Lurene said, "I think I know who did it, but because it was such a tragedy they never talked about it."[108] Susa and Jacob had eleven children together, and only two daughters: Lule, their first child together, and Beulah.

Susa rarely talked or wrote about the many sad tragedies in her life. She was a survivor, and she soldiered on. But three months after Beulah's death, she wrote to Jacob from Omaha that she had dreamed of Beulah for three nights. "I hugged her and begged her to stay with me. ... How I long to be worthy to be with her in eternity." In another dream, Beulah told her "she would have to go back to Heaven now."[109] Jacob replied, "Your reference to our darling Beulah

---

106. Susa Young Gates to Jacob Gates, box 9, fd. 13.

107. Jacob Gates to Susa Young Gates, box 7, fd. 1.

108. Lurene Gates Wilkinson, interview by Romney Burke, Aug. 5, 2007, transcript in author's possession.

109. Susa Young Gates to Jacob Gates, various letters, box 9, fd. 13.

made me so sad and lonely. ... I so long for her sweet presence some-time that I can hardly restrain my tears."[110]

After three years of teaching at the state agricultural college in Logan, John Widtsoe received a scholarship at the University of Göttingen in Germany to obtain a doctorate. Leah pressed the fam-ily to send Lule with them to pursue her musical training in Europe. "I can't give up the idea of her going with us [to Germany]."[111] Fi-nally, Jacob acceded, with the stipulation that Lule obey four things: "Pray, observe the Sabbath, pay your tithing, and write home every Sunday."[112] On August 6, fifteen days after her sister died, Emma Lucy Gates joined her half-sister and her new brother-in-law for the journey to Germany via England and Holland. In England they were feted by the wealthy Henry B. Bruce, twice mayor of Leicester and husband of Jacob's aunt, Sarah Forsberry Bruce.

In Göttingen, Germany, John quickly began his studies, which he pursued with abandon, finishing in a little over a year a course of work that should have taken two or three. Emma Lucy studied with a piano professor, who one day heard her singing during a break and was so impressed with her "voice of a generation" that he felt she should continue with vocal training, "even if she had to give up her piano work."[113] Leah, who was pregnant, was having mild health issues. She wrote to her mother that "John and Lule have admin-istered to me," and the next month she received another blessing when Lule washed and anointed her, after which John blessed her and "sealed the blessing."[114]

In early October 1898 Susa left to attend two meetings in Omaha. She was the guest for three weeks of Mary Moody Pugh, who "al-most gasped for breath" when she found out that Susa was Brigham Young's daughter.[115] While there, Susa delivered a talk—"The Neces-sity of Instructing Children Concerning Their Prospective Conjugal and Parental Duties"—to the Sixth Annual Meeting of the National Household Economic Association. That night she wrote to Jacob, "I

110. Jacob Gates to Susa Young Gates, box 7, fd. 1.
111. Leah Widtsoe to Gates Family, box 13, fd. 12.
112. Jenson, "Susa Young Gates," 137.
113. Johnson, "Emma Lucy Gates Bowen," 347–48.
114. Leah Widtsoe to Susa Young Gates, various letters, box 13, fd. 13.
115. Susa Young Gates to Jacob Gates, box 9, fd. 13.

cant tell you the sensation my paper created."[116] No transcript of the talk has survived, but a reporter for the *Omaha World Herald* reported:

> Inclosed please find the address of Mrs. Susa Young Gates which I borrowed yesterday. I am very sorry that space forbade the publication of the address in full, as it is worthy of publication, and should be read in every home in the land, or better still, read and framed for future use and inspiration. ...Such thoughts can only originate in the mind of a noble, refined, intellectual woman, a mother, for she knows whereof she speaks.
>
> I have no sermon to preach, for newspapermen are trained to listen and be silent ... if the women—mothers—of Omaha would give the subject as presented by Mrs. Gates careful attention they would not alone raise monuments to themselves, and their posterity, but also to Him who did not disdain to take the most lowly by the hand of good fellowship and love and help them onward and upward. There is much work to be done in Omaha, in the home and on the streets, than the good mothers of Omaha dream of. ... The work as mapped out by Mrs. Gates must of necessity be largely conducted by woman. And who is so well adapted to advise the boys and girls as mother—she who is the holy of holies. To Mrs. Gates you can say that one man at least in Omaha appreciated what she had to say.[117]

The Women's Congress of the National Council of Women was held October 24–29 in Omaha, in conjunction with the Trans-Mississippi and International Exposition (June 1–November 1), a world's fair aimed at promoting the development of Omaha. In addition to Susa, who represented the YLMIA, Jane S. Richards, Emmeline B. Wells, Maria Y. Dougall, and Minnie J. Snow were also a part of the congress.

The goals of the NCW were summarized in the *Young Woman's Journal* the following January. As the United States shifted from the Gilded Age to the Progressive Era, hundreds of reform groups, benevolent societies, and other organizations, often founded and led by women, sprang up to respond to social ills and injustice. Cities grew denser, more Americans became wage laborers, and children, once kept busy by farm chores, now found themselves with leisure time,

---

116. Gates, Autobiographical sketches, box 3, fd. 35.

117. Eugene O. Mayfield, "Women and the Home," *Omaha World Herald*, Oct. 15, 1898.

something adults thought dangerous for America's youth. Therefore, the *Young Woman's Journal* explained, the NCW brought together many of these groups "to disseminate more widely the knowledge of the magnitude and variety of woman's work for humanity, to the end that public sympathy for it may be increased and a more general public support secured." It also worked to "perfectly concentrate the efforts of individual organizations so that the united whole will produce more general benefit," both for women's rights and for the world as a whole.[118] Susa felt strongly that the women of Utah were making a difference in the national fabric of women's rights, and that prejudice against the LDS Church because of polygamy was beginning to abate as a result of their influence.

With Susa's frenetic life, travels, family—complete with the joy of birth and tragedy of death—her involvement in national organizations, and her writing, it is easy to overlook the most important thing in her life: her faith. She was so dedicated to Mormonism that she wrote at times to her husband that he came second only to God. Susa often wrote about her dependence on God, and she ascribed any glory to him. After speaking at the women's congress and receiving acclaim, including from the wife of the governor of Georgia, Susa said, "But all their praises slip off my back like water—for I know it was God who deserves the praise."[119] This was a common refrain in her life, and she saw herself as an ambassador both for Mormonism and for God.

Susa traveled more and farther in 1899 than ever before. On February 5, she and Zina Young Card left Salt Lake City by train for the triennial meeting of the NCW in Washington, DC. Twenty-two pages, almost half of the issue, were devoted to reporting this event in the May 1899 *Young Woman's Journal*. Susa had been invited by the president of the NCW, May Wright Sewall, to serve as pro-tem chair of the Press Committee for the duration of the meeting in Washington. Sewall offered the post to Susa because of her "comprehensive grasp of the possibilities of the Council," but she did not want to make the appointment public because of the "strong prejudice" against Mormons because of polygamy. Sewall

---

118. Susa Young Gates, "Women's Congress," *Young Woman's Journal*, Jan. 1899, 17.
119. Susa Young Gates to Jacob Gates, box 9, fd. 13.

herself loathed polygamy and told Susa as much in her invitation to chair the press committee.[120]

Susa and Zina made it as far as Denver, when their train was stuck in a blizzard for thirty-six hours. Susa wrote that they "deserved to be [stuck] for starting on a journey on the Sabbath Day." They traveled via New York City, where they arrived seven hours late in another "blinding snow-storm."[121] They spent a day with their half-sister Jeannette Easton and her husband, Robert. Bad weather plagued them virtually the entire time they were in Washington. They arrived nearly at midnight and made their way to the home of Mrs. Belva Lockwood, where Susa's mother was lodging with Lula Greene Richards. The next day, with a combination of walking in a blizzard with freezing wind and getting carriage rides however they could, they arrived several hours late for the opening of the meeting.

Besides Susa and Zina, the Utah delegation included Emmeline B. Wells, Martha Horne Tingey, Minnie J. Snow, her daughter Mabel, Ann M. Cannon, and Lucy Bigelow Young. Lula Greene Richards joined the delegation as a guest. President May Sewall had also invited Hana Kaaepa, a native of Hawai'i living in Utah in the Polynesian colony of Iosepa. In that first week, the deposed Queen Lili'uokalani of Hawaii, who was living in Washington at the time, hosted a dinner for Hana, which Susan B. Anthony, May Sewall, Emmeline B. Wells, Lucy B. Young, and Susa attended.

Speakers addressed the crowd on topics such as coeducation, citizenship, patriotism, moral reform, war and peace, religion, and domestic science. Susan B. Anthony spoke on the "Retrogression in Equal Rights."[122] Susa introduced Hana Kaaepa in a talk on "The Hawaiian Woman." Kaaepa addressed the audience in English, "asking the ladies to use their influence in giving the franchise to the women of her nation when it was extended to the men."[123] Elections were held, and Fannie Humphreys Gaffney of New York was elected to replace May Wright Sewall, who had served as NCW president for the previous two years. (Sewall began service as president of the

---

120. Sewall to Gates, Jan. 27, 1899, box 42, fd. 6.
121. Susa Young Gates, "The Recent Triennial in Washington," *Young Woman's Journal,* May 1899, 195–96.
122. National Council of Women files, box 42, fd. 6.
123. Gates, "Recent Triennial," 204.

International Council of Women in 1899 and continued in that office for five years.) Emmeline B. Wells was elected as second recording secretary.

Down the street at the US Capitol, a major political battle was being waged over polygamy. B. H. Roberts had been elected a member of the US House of Representatives from Utah in 1898. But because Roberts was a practicing polygamist, in defiance of federal law, Congress refused to seat him. Roberts, a Democrat opposed to women's suffrage, lost the hearings and his seat. Most of the Utah delegation to the National Council of Women were Republican and in favor of female suffrage, and so had not voted for Roberts. But they still believed he had been legally elected and deserved his seat. Once again, polygamy was thrust into the national spotlight, and the women of the NCW debated two resolutions put forth by members.

The majority report read, "Whereas, The National Council of Women of the United States stands for the highest ideals of domestic and civic virtue, as well as for the observance of law in all its departments, both state and national; therefore, Resolved, That no person should be allowed to hold a place in any law-making body of the nation who is not a law-abiding citizen." The minority report called out polygamy and legislation against the LDS Church: "Whereas, The passage of the Edmunds bill (so-called) established the law of monogamic marriage as binding upon all citizens of the United States, therefore, Resolved, That no person should be allowed to hold a place in a law-making body of the nation who is not in this, and in all other matters, a law-abiding citizen."

Spirited, but civil, debate ensued. The first person to speak was "sweet, modest, diffident Annie M. Cannon." Cannon slyly separated Roberts from the church and aligned him with the Democratic Party: "Polygamy is a past issue; we have agreed to abide by the law. The election of Mr. Roberts has no place in the Council. He was not a candidate of the Mormon Church. He was nominated in a Democratic convention (by an avowed non-Mormon) and elected by Democratic votes. Many Mormons voted against him; many non-Mormons voted for him." Susa followed and said that, whatever the outcome of the vote on the resolutions put forth, "we should still respect and love these women [the delegates], no matter what their actions might be." But Susa seemed stung by the resurfacing of polygamy and the inferences made against members of the church, "as if it were the honesty and sincerity of our people and ourselves which were on trial." One Utah delegate suggested an amendment to the resolution that would disallow any man who broke the seventh commandment—"Thou shalt not commit adultery"—to hold a seat in Congress, to which Susan B. Anthony responded that such a law would probably leave the country without a law-making body. The majority report passed with thirty-one votes; sixteen were in favor of the minority report.[124]

It was "a week, never to be forgotten." Even the inclement weather turned out to be a blessing in disguise, since the atmosphere at the meeting was "cozy" and few attendees ventured far from the gathering. Another highlight of the week was the walk to the White House where Susa and the others were received by President William McKinley in his private office.

Susa and Jacob wrote their usual tender letters to each other. Both Sewall and Anthony wanted Susa to go to the International Council of Women meeting in London in June. Because of her organizational skills, Susa was highly regarded among the leadership of both the national and international councils of women. Maria Purdy Peck, the vice-president-at-large of the NCW, wrote to Susa, "I often think of you, your dispassionate judgment, your self-possession, your strong character. Would that we had many, many more of this sort."[125] Susa wanted to go to London, but money was always an issue. Jacob was "most discouraged" after a mining claim he made in Vernal, Utah, had "been jumped" because he had not done the work required of the claim during 1898. He detailed his plan to her to dispose of more property to "turn on my debts."[126] Despite the financial challenges, Susa, who always viewed her civic responsibilities as a mission, postulated, "But if I go on a mission with the missionary spirit, God will take care of me, I know that!"[127]

Happy news arrived from Göttingen. Leah had given birth on

124. Account of the resolutions and debate taken from Gates, "Recent Triennial," 205–07.
125. Peck to Gates, box 42, fd. 7.
126. Jacob Gates to Susa Young Gates, various letters, box 7, fd. 2.
127. Susa Young Gates to Jacob Gates, various letters, box 10, fd. 1.

April 2, 1899, to a daughter, Anna Gaarden Widtsoe, named in honor of John's mother. During her pregnancy, Leah assured her mother that she needed expressions of her love as much as ever. She proclaimed, "It is such a happy relief, isn't it, Mother, if one is happily married." Just before Anna's birth, John wrote to Susa, "I am desperately in love with Leah," which certainly endeared him further to his mother-in-law.[128] In the fall John received a master's degree and his PhD, magna cum laude. Emma Lucy, who by now had acclimated herself to Germany and the German language, applied to the Royal Conservatory of Berlin to continue her vocal studies. John and Leah felt that Emma Lucy should not go to Berlin until she can live "with someone we know," so her grandmother Lucy Bigelow Young agreed to travel to Berlin and act as Emma Lucy's chaperone.[129]

Susa decided she would attend the International Council of Women (ICW) in London that June, her first trip to Europe. The ICW was established in Washington, DC, at the same time as the NCW. It was comprised of women from fifty-three organizations representing nine countries. Many of the women in the NCW in the United States also joined the ICW. Apart from holding annual executive meetings, the ICW had done little until this first conference away from the NCW was organized.[130]

Susa left Salt Lake City for Europe at the end of May, sailing on the *S.S. Waesland*. She missed Jacob and wrote aboard the ship, "The happy thought of being yours for all eternity, rests at my heart like a sweet benediction."[131] Henry B. Bruce met the group, just as he had met Leah and John Widtsoe when they arrived in Europe. He invited the party to stay with him and his wife in Leicester. In addition to Susa, her mother-in-law Emma Forsberry Gates, Lucy Bigelow Young, Elizabeth Claridge McCune, and "the two girls," presumably Clara Holbrook and Josephine Booth, Americans who were staying in

---

128. Leah Widtsoe and John A. Widtsoe to Susa Young Gates, various letters, box 10, fds. 13–14.

129. Leah Widtsoe to Susa Young Gates, box 13, fd. 13.

130. Susa, just as she had for the NCW, wrote an extensive article on the ICW for the *Young Woman's Journal*. Susa Young Gates, "International Council of Women," *Young Woman's Journal*, Oct. 1899, 435–50.

131. Susa Young Gates to Jacob Gates, box 10, fd. 2.

Germany, were traveling to the conference.[132] Susa's nephew Daniel H. McAllister met them in Leicester. He had just arrived in England to begin a mission for the church. After several days most of the group left for London. Daniel proceeded on to a mission assignment, and Emma stayed with her sister in Leicester, where she spent a year living with the Bruces. Lulu joined the group in London.

Elizabeth McCune insisted that the group stay at the Palace Hotel in London, and she helped to underwrite Susa's expenses. McCune had been a close friend of Susa since the early 1870s in St. George and was married to mining magnate Alfred W. Mc-Cune, one of Utah's first millionaires. In addition to Susa's group, Emmeline B. Wells, Margaret Caine, Jean Clara Holbrook, and at least seven other women from Utah were part of the ICW.[133] Lydia Mountford was also at the conference and took Susa to see the great sights of London, including St. Paul's Cathedral, Westminster Abbey, Palace of Westminster (home of the British Parliament), Hyde Park, and the Prince Albert Memorial.

Intrigue began before the meetings commenced, as Susa was summoned to see May Wright Sewall, vice-president of the International Council of Women, who told Susa

a most extraordinary story. The first lot of programs [Sewall] received in America had my [Susa's] name on and in places of high honor: the second lot had left out my name everywhere. She at once wrote demanding it should be replaced. Then came a letter saying a Mrs. [Harriott] Blatch—an American woman and daughter of Mrs. Elizabeth Cady Stanton had told the ladies here that I was a most dangerous and subtle women; that I was a daughter of Brigham Young, clever, ect., ect. and then followed a description of the time we had in Washington, & how we simply carried everything before us, our opponents not being able to do a thing. There was more about me, which I wont bother to repeat. This so frightened the ladies here that my name was stricken out entirely. Mrs. Sewall wrote, demanding that my name should be restored, telling what an able and so forth kind of a woman I was, that you and I had never been in polygamy, ect., ect. That we as a people had given it up & that there was much more to Mormonism than polygamy. That we

132. Gates, "Lucy Bigelow Young," 197.
133. Gates, "International Council of Women," 437.

were not trying to teach our religion (by the way I forgot to tell you [Jacob] that Mrs. Blatch had told them we were only using the Council as a tool to cover our proselyting schemes) any more than other religious faiths were theirs. My name was put back; but Mrs. [Louise] Creighton, the wife of the Bishop of London, had utterly refused to preside when I should speak, so I was moved back to an inferior position.[134]

Susa said nothing of this controversy in her article for the *Young Woman's Journal* on the ICW, and called Creighton an "exceedingly shrewd and determined leader. In many respects she was the brightest of all the brilliant coterie of English representatives."[135]

The conference began June 26, and Susa delivered her speech two days later on "Scientific Treatment of Domestic Service." Her talk was, even more than usual, a product of its time, and rooted in beliefs about social hierarchy. She said that "rational and scientific training for domestic service ... involves two necessary conditions: first, the training of both mistress and maid; and second, the fostering of a warm human sympathy between them as correlative factors in home-making." She concluded "that scientific treatment of domestic service will be attained only when both served and server have been trained empirically, rationally, and ethically."[136]

Much like its American counterpart, the NCW, presentations were categorized under topics like education, professional life, legislative and industrial, political, and social. There was a continual round of receptions, garden parties, and luncheons for the delegates. The high point of the conference was the "drive-by" tea with Queen Victoria, arranged by Lady Aberdeen, president of the International Council of Women. The event was held at Windsor Castle. The delegates "passed into the inner courtyard, where we were arranged in a long semi-circle, awaiting the entrance of the Queen." The Queen was helped into her carriage by her Indian servant, stopped to talk with Lady Aberdeen, and then rode slowly by, "bowing, smiling, and speaking cordially to all as she passed on down the driveway."[137]

---

134. Susa Young Gates to Jacob Gates, box 10, fd. 2.
135. Gates, "International Council of Women," 442.
136. Gates, "Scientific Treatment of Domestic Service," *Young Woman's Journal*, Sep. 1899, 402–05.
137. Gates, "International Council of Women," 449.

After the conference concluded, Susa left for Göttingen with daughter Emma Lucy, mother Lucy, and family friend Kate Thomas. There, Susa met and held her first grandchild, Leah and John's daughter, Anna. Nine days later on July 17, the group left for Berlin. While there, Susa, at the request of Brother Christensen, branch president in Berlin, traveled with him to talk with the Saints in Stettin, today Gdansk, Poland. She wrote to Jacob, "I have promised to give my voice and talent to the Praise of His Holy name and for the building up of His Zion." Susa decided to stay in Berlin until August 26, instead of sailing home on August 3 as planned.[138] Jacob had written earlier, "I am counting up the time when you will start for home, but I dont want to be selfish and cut off any of the possibilities of travel for you. See all you can while in Europe."[139]

Jacob was distracted by problems at home. He had to make another filing on his coal mine and was working on the family cabin. The Gates boys, always busy, had some injuries and health scares. "We have had a regular hospital the last week." Cecil's fingers had been scorched from pistol caps in his pocket. He had also had "a billious spell [vomiting]." Hal fell off his horse and was on crutches. Frank needed a tonsillectomy, but at age six years consented to have only one tonsil removed. Brigham had "inflammatory rheumatism." There was an outbreak of scarlet fever in Provo, so Jacob moved the boys to the family cabin. It is no surprise then that Jacob was dismayed when he found out that Susa did not plan to be home until September, commenting that four months is a long time for her to be away. He had "neglected all at home for the sake of the children" and determined on July 30 to leave the canyon right away.[140]

In Berlin Susa accompanied Emma Lucy to the home of Professor Schulze of the Berlin Conservatory. They talked about the possibility of arranging summer lessons so Emma Lucy could audition for admission in the fall. Emma Lucy sang for the professor, who admitted that her voice was "pretty," but not "strong enough for great halls and choruses." Even if her voice never strengthened, however, Emma Lucy would be a good teacher and so, "It would be a great pity not

---

138. Susa Young Gates to Jacob Gates, box 10, fd. 3.
139. Jacob Gates to Susa Young Gates, box 7, fd. 2.
140. Jacob Gates to Susa Young Gates, box 7, fd. 2.

to train it, for it is so pretty." Susa said that the family simply wanted Emma Lucy to be as well-trained as possible. If that included becoming "a great singer," it would be fine, but if not, she could always teach as a career and the family "would not be in the least disappointed." Susa asked what the professor thought Emma Lucy's chance of acceptance to the conservatory for that fall might be; he said that she would definitely be admitted because he made the decisions.[141]

Shortly before returning home, Susa wrote to Jacob, "I think you will never find me leaving you and the boys again. I feel as if this was the gratification of the crowning desire of my life—to see Europe!" She decided to return as planned. She had seen the world and found, "All is vanity! Except my home and religion."[142] Priorities were never a question with Susa. Jacob exulted, "Thank God for my beloved wife. I shall have you forever and forever I know and all my children also."[143] After telling Jacob it would be a few more weeks, she set sail from Europe on August 3 after all, perhaps missing her family too much to lengthen her trip. She was back home in Provo twenty days later, nearly three months after her departure.

In the past decade, Susa had become a published author in one of America's most prominent national magazines, she had edited her own religious magazine for young women, authoring many of its pages, and she had joined or initiated multiple state, national, and international organizations. She had traveled extensively throughout America and sojourned to Europe, delivering several major addresses. She had met and mingled with the major figures in women's suffrage. She had borne the last four of her thirteen children, and she had become a grandmother. She had met the president of the United States and associated with two queens, deposed Lili'uokalani of Hawaii and Queen Victoria, the most powerful monarch on earth. In twenty-five years she had come a long way from the brutally hot, wind-swept, red sandstone hills of St. George. And she would yet travel a great deal farther.

---

141. Susa Young Gates to Jacob Gates, box 10, fd. 3.
142. Gates to Gates.
143. Jacob Gates to Susa Young Gates, box 7, fd. 2.

Young Woman's Journal

When Susa and her family returned from Hawai'i at the end of the 1880s, there were three church-related magazines targeted to specific interest groups. The *Juvenile Instructor*, dating from 1866, was geared toward the Sunday school and the children of the church. It was owned and edited by George Q. Cannon, apostle and counselor in the First Presidency. In 1901, at Cannon's death, it would be taken over by the Sunday school and continue until 1929.

The *Woman's Exponent*, devoted to women's issues, was founded in 1872 under the editorship of Louisa Lula Greene as a semi-monthly publication. It was later published monthly and served as the de facto organ of the Relief Society. Beginning in 1877, it was edited by Emmeline B. Wells, who in 1910 would become, at age eighty-two, general president of the Relief Society. The journal ceased publication in 1914 due to financial difficulties.

Junius F. Wells, president of the Young Men Mutual Improvement Association (YMMIA), started the *Contributor* in 1879 as a venue for the young men and initially the young women of the church. By 1889 it no longer targeted the young women. The *Contributor* was purchased by the Cannon Publishing Company in 1892, but ceased publication in October 1896, three months after the untimely death of George Q. Cannon's son Abraham, who handled most of the business activities of the firm.

A fourth journal, aimed at the Young Ladies Mutual Improvement Association (YLMIA), was founded in 1889 by Susa Young

Gates, who also functioned as editor. She nurtured the journal, at some physical and mental cost to herself, for over a decade.

The seeds of the new journal were planted when Susa wrote from Lā'ie to her "other mother," Zina D. H. Young, expressing her interest in pursuing her "literary labors and aspirations." Jacob had told her, "Su I wish you would get a position on the *Exponent* as Associate Editor. Not assuming any duties that would require your absence from home oftener than one day out of a week; but for you to come in under Aunt Em [Emmeline B. Wells], and you two together to take a renewed hold on the little paper." Jacob thought that this would be preferable to "any other position he could think of" and recommended that Susa ask for "shares in the stock." Susa prayed that "any desire for self-aggrandizement" would be taken from her. She asked her "dearest Aunt Zina, give me your counsel. What shall I do? What steps shall I take?"[1]

Susa and Jacob had been married for eight years, and he had certainly come to understand her consuming interest in writing. He watched as she had labored late into the night by candlelight during her limited spare time in Hawai'i, writing articles for the *Juvenile Instructor*, the *Woman's Exponent*, and *Godey's Lady's Book*. But while he was supportive, it seems unlikely that this idea to try her hand at editing originated with Jacob. Instead, it was most likely a ploy by Susa to deflect from herself her vaunting ambition, placing it instead on her unwitting, but loyal husband. Susa was, after all, sensitive to gossip and accusations that she was too involved in her writing and insufficiently dedicated to her home and family.

She did not wait for a response from Aunt Zina; the same day she penned a letter to Emmeline B. Wells, offering her help as a "subordinate editor of the *Exponent*," and couching her request in the language of concern because of Wells's "many arduous labors." Susa offered, after she returned from Hawai'i, to travel to Salt Lake City from Provo every week or two for the day, and to take on an editorial department where she could work from home. Susa, never noted for her timidity or modesty, forged ahead, saying that she "should like to invest some money in the matter" and, further, that she "would

---

1. Susa Young Gates to Zina D. H. Young, May 5, 1888, box 77, fd. 12.

wish to see the paper improved as to paper, cover, & etc." There were, in addition, "many little items" to improve which Susa did not have time to delineate. Susa assured Emmeline, "I am confident that the result would be most gratifying to you, and pleasing to all the old contributors as well as hundreds of new ones." Susa offered her assistance in a "spirit of love and humility" with a "humble earnest desire."[2] If Wells wrote a response, it has not survived, which is a shame given that Susa had advised a highly revered woman twenty-eight years her senior, who had edited her own journal for eleven years, what needed to be done.

A letter from Susa's close friend, Romania B. Pratt, disabused Susa of the notion that Emmeline would welcome her on the staff of the *Exponent*. Romania frankly assessed the situation to Susa: The *Exponent* had started with a large board and had been edited since 1877 by Wells. Initially, according to Pratt, Wells had reported regularly to the board, but over time she became increasingly independent. Reports and board oversight eventually all but vanished, and "now [Wells] virtually owns the whole thing and I presume would resent it as an impertinence for anyone to ask her the questions you propound." Perhaps understanding Susa's need for independence, Pratt suggested that working on the *Exponent* would not be "your best situation." Rather, she recommended that Susa "branch out and take the fruitful and waiting field of the Y.L.M.I. Association." The young men had their own journal, why not the young women? Romania posited that the main reason a journal for the young women did not already exist is that "no one yet has had the energy to commence the work." Susa should proceed "quietly" under "proper [priesthood] authority" to set the stage. Romania counseled that the work would be "not only self supporting but actually remunerative" and that it would "pay you handsomely if well canvassed." Furthermore, there was no reason the magazine could not be edited from Provo.[3]

Susa had also written to her close friend, Apostle Joseph F. Smith, who suggested that Susa contact Wilford Woodruff, president of the Quorum of the Twelve and de facto head of the church, about

---

2. Susa Young Gates to Emmeline B. Wells, May 5, 1888, box 79, fd. 1.
3. Romania Pratt to Susa Young Gates, June 26, 1888, box 78, fd. 6.

her plans.[4] Smith suggested, in addition, consulting with the general presidency of the YLMIA.[5] Smith felt the issue should be "conducted from the inception of it to its completion by home-female talant." Susa should "seek good and wise counselors" and warned that "self-aggrandizement must of course not figure in the scheme." In keeping with Mormon tradition, he reminded her that "our community is different to any other. Our prosperity lies in our own union, cooperation, and mutual benefit. There is no independent."[6] It is telling that two of Susa's closest friends, people who knew her better than most, warned her to proceed "quietly," under the "proper authority," and to avoid "self-aggrandizement."

Susa followed Smith's advice and wrote to Woodruff, asking for his input and enclosing a letter to be forwarded to the YLMIA general presidency if he concurred with the proposal for a new journal for young women. Susa said that after considering Romania's "completely new suggestion," Jacob "decided that if the presidency of the Church, and the authorized members of the Y.L.M.I.A felt to add their co-operation and faith to such a scheme, he was willing I should undertake to fulfill a practice of that mission."[7]

Once again, given the relationship between Jacob and Susa, it is unlikely that Jacob made the decision to have Susa undertake the initiation of the *Young Woman's Journal*. Rather, Susa herself no doubt made this decision, and with Jacob's usual deference, he assented. Susa may have been following Romania Pratt's advice about following proper priesthood channels by letting Woodruff know that Jacob approved of the plan.

Susa's letter to the YLMIA presidency, forwarded by Woodruff, stated that her "great desire" was to be a "benefit and help in a literary way to my sisters in their lives and labors." For nine years with the "direct sanction and approval" of her husband, she had engaged in "labors of the pen," never allowing her "literary pursuits to interfere with

---

4. Woodruff would become president of the church in 1889, and the First Presidency would be reconstituted then.

5. The presidency at that time were President Elmina Taylor and her counselors, Maria Y. Dougall and Mattie Horne Tingey.

6. Joseph F. Smith to Susa Young Gates, Aug. 1888, box 77, fd. 12.

7. Susa Young Gates to Wilford Woodruff, Aug. 23, 1888, box 77, fd. 12.

the rights and priviledges of my husband and children." She asked rhetorically, "Am I a worthy instrument to perform this great labor?"[8]

Susa had developed great confidence in her writing abilities because of the faith expressed in her by her husband, who suggested "that I should assume the duties of Editor." She recommended that a broad-based board be appointed under the direction of the priesthood, that a business manager be appointed, and that printing be done "at the *Juvenile [Instructor]* office in Salt Lake City." She said, "Although I have capital sufficient to start such an enterprize yet it would seem wiser to me to create a Stock Co. among the A.'s [Mutual Improvement Associations] and let each Society hold an interest, receiving of the profits if there be any." In this manner, the individual associations would have a vested interest in the success of the endeavor.

She then outlined to the YLMIA presidency her vision of the magazine: sections devoted to literature, poetry, reports, health, "topics of the time," fashions, cooking, housekeeping, and a correspondents' club, among others. The magazine would represent the young women of the church as the *Contributor* represented the young men, but would "yet partake of the light and pleasing character of the *Juvenile Instructor*."[9]

Woodruff gave his assent to begin the journal, instructing Susa that it should be "commenced upon business principles." Subscriptions should be sought, and costs of publication should be determined. The "venture" should "stand on its own resources, independent of any aid from the Church" beyond "moral support." This was in keeping with church policy regarding the other three magazines, which were all owned and edited by individual church members. This was also a time of great financial difficulty for the church, which had had its properties escheated as a result of the anti-polygamy legislation of the Edmunds–Tucker Act of the previous year. With regard to Susa's editorship, Woodruff wrote that "we would suppose that your ability and talent would eminently fit you for that position."[10] Susa began to reach out for support. She told half-sister Maria Y. Dougall, "I

8. Gates to YLMIA presidency, box 77, fd. 12.
9. Gates to YLMIA.
10. Woodruff to Gates, Oct. 2, 1888, box 77, fd. 12.

have got plenty of money to establish the matter, but what I wish is the blessing, approval, assistance and earnest co-operation of the women in whose interests I wish to spend my time and abilities."[11]

With the approval of the First Presidency and the YLMIA general presidency, the magazine would begin after Susa returned from Hawai'i, which occurred in May 1889. Susa, in the company of Elmina S. Taylor and Dougall, was set apart as editor of the new journal by George Q. Cannon that summer. Shortly afterwards several letters from Cannon's son, Abraham, business manager of the *Juvenile Instructor*, finalized arrangements for George Q. Cannon and Sons Co. to publish the new magazine, which debuted in October 1889. In 1929, forty years later, in the final issue of the *Journal*, Susa reminisced, "The real purpose in establishing the *Journal* was to provide an outlet for the literary gifts of the girl members of the Church while presenting the truths of the Gospel of Jesus Christ as a factor in religious, domestic, social and recreational life through articles and stories, departments and editorials."[12]

The initial subscription cost was $2.00 per year; in 1900 that was lowered to $1.00 per year as a result of increased subscriptions.[13] The original press run was approximately 1,500 copies. Subscriptions trickled in slowly at first. Susa enlisted her mother, who hitched up her horse and buggy and traveled north to south throughout the territory, gathering subscriptions. Susa hoped for a broad readership and, to boost circulation, pled for each young girl to have her own subscription. "Girls," she wrote, "let me make one request of you: Don't lend your Journal. You do an injustice to yourself, as well as to the magazine."[14] At the end of 1897, when the YLMIA general board assumed management of the *Young Woman's Journal*, fewer than 2,000 copies were being printed. During 1900, the last year of Susa's editorship, the subscription list was 8,000, and a press run of 10,000 was planned for 1901.

The first six issues were only thirty-six pages long, but the magazine then expanded to forty-eight pages for the next several years.

11. Gates to Maria Y. Dougall, box 77, fd. 12.

12. Susa Young Gates, "Hail and Farewell," *Young Woman's Journal*, Oct. 1929, 678. Hereafter the Journal will be cited as *YWJ*.

13. Susa Young Gates, "New Year's Greetings," *YWJ*, Jan. 1901, 38.

14. Gates, "Editorial Department," *YWJ*, June 1891, 429–30.

Susa later wrote that there were two things of "paramount importance" to her. "First … the spirit of the magazine should take precedence above the forms in which the words might be cast." That is, message prevailed over syntax. "Second, from the first number the regular contributors must be home writers, and in harmony with the spirit of the associations," that is, the individual ward and stake organizations of the YLMIA.[15]

She claimed to welcome submissions from the young women of the church, but over the years few such articles appeared. Susa bore the brunt of the effort required to launch the new journal, but with at least lip service maintained fealty to the YLMIA general presidency, since the publication did serve the association. Susa wrote that from the outset Elmina S. Taylor "carried the moral responsibility of the young publication." Taylor worked so hard, in fact, that she told Susa on repeated occasions that "the journal would be the death of her." Later, in 1897, a board was formed to distribute responsibilities more evenly.[16]

Although money was a constant concern, Susa made it clear that she was not interested in dealing with the business aspects of the enterprise. "[A]ll communications of a business character" should be directed "to the *Juvenile Instructor* Office, Salt Lake City," where they would find a clerk whose responsibility included "non-arrival of Journals, stoppage of subscriptions, renewal of subscriptions, lists of names, payment of money, instructions as to agents' duties and per cent." She reminded readers that "the editor of the Journal has nothing whatever to do with the business part of the enterprise." And, as far as local canvassers were concerned, "it is nothing to the editor whether you do your duty as an agent of the Magazine or not; that matter lies between yourselves and the YLMIA Presidency of the Church. The editor is under the same surveillance and bears the same duty of obedience to that authority as yourselves."[17]

Several people acted as business manager for the *Journal* over the years, including Abraham H. Cannon, Estelle Neff, and Ellen Jakeman. The March 1891 issue announced the appointment of Jakeman

---

15. Gates, *History of the YLMIA*, 107.
16. Gates, 108.
17. Gates, "The Editor's Department," *YWJ*, May 1890, 285–86.

as business manager, to which she was duly set apart by George Q. Cannon.[18] Eighteen months later, Jakeman was out. "There were some matters of difference in a business way between the editor and the business manager; but we now take the occasion to say that Sister Jakeman performed most excellent service for it while laboring in the interests of this journal."[19] Jakeman felt that she was not being compensated fairly for her work, but Susa, who had given her a one-third interest in the *Journal*, disagreed. Susa did not list Jakeman as a business manager in her history of the YLMIA two decades later.

Jakeman was not the first person with whom Susa had differences of opinion regarding management of the *Journal*. Early on she clashed with both Apostle Abraham Cannon and YLMIA president Elmina Taylor. Cannon wrote Susa about her criticisms of a proposed contract: "I have done the best I knew how in this matter … and now I must ask you to have something prepared which will suit you fully, and … I will see if I can agree to it. I cannot, however, spend more time upon this thing at present. In fact, the longer the thing is postponed the more desirous I am that you retain the whole affair, and I will do all I can to assist you with its management. I fear that Sister Taylor herself feels very much grieved at your last communication to her, and she almost feels to have nothing more to do with the magazine."[20]

Cannon also found himself in the middle of Susa and Jakeman's dispute. He advised Susa to meet with Jakeman "and settle the matter between yourselves … even though it should require some sacrifice of feelings on your part. … Personally I think you are both in the wrong to some extent."[21] Susa wrote to Jakeman that "she still disagree[d] with many of your expressed views as to the settlement of those difficulties," but she submitted to Cannon's request, not because she was admitting any wrongdoing, but "I do have an earnest desire to comply with the words of those who are set to counsel me."[22]

Money was always a challenge, especially in the early days of the journal as debts were incurred due to a low subscription rate. But

---

18. Gates, 285.
19. Gates, "Editorial Department," *YWJ*, Sep. 1892, 563.
20. Cannon to Gates, Dec. 9, 1891, box 36, fd. 3.
21. Cannon to Gates, box 36, fd. 3.
22. Gates to Jakeman, Oct. 15, 1891, box 36, fd. 3.

Apostle Cannon remained optimistic, even as unsold back issues piled up on the shelves. In October 1892 he proposed a three-way partnership, with himself, Susa, and the "associations" to each own one-third of the magazine. Cannon and Susa signed the agreement, but Elmina Taylor did not want the associations to be incorporated, and she was unwilling to be personally involved financially.[23]

Abraham Cannon died unexpectedly in July 1896, at the age of thirty-seven, throwing the *Journal* into uncertainty, since it remained several thousand dollars in debt. Susa took a trip north to sell back copies, "which were at the same time the assets and the cause of the liabilities of the concern," raising $700.[24] Other board members also took it upon themselves to sell back issues, and a $500 contribution from Susa's wealthy friend, Elizabeth McCune, helped to avert ruin. After Cannon's death, there was a hiatus of three months (October-December 1896) when no issues of the journal were printed. They resumed again with volume eight in January 1897. By the end of the year the general board of the YLMIA had assumed management of the magazine, and business and literary committees, made up of board members, had been formed.[25]

Susa initially wrote a preponderance of the issues, but with time this changed. She employed a host of pseudonyms, including the usual "Homespun." Other noms de plume, which she acknowledged, include "Mary Foster Gibb, Dr. Snuffbottle, Mary Howe, Aunt Amelia, etc." Skurlock was probably Susa, as well. Often Susa used no name at all in her articles, which were just "slipped in, nameless."[26] Susa likely used pen names and published unsigned articles to hide just how much of the magazine was, at least initially, her work.

Many women who would later emerge as significant female Mormon writers "had their initial training in the *Journal* pages," including "Josephine Spencer, Kate Thomas, Annie Pike Greenwood, Susa Talmage, Christine D. Young, Ruth M. Fox and Leah D. Widtsoe." Numerous male luminaries also contributed articles

23. Gates, *History of the YLMIA*, 107.
24. Gates, 108–09.
25. Gates, "New Year's Greetings," 38.
26. Gates, "Hail and Farewell," 677–78.

for the early *Journal*, including Joseph F. Smith, George Q. Cannon, Orson F. Whitney, James E. Talmage, and John A. Widtsoe.[27]

The magazine initially consisted of several departments, including Literary; Our Girls'; House and Home, Dress; Health and Hygiene; and Editor's. Later additions included Our Shopping; Current Issues; The Sunday Chapter; Professional and Business Opportunities for Women; Constitutional Government; Young Mother's; Fashions Sensible and Pretty; Confidential Talks with Girls; and Stories of the Standard Operas. Several of the departments were short-lived.[28]

The Literary Department was first, beginning generally with a story, a serial, or a poem. The May 1891 issue, for example, carried three serial stories at the same time. Beginning with volume two, pictures and life sketches of prominent women in the YLMIA appeared at the beginning of each issue, including Elmina S. Taylor, Maria Y. Dougall, and Mattie Horne Tingey, and continued intermittently for several years.

Frequently reported were previously unpublished speeches of Brigham Young, which had probably been first transcribed in shorthand by Susa. The Our Girls section was timely advice to the young women of the church, written by the general presidency of the YLMIA. These messages were often of a spiritual nature; for example, on March 14, 1890, Zina D. H. Young spoke in tongues, interpreted by Dr. Ellis Shipp, at a conference of the Salt Lake Stake YLMIA in the Assembly Hall in Salt Lake City.[29] Readers were told women should not receive presents from men, unless they are closely related. "Good language ... should be rendered smooth and pleasing by proper modification and accentuation." The best age for marriage is between nineteen and twenty-five for women and twenty-two to twenty-eight for men, although there is "no set time." However, "girls under sixteen or over thirty and men under eighteen or over thirty-five are not as a rule so well prepared for marriage either physically and mentally."[30]

House and Home, often authored in the early days by May Greenhalgh and later by Leah Dunford Widtsoe, Susa's oldest

27. Gates, *History of the YLMIA*, 111.
28. Gates, 110–11.
29. "Our Girls," *YWJ*, Apr. 1890, 226.
30. "Confidential Talks with Girls," *YWJ*, Jan. 1897, 196–97, 200; Sep. 1897, 570.

daughter, offered commonsensical advice, such as, housewives need a "system. ... A place for everything, and everything in its place." "[D]o not exhaust yourself one day so that you may be unfit for work on the next." "Avoid unnecessary labor, and be more systematic" in housekeeping. One can learn how to hang pictures and wash clothes. "Establish better ventilation in the home." "Every kitchen should be a Domestic Laboratory and every woman that works therein should be a trained Domestic Chemist."[31]

Cooking Recipes included items as diverse as Indian pudding, scones, curried tripe, prairie chicken, venison chops, and oyster omelets. Readers were told to establish a regular hour for eating. "Don't have dinner, where flower's are in season, without some modest floral decoration," and "Serve every meal in such a way as to make it appetizing."[32]

Hygiene was initially written by Dr. Romania Pratt, but other authors included "Cactus" (Julia Macdonald), a medical student from Utah at the University of Michigan; Hannah Sorenson, a trained midwife from Denmark; and Dr. Snuffbottle, Susa herself. Sometimes letters were printed that were deemed to have good advice, and speeches on practical living were reprinted. In retrospect, much of the counsel seems obvious, such as the necessity for clean air, proper food, and pure water, along with avoidance of alcohol and adherence to the Word of Wisdom, but other recommendations are dated: Mothers of neonates cannot nurse while angry. Corsets are to be shunned because of their ill effects. Diphtheria can be cured by consecrated [olive] oil, and brown bread can overcome constipation. Bathe "at least twice a week, in cold water." It is appropriate to bathe in the morning, but not just before or after a meal. The hair "must be supplied with moisture artificially," preferably with Vaseline (petroleum jelly), since "nothing has ever been discovered which is so good for the promotion of the growth of the hair as ... Vaseline."[33]

---

31. "Systematic Housekeeping," *YWJ*, Nov. 1889, 55; Feb. 1890, 153; "Economy in the Home," Sep. 1896, 574–76; "The Home," July 1898, 330; "First Lessons in Cookery," June 1899, 276.

32. "Hygiene," *YWJ*, Oct. 1896, 24; "Home Economy," Sep. 1897, 566.

33. "Systematic Housekeeping," *YWJ*, Feb. 1890, 153; "Health," June 1890, 323; "Dress," Aug. 1890, 421; "Health," Oct. 1890, 32; "Bathing," Nov. 1896, 90; "Fashions Sensible and Pretty," Nov. 1896, 96; "Confidential Chats," Aug. 1898, 381.

The Fashion or Dress section encouraged simplicity in clothes, with preference given to Utah home industry. A dress should be at once "artistic and hygienic." Walk with "an active chest." "The horrid bustle ... has been banished." "Corsets and petticoats are foes to beauty," and corsets have been replaced by "compromised bodice." "Ear boring" [pierced ears] is decried as "semi-barbarous." "Do not get kid [goat] gloves for school or shopping wear," since dog and pig skin last three times longer. Every woman should have "one good, well made black gown." One entire article was dedicated to "commonsense" underwear. Buy patterns for dressmaking from a reliable firm. "Never buy an article because it is cheap." Avoid hats with birds and gaudy colors. Do not allow "the tyrant—Fashion—to make the body suffer."[34]

The Young Mothers' Department did not appear officially until volume eight in 1897, but there is an abundance of advice for mothers throughout the *Journal*, since there was no strict segregation between the YLMIA and the Relief Society. In fact, Susa used the *Journal* to encourage young women to continue in the YLMIA after marriage.[35] They were taught about lactation and weaning. Counsel was given to young mothers that babies need a bath at the same time every day. "Rocking a child to sleep is injurious to him," and "keep baby as quiet as possible during the first year of his life."[36]

The Editor's Department was used by Susa to pontificate each month on a subject of her choosing. Early on, the girls were advised that this is "your magazine." Every young woman should subscribe and solicit at least one other girl to subscribe as well. "Make your parents your confidants," especially if "they possess the Holy Spirit." Gratitude is expressed to the *Deseret News, Exponent, Contributor, Utah Enquirer, Home Sentinel,* and the *Salt Lake Herald* for their help in publicizing the *Journal.* Because of the challenges of the modern world, "it is wiser in us to lead, not follow where the world may

---

34. "Dress," *YWJ*, Feb. 1890, 157; "Dress," July 1890, 373, 378, 380; "Dress," Aug. 1890, 421; "Dress," Dec. 1890, 130; "Dress," Feb. 1891, 233; "Commonsense Underwear," Feb. 1899, 77; "Fashions Sensible and Pretty," Sep. 1896, 566; "Home and Kitchen," Sep. 1896, 573; "Our Girls," Sep. 1896, 580; "Hygiene," Oct. 1896, 24.

35. See, for example, "Young Ladies Conference," *YWJ*, June 1890, 326; "Our Picture Gallery," Mar. 1891, 242; and "Reward of Faith," Apr. 1893, 333.

36. "The Babe and the Mother," *YWJ*, Jan. 1899, 30–31.

choose to go." "How blessed is the knowledge that God orders all things for our good! To know that the storm is as necessary as the sunshine, the pain as useful as the pleasure. Accept your lot, dear friend, striving always to better it with the highest aims."[37]

The Sunday Chapter provided lessons for the "associations" to use in their own meetings. In November and December 1891, O. H. Huntington wrote about the life of Joseph Smith and his personal dealings with him. The next two months were devoted to miraculous healings in modern times.

"The World: As Seen Through a Woman's Eyes," by Lucy Page Stelle, presented a potpourri of women's issues throughout the world. One sample, from January 1891, covers a range of news. For example, Queen Victoria has just returned to Windsor Castle from a trip to Scotland. The memoirs of Queen Natalie (presumably of Serbia) are almost completed. Queen Nagarherita of Italy is stout with entirely gray hair. The Czar of Russia is chagrined with allegations of infidelity by the husband of his aunt, Queen Olga. Lady Roseberry, née Rothschild, has died. A scandalous affair between Charles Parnell and Mrs. O'Shea has occurred in Dublin. Lady Dilke is interested in labor unions in England. Baroness Margaretha von Lilienkreutz has become a member of the Salvation Army in Berlin. Artist Rosa Bonheur has been interviewed at her home in France. There are now several fire brigades in England formed entirely of women. Miss Susan B. Anthony will be coming to Washington, DC, for the annual meeting of the Association for women suffrage. And Miss Phoebe Couzins has been named secretary of the women's department of the World's Fair, to be held in 1893.[38]

Programmes began late in volume one in 1890, giving the various ward and stake associations the opportunity to send in reviews of their activities to stimulate the exchange of new ideas. Current Events began in the second volume, with a letter from famed Mormon pioneer Mary Fielding Smith to her sister, Mercy R. Thompson,

---

37. "Editor's Department," *YWJ*, Oct. 1889, 32; "Pioneer Sketches," Dec. 1889, 81; "Literary Department," Apr. 1890, 196; "The Editor's Department," Apr. 1890, 235; "The Editor's Department," June 1890, 334.

38. "The World: As Seen Through a Woman's Eyes," *YWJ*, Jan. 1891, 174–78.

submitted by Mary's son, Apostle Joseph F. Smith. John Nicholson outlined his thoughts about the "Indian question."[39]

Midway through the second year a several-page feature entitled Our Shopping Department began, giving an extensive review of shopping venues in Salt Lake City and environs. This advertising section, however, did not survive long. Young women were asked to identify themselves as readers of the *Journal* when they visited the advertised establishments and to report any problems with service to the editorial staff.

For the first twenty years of the YLMIA, each individual ward and stake was "more or less a law unto itself."[40] Correlation, commonplace today in the LDS Church, was far away. There was no coordination of lessons, and the programs were uneven in quality. In 1892 Susa offered a proposal to the general board of the YL-MIA: systematized lessons in a guide available for all wards and stakes. Susa wrote most of the first two guides; Maud May Babcock helped write twelve lessons on physical exercise. Three courses were presented in each year's guidebook, with a Theological Department each year, and the other two subjects drawn from a variety of topics, including history, human physiology and hygiene, ethics, home, and literature.[41] The first guide appeared in 1893 and was considered a great success. The second guide was published in pamphlet form two years later and consisted of more difficult lessons. Beginning in 1897 the lessons were published in the *Journal,* which explains in part the large increase in circulation that began that year.

The *Young Woman's Journal,* along with the *Woman's Exponent,* represented a tradition in Mormonism called "home literature," a phrase made popular in the late 1880s by Orson F. Whitney, a Salt Lake City essayist, poet, bishop, and future apostle. In an article in the July 1888 *Contributor,* Whitney wrote, "The formation of a home literature is directly in the line and spirit of this injunction [to "seek learning, even by study and also by faith," enunciated by Joseph Smith]. Literature means learning, and it is from the 'best books' we are told to seek it. This does not merely mean ... [scripture],

39. "Current Issues," *YWJ,* June 1891, 422–25; "Current Issues," Feb. 1891, 218–20.
40. Gates, *History of the YLMIA,* 179.
41. Gates, 182–84.

Church works and religious writings—though these indeed are 'the best books,' ... but it also means history, poetry, philosophy, art and science, languages, government—all truth in fact, wherever found."[42] This was "a historic call for Mormons to produce a literature worthy of national attention, while embodying uniquely Mormon values—a 'home literature.'"[43]

Since the coming of the transcontinental railroad in 1869, there had been an increasing encroachment in Utah Territory of "gentiles" and "gentile values" felt by Mormon leaders. Brigham Young was particularly concerned about the influence of "outsiders," and Susa followed in her father's footsteps. Historian Terryl Givens noted that "women's leaders like Emmeline B. Wells and Susa Young Gates had both been urging and modeling a resistance to gentile values."[44] Home literature by, for, and about Mormons became an integral part of defending Mormon beliefs, traditions, and peculiarities. Its effects have not echoed down through the twenty-first century, but they had considerable influence in the reform-minded people of the Progressive Era. Eugene England opined that with its "highly didactic fiction and poetry," it provided "little [of] lasting worth."[45] Likewise, Givens declared that home literature "did not immediately produce any lasting literary monuments, but it did set Mormonism on a course of studied engagement with literary expression that continues to the present."[46] Even at the time, home literature's domain was limited to Mormon audiences. Before the beginning of the twentieth century, for example, there were only the two articles written by Susa published in the national media—her piece on "Tropical Dresses" in Hawai'i and her article on "Family Life Among the Mormons."[47] Other articles were rejected, including a

---

42. Whitney, "Home Literature," 205.

43. Givens, *People of Paradox*, 192. Mormon scholar Eugene England identified four periods in Mormon literature, including Foundations (1830–80), Home Literature (1880–1930), The Lost Generation (1930–70), and Faithful Realism (1960–present). England, "Mormon Literature."

44. Givens, *People of Paradox*, 172.

45. England, "Mormon Literature," 461.

46. Givens, *People of Paradox*, 285.

47. Susa Young Gates, "Tropical Dresses," *Godey's Lady's Book*, July 1887, 62; Gates, "Family Life."

series she proposed on Brigham Young for *Ladies' Home Journal*.[48] Susa and the *Young Woman's Journal* were especially influential in promoting and developing home literature.[49]

Brigham Young, in conjunction with his worry about "outsiders" flooding the state, embarked on an ambitious campaign in the late 1860s and 1870s to promote a cooperative economic model that would make the Latter-day Saints self-sufficient. These were the beginning steps to what became ZCMI, the church-owned department store. Susa took up her father's ambition and promoted home industry to readers. They were encouraged not to purchase expensive items of fashion imported from the East, but to make do with what was produced at home, and she reminded them of what her father and his successors said to "patronize home industries." Susa blamed a lack of support for local merchants and goods for rising personal debt among the Latter-day Saints. How much better off would the church and its members be, she mused, if "we refuse to eat or wear Eastern goods of all kinds possible that can be manufactured at home?"[50] Susa's criticism of debt came at a time when the LDS Church was struggling under crippling economic pressure, and only a fraction of church members paid tithing. Over the next several years, LDS presidents Lorenzo Snow and Joseph F. Smith would embark on aggressive campaigns to boost tithing receipts and lift the church out of debt.[51]

The *Young Woman's Journal* promoted Mormon values without apology. The major themes appearing in the *Journal* under Susa's editorship reveal her beliefs about her faith, home life, parenting, marriage, relationships, and the roles and responsibilities of women in American society. Even when the words are not her own, they are consistent with her thoughts.

One recurring theme was the importance of the YLMIA. The young women were reminded frequently that the YLMIA had first been established by Brigham Young as a "retrenchment society." They were instructed: "It is your duty, sisters, to live near to the Lord, and retrench from everything unbecoming a Saint or displeasing

48. Edward Bok to Susa Young Gates, Dec. 23, 1891, box 39, fd. 23.
49. See Tait, "Mormon Culture Meets Popular Fiction."
50. "The Editor's Department," *YWJ*, July 1893, 477; "Home Industry Versus Getting Out of Debt," May 1897, 384–86.
51. See Quinn, *Wealth and Corporate Power*, 109–12.

to God and His servants. Seek to be guided by His spirit. Improve yourselves so that you may become refined and cultivated daughters of Zion, setting an example worthy of imitation. This is the object of these Associations."[52] Furthermore, one's responsibilities to the YLMIA did not cease with marriage. In fact, at that point the work of the YLMIA became even more important to the young women of the church. "Do not leave the association as soon as you are married for you then need the good spirit that is found in these meetings more than at any other time."[53]

No other theme is reiterated with greater clarity and frequency than the importance of marrying within the faith in the temple. Time and again stories and serials, dealing with both true and fictional accounts, sharply paint the hazards of marrying outside the faith, or even inside the faith (but outside of the temple). "The young men and women should be taught that it is a calamity to marry outside of the Church, and if they understood the gospel thoroughly they would never do it." Young women are counseled, "Be careful whom you choose for husbands, for if they are not of your faith, your misery will only be increased as years fade into the great eternal day." The choice of a husband should be prayed about, and it is a decision of eternal consequence. "Make marriage a matter of prayer; look for a man who is worthy to take you through the temple. ... Never marry outside of the holy covenant; it would be an injury to your posterity, you would rob them of a birthright."

Young women were warned about the dangers in associating with men not of their faith. "Girls, I entreat you not to accept the attention of strangers, those not of our faith, no matter how polite and affable their manners may be. How many of our innocent, trusting girls have been deceived, betrayed by the wolves in sheep's clothing, who fascinated them with their oily tongues and polished manners." And if young women find non-Mormons more sophisticated or worldly than their fellow church members, beware.

But guard your virtue and affection sacredly until you find a man worthy of your love and confidence, one that will take you to the house of the

---

52. "Reminiscences of Our First Organization," *YWJ*, July 1895, 484.
53. "Young Ladies Conference," *YWJ*, June 1890, 326.

Lord [the temple] where you can be united for time and eternity, even if his exterior is not quite as smooth, if his heart is right before God. You with your refining influence can help to rub off the roughness without till you find the diamond within. But beware of those that come to you with insinuating address and polished manners, and under the pretense of love seek to take undue liberties with you.

To expect to change a husband's behavior after marriage is an illusion. "Girls often think they can reform men after marriage; but, alas! how few ever realize their hopes. The time to reform them is before, not after marriage. Look around you and profit by the sad experience of those who married men who only drank occasionally, but who today are *drunkards'* wives" (emphasis in original).[54]

There were, Susa believed, too many young women who were not following the counsel of church leaders. "How many instances have there been where our girls have linked themselves with unbelievers, gone away with them, stayed a few years, then returned to their old home and friends, broken in health and spirits, burdened with a family of children, poor, and deserted by their natural protector. And yet these many cases of woe appear to be no warning to others, who seem anxious to go and do likewise." One wonders if Susa felt that this description applied to her sisters. With the issuance of the Manifesto forbidding plural marriage, there was a natural concern about a presumed surplus of marriageable young women. Nonetheless, it is better, according to counsel in the *Journal*, to remain unyoked, rather than unevenly yoked. "The question is becoming too frequent, 'Is it not better for our girls to marry those outside our faith than to remain single?' Let me shout the answer in your ears again and again. No! No! No! Better live the whole life out singly and in old maidenhood than to sell your birthright for a miserable mess of pottage. ... Apostle F. M. Lyman ... sends his voice out to you ... 'Let our girls wait till they get to eternity to marry, rather than marry outside of their own Church.'"[55]

54. "Our Girls," *YWJ*, July 1894, 501; "Y.L.M.I.A. Conference of Utah Stake," Nov. 1895, 85; "Y.L.M.I.A. Conference of Box Elder Stake," Nov. 1895, 81; "Influence of Association," June 1891, 431; "To the Young Daughters of Zion," Jan. 1892, 182; "Influence of Association."

55. "Relation of the Sexes," *YWJ*, Sep. 1893, 553; "Editor's Department," Nov. 1893, 92. The serial story "Donald's Boy" put the importance of temple marriage bluntly. The

Other consistent themes included miracles and spiritual gifts. The two most commonly discussed in the *Young Women's Journal* were speaking in tongues and healing the sick. Miracles in Mormonism are considered a manifestation of God's love for those who have been faithful. If not considered too personal or sacred, they are often shared to promote the faith of other church members. The *Journal* published a story from a reader about Susa's mother, Lucy Bigelow Young, healing an elderly woman who was dying. After Lucy "commanded her in the name of the Lord to arise and be made whole," the woman stood and walked, and within a few days was attending the temple.[56] Several examples of speaking in tongues, and those tongues being interpreted by another present, appear in the *Journal*, including the story above of Zina D. H. Young speaking and Dr. Ellis Shipp translating.[57]

The *Journal* in virtually every issue promoted the Word of Wisdom, often by stories which detailed the woes of not adhering thereto, particularly regarding alcohol. The Word of Wisdom, the Mormon health code, had long vacillated somewhere between good advice and strict commandment.[58] Some Latter-day Saints, including church leaders, would continue to use coffee, tobacco, and liquor after the Word had been introduced by Joseph Smith in 1833. But Susa and Jacob had decided early in their marriage to obey it strictly, and Susa preached its benefits to others. In one story, when a woman confesses that she sometimes has wine, her neighbor and fellow Mormon replies coolly, "We have a few true Latter-day Saints left who do not allow wines upon their tables, and who never allow it to pass their lips."[59]

Coffee and tea, although not as taboo in the pages of the *Journal* or in broader LDS culture, still was counseled against in the magazine.

protagonist, Phylis, is dating a non-Mormon, and her wise Aunt Ellen advises, "While it is a woman's duty to marry and become a mother I should remain an old maid to the end of my days rather than marry an outsider, and I know it would be more pleasing in the sight of God." "Donald's Boy," *YWJ*, Feb. 1895, 211.

56. "Dear Sister Susa Y. Gates," *YWJ*, Oct. 1890, 34.

57. "Our Girls," *YWJ*, Apr. 1890, 226. Other examples, among many, include "Y.L.M.I.A. Conference of Utah Stake," Nov. 1890, 86; and "Conference Minutes," May 1891, 221.

58. See, for example, Peterson, "Historical Analysis"; Alexander, "Word of Wisdom."

59. "Lead Us Not into Temptation," *YWJ*, July 1898, 312.

In an article by Susa's daughter Leah, partaking of coffee or tea was condemned as not only breaking "the Word of Wisdom but the laws of health," and girls were advised that if they "thoughtlessly formed that habit because mother or father does, stop it immediately."[60]

The two exceptions to this strict prohibition were for missionaries and for health purposes. Some Saints took coffee for headaches, and missionaries sometimes drank what was offered to them if to refuse would be impolite. Even Susa may have drunk tea at a reception at Windsor Palace hosted by Queen Victoria. She wrote in her lengthy report on the International Council of Women, "We all hastened into the great hall, where delicious tea ... was served to every one. ... Yes, every one! We do not drink tea ... but we knew 'our manners' too well to refuse such a lovely invitation from such a lovely lady."[61]

The *Young Woman's Journal*, under Susa's editorial hand, also strongly promoted the LDS prohibitions against fornication and adultery and instilled in readers Susa's sense of fidelity and virtue. The *Journal* reprinted speeches on the LDS law of chastity and published serial stories about women who were "pure and chaste as lovers." Again, the young women were cautioned about whom they might choose as a marriage partner, and were told that the men who truly love them "honors God and His laws above all earthly things." It was not only a woman's right, but her duty, to "demand from the husband and father the same purity of life and character that she herself maintains."[62]

Susa also had an interest in fashion, and the *Journal* published pieces on both the practical ("ruffles and bustles" are "things of the past") and the spiritual effects of clothing and dress. Fashion sense mattered and how young ladies presented themselves was important, but it was a "serious evil" to get too caught up in fashion trends which were "apt to starve the soul and deaden the ennobling, self-sacrificing qualities" that Latter-day Saint women were expected to have. Girls had to have a sense of thoughtfulness when choosing clothing and

---

60. "Hot Drinks for Breakfast," *YWJ*, May 1898, 235.

61. "International Council of Women," *YWJ*, Oct. 1899, 449–50.

62. "Y.L.M.I.A. Conference of Box Elder Stake," *YWJ*, Nov. 1890, 81; "Love, Courtship and Marriage," June 1890, 313; "Woman's Power," Aug. 1890, 405; "Address of Mrs. Mattie Horne Tingey," Sep. 1893, 548.

dressing, since "many womanly ailments exist" because of "thought-lessness" in fashion.[63]

Brigham Young had a marked aversion to medicine and physicians, a prejudice he passed on to Susa and which often appeared in the pages of the *Journal*. Even when her two young sons were dying in Hawai'i, there is no evidence that Susa sent for medical help. Instead, many of the medical myths of the era pervaded the pages of the *Young Woman's Journal*. "Never fall into the vile practice of sleeping with your head smothered up by the bed clothes, for the poison you thus imbibe will injure you far more than so many poisonous medicine taken into the stomach." Other advice was more practical, if still delivered with a strident tone: "That most beloved of all girlish loves, candy, is just so much poison to her system." Pure air, pure water, and proper foods were all extolled in the *Journal*, and "good, homemade brown bread" was supposed to "form the foundation" of a young girl's diet.[64]

A "great amount of sickness" came from food, bad habits, intemperance, and weakness. Susa coupled these beliefs in health with her belief in the Word of Wisdom. "Sending for a doctor … shows a lack of faith," and Susa felt it "a shame" that the Latter-day Saints neglected "the gifts of healing" that were available to them. Foreshadowing a strong criticism of medicine that persists in some quarters even today, the *Journal* reported that "doctors and druggists are getting enormously rich, and they are doing it at your expense." In fact, it would be better for a child to die and go into the celestial kingdom than be healed by a gentile, and "glorious will be their resurrection."[65]

The *Journal* also put a premium on "good manners" and in a serial story, likely written by Susa, the heroine Gwyn Lloyd is praised for her "truthfulness, her simplicity, her candor, and above all, her intrinsic faith in God," which "are safe-guards to her character," rare qualities "even among our highly-favored people."[66] Differences between men and women were emphasized, and the girls were told

---

63. "Dress," *YWJ*, Apr. 1890, 231; "Fashion," May 1891, 374; "Letter to the Young Women of Zion," Feb. 1891, 230.

64. "Diet," *YWJ*, Nov. 1891, 83–84.

65. "Our Sunday Chapter," *YWJ*, Mar. 1891, 278–80; "Evil Tendencies," Apr. 1891, 322.

66. "To the Officers and Members of the Y.L.M.I.A. Associations," *YWJ*, Oct. 1890, 28; "Lights and Shades," Nov. 1890, 50.

they should never try to act like a man or "be mannish." They should accept adversity in life, "be patient in affliction, brave in danger and humble in peace and prosperity." Playing games was considered acceptable, but card games, "noisy, provocative of quarrels, and has not the sanction of the best society," were not, nor did they have the "approval of the authorities of the Church." Deference to church leaders was also a common theme, as seen in the proscription against round dancing or waltzing.[67] After several reasons were given why round dancing was not acceptable, including how frequently partners touched one another, Susa exclaimed, "But there is one simple yet most potent reason why our young people should not indulge in round-dancing … it is against counsel! … Our leaders have condemned it, and that should be enough for our Mutual Improvement girls and boys."[68]

Susa valued ladylike behavior and wrote often about striving for womanhood. "Remember that perfect womanhood is the object for which you are laboring, and everything which will tend to your development physically, mentally and morally, should be adopted by the associations. Especially we would recommend … good manners, chaste language, reverence for God and sacred things, filial duty, respect for age—indeed, educate the heart equally with the mind." Women should never try to mimic or act like men, but ought to be "gentle, kind, loving, forgiving, full of mercy and charity." As she tried to define womanhood, she also explained that "we will take for granted that every young lady understands the duty of obedience to parental authority, and in the home is striving to become polite and refined in conversation and manners.[69]

A common method employed by numerous authors in the *Journal* was to create an older female character, most usually an "aunt,"

---

67. The waltz, a form of round dancing, became increasingly popular in the mid-nineteenth century. Round dancing involved closer physical contact between partners than previous dances, which mostly involved holding hands. Because of the increased level of physical intimacy, some more conservative elements frequently disparaged the new dance.

68. "Woman's Power," *YWJ*, Aug. 1890, 407; "The Editor's Department," June 1890, 334; "Winter Amusements for the Young People," Jan. 1893, 191; "Shall We Waltz?" Feb. 1900, 89–90.

69. "Our Girls," *YWJ*, Oct. 1890, 28; "Woman's Power," Aug. 1890, 407; "The Art of Good Behavior and How to Acquire It," Jan. 1893, 177.

who was developed as an experienced, sympathetic, wise, moral source of truth to whom the young reader could relate and whose teachings she could trust. In the story "Too Great a Responsibility" by Skurlock—probably Susa—seventeen-year-old Hazel and her friends "make sport" of "steady" Mr. Winfield because he is so "credulous." Her listener, "a comely matron of forty-five," defends the young man, believing that "he has faith enough in human nature to take the best view of all their words and actions."[70]

The story of Aunt Ruth, in the melodramatic serial, "Aunt Ruth's Story," touches on many of the themes common to the journal. It describes in harrowing detail the "dreadful story" of poor cousin Clara, who faithfully attends Sunday school and the YLMIA, but is swept off her feet by a "dashing young man" with "extravagant habits." The young man, Mr. Brown, even converts to Mormonism for Clara and takes her to the Endowment House.[71] Over the ensuing years Clara finds that her husband is a thief and a murderer who has abandoned a wife and children in another state. He commits suicide, and Clara returns home to her family broken-hearted. The moral of the story is clear, and Aunt Ruth makes sure her young listeners are duly impressed.[72]

Women's progress and rights were also promoted. Women in Utah were granted suffrage in 1870, but lost it under the Edmunds–Tucker Act of 1887. In the pages of the *Journal*, Susa was unapologetically pro-suffrage. Women had "obeyed the laws of her country as faithfully" as the men, and they "make themselves acquainted" with politics. If Utah were to enter the Union as a state, it must be with "*all* our citizens, or we will remain outside." Education for women was also strongly advocated. Susa knew first-hand from her marriage to Alma Dunford what it was like to be attached to an alcoholic unable to properly care for his family. She, like other women of her era, believed that women needed to be able to care for themselves. "It is very important also that our girls should learn some useful trade or profession. Why should they not be taught to be

---

70. "Too Great a Responsibility," *YWJ*, Sep. 1890, 478.

71. The Endowment House in Salt Lake City hosted temple rites until temples in the territory were completed. It was demolished in 1889.

72. "Aunt Ruth's Story," *YWJ*, Oct. 1892, 2–15.

independent and self-sustaining as well as men?"[73] Susa published, under the pseudonym of Mary Howe, a series on "Professional and Business Opportunities for Women," outlining prospects for female employment in such diverse fields as medicine, law, stenography and typewriting, retouching for photographers, dentistry, and merchandising.[74]

Susa, who both loved to read and write, and who had corresponded with Leo Tolstoy through his daughter, had conflicted feelings about novels. This, like so many other of her traits, followed her father's thinking. Brigham Young had spoken on occasion about novels and had said that, in an ideal world, novel reading would be forbidden, but he also said that he "would rather that persons read novels than read nothing."[75] Presumably Susa was aware of the irony that she spent her whole life writing fiction despite sometimes condemning it, but since her stories painted clear moral pictures in support of LDS values, she may have felt that her work was different.

At least one article in the *Journal* reported that fiction reading had produced "greater morality, towards a greater love for god, man and nature" and had helped to unite "individuals in a common brotherhood, and not only individuals, but nations," and had "given us larger sympathies and broader minds." But such thinking was tempered in the next article, written by Susa herself, by warnings that novels had to be chosen with the utmost care. Novel reading could be addicting and should only be done on occasion, provided the book emphasized LDS values.[76] It is telling that what is probably the most dramatic—or melodramatic—story Susa wrote for the *Journal* was the first article on the first page of the first issue in October 1889. In "Whatsoever a Man Soweth," written under her best-known pseudonym, Homespun, virtually everything that happened to the pathetic Leonard Fox occurred because of novel reading. At the

---

73. "Woman's Progress," *YWJ*, Sep. 1891, 551–52; "Statehood for Utah," Mar. 1892, 261; "Maidenhood," Sep. 1891, 577.

74. The series was published throughout volume three of the journal, October 1891–September 1892.

75. *JD*, 9:173. See also another speech by Young, *JD*, 15:224.

76. "The Influence of Fiction on Education," *YWJ*, Nov. 1900, 488; "Another Phase of the Question," Nov. 1900, 497–501; "What to Read," Aug. 1898, 362; "Mental Hygiene," May 1893, 370–71.

outset his mother warns him, "If you don't stop reading them trashy novels day after day and day after day you'll go clean crazy." Leonard descends into a miserable existence: he attempts suicide after his girlfriend spurns him, and he marries a Swedish immigrant but abandons her for his studies while she is pregnant. Finally Leonard "awakens" from his filthy novel habit, which "had been almost as debauching as drink," and "warns every young person he meets never to read novels." Even Susa allows that this might be overkill, and she concludes, ""I only wish we had novels or stories written by our own people with proper lessons taught therein."[77]

Susa spent considerable time writing and editing for the *Young Woman's Journal*. She fretted over its financial status and had to travel, usually at least twice a month, to boost subscriptions, solicit material, and resolve conflicts. When she was recovering from pregnancy or poor health, she would dictate from bed to Lule, who had "abominable English and penmanship," and her work would be corrected by Abraham Cannon or Estelle Neff. By 1900, Susa was not well, and she resigned as editor.[78] She was paid $1,000 for "my long unpaid labor and loss." In addition to all the other joys and challenges in her life (see chapter nine), the decade when she oversaw the *Journal* sapped her of good health, and as the new century proceeded, Susa's health would continue to decline.

---

77. "Whatsoever a Man Soweth," *YWJ*, Oct. 1889, 2–10, 45–50.
78. Gates, "Hail and Farewell," 677–78.

11
Illness

On February 20, 1900, Jacob wrote to Susa, who was most likely in Salt Lake City, that their youngest child and namesake of his grandfather, was coughing. Five days later, three-and-a-half-year-old Brigham Young Gates died, the eighth and last of Susa's children whom she lost in childhood or adolescence. She had given birth to thirteen children; five survived into adulthood and outlived her. Susa did not write much about young Brigham's death, just as she had not written much about her children's deaths since she lost Karl and Jay in Hawai'i. Fourteen months later, Abbott, the young son of Mabel Young Sanborn, Susa's younger sister, died. Susa noted that Abbott died very much like Brigham, presumably of Bright's disease (chronic inflammation of the kidneys). With Brigham's death, Susa and Jacob's large family had dwindled to just three sons left at home—Cecil, Harvey "Hal," and Franklin. Despite her frequent absences from home, Susa seems to have always had these young men in mind, once referring to them as "sweet Cecil, brave Hal, and comical little Frank."[1] During her travels, Susa would send them counsel regarding the importance of household chores, study, music practice, and especially a well-balanced diet.

Among her many other responsibilities, Susa taught a class in Sunday school for young women in her ward in Provo. On the occasion of her forty-fourth birthday on March 18, 1900, the young women paid her homage with a tribute:

---

1. Susa Young Gates to Jacob Gates, Mar. 1902, box 10, fd. 10.

Our dear Teacher, yea Mother, for you have been more than a teacher to us, we meet today to … commemorate your birthday. Your precepts have taught us much, but your well spent life more. It has taught us, That it is good to be well born; That inherited character is a strong foundation for other attributes and virtues to build … upon; That Humility … is that … root, from which all heavenly virtues shoot; That a true mother can also be a splendid public servant … you will live for generations after your body is laid in the tomb, especially will you live in the hearts of those who know you best.

> May your birthdays be many and sweet
> And your life's labor be complete
> When the Savior is ready and waits
> To welcome dear Susie Young Gates.[2]

In late September 1900 Susa traveled to Toronto, Canada, for a meeting of the National Household Economic Association of the United States, which had been organized at the time of the World's Fair in Chicago in 1893 "for the betterment of the home in all the details of every-day life."[3] In the absence of the president of the organization, Dr. Mary E. Green, who was mourning the recent death of her husband, Susa was asked to give "the response of welcome," for which she reports she was congratulated by everyone. She paid tribute to Queen Victoria: "We all realize the influence of your good Queen across the water, whose life has been so pure, so beautiful. There is not a hamlet, not a home in all our States, which does not feel the influence of her beautiful life." Despite what she considered a successful trip, Susa lamented in a letter to Jacob that she prayed "for the time when we can travel together." She missed home and wrote, "I would rather be your wife and the mother of your children to anything else on earth."[4]

Susa, who had previously met President William McKinley, attended his second inauguration in March 1901 in the company of Emmeline B. Wells, general president of the Relief Society, and met McKinley two more times. Before departing Salt Lake City for Washington, DC, they were given a priesthood blessing by

---

2. Sunday School class letter, box 3, fd. 26, SYGP (CHL).
3. "Household Economics," *The Globe*, Oct. 3, 1900.
4. Susa Young Gates to Jacob Gates, Oct. 2, 1900, box 10, fd. 4.

high-ranking LDS authorities. Emmeline was blessed by Joseph F. Smith, Susa by Anthon H. Lund. The blessings were given at the instruction of Lorenzo Snow, president of the church, who said that the two women "were going on missions for the benefit and up-building of the Kingdom of God."[5]

Although universal suffrage for women was not enacted in the United States until 1920 with the 19th Amendment to the Constitution, Republican women under the auspices of the Women's National Republican Association were to have "their distinct and separate part in the inauguration of President McKinley." The program listed Mrs. Susa Young Gates of Utah, explaining "Why Utah Went Republican."[6]

Susa lodged once again with Belva Lockwood during her month-long stay in the capital and met with many prominent people, including William H. King, US representative from Utah; Ida Husted Harper, journalist and suffragist; Gilman Bigelow Howe, Susa's distant cousin who had written the Bigelow genealogy; Fannie Humphries Gaffney, president of the National Council of Women; May Wright Sewall, president of the International Council of Women; Kate Waller Barrett, vice-president of the Florence Crittenton Mission for unmarried mothers; Willard Young, Susa's half-brother, West Point graduate, and Spanish-American War hero; and Joseph L. Rawlins, US senator from Utah.

Susa attended Press Club meetings of the National Council of Women (NCW) as well. After receiving a ticket from Senator Rawlins, she attended the inauguration of President McKinley on March 4, waiting three hours in the rain for the services to begin. She went to the White House the next day, but the president was too busy to see private callers. She joined a delegation from Illinois, however, and was able to shake the president's hand. Six months later McKinley was shot by Leon Czolgosz in Buffalo, New York. He died eight days later, becoming the third US president to die from an assassin's bullet.

Susa sent Jacob a telegram on March 6, explaining that Major James B. Pond, Civil-War-hero-turned-lecture-manager, had asked her to come to New York City at his expense to speak with his friends,

5. Gates to Gates, Feb. 1901, box 10, fd. 5.
6. "Inaugural Banquet," box 42, fd. 9, SYGP (CHL).

who were wealthy and well-connected. Pond had previously managed Ann Eliza Webb Young, Brigham's fifty-second wife, who divorced Young and later made a living from anti-polygamy/anti-Brigham Young lectures. Pond would manage the 1902 eastern states concert tour of Emma Lucy Gates.

Should Susa go to New York City, or should she come home? As usual, Jacob replied, "Go, but hurry home." Susa wrote that "Aunt Em"—Emmeline B. Wells—"scolds me for being in such a hurry, when I am doing so much good, and have come so far and spent so much money. ... But I cant help feeling I am doing missionary work." Two days later, she added, "But this mission still seems to press upon me as unfinished."[7]

In New York City Susa spoke at a gathering of the rich and intellectual neighbors of Major Pond, giving a "simple, modest talk on Utah." Susa reports that she was "simply overwhelmed with compliments and praise." In addition, she said she had never had so many opportunities to preach and proselytize. She visited Asenath Adams, mother of Maud Adams, a Utah native and one of America's most famous actresses of the time. She also saw Ida Bamberger of Utah, wife of Simon Bamberger, one of Utah's wealthiest men and the state's future governor and its only Jewish governor. Susa visited the "Ghetto" with Bamberger, a Jewish neighborhood in New York. She also met with Frank J. Cannon, former US senator from Utah; Charlotte Perkins Gilman, feminist, novelist, and social reformer; Linda Hull Larned, prominent author and household economist; and Newell Dwight Hillis, pastor of Brooklyn's Plymouth Church, whom Susa considered the most famous preacher in America. She spent two hours with Hillis explaining Mormonism.[8]

Finally, after being gone for a month, Susa left for Utah on March 20. This particular trip highlights several features of the many trips Susa made during her life. She rarely traveled alone. Money was always a concern. And she was not reluctant to ask for financial help, often from church sources, and would frequently ask Jacob to send her money. She usually wrote to Jacob every day or two, sometimes twice a day. She nearly always expressed homesickness and gave

---

7. Susa Young Gates to Jacob Gates, various correspondence, Mar. 1891, box 10, fd. 6.
8. Gates to Gates.

advice to various family members. She considered her trips as "a mission," and was never reluctant to praise the glories of Mormonism. She maintained a hectic schedule while traveling, sometimes getting by with two to three hours of sleep at night. She met and mingled with the rich and famous of the world. But she was effusive in her praise of her husband, whom she viewed as superior to every man she met. She was almost without exception gone longer than she had anticipated. She would write to Jacob, who often bemoaned the length of her trips, but who almost always acceded to her pleas to stay longer.

In 1901 Jacob confessed, "When you are away, I am not content to await patiently the slow return of the appointed time, but I chafe and fret in my spirit for my absent one and then when the 'appointed time' takes wings and soars away again, I can hardly endure it. If you are doing good I ought to be content, I will be." He said that he was growing tired of being both father and mother to the boys. "No one but me to see that they are bathed, only me to see that their clothes are ready and mended up for Sunday and conference. What is the result—you can imagine. I sometimes feel a little discouraged at the lack of home life that we have. I hardly know how to remedy the matter, but ... we will talk it out and adopt some way whereby both you and I will be more satisfied, by getting more comfort out of home, children and each other."[9]

By the beginning of 1902 Emma Lucy, who increasingly went by Lucy, had been studying voice for three years in Germany and felt ready to begin a concert tour in the United States, to be arranged by Major Pond. She and Susa left Salt Lake City on January 21 for New York City, and arrived four days later. In less than a century, a journey that would have taken several months now took days, and often in comfort.

In New York, Emma Lucy would share the stage with Florizel, a child prodigy violinist. The original schedule called for concerts at Carnegie Hall, Boston, Washington, DC, and Philadelphia, all within a week's time. Although Emma Lucy was reportedly well-received by the audience, the critics, particularly in New York City, were brutal, and she was, according to Susa, "unmercifully roasted."

---

9. Jacob Gates to Susa Young Gates, various letters, 1901, box 7, fd. 3.

The critics in Boston were somewhat kinder, but hardly laudatory. They reported that, although she had a "good voice," she was not yet ready for public appearances. Emma Lucy was "discouraged and homesick." The remainder of the tour was cancelled, not only because of bad reviews and lagging ticket sales, but also by the illness of Florizel, who required ear surgery."[10]

Initially, Lucy wanted to return to Europe immediately, but plans were eventually made for her to remain in New York City, where she stayed until April and took lessons from several prominent voice teachers. By the time Florizel had recuperated, plans to continue the tour had fallen apart, and Pond had lost several thousand dollars. From Utah Jacob opined that "it was rather cruel to put our sensitive, tenderhearted child to such tests," but concluded, "it will suggest to Lule the fact that she has something left to learn, and keep her from getting proud." Jacob's letters throughout February continued to pour out his love for Susa, and he repeated often how much he missed her.[11]

In New York City Susa also visited with Lydia Finkelstein Mountford, the Holy Land lecturer born in Jerusalem to a Russian, presumably Jewish, family. Beginning in the 1880s, Mountford had begun worldwide presentations of Bible stories with characters in full costume depicting life in ancient Jerusalem, and in the 1890s, Susa's young children, Beulah and Franklin, had acted in Mountford's pageants when she visited Utah. Susa reported that during this visit, Mountford was with her "man," and she assumed that Mountford was leading a double life.[12]

While Lucy remained in New York City, Susa traveled to Washington, DC, for the fourth triennial meeting of the National Council of Women (NCW), held from February 19 to 25. Mrs. Alder, the chair of the press committee, was not present, so Susa, as assistant chair, assumed responsibility for speaking with the press. It was during this meeting Susa was named chair of the Press Committee of the National Council of Women. Susa was stressed during this time, for not only was she handling the press responsibilities

---

10. Susa Young Gates to Jacob Gates, various letters, Feb. 1902, box 10, fd. 9.

11. Jacob Gates to Susa Young Gates, various letters, Feb. 1902, box 7, fd. 4.

12. Susa Young Gates to Jacob Gates, Feb. 2, 1902, box 10, fd. 9.

for the meeting, but she was a speaker on the topic, "Can a Mother Forget Her Own?"

Susa came under particular opprobrium for her press coverage of the meeting in Washington, which some women felt promoted LDS talks over others. Elizabeth B. Grannis, president of the National Christian League for the Promoting of Social Purity, complained to Susa that "the "Morman women's talks" were given a column in the newspaper, but "not a line" was given to Mrs. Grannis's paper, which was the official paper from the Christian League in Washington. She stated that she was "quite incapable of appreciating the depth of intrigue of the Morman Chairman of the Press Committee."[13]

Susa took offense and shot back a lengthy rejoinder to Grannis, insisting that she had no "thought of being either partial or unjust to any human being," but she was put "in this dilemma" due to her "inexperience and the rush ... of the reporters." Susa then pivoted to self-pity, writing that she did not know "why I should have taken up this work" since "almost all of my people are opposed to my doing so." Mormon women, Susa explained, were still smarting over the poor treatment and "the suspicion and scorn with which they are met by many women of the world." Most of Susa's friends, she insisted, wondered why LDS women should continue to pay membership dues to an institution where they are "confronted constantly with these very misrepresentations" to which Grannis had subjected Susa. Susa concluded with Grannis's claim that the church spent large sums of money to send Mormon women to Washington to influence the NCW. Susa, for whom money was always scarce, took particular exception to this and exclaimed, "I only wish to goodness it were true!" and she explained that, with rare exception, she had to pay her own way. She wondered "why should I persist in taking up the Council work when they want me so much at home and when there is so much good work waiting to be done here? The only answer I can give you is that I am a devoted believer in the Council."[14]

Despite Grannis and her letter, Susa told Jacob that the president and the vice-president of the organization both queried, "What

13. Grannis to Gates, Apr. 26, 1902, box 42, fd. 12.
14. Gates to Grannis, May 4, 1902, box 42, fd. 12.

would the convention or we have done without Mrs. Gates?"[15] While in Washington, Susa continued to visit with high-ranking and prominent officials, including George Sutherland, US Congressman from Utah and future justice of the US Supreme Court. Sutherland obtained for Susa an autograph from the new president, Theodore Roosevelt, who had taken office after McKinley's assassination. Susa also visited Anna Howard Shaw, president of the National Women's Suffrage Association; Rachel Foster Avery, one of the organizers of the International Council of Women; Susan B. Anthony; and Clara Barton, founder of the American Red Cross.

During the meeting, Susa received the sad news that her daughter Leah had just lost her firstborn son, John Jr., in Utah. John was only ten months old and, after he contracted "an infectious disease from a neighbor," had been ill for some time.[16] His father was so distraught, he was confined to his bed "with what threatened to be nervous prostration."[17] Susa was also pressured to entertain the several members of the Utah delegation, and the usual financial problems loomed. But, despite these challenges and the heartbreaking news of John Jr., Susa seemed to sense light at the end of the financial tunnel she and Jacob had wallowed in for years.

The most promising proposal was for their daughter Lucy to spend the next year in New York City, chaperoned by Jacob, who had been called by the First Presidency[18] to serve as a missionary in the Eastern States Mission, headquartered in New York City. Susa, anxious for more reasons to visit the East Coast, insisted, "You *must not* fail to go on your mission. ... The way is clear to pay your debts" (emphasis in original). A month later Susa told Jacob to sell a parcel of property they owned in Salt Lake City. "I am so anxious to see you cleared of all debt, and ready to go on your mission [with Lucy] next fall." Susa also hoped to return to Brigham Young Academy to teach Domestic Science, but the administration at the academy waffled, indicating that they would not be able to pay more than a $40 salary per month, which Susa and Jacob felt was not enough.

---

15. Gates to Gates, Feb. 1902, box 10, fd. 9.

16. Widtsoe, *Sunlit Land*, 235. See also Parrish, *John A. Widtsoe*, 381.

17. "Agricultural College," *Salt Lake Herald*, Feb. 9, 1902, 10.

18. Lorenzo Snow had died in October 1901, and the new First Presidency was Joseph F. Smith and counselors John R. Winder and Anthon H. Lund.

The university administration also worried that Susa's age, forty-six, might be a problem.[19]

Susa returned to New York City from Washington and initially lived with Lucy at Major Pond's home in Jersey City, New Jersey. But the time involved to commute into New York City was too great, so, at the invitation of the mission president, John McQuarrie, they moved to the mission home of the Eastern States Mission. Susa continued her customary round of visits, including to Asenath Adams and Charlotte Perkins Gilman. She attended church in New York and wrote to Jacob that she and her half-sister Maria Young Dougall had spoken in tongues.[20]

When she finally planned her trip back to Utah, Susa passed through Rochester, New York, where she visited with Susan B. Anthony, who was also hosting Ida Husted Harper. From there she proceeded to Indianapolis and spent several days with Mrs. May Wright Sewall at Sewall's insistence. After her train had pulled into the Indianapolis station, Susa called for a taxi, expecting a carriage, but instead found an automobile; it was her first car ride. Sewall, whose formality even Susa wrote "chills me and repels me," handpicked Susa to represent her on behalf of the United States at the International Council of Women (ICW) meeting in Copenhagen.[21] Susa finally left Sewall's home for Utah, stopping in Chicago briefly where she met Lucy, who had arrived there in the company of Wesley Young, a cousin living in New York. The three continued to Provo, where Wesley spent several months helping to take care of the Gates boys.

During Susa's absence, her family continued to flourish under Jacob's care. Several neighborhood boys in Provo had formed a juvenile band. Cecil played trombone, Hal played drums. Young Franklin, who was quite ingenious, not yet nine years old, wanted to play, but was told he was too young. He took a hose, cut holes in it, and taught himself to make tones. He was rewarded for his efforts with a brass horn, which his father said was bigger than Frank himself, and he

---

19. Gates to Gates, various letters, Feb.-Mar. 1902, box 10, fds. 9–10.
20. Gates to Gates, Mar. 18, 1902, box 10, fd. 10.
21. Gates to Gates, Apr. 22, 1902, box 10, fd. 11.

was allowed to join the band.[22] Lucy wanted to continue to sing and tour, and Pond had planned to sponsor a Utah concert tour for her during the summer of 1902. Pond eventually stepped aside, and Jacob managed the tour himself. Lucy and her father toured southern Utah in a series of concerts. They made $625 and cleared $500.

While Jacob and Emma Lucy were beginning their concert tour, Susa confronted the "great howl [that] went up from every corner of the globe" after word leaked out that May Sewall had chosen Susa to represent her at the ICW in Copenhagen. Even Susan B. Anthony, who had always been on friendly terms with Susa, said that sending a Utahn, a Mormon, and a daughter of Brigham Young might taint the good name of the council. Susa was given strict instructions by Sewall that she was not to be interviewed or introduced at the meeting as either a daughter of Brigham Young or a Utahn.[23] The howl soon dissipated and Susa remained the choice to attend the meeting, which meant paying for her travel. She asked church leaders for funding, and Bathsheba Smith offered $100. Joseph F. Smith said that through the *Deseret News* Susa could get train passage to and from New York City. He talked with other leaders and they thought it important for Susa to attend the meeting. Emmeline B. Wells, Reed Smoot, and Anthon Lund favored the proposition, and so at least some funding was secured from the church for Susa's travel and expenses.

Susa left Provo on June 19 after she had been home barely two months. She was not indifferent to Jacob's feelings, or her children's, about her long absences. She begged Jacob to "forgive me if I do not my full duty by them." She described feelings of inadequacy, saying it was a "terrible responsibility" to be the sole representative from America. She reached New York and sailed on a German steamer, the *Frederich der Grosse,* and said that nearly everyone on board spoke only German. Susa, outgoing and anxious to act as a missionary for the church, was disappointed that she could not go about her usual efforts to get to know fellow travelers.[24]

The steamer chugged down the River Weser and landed in Bremen in northern Germany. From there Susa went via Hamburg and Kiel

---

22. Jacob Gates to Susa Young Gates, June 1902, box 7, fd. 7.
23. Susa Young Gates to Jacob Gates, various letters, 1903, box 10, fd. 14.
24. Gates to Gates, various letters, June 1902, box 10, fd. 12.

to Copenhagen. At the meetings a plethora of causes was brought up by various national councils: eligibility of women to serve on education commissions, suppression of houses of ill repute, "education and supervision of midwives," women's suffrage, improvement of penal laws concerning minors, "abrogation of the political restrictions placed on women," and admission of women as regular students at all universities, among other issues. An overarching concern was that of advocating for peace. At the behest of the NCW, May 15, 1902, had been set aside as the day for peace demonstrations throughout the United States, and, indeed, in most large cities of America, peace marches had taken place.[25]

After this success in the United States, the NCW raised the issue of setting an annual date for worldwide peace demonstrations. Although many representatives at the ICW thought this a good idea, those on behalf of England opposed the measure since British soldiers had recently departed for South Africa to fight the Boer War.

During Susa's time in Copenhagen, things went smoothly, although there would be considerable fallout in the months to come. As was her usual custom, Susa met with several prominent church members, including historian Andrew Jenson; Apostle Francis M. Lyman; her nephew, Levi Edgar Young, president of the Swiss Mission; and Hugh J. Cannon, president of the German Mission. She spoke at several church meetings in Copenhagen, and her remarks were translated by Andrew Jenson.

Susa was supposed to leave for England on July 16, prior to returning to the United States, but then another opportunity arose. Madame Chapponier-Chaix from Geneva, Switzerland, invited Susa to visit her at her lakeside home. Susa felt this would be an excellent opportunity to meet more influential people. She wrote Jacob, "I came out for a certain object, and I must not only half do my work." Susa felt that going to Geneva would be an excellent opportunity to meet more influential people, not just in Switzerland, but she could also get a letter of introduction to the French council as well. This "permits me to do so much good."[26]

---

25. NCW, July 1902, box 43, fd. 2, SYGP (CHL).
26. Susa Young Gates to Jacob Gates, various letters, box 10, fd. 12.

Susa became ill the day after arriving in Geneva, which she ascribed to Danish food, too much meat and not enough bread. Her illness was, she claimed, due to "errors in diet," not "overwork," and she refused to see a doctor. She remained in Geneva until the first week in August and spent a day sightseeing in Paris.

Since her departure for America was already delayed, Susa reasoned that it would be a good idea to remain in London for the coronation on August 9, 1902, of King Edward VII, eldest son of Queen Victoria and Prince Albert. She felt this would be important, so that she could write about the coronation for the *Deseret News*, which had partially funded her trip. She reported a "fine time" on Coronation Day to Jacob.[27]

The day after the coronation, Susa, who still was not well, received a priesthood blessing from Apostle Lyman, which she described as "lovely." In her letter to Jacob the next day, she did not talk about the content of the blessing, which is mystifying in view of the importance which Susa later attached to it. She likely did not want to worry Jacob, though she did admit that Lyman was "quite uneasy" about her health.[28] Susa finally wrote about the blessing twenty-seven years later, in the final issue of the *Young Woman's Journal*. She revealed that Lyman had seemed to tell her that she would die soon, but then hesitated, and reversed himself:

> President Lyman began his blessing by dedicating me to the Lord, adding that I ought not to shrink from going on the Other Side for there was much greater scope for any gifts and talents I might have there, and that my father and the Prophet wanted me there—then he paused and after a few silent moments he began again by saying there had been a council held over there, and it was decided that I should remain on earth to be a help to my husband and family and to take up a work that had not been done so far in the Church.[29]

Susa interpreted the work that "had not been done so far" to be genealogy. A few weeks after he gave her the blessing, Lyman wrote to Susa and explained, "I have nothing to retract from the blessing the

---

27. Gates to Gates, Aug. 10, 1902, box 10, fd. 12.
28. Gates to Gates, Aug. 11, 1892, box 10, fd. 12.
29. Susa Young Gates, "Hail and Farewell," *Young Woman's Journal*, Oct. 1929, 677.

Lord gave you. It was not all told by any means."[30] What exactly was "not all told" remains unclear.

Susa's declining health in the early years of the twentieth century remains something of a mystery. Some writers have speculated that she may have suffered from a nervous breakdown, but she was never hospitalized, nor would she ever have allowed herself to be. She blamed her poor health on a European diet. In the pages of the *Young Woman's Journal*, she extolled bread as essential to good health, but found it lacking in Europe. She also thought Europeans ate too much meat. But there are signs that her health was already suffering before she set out for Copenhagen. Her mother wrote to her from Berlin in June 1900: "Throw off all tension and prostrait yourself upon your bed, and have a perfect rest for a few days, every time you are sick."[31] In the aftermath of Emma Lucy's unfortunate concerts in the winter of 1902, Jacob wrote to Susa, "The uncertainty of matters is trying ... but more so no doubt because of your condition, not being well."[32] Susa had several blessings, including the one from Lyman that came to mean a great deal to her. She would later write that she was near death, and that she was given morphine, which suggests the seriousness of the problem, since Susa usually eschewed any medicine she did not consider natural. Whatever the cause of her poor health, she rested in Geneva in Switzerland, but thereafter largely functioned as she had before.

Lyman's blessing grew in significance to Susa over the ensuing years. Whether her perception of the experience changed, or whether in the moment she neglected to describe fully its meaning, is unclear. Regardless, the blessing appears to have been a turning point for Susa, one where she felt her life was in danger and needed a new direction. Thereafter, genealogy became a consuming interest, and she was convinced that her survival pointed her toward genealogy and temple work, themes which dominated the last years of her life, and would soon lead to major changes in her and Jacob's lives.

After her time on the European mainland and her coverage of

---

30. Gates to Gates, various letters, Aug.-Sep. 1902, box 10, fd. 12.

31. Lucy Bigelow Young to Susa Young Gates, miscellaneous correspondence, box 1, fd. 7.

32. Jacob Gates to Susa Young Gates, Feb. 1902, box 7, fd. 5.

King Edward's coronation, Susa visited Jacob's uncle Henry Bruce in Leicester, then she sailed to New York City with Francis Lyman's first wife, Rhoda Taylor Lyman. Susa finally arrived home in Provo at the end of August. Once there, if she was hoping to rest and recuperate, it was difficult to do so.

Susa came under fire for her press releases reporting the activities of the meetings in Copenhagen. Susa was often informal, personal, and conversational in her reporting of professional activities. Henni Forchhammer, president of the Danish Council of Women and nominally in charge of the meetings in Copenhagen, wrote to Susa in mid-September, "Now about your notes, I think what shocked people was partly their being so personal, we are not used to so much personality in our way of writing this side of the Atlantic and I think some did not think the tone quite dignified for a sort of official document."[33] Susa was effusive in her praise of all the women whose activities she wrote about in her press releases, but there were a couple of observations which were not appreciated. Frau Stritt, president of the German Council, was described by Susa as "a most devoted Council worker … beautiful, graceful and young," but "frank and outspoken, she tells exactly what she thinks, and whatever bitter drop there may be in her nature, it [is] always found under her tongue, never in her heart." Of Matina Kramers, corresponding secretary of the Dutch Council, Susa wrote that she is "one of the most independent young women ever produced by modern emancipation … a tender flower of deep sympathy and love" which "sends out from its hidden recess a fragrance, softening the other wise harsh outlines into a very womanly character." And in an attempt at a left-handed compliment to her Danish hostesses, Susa asked, "What about these Danish women? They are finer, apparently than their northern and southern neighbors and broader in culture."[34]

During the October 1902 general conference, a call was extended to Jacob Gates to serve as a missionary in the Eastern States Mission in a letter signed by all three members of the First Presidency. Susa received her own missionary assignment, issued five months later in March 1903. She was called to the "United States." Jacob spent his

33. Forchhammer to Gates, Sep. 1892, box 43, fd. 3.
34. Press releases, 1902, box 43, fd. 2, SYGP (CHL).

time as part of the Brooklyn Conference in New York City. However, their mission was short-lived and infelicitous, due at least in
part to Susa's health. Jacob was released in March 1903, shortly after
Susa had received her own call.

During their brief stay in New York, Susa was involved in another unpleasant imbroglio regarding the Copenhagen meetings,
this time with May Wright Sewall, president of the ICW. Susa had
represented Sewall at the meetings, and had agreed not to discuss
her background as a daughter of Brigham Young, a Utahn, or a
Mormon. Susa only reluctantly kept her word to not speak of these
things at the conference. But Sewall heard from others that Susa
had spoken at LDS meetings while in Copenhagen. Apparently
a "disturbance" had rippled through the ICW meetings as word
spread that a "Mormon woman" had "very imprudently" attended
her own worship services. Lady Ishbel Aberdeen, former president
of the ICW, wrote to Sewall that Susa's willingness to address LDS
gatherings "much disquieted many of our friends." Sewall chastised
Susa, "This opportunity abroad should in no way be used directly or
indirectly for the promulgation of your religious opinions," and she
reminded Susa, "You were going for the Council and the Council
only." Sewall even counseled Susa to leave Mormonism to "emerge
into a whiter light."

Susa vehemently defended herself in a twelve-page typewritten
letter. For the first time she spoke about the seriousness of her health
problems, saying that "my illness, far from being feigned, was of the
most violent and dangerous character," requiring eleven days of morphine for "screaming agony." She had been, she insisted, "near the
death portal." Susa had waited until after the conference to speak at
any church meetings and she had kept her promise not to bring up her
faith at the conference itself. Susa fell back on some of the same argu-
ments she had mustered before in her defense: that other LDS women
wondered why Susa bothered with the NCW and the ICW at all,
given the shabby treatment many Mormon women felt they received
from the groups. It was only at Sewall's urging, Susa wrote, that she
continued with the women's conferences instead of doing "the work
which seems as important and far more agreeable in my own Church
and in defense of its interests." Susa, who to others blamed her illness

on her diet, now told Sewall that "it was the nervous strain caused by this pressure" of the ICW that caused her ailments. Finally, Susa responded to Sewall's call to leave the church with a little preaching of her own: "I sometimes feel a longing for the time when your great soul can see the Truth in all its glory and significance."[35]

Two months later, this conflict was rekindled when Susa missed the meeting of the executive committee of the ICW in New Orleans. Susa's absence was such a disappointment for May Sewall that, when she wrote to Susa, she alluded to the subservience of LDS women: "I cannot excuse your absence, even although your idea of wifely obediance demanded it." Susa's absence from the meeting was not the only problem, however. She had issued press releases about the meeting in New Orleans, and she had made references to the National Association of Colored Women (NACW), which was a member of the National Council of Women. Sharp-eyed segregationists had omitted these references from newspapers in New Orleans, but they appeared in newspapers in Cincinnati. From there they spread "like wildfire," according to Sewall, and caused considerable controversy. Sewall abandoned all pretense and, despite her previously cordial relationship with Susa, made her feelings known. She said that the three largest threats to the International Council of Women were "colored" women's leagues, LDS Relief Societies, and the LDS Young Ladies' Mutual Improvement Association. In short, Mormon women and black women, while not forbidden entirely from the councils, were not welcome.[36]

The final blow came when the new president of the NCW, Mary Wood Swift, refused to communicate with Susa. Susa realized she had been cut off from the officers of the council, and so she resigned as head of the press committee. Sewall, who was no doubt relieved, placated Susa by insisting that she "did right" to appoint Susa to represent her in Copenhagen, despite the fallout from Susa attending LDS meetings. Sewall concluded that "your impulsiveness is the only thing which I ever fear."[37]

---

35. Susa's conflict with Sewall is detailed in their correspondence, Jan. 1903, box 43, fd. 5.

36. Sewall to Gates, Apr. 4, 1903, box 43, fd. 7.

37. Sewall to Gates, May 1903, box 43, fd. 8.

After nearly constant travel and a serious health crisis, Susa was back in Utah in April 1903. Both she and Jacob had been released from their mission. Jacob remembered his time in New York as filled with "pain and distress of some sort." In addition to Susa's health problems, Jacob was likely worried about finances. While Susa settled in Salt Lake City, he returned to Provo, where he lived in his store to save money. Susa wrote that he was "worried over his unsettled business conditions." Jacob would say that he was "rich in the affection of my family, if not in the things of this world."[38]

As soon as she returned to Utah, Susa decided that she no longer wanted to live in Provo. Perhaps spurred by her blessing while in England, she decided she wanted to "work in the Temple; and I don't want to live in Provo any more." She gave Jacob multiple reasons for moving: a desire to live near her mother and sister Mabel in Salt Lake City; availability of a temple, which was becoming increasingly important to her; and fatigue with having "to run back and forth" between Provo and Salt Lake City, sometimes several times a week. She promised, "I will get well if you will let me have something to live for," referring to a home in Salt Lake City. She proposed building "a little place down here on my lot."[39]

Jacob sold the family home in Provo for $2,500. Susa reminisced about the "dear, beloved, uncomfortable old home," but seemed to suffer no recriminations in leaving. With Jacob still living in Provo and Susa's precarious health, the new house would not be built until the next year. Susa was impatient to begin construction, but did confess to "my own precipitate, impulsive nature," contrasting it with Jacob's "sound slow judgement and prudence." She agreed to the year-long delay with the proviso to Jacob that "you pay your tithing, and God will impress you to do just the right thing."[40]

Susa decided to go to Logan to stay with her daughter Leah and son-in-law John Widtsoe. There she would begin to recuperate and regain her health. "Leah waits on me hand and foot," aided by "my good nurse Cecil."[41] Summer 1903 was a difficult one for the Gates

---

38. Jacob Gates to Susa Young Gates, various letters, box 7, fds. 9, 13.
39. Susa Young Gates to Jacob Gates, Apr. 20, 1903, box 10, fd. 14.
40. Gates to Gates.
41. Susa Young Gates to Jacob Gates, June 1903, box 7, fd. 10.

family. Susa put part of the problems to Jacob succinctly: "I realize that you are in debt and that my health is poor." But in addition to those challenges, and the stress of building a new home, their children added to their stress. Jacob and Susa's second-oldest son, Harvey ("Hal"), had some behavior problems, and returned to Provo where he lived with a family named Shelton. Hal, age fourteen, was not paying for his room or board, and apparently John Widtsoe disapproved. Susa wrote to Jacob in Provo that "John's sharp and satirical allusions to our family affairs and government are very trying to me."[42] Frank, who had just turned ten years old, had been living with four different families in Provo.

While in Logan, Susa often went to the temple in the morning and rested in the afternoon. She wrote to Jacob, "The Temple work is the greatest work for the Latter-Day Saints to do, only we dont realize it." Contemporary sources suggest Susa was ill for most of 1902 through 1904. It is obvious from Susa's own observations that menopausal symptoms constituted a large part of her poor health, but not all. She described no emotional or mental problems, which would tend to indicate that a "nervous breakdown" probably did not occur. Multiple observations indicate varying symptoms and states of well-being: feeling a little stronger; constipation, exacerbated by hemorrhoids; lack of strength to write; remaining in bed; not getting out of bed much; feeling much stronger; a lack of "nervous force" in bed most of the time for up to two weeks at a time; certainly reaching the change of life; pain in the pit of her stomach; a week lying in bed with stomach trouble; yellow eyes and skin; pain in the uterus with activity; erysipelas; and dizziness.[43] Her weight varied between 126 to 137 pounds. Jacob advised his wife that her job was to get well, and Susa replied that he would have to "leave this question of diet to the Lord and me."

Susa did not always appear acutely ill. She wrote from Logan that people who did not know her were often unaware that she was sick. Susa relied heavily on her faith throughout her convalescence. Blessings of healing from church members were an important factor in Susa's life, and she received several from many people, including

---

42. Gates to Gates, box 10, fd. 14.
43. Gates to Gates.

Elder J. Golden Kimball of the Seventy; the "Temple sisters," who washed and anointed her; her brother-in-law William Dougall; and John Smith, Patriarch to the Church.

In fall 1903, Susa returned to Salt Lake City. By mid-February 1904, she felt well enough to attend Elizabeth McCune's "grand party" in the McCune "palace." She told Jacob, "Everyone was so kind to me, from President [Joseph F.] Smith to the last ones there, and seemed so pleased to see me once more in society. Its (sic) over a year since I spent a social evening."[44] She was also passing the time by working on Gates family records for temple work. She warned Jacob, "There is a tremendous work for you to do in the Temple, my love. And I feel that your father is urging me on to do what I can and stir you folks up to do all you can."[45] In April Susa attended all sessions of general conference, the first time she had done so in two years.

Jacob kept busy with a second-edition translation into Hawai'ian of the Book of Mormon, which he began in 1903 under the direction of the First Presidency. The first edition of the Book of Mormon in Hawai'ian was translated from 1851 to 1853 by George Q. Cannon, with the help of native Hawai'ian Ionatana Napela. Jacob was thrilled by the work, and he "can hardly take time to eat or sleep, he enjoys it so much."[46]

By June 1904 Susa felt like she was largely back to her normal state of health. She wrote to May Sewall, "I am able now to attend to some work." Later in the year Sewall received word from Mary Burke East, former council secretary who had visited Susa, that Susa is "perfectly well," looking "as young as a girl."[47] East reported that Susa had moved into a beautiful new home in Salt Lake City. This was the home, located at 226 West 600 North,[48] which Jacob had promised to build for her. Sewall was anxious to know about Susa's interest in the council. Susa returned to work as chair of the Press Committee of the NCW.

Susa's decision to return to the NCW was remarkable, given recent events. The Reed Smoot hearings in Washington, DC, had

44. Gates to Gates, Feb. 13, 1904, box 10, fd. 15.
45. Jacob's father died in 1892.
46. Susa Young Gates to Cecil Gates, Apr. 1904, box 24, fd. 12.
47. Gates to Sewall; Sewall to Gates, various correspondence, box 43, fd. 9.
48. Today 700 North.

rekindled anti-Mormon sentiment, especially around polygamy, and people across the country could follow the conflict in newspapers in every state. Smoot, an apostle, had been selected by the Utah State Legislature as a US senator.[49] He had lived in Provo and was a life-long friend of Susa. Smoot was not a polygamist himself, but his election was challenged by senators who believed Smoot's loyalty as an LDS apostle would be to his church first, his country second. US senators and congressmen have the power granted to choose not to seat members; the House of Representatives had refused to seat B. H. Roberts, a polygamist, in 1898.[50] Now hearings in Washington were held to determine if Smoot should be granted his seat; they would drag on for three years before Smoot, unlike Roberts, was allowed his office.

In large part because of the attention of the Smoot hearings, May Sewall had written to Susa earlier that, because of the volume of inquiries she fielded on the participation of LDS women's groups in the NCW and ICW, she felt the "absolute necessity to express my views publicly on Mormonism." Resolutions to exclude Mormon women from both councils had been recommended. Sewall said she would have consulted Susa before making any statement, had Susa's health been better.

Sewall answered several questions that she had been most frequently asked: How can she associate with Mormons, and what effect will they have on the NCW? Sewall's answers were remarkably even-handed, although not necessarily partisan to Mormon interests. Mormon women, she said, came into the council not as Mormons, but as "representatives of educational and philanthropic societies." She also explained that questions about the moral worthiness of any member of the councils should be treated as individuals and not because they were members of a specific church. Sewall had visited Utah in 1901, and she answered charges of immorality among the Mormons by explaining that she was amazed at the "Puritanic forms which prevailed in family and societal life" there. She then paid tribute to Mormon women and said, that as far as she was concerned,

49. Until the passage of the seventeenth amendment to the US Constitution in 1913, US senators were selected by state legislators, not directly by voters.
50. Bitton, "B. H. Roberts Case"; Sillito, *B. H. Roberts*.

her Mormon friends were observing the laws of the land regarding plural marriage and had declared "their belief that this [polygamy] was a system justified for a period for a distinct purpose."[51]

In 1905, with her health restored, Susa resumed her frenetic pace of life. Just as she did so, she faced another loss. On February 3, 1905, her mother, Lucy Bigelow Young, died in Salt Lake City at age seventy-four. She had spent time in Germany as the president of the Relief Society of the German Mission, then had returned home to America with her granddaughter Emma Lucy Gates in 1901. She lived with Susa's younger sister Mabel in Salt Lake City but, because of Lucy's "rheumatism" and her oldest daughter Dora's insistence, had spent the winter of 1904 in Pasadena, California, with Dora and her children, Harold and May. Confined to a wheelchair, Lucy found comfort in planning a new home at 709 North First West in Salt Lake City, near Mabel's home, and just around the corner from Susa and Jacob's new house. Lucy moved into her new home in December 1904, but she succumbed to pneumonia just a few weeks later, surrounded by all three of her daughters.

Lucy had written a note to Professor Haag, president of the Berlin Conference of the church, several years earlier with paeans of praise regarding her husband, Brigham, who had predeceased her by twenty-eight years. She wrote, "I know of no words in which to express my conception of his character as a husband and father. However, if I could have for a few short moments the pen of the most talented author or the tongue of an angel I would proclaim my estimate of him in letters of gold to all the world. In this particular, as in all others, he excelled all men. He was never commanding or authorative. He was gentle as a lamb with his wives and family. Loving and inoffensive as an angel."[52]

Susa wrote in the manuscript of Lucy Young's biography that, shortly before Brigham's death, he had talked to her about Lucy. "Daughter, your Mother never gave me a cross word in all her life, nor ever refused to take my counsel."[53] Speakers at the funeral included Arnold H. Schulthess of the German Mission; Dr. Romania

---

51. Sewall to Gates, box 43, fd. 9.
52. Gates, "Lucy Bigelow Young," 239.
53. Gates.

B. Penrose; Maud May Babcock; and Joseph F. Smith. Smith spoke
about the work of departed Saints in preaching the gospel in the
spirit world, words reminiscent of feelings he obviously carried for
many years and which were eventually canonized as official LDS
scripture in the Doctrine and Covenants Section 138.

Shortly after her mother's passing, Susa turned her attention to
the ongoing Smoot hearings, where two of her close friends, Smoot
himself and church president Joseph F. Smith, were being excoriated
in the national press. Smith had testified before Congress for three
days in March 1904. Because some evidence emerged during the
hearings that plural marriages had continued after the 1890 Woodruff Manifesto, Smith issued the Second Manifesto, which forbade
any additional plural marriages, including those performed in other
countries, such as Mexico and Canada, and threatened excommuni-
cation for church members who disobeyed.[54]

Susa defended her friends and her faith in a scathing editorial
published in the *New York Sun* and reprinted in the *Deseret News*.[55]
She argued that the LDS version of polygamy was vastly superior
to the de facto polygamy practiced by many non-Mormons who
strayed from their marriage vows into adulterous relationships. She
decried the slander, vilification, and ridicule heaped upon Joseph F.
Smith in the press. Smith had married five wives before the Manifesto and had fathered eleven more children after the issuance of the
1890 Manifesto. Susa called his life "an open book, into which God,
angels and men may look without shame or regret." He had always
exhibited the "deepest integrity" and the "highest morality" and had
simply done what he thought was right, for which he had been un-
justly "disgraced, dishonored and destroyed." Susa also detailed the
history of Mormon persecution, which had led to the deaths of both
Smith's father and uncle, Hyrum and Joseph Smith, in 1844. Ad-
dressing herself primarily to women and ministers, Susa asked, "Will
the American people be content forever to accept the statement of
our enemies about us?" Why do those people who feel the Mormons
are misguided "not come with outstretched, merciful hands, instead

54. For more on the Smoot hearings, see Flake, *Politics of American Religious Identity*, and Paulos, *Mormon Church on Trial*.
55. *New York Sun*, Mar. 30, 1905; *Deseret News*, Apr. 6, 1905.

of piercing the soul with ridicule and oppressing the heart with scorn and hatred?" If Mormons are misguided, the way to combat the error is with "generosity and frank, brotherly dealing ... [which] are the weapons which ever disarm error and destroy impostures." It was vintage Susa, and she continued by bearing testimony of the divinity of the mission of Joseph Smith, the existence of spiritual gifts within the Church, and of her acceptance of and support for Joseph F. Smith as the spokesman for God on the earth. She concluded, "Do not fan the flames of prejudice against us until murder and mobocracy again stalk abroad in our midst. ... I cannot be silent when the voice of the assassin is heard in the land."

In June 1905 Susa became the fourth president of the Daughters of the Utah Pioneers, a position she held for three years. The group had been organized four years earlier to preserve the history of the pioneers of the State of Deseret and Utah Territory and their descendants. Membership was open to women over the age of eighteen who had immigrated to Utah Territory between July 24, 1847—the date of the entry of the first pioneers into the Salt Lake Valley—and May 10, 1869—the completion of the transcontinental railroad. The descendants of these women, naturally born or legally adopted, were also invited to join. Susa, always interested in history, was especially invested in the preservation of relics, particularly those relating to Joseph Smith and Brigham Young. She managed to obtain for the society a small room as an office in the old *Deseret News* building, as well as a room just north of the parlor in the Lion House, for a relic exhibition.[56]

Susa's health had improved so much that she began to travel again. Jacob had gone to Mexico on a business trip for several weeks in May, and Susa accompanied Emma Lucy to Portland, Oregon, in August to sing at a concert at the Lewis and Clark Exposition, celebrating the centennial of the Lewis and Clark Expedition. While there, they were introduced to the private secretary of Anthony Bailey, partner of the Barnum and Bailey Circus, who gave them a tour and explained the inner workings of the circus.[57] Emma Lucy had been asked to give a benefit concert at Brigham Young University,

---

56. Daughters of Utah Pioneers, box 37, fd. 15, SYGP (CHL).
57. Susa Young Gates to Jacob Gates, Aug. 23, 1905, box 11, fd. 1.

but the family had to decline. They explained that Emma Lucy had four benefactors, who were not identified, who had been helping to underwrite her continued musical studies, and she was not at liberty to determine her own concert schedule.[58]

Because of staffing shortages at the *Young Woman's Journal*, Susa agreed to write several editorials and articles in 1905. One of her articles, "The Open Door for Woman," related the history of the organization of the Relief Society in Nauvoo, Illinois, by Joseph Smith, whose first wife, Emma, was made first president of the new society.[59] Unlike other early members of the Relief Society, including Eliza R. Snow and Elizabeth Ann Whitney, Emma Smith never joined with Brigham Young and never traveled west to Utah. Instead, she remained in Nauvoo, married non-Mormon Lewis Bidamon, and eventually joined the Reorganized Church of Jesus Christ of Latter Day Saints, with her son, Joseph Smith III, as its leader.[60] Susa, not surprisingly as a daughter of Brigham Young, was critical of Emma.

She criticized Emma three times throughout the article: "Ah, that she had always remained true to her calling and election"; "And [Joseph] was yet to find that even some of these women, and the woman he loved best on earth among them, would shrink, falter and betray, when the crucial test of the highest principle in the gospel was applied to their weak, trembling hearts"; and finally, "But there came a time, not long before his [Joseph's] death, when [Emma] opposed him and finally helped to betray him. We do not judge, we only pity and pray." However, several years later, Susa wrote of "the unusual strength and brilliancy of ... Emma Hale Smith."[61]

It is perhaps easy to see why Susa might not have been sympathetic to Emma. Emma had not accepted the leadership of Brigham Young as her husband's successor. In fact, Emma and Brigham clashed over several issues, shortly after Joseph Smith's death. Susa was hardly the only LDS writer to criticize Emma, who was often seen as a traitor who had betrayed her husband, first by refusing to travel west, then by marrying outside of the faith, and finally by

58. Susa Young Gates to George Brimhall, Sep. 22, 1905, box 35, fd. 4.

59. Gates, "Open Door for Woman," *Young Woman's Journal*, Mar. 1905, 116.

60. Today the church is called the Community of Christ. I use Reorganized or RLDS for the church, since that was its name throughout Susa's lifetime.

61. Gates, *History of YLMIA*, 26.

denying that her husband ever practiced polygamy. But historians have since been kinder to Emma, who now has a much more exalted reputation than she did during Susa's lifetime. Emma had undergone incredible hardships and deprivation, including the death of her thirty-eight-year-old husband at the hands of a mob when she was pregnant with their eleventh child. Six other children of Joseph and Emma had previously died at birth or in infancy. Their marriage had also been strained by the introduction of polygamy.[62]

Soon after the recovery of her health, Susa wrote to Susan B. Anthony, long-standing president of the National American Woman Suffrage Association, and asked her to contribute to or endorse a book she was working on. Susa's request does not survive, but two angry responses from Anthony do. Anthony fired off a letter to Susa saying she had read together with the Reverend Anna Howard Shaw the "preface and introduction" of Susa's work and did not want her name "on any part of your book." Anthony must have read the letter a second time and forgotten that she had already responded, since she wrote again to Susa a few months later to say she had just come across Susa's letter of July 18, 1905. She lambasted Susa, "Now you, with others, never seem to discover the difference between endorsing a movement and its affiliation with the National Council. ... When you come to say that polygamy is endorsed or required by the religious faith of a people, that is going too far and making it too respectable." Years later, Susa noted in the margin of the letter, "Miss Anthony's last painful letter to me."[63]

That winter, Susa was invited to celebrate the 100th anniversary of Joseph Smith's birth. Thirty people traveled by invitation of the First Presidency to Sharon, Vermont, for the unveiling of the obelisk monument and the dedicatory services. Two of the three members of the First Presidency attended (Joseph F. Smith and Anthon H. Lund), as well as five apostles (Francis M. Lyman, John Henry Smith, Hyrum M. Smith, George A. Smith, and Charles Penrose), and George F. Richards, who was ordained an apostle a few months after the celebration. Susa was one of five women in the group, along with three Smiths: Julina C., wife of Joseph F. Smith; Ida B., wife of

---

62. For more on Emma Smith, see Newell and Avery, *Mormon Enigma*.

63. Anthony to Gates, Aug. 23 and Dec. 21, 1905, box 43, fd. 9.

Hyrum M. Smith; and Edith A., daughter of Joseph Smith's cousin, Elias A. Smith, who was also one of the attendees. The fifth woman was Alice Richards, wife of George F., who brought her infant son, Oliver L. Richards. Emma Lucy was present for the ceremony and sang a solo, *O Ye Mountains High*. Annual festivities commemorating the "Vermont Party" were celebrated at the Lion House in Salt Lake City until at least December 1908.[64]

On Sunday, March 18, 1906, just three months after Susa's trip to Vermont, a party took place at the Lion House to celebrate two events, Susa's 50th birthday and the 50th anniversary of the completion of the Lion House. The invitations reminded the prominent invitees that Susa had been the first child born there. No gifts were allowed.[65]

Susa also joined the newly formed Civic Improvement League to "work together on social, cultural and environmental matters" affecting Salt Lake City.[66] Committee members battled for increased paving to alleviate muddy streets and lobbied for changes in sewer ordinances to allow for more pipe to be laid. They encouraged the legislature to pass a bill, which it did in 1911, creating "a new nonpartisan city commission." The commission represented a broad-based group from both political parties. Besides Susa, a staunch Republican, multiple prominent citizens of Salt Lake City were part of the group, including William H. King, former Democratic congressman; Orlando W. Powers, a former Democratic federal judge; Episcopalian Bishop Franklin S. Spalding, an outspoken critic of the LDS Church; Frank B. Stephens, former city attorney; and Nephi L. Morris, president of the Salt Lake Stake and Republican businessman.

A year later in April 1907, Horace H. Cummings, General Superintendent of Latter-day Saint Schools, wrote to Susa. He asked her to chair a committee to oversee new instructions for the use of "matrons/lady superintendents" to aid the girls in church schools. Other committee members included Alice Reynolds (Provo), Zina Y. Card (Salt Lake City), Sarah T. Evans (Ogden), and Johannah Moen (Logan).[67] Just five months later the committee submitted its

---

64. Lion House Vermont party, box 3, fd. 18, SYGP (CHL).
65. Fiftieth birthday celebration, box 3, fd. 27, SYGP (CHL).
66. The league was formed in March 1906. Alexander, *Utah*, 286.
67. Cummings to Gates, Apr. 23, 1907, box 58, fd. 5.

report, "Church School Guidelines for Young Women," with lessons
outlined for the first year:

Special Regulations for Student Life
Rules of Behavior
The Gospel of Work for Girls
Hygiene of Dress
Underwear and Footwear
Personal Cleanliness
Modesty
Care of the Body
Nervous Disorders
Special Health of Girlhood
Ideal Girlhood[68]

In 1907 both sons Cecil and Harvey were called as missionaries,
Cecil to the Eastern States, headquartered in New York City, and
Harvey to the Northwestern States in Portland, Oregon. This further
stretched family finances, and Susa wrote, "You dont know how close
Papa is ... for money. We must not spend one cent we dont have to."[69]

Other biographers and family members have asked: Was the
Gates family poor? Granddaughter Lurene said that growing up, she
did not perceive any significant deprivation in the family. Her grandparents had a comfortable home in Salt Lake City, and Susa spent
most of her summers in their cottage in Brighton Canyon.[70] Jacob
and Susa often found themselves under multiple economic pressures.
They sent Leah to New York to study at the Pratt Institute, and they
provided for the musical education in both the United States and
Europe for Emma Lucy and Cecil. They supported Cecil on his mission and Harvey on two separate missions. Jacob and Susa also sent
monthly checks to support their son Franklin and his young bride,
Florence, on their mission as newlyweds in Hawai'i (1913–15).

Jacob was frequently behind in his payment of tithing, and there
are several warnings from Susa to Jacob to bring his tithing up to
date. Susa probably summed up their financial situation best when
she wrote, "I have thanked the Lord on my knees more than once

68. Circular letter to church school matrons, box 35, fd. 4, SYGP (CHL).
69. Susa Young Gates to Cecil Gates, July 18, 1907, box 11, fd. 1.
70. Lurene Gates Wilkinson, personal communication with the author, Feb. 2009.

that he had kept my husband and our family comparatively poor, and that we have all learned the good discipline of struggle, deprivation, hard work, and rigid self-denial."[71] The family was not destitute, and both Susa and Jacob were always hard at work, but they were by no means well-off.

In Portland, Harvey, who had frequently caused concerns for his parents, had a run-in with Ellen Jakeman, whom Susa had clashed with during Jakeman's brief tenure as *Young Woman's Journal* business manager.[72] The exact nature of Harvey's conflict with Jakeman is not clear, but it only added to his parent's concerns. Harvey had also fallen in love on his mission.[73] Susa, who was "very deeply engaged in my writing" at the family summer home in Brighton, Utah, asked Jacob to write Harvey and have him confide in his mission president about the romance. Susa opined, "It is his [Harvey's] moral duty to either drop all his love-notions or to have the approval of his presiding officer." Furthermore, Susa, ever the Republican, felt that Harvey should "not to go too far in announcing himself as a Democrat. He may become quite a power at home politically and there is no sense in his being on the wrong side of the question." Susa had high expectations for Harvey because of his "brilliant gifts."[74]

Susa's frustration toward Harvey did not extend to Cecil. Perhaps it was the thrill of being able to visit Cecil on his mission, or perhaps Cecil had caused less trouble, but Susa extolled her "precious, noble eldest son." She was in Camden, New Jersey, visiting Cecil, when she wrote to Jacob that Cecil had lost his stutter and become "a manly, modest, pure, lovely man!" with "gifts and charms that gladden his mother's heart."[75]

In June 1908 the Gateses hosted an evening with Senator Reed Smoot at their home.[76] About this time, Susa had her feelings deeply hurt. The cause is not clear. Emmeline B. Wells wrote to Susa,

71. Gates, *Why I Believe*, 20.
72. See chapter ten.
73. Missionaries in the early 1900s had different rules and expectations, and while Harvey's romance would not have been encouraged, it was not considered taboo as it would be today.
74. Susa Young Gates to Jacob Gates, various letters, Aug. 1908, box 11, fd. 1.
75. Gates to Gates.
76. David O. McKay, a new apostle and future ninth president of the church, sent regrets, box 58, fd. 6.

thanking her for the Smoot soiree and indicating that she knew of Susa's bruised feelings. Wells hoped that she was not the cause and offered to help Susa in any way she could. She told Susa, "There are few women in the world as capable of doing things as *yourself*—and you must not lose faith in your ability to do—because there will be more and more that will need doing" (emphasis in original).[77] Emmeline and Susa had crossed paths many times over the years. However, in public they usually surfeited one another with praise.[78] Wells once wrote of Susa: "An admirer of Mrs. Gates has said of her, 'That one of the striking elements of true greatness in this gifted woman's character, is the rare quality of a sincere appreciation, and marvellous generosity, towards others pursuing the same lines of study or activity, and who might be counted rivals. This exceptional attribute adds a potent charm to her personality and bears the stamp of true nobility of soul.'"[79] Susa responded in kind, later saying of Emmeline, "She was the incarnate figure of tender, delicate, eternally determined womanhood, arrived and triumphant."[80]

In 1908 Susa and Lucy O. Clark of Brigham City, Utah, were named as alternate delegates to the Republican National Convention in Chicago. Susa's status as an alternate delegate was duly noted in the press, including *Leslies Weekly* and a Chicago newspaper that Susa clipped and saved.[81] It is not hard to see why Susa was amused by the article. Published under the headline "Cramming It Down," the paper expressed hope that the delegate for whom Susa was alternate would allow her to sit in his place, at least a part of the time during the convention, because of "novelty" and "gallantry." Susa acting as a delegate would "vindicate in a way Brigham Young's fierce claim that he would 'cram polygamy down the throats of the American people.'"

A few years previously, Susa had been appointed by Utah Governor John Cutler to the nine-member board of trustees at the

---

77. Wells to Gates, June 15, 1908, box 58, fd. 6.

78. Susa and Emmeline B. Wells's sometimes-contentious relationship is outlined in Madsen, *Emmeline B. Wells*, 284–85, 396, 398, 454–55, and 469–70.

79. From transcript on *Young Woman's Journal* stationery, in box 1, fd. 10, SYGP (CHL).

80. Gates, "Utah." See also Madsen, *Emmeline B. Wells*, 488.

81. *Leslies Weekly*, June 25, 1908, and "Cramming it Down," undated clipping, both in box 1, fd. 9, SYGP (CHL).

Agricultural College of Utah in Logan, where her son-in-law, John
A Widtsoe, was on the faculty. Susa also served on the three-mem-
ber committee on Domestic Science and Arts with her close friend,
Elizabeth McCune, and John Dern. She was appointed to a second
term in 1909, but resigned in April 1911, citing "home cares" and
"public responsibilities."[82]

In February 1909, Widtsoe, now president of the college, asked
his mother-in-law for her help in getting a bill passed by the state
legislature to fund a new building for women, since existing facili-
ties were inadequate. Much of Susa's work in 1909 was directed at
improving the college for women. She wrote to officials of multiple
universities throughout the country, asking: (1) Do you have formal
classes in ethics for female students? (2) What provisions do you
have for supervision of female students? The president of Delaware
College in Newark, Delaware, replied that since their institution
does not admit girls, "we are not bothered with the necessity of having a Dean or Matron to look after them."[83]

In May and June 1909 Susa and her friend Elizabeth McCune
undertook a four-week trip to the Midwest and East to visit insti-
tutions of higher learning "for the purpose of gathering information
that will enable this Institution to build and improve the School of
Domestic Science and Arts which forms an important part of the
work done by the Agricultural College of Utah." They traveled to
Lincoln, Chicago, Evanston, Boston, New York City, Philadelphia,
and Washington, DC.[84]

In the capital, through the auspices of Reed Smoot, they observed
experiments being conducted in the laboratories of the US Department of Agriculture. The trip, although productive, was tiring, and
Susa lamented in a letter home to Jacob, on June 7, "Home is the
sweetest and dearest place on this earth, and you are the very sweetest and dearest husband on earth. I never realized how much I would
miss you." After two decades of frequent travel, she lamented to her
husband that "travel and theaters and dinners have all become very
wearisome to me." While she was away, her first novel, *John Stevens'*

82. Gates to Governor Spry et al., Apr. 8, 1911, box 34, fd. 4.
83. George A. Harter to Susa Young Gates, Mar. 23, 1909, box 34, fd. 6.
84. Widtsoe, general letter, May 19, 1909, box 34, fd. 6.

Courtship, was about to be published, so she urged Jacob to call and find out how things were going with the printing.[85]

In Philadelphia Susa was able to visit her son Cecil in Camden, New Jersey, on his mission. Susa had to cover her own expenses for part of the trip, but the agricultural college allotted her and Elizabeth $600 for reimbursement, provided they kept a strict accounting of all expenditures. After the trip Susa dutifully submitted a four-page itemization of expenses, including 25 and 30 cents for porters to carry their luggage. Just above her signature, Susa penned, "No more trips where one has to keep itemized accounts, thank you."[86] Back home, Susa immediately went to the Gates family cabin in Brighton, in the mountain east of Salt Lake City, to rest and relax. This was Susa's precious retreat, where she spent most of her summers beginning in the late 1890s. Typical of her feelings about Brighton, she had written previously to Jacob, "This is the first time for months that I have felt the strain lifted, and my mind ready to relax."[87]

Susa's work on behalf of the Agricultural College was successful, and when she resigned from the board two years later, the student newspaper remembered that during her tenure "far-reaching changes" were made in which she took "an active and prominent part." She rendered "invaluable service," while at the same time "the interests of students and faculty" were safeguarded. "Her best efforts" were in the School of Home Economics, where Susa's "main business" was obtaining appropriations for a new "Woman's Building," considered to be the "most satisfactory and up-to-date building for the teaching of the science of homemaking in the western country." Susa also insisted that a women's gymnasium be included in the new building.[88]

Susa was juggling multiple responsibilities, and in late 1909 she made another trip, this time to Arizona as a member of the general board of the Young Women's MIA. Susa was well-known as a captivating public speaker. In one of the MIA meetings in stake conference in Thatcher, Arizona, she asked for a show of hands how

85. Gates to Gates, June 7, 9, 1909, box 11, fd. 1. For more on Susa's writing, see chapter twelve, herein.
86. McCune and Gates, Expenses, box 34, fd. 5, SYGP (CHL).
87. Gates to Gates, box 11, fd. 1.
88. *Student Life*, Senior Class Issue, Apr. 21, 1911, 1 (published by the students of the Utah Agricultural College).

many people in the congregation of approximately 1,000 had ever read the Holy Bible cover to cover. In the congregation was fourteen-year-old Spencer W. Kimball, son of stake president Andrew Kimball and future twelfth president of the church. Spencer reported that only five or six people raised their hands. Susa encouraged her listeners to remedy the oversight, and Spencer later wrote as LDS Church president, "I was shocked into an unalterable determination to read that great book." That evening he trudged home, took the family Bible, climbed the stairs to his room in the attic, and, by the light of a kerosene lamp, started at Genesis. He read faithfully every day, and one year later, he completed both testaments. "For more than half of a century now I have continued to be grateful to Sister Gates for the inspiration that provoked me to read the Holy Bible my first time."[89]

89. Kimball, "Reading, a Sacred Privilege," *The Friend*, Nov. 1978.

Novels, Poetry, and Short Stories

No matter how busy she became, Susa was always writing. She would write late into the night by candlelight while with her husband on a mission in Hawai'i. Later, when electricity came to Salt Lake City and the Gateses home was wired, she continued to write. She would spend summers up Big Cottonwood Canyon in the mountains at the family cabin in Brighton, writing there.

Susa published countless stories, editorials, and essays, almost always in LDS-themed periodicals, though a few essays and editorials appeared in national publications. Her first novel, *John Stevens' Courtship*, was published in book-form in 1909. It was among the first published novels written by a Mormon woman. The story was initially published as a serial in *The Contributor* in 1895 and 1896.[1]

W. J. Lewis, who worked for the Deseret News bookstore, which published *John Stevens' Courtship*, wrote to Susa on June 23, 1909, amending the previous printing contract. Three thousand copies of the book would be printed for $1,170. Upon delivery of the manuscript, Susa would pay $220 to the publisher, which would be the exclusive distributor for the book. The remainder of the publishing costs would be paid for from the sale of the book, which would cost $1.00 per copy. In the preface Susa wrote that "the theme of this book" is a "story of love … to show that there is plenty of romance

---

1. Other Mormon women had also published novels, just not as printed books. Emmeline B. Wells, for example, had written the serialized *Hephzibah* in the *Woman's Exponent* in 1889.

and color in every-day life." Her "chief justification for the writing of this book" was to perpetuate memories of the pioneer days.[2]

The subtitle of the book is *A Story of the Echo Canyon War*, today known as the Utah War. Susa relied heavily on the history of the war, or at least the history that was available at the time, which she interwove with the plot. In July 1857 President James Buchanan, having heard multiple rumors of a Mormon insurrection in Utah Territory, replaced Brigham Young as territorial governor with Alfred Cumming of Georgia. Buchanan deployed an army of 2,500 American soldiers to accompany Cumming to Salt Lake City, a fact unknown to Young until messengers brought him the word that the Army was already on the move. Young dug in his heels and determined that the Army would not enter the Salt Lake Valley that year. The troops were effectively stopped at Fort Bridger in Wyoming, where they spent the winter. Lot Smith was encouraged by Young to harass the federal troops "in every way possible," including stampeding their animals and burning their supply wagons. The US army did enter the Salt Lake Valley in the spring of 1858, at which time thousands of the Saints abandoned their homes in Salt Lake City to move to Provo and points south for several months. Young brokered a deal that guaranteed the federal troops would be separated from the body of Mormons by at least twenty miles, and the bloodless conflict was resolved.[3]

It was against this backdrop that John Stevens, the eponymous hero of the novel and a trusted advisor of Brigham Young, is frequently absent on assignments given to him as one of the chief officers in the Utah militia. Two young orphan women, Diantha Winthrop and Ellen Tyler, both feel great affection for John. Diantha lives with her brother, who is also the local ward bishop, and Ellen lives with her Aunt Clara. Despite the taboo of mingling with the federal soldiers, both Diantha and Ellen meet black-hearted Captain Sherwood of the army. Diantha is able to withstand Sherwood's wiles, but Ellen grows close to him and is eventually abducted. While ensconced with Sherwood in a remote cabin, Ellen is shot and killed by jealous

---

2. Gates, *John Stevens' Courtship*, preface (hereafter cited as *Courtship*).

3. For more on the Utah War, see MacKinnon, *At Sword's Point*. The quoted line is taken from *Courtship*, 114–15.

Louisiana Liz, a prostitute who had been involved with Sherwood. When John finally tracks Ellen down, Aunt Clara sadly questions him about her: "Dead or disgraced?" to which John replies, "Both!" John then serves a two-year church mission and returns home to marry Diantha.[4]

Susa said John was a "composite" character, although his appearance with a long beard closely resembled Joseph F. Smith, whom Susa had long admired. On one of his missions, John is stopped by a pistol-waving soldier and asked if he were a "damned Mormon." John responded "Yes siree! I am a 'Mormon!' Dyed in the wool!" The soldier unexpectedly replied, "Well, you're a damned good feller."[5] This is virtually a verbatim lifting of an experience Joseph F. underwent when, at age nineteen, he was stopped by desperados in California as he was returning from his first mission to Hawai'i. In response to the question of whether he was a Mormon, he reportedly replied that he was indeed a dyed-in-the-wool Mormon, at which point the troublemaker put down his gun and let Joseph pass. Susa described Aunt Clara as a figure known to many pioneers. The character of Diantha, she said, was based on a woman yet living in the prime of her life.

It is noteworthy that Susa plotted the death of one of the two young women in the novel, instead of proposing that John could marry both of them in a polygamous relationship. Polygamy as a practice among church members was at its height during the Utah War. By 1909, when the novel was published, the church was trying hard to shed its polygamous past. Knowing this, Susa would have avoided a polygamous solution for the hero of the novel. But suffering a violent death for sexual indiscretion seems a harsh penalty for Ellen. Why did "blood atonement," a commonly held nineteenth-century LDS belief that some sins are so heinous that they can only be paid for by the death of the sinner, seem to prevail rather than repentance and forgiveness?

John Stevens' Courtship is a morality tale. Susa used the novel to move along the same agenda that she had written about during her

---

4. *Courtship*, esp. 158, 338. Liz is also identified as an "octoroon," adding a racist element to the narrative.
5. *Courtship*, 163.

eleven years as editor of the *Young Woman's Journal*. "Utah," in the novel, "is the home of beauty and goodness." It is a mountain retreat "where none can molest us, or make us afraid." Mormons have long suffered persecution and continue to do so. "What cowardly fool and lying trickster has persuaded the President of the United States to send out here the flower of the American army to subdue, or perhaps destroy, this innocent, loyal, and simple people?" Susa asked in the book. "How is it that men are so easily prejudiced against our people?" Mormons in the novel are obviously misunderstood. One army captain "expected to find a seditious and priest-ridden community," but instead encountered only "a handful of wronged and hunted religionists." The world at large fails to appreciate the charm of Mormon leaders. "Who could resist the magnetic courtesy and geniality of the 'Mormon' leader [Brigham Young] when he chose to exert it!" Nevertheless, the Saints have always been loyal to the US government. "After we came here, we planted the flag of our country upon our Ensign Peak within twenty-four hours" because "'Mormons' are a lawful and loyal people, and have ever been."[6]

A recurring theme for Susa was the importance of her New England Yankee heritage. The members of the Peace Commission sent by President Buchanan to investigate are told "that those people down there mostly of pure New England descent. ... Yankees they are, most of them." And in addition they are Puritans "from New England's wave-washed shores." God will fight the battles for his Saints. "I have heard President Young say many times since we entered the Valley that we should not have to fight any more battles, for God would fight them for us." Then the warning, "But hands off! Do not send your armed mobs into our midst. If you do, we will fight you, as the Lord lives. Do not threaten us with what the United States can do and will do, for we ask no odds of them or their troops. We have the God of Israel ... on our side; and let me tell you, gentlemen, we fear not your threats."[7]

The overarching message of *John Stevens' Courtship*, however, is the importance of premarital chastity and of marriage within the faith. Susa's John knows "that in strictest chastity only there was

6. *Courtship*, 19, 26, 75–76, 80, 95–96, 158, 182–83.
7. *Courtship*, 62, 129, 168, 183.

safety and peace for either man or woman in this life or the life to come." He says that "it is the paradox of human nature that man, who should be the protector of woman, is too often her assailant; and that the kindly virtues of a woman which make her the best of wives and mothers, too often renders her the easiest prey to a wicked man." John expresses anger "that any one should seek to entangle our girls and draw them away from the safety and purity of their own innocent happy lives." Diantha and Ellen vie throughout the novel for John's attention. Diantha warns Ellen, "And especially do I begin to see how unsafe we are associating with any man outside this church and kingdom." She believes that "married people should be mated on … three planes … the physical, the mental and the spiritual." Most important of all, "It is not right for the believer to mate with the unbeliever." In fact, "God sets a curse on those of His chosen people who marry with unbelievers."[8]

Susa's prose is often florid, forced, and over the top. The mountain camp at the beginning of the novel is "an emerald-tinted valley with a silvery lake empearled on its western rim before them, cupped in a circle of embracing hills and snow-covered crags. The summits of the eastern and western hills were crowned with pine, which here and there, like dusky sentinels, traced their lines down, down to the water's edge. That gleaming, brilliant, silent water!" An early physical description of Diantha had "her columned throat pulsat[ing] with bounding life under the snowy skin, as she moved her pretty head from side to side, while the crown of her yellow hair which was coronaded in heavy braids around and around the shapely head, broke into tiny curls on her temples and at the white nape of the neck, and was a glittering mass of spun gold in the dancing flames which heightened both color and quality of that mass of silken charm."[9]

The novel was praised within church circles. Joseph F. Smith pronounced it "entertaining and interesting."[10] Other encomiums came from general authorities Charles W. Penrose, Heber J. Grant, Jonathan G. Kimball, and Joseph W. McMurrin. George H. Brimhall lauded the "faith-promoting character of the book," and Lewis A.

---

8. *Courtship*, 87–88, 101, 137, 233, 242, 306.

9. *Courtship*, 18–19, 29.

10. Transcript of note from Joseph F. Smith, box 104, fd. 4, SYGP (CHL).

Merrill pronounced it more effective "than listening to a sermon." Emmeline B. Wells said the book "deals with facts and fiction ingeniously mingled." The novel was adopted by the boards of both the Young Men and Young Women Mutual Improvement Associations for their reading courses.[11]

Susa's second work of fiction, a historical novel called *The Prince of Ur,* appeared originally in serial form in the *Relief Society Magazine,* which Susa began to edit at its inception in 1914. There were sixteen chapters in the book, delivered in twenty-two installments, beginning in the January 1915 issue and ending in October 1916. Susa's original outline, dated June 1911, listed only nine chapters and mentioned no co-authors. *The Prince of Ur* was first issued as a book after Susa's death and listed her daughter Leah Widtsoe as coauthor.[12]

The serial edition and the book version have some minor variations, undoubtedly made by Leah. Most of these changes are small: a "light wind" becomes a "strong wind," Lot goes from Abram's "kinsman" to his "nephew." A few lines of informal discourse are rendered more formally, sometimes in King James-style English. Leah did add a handful of small paragraphs in the book edition.[13]

Abram, later known as Abraham, occupies a central place in Mormon theology because of the Abrahamic Covenant, by which the blessings of the covenant people of God are dispensed. Abram's story is recounted in the book of Genesis in the Old Testament, but has been supplemented in Mormonism by the Book of Abraham, which forms part of the Pearl of Great Price, one of four books of canonized scripture. In July 1835 Joseph Smith had purchased Egyptian mummies containing rolls of papyrus with hieroglyphics. From the papyri, Smith produced the Book of Abraham, from which Susa fashioned her novel.

Abram was born in Ur of the Chaldees to Terah, the high priest of Ur and vice-regent under the great hunter Nimrod, king of

---

11. *John Stevens' Courtship,* letters and promotional material, box 104, fd. 4, SYGP (CHL).

12. Gates and Widtsoe, *Prince of Ur.*

13. Compare Gates, "Prince of Ur," *Relief Society Magazine,* Jan. 1915-Oct. 1916, 149, 335, 365, 494, 499, to Gates and Widtsoe, *Prince of Ur,* 59, 69–70, 90–91, 107, 157, 232 (hereafter cited as *Prince*).

Babylon. At the beginning of the novel, Abram has returned to Ur after an absence of twenty years. He meets his enemy and kinsman, Mardan, who informs him that Nimrod will return soon from battle to dedicate the new ziggurat of Ur, built to the Moon-goddess. This is anathema to Abram, who believes in Jehovah as the one true God.

Beautiful Princess Sarai, also a believer in Jehovah, is at odds with her kinswoman Ischa, who worships the Assyrian goddess Ishtar. Ischa owns a black female slave, Zillah, whose husband, Azzi-Jaama, is a master sculptor described as having "the most skillful cunning in artificing brass and metal that hath been seen in all the valley of the Euphrates." He has fashioned stone and gold idols to the pagan gods under the direction of Terah, Abram's father. Abram is sick at the thought of the human sacrifices which will accompany Nimrod's dedication of the new temple of Ur. Nimrod lays claim to the priesthood, because "his father's father Ham stole the robe and the sacred garments from our forefather Noah's body."[14]

As Nimrod returned to Ur to dedicate the new temple, he "determined … that the human sacrifice to be offered up should be sufficiently large and imposing to gratify the deepest blood-lust amongst his restless, fiery-tempered soldiers." Mardan has arranged for the sacrifice of three Cushite virgins, daughters of the sculptor Azzi-Jaama, as well as their infant half-brother, son of Azzi-Jaama and Zillah, servant of Ischa.[15]

Abram introduces himself to Nimrod, who turns furious, because he thought that Terah had eliminated Abram as a threat to Nimrod years before. Nimrod thunders that Terah has deceived him and attempts to kill Terah. Abram intervenes and stops the attack. When Sarai appears before Nimrod, he is ravished by her beauty and "seized her quivering body in his huge arms," Abram intervenes again, and he has to plot a sudden flight from Ur for himself and his followers, since "[h]is own life has been forfeited by his double attack upon the person of the king." He cannot escape in time, however, and is taken prisoner by Mardan and the king's guard. Mardan is also ordered to bring Sarai that night to Nimrod.[16]

---

14. *Prince*, 73, 101, 122.
15. *Prince*, 103–04.
16. *Prince*, 123, 127.

Nimrod learns that Abram's nephew Lot is planning with the shepherds of Terah to rescue Abram that night and they plan to flee into the wilderness. Nimrod decides that if Abram does not help him with the priestly duties of sacrificing the three daughters of Azzi-Jaama, Abram himself will also be offered that evening as a human sacrifice.

The Cushite daughters of Azzi-Jaama, along with his infant son, are duly sacrificed. Zillah, seeing the hand of Mardan in these nefarious doings, kills both herself and Mardan by jumping from the tower of the ziggurat. Abram is bound on the sacrificial altar, but as Nimrod extends his hand to plunge his knife into Abram, "it was struck from behind with a darting bolt of fire." An earthquake strikes and Abram is freed from the altar. Ur stands in ruin, and the ziggurat is "a smoking pile of dust and disaster." The next morning Abram encounters Sarai with the rest of his followers, and the exodus to Haran begins. Here the story ends. Abram was renamed Abraham by Jehovah. Abraham's further adventures are left untold in Susa's novel.[17]

In addition to her novels, Susa wrote poetry, short stories, plays, editorials, essays, newspaper columns, and lyrics to music, much of which was composed by her son B. Cecil. Susa may have written as many as thirty-plus poems and forty-five short stories, though this is uncertain as Susa published in multiple journals over several decades, often with a pseudonym.[18]

R. Paul Cracroft has probably written more about Susa's poetry than any other author. Susa was not a particularly adept poet, as Cracroft noted. In fact, he said that Susa "had only a limited familiarity with poetry and poets."[19] Susa's greatest strength in her writings was her editorials, which appeared primarily in the *Young Woman's Journal* and the *Relief Society Magazine.* According to Cracroft, Susa "wrote much [poetry], but left little of merit." For this reason, he paid "only cursory attention" to her poetry in his thesis.

---

17. *Prince*, 241.

18. Richard H. Cracroft, "Susa Young Gates," in Ludlow, *Encyclopedia of Mormonism*, 3:832.

19. Cracroft, "Susa Young Gates," 64.

He felt that rhyme was so important to Susa that the message was often subverted.[20]

Susa's poetry appeared in multiple journals and magazines over a period of four decades, including the *Woman's Exponent*, the *Improvement Era*, the *Young Woman's Journal*, and the *Relief Society Magazine*. Susa's favorite poet was Alfred Lord Tennyson.[21] She wrote poems about nature, Mormon history, church doctrine, and family relationships. She often wrote poems for special social occasions. And she sometimes engaged in doggerel.

When Susa began writing poetry is open to question. A notebook from her first year as a student at Brigham Young Academy (1878–79) contains multiple poems, which she claimed were her first attempts at poetry.[22] However, in the first year of the *Young Woman's Journal* a poem appeared entitled "My Valentine," written by "Hope," a pseudonym for Susa, which is dated February 14, 1872.[23]

Susa sent poems to several grieving mothers whose young children had died. Her friend Mary Schwartz Smith, a polygamous wife of church president Joseph F. Smith, had lost a son. Susa wrote for her, "From a Mother to Her Babes":

Thou camest to my lonely heart
Like dew to thirsty flower.
With silver glistened every cloud,
Through baby's matchless power.
Oh, must thou leave me dearest one
And in the grave lie sleeping?
Behold my heart with anguish torn
My soul is faint with weeping.
God speaks! I hear! My angel boy
Go back when thou wast given.
You hold within those tiny hands
A chain from me to Heaven.
Oh hear me, bear me Father God

---

20. Cracroft, 63–67.

21. Gates, "Tennyson and the Life Beyond," *Relief Society Magazine*, Oct. 1920, 610–11.

22. Brigham Young Academy rhymes, box 99, fd. 27, SYGP (CHL).

23. Hope [Susa Young Gates], "My Valentine," *Young Woman's Journal*, Feb. 1890, 137.

Upon thy tender Bosom!
Let angels guard with gentle care
My John, my earthly blossom.[24]

Susa and Jacob worried about son Hal during his entire adult life.
In 1914 Susa wrote a tender poem entitled "Hymn of the Mothers
of Men":

For our recreant sons we pray, O Lord,
For our sons who will not pray.
Who scorn their mother's teachings, Lord,
And shame thee day by day.
For our wastrel sons we cry, O Lord,
For our sons who will not cry.
For they serve the god of their appetites, Lord,
And they love and believe a lie.
Be merciful unto them, we pray—
We the mothers of men.
For our reckless sons we plead, O Lord,
For our sons who will not heed,
They choose to walk in the darkness, Lord,
For thy cross they see no need.
But these are thy sheep on the hillside, Lord,
They're lost and cold and numb—
And the storms and darkened gloom, dear Lord—
Have beaten them silent and dumb.
Be merciful unto them, we pray—
We, the mothers of men.
These are thy sheep—go forth, O Lord,
For the saved are folded well.
But our sons on the hillside need thee, Lord
Lest they fall into deepest hell.
Reach out thine arm to these erring ones,
Strike close, while they still have youth—
With the quivering shame of repentance, smite
Their souls with the sword of Truth.
Be merciful unto them, we pray—
We, the mothers of men.
Into the silence and gloom we peer,

---

24. In autobiographical sketches, box 3, fd. 35, SYGP (CHL).

(We are the mothers of men,)
But thy love gives hope and thy word gives cheer,
That our sons will come back again,
In the silent sweep of Eternity's round,
They have felt life's direst loss—
Broken and maimed they will all creep back
To our arms and to thy cross.
Be merciful unto them, we pray—
We, the mothers of men.[25]

One of Susa's loftiest poems was also written in 1914. Titled "Consecration," she offered herself as a "block" in the "shrine" of God:

O Builder, let me fill my little niche
With feeble work or strong—
A word of help, a broken crust—choose which—
Or e'en one little song.
Nay, Builder, better—let the midnight toll
No deed of mine today,
If in the doing of it, some weak soul
Would find seeds of decay.
If, Builder, in some hidden tower-stair,
Thou needst a block like me,
On which may climb the toilers upward there,
O, there I fain would be.
Not deeds alone, calm Builder of the sun,
I offer on thy shrine,
But heart of passionate desire to learn
The patience that is Thine.[26]

In 1917 the "Clique," a group of five or six close friends, spent a week together at Elizabeth McCune's new mansion in Salt Lake City. Members Alice K. Smith, Augusta Grant, Ann Groesbeck, Elizabeth McCune, and Susa Young Gates reported a grand time. They had their picture taken together, and Susa composed a lengthy poem celebrating the event, called "The House that Elizabeth Built." The first verse reads:

25. Gates, "Hymns of the Mothers of Men," *Improvement Era*, Jan. 1914, 226.
26. Gates, "Consecration," *Young Woman's Journal*, Oct. 1914, 594.

This is the palace that Elizabeth built.
These are the women that Elizabeth asked
To spend a week in the palace that she built.
These are the dresses all striped and fine
That Elizabeth bought for the women that time
To wear in the house that she built.
This is the limousine, luxurious and new
That the women all christened and rode for the view.
Dressed in their gowns all striped and new
While spending a week in the palace that Elizabeth built.
Gone are the strawberries, delicious and real,
Likewise the peas, the lamb and veal
The omelet Spanish with all of the trimmings
And buttermilk on ice that were served to the women
All striped and fine that Elizabeth asked
To stay with her that time, in the house that she built.[27]

One of Susa's most clever poems, which demonstrates a compendious knowledge of famous figures, is the somewhat tedious, punnish, doggerel, "What, When, Who?", which appeared in the *Young Woman's Journal* in 1894:

Pray, what did T. Buchanan Read?
At what did E. A. Poe?
What volumes did Elizur Wright?
And where did E. P. Roe?

Is Thomas Hardy nowadays?
Is Rider Haggard pale?
Is Minot Savage? Oscar Wilde?
And Edward Everett Hale?

Was Laurence Sterne? Was Hermann Grimm?
Was Edward Young? John Gay?
Jonathan Swift? And old John Bright?
And why was Thomas Gray?

Was Francis Bacon lean in streaks?
John Suckling vealy? Pray,
Was Hogg much given to the pen?
Are Lamb's Tales sold today?

27. The complete poem is scanned and available online at the LDS Church History catalogue, "House That Elizabeth Built," box 99, fd. 29, SYGP (CHL).

Did Mary Mapes Dodge just in time?
Did C. D. Warner? How?
At what did Andrew Marvell so?
Does Anthony Whymper now?

What goodies did Rose Terry Cooke?
Or Richard Boyle beside?
What gave the wicked Thomas Paine?
And what made Mark Akenside?

Was Thomas Tickell-ish at all?
Did Richard Steele, I ask?
Tell me, has George A. Hale suit?
Did William Ware a mask?

Does Henry Cabot Lodge at home?
John Horne Tooke what and when?
Is Gordon Cumming, Has G. W.
Cabled his friends again?[28]

Susa penned the following unnamed poem and tucked it in a cookbook given to one of her daughters. It has been preserved by her granddaughter, Lurene Gates Wilkinson:

You know your friends may oft recall
Your virtues one by one.
"She's sweet, she's good, she's fair, she's tall,"
Then speak of deeds you've done.

But, oh, my girl, there's such a world
Of praise beyond all looks
With which your friends close all remarks,
"You know how well she cooks!"

And so we're judged, we women folk,
Not as saints or sinners,
But simply by the speed and skill
With which we cook our dinners!

Be happy, dear, and may good cheer
Within your household flourish,
And every hope and every truth
With care and patience nourish.[29]

28. Gates, "What, When, Who?" *Young Woman's Journal*, Apr. 1894, 360.
29. Gates, n.d., copy in author's possession.

Susa encouraged the poetic prowess of her progeny. When grand-daughter Lurene at age twelve sent her a poem, "Grandma Dear," Susa sent a piece by the name of "Grandmother Replies":

Grandma Dear

Oh! A grandmother is a wonderful thing,
With a tender way all her own.
The sweet smile on her face, the cheer on her brow
Belongs to her all alone.
How sweet and loving she always is;
How cheerful she is through the day;
She is ever ready to help us
Whenever we come to stay.
So on this dear day that is meant for all mothers
I'm sending my love to my father's dear mother. —Lurene Gates

Grandmother Replies

Have you a little grand-girl
With gentle eyes of blue
Who writes her loving heart out
In verses just for you?
No? Then I am sorry, sorry,
For your luckless, hapless plight.
I hate to crow, and yet you know—
I have this dear delight.
My darling grand-girl sits and dreams
About a thousand things;
Of stars and flowers, of hills and streams,
About them all she sings,
But most of all she thinks of love
Of father and of mother,
What she can write to give delight
To her proud and glad grandmother. —Susa Young Gates[30]

Susa wrote dozens of short stories, published in multiple journals, including the *Juvenile Instructor, Young Woman's Journal, Improvement Era, Woman's Exponent,* and *Contributor.* They are, for the most part, simple in plot, moralistic, gospel-centered, and sometimes

---

30. "Grandma Dear," and "Grandmother Replies," *Juvenile Instructor*, Sep. 1927, 522.

implausible. Susa throughout her life made efforts to improve her writing skills, beginning in 1892 with her attendance at summer school at Harvard University. As late as 1913, at age fifty-seven, she took a correspondence class in short story writing from Joseph Berg Esenwein, an editor and writer who also managed the Home Correspondence School in Springfield, Massachusetts. Reviews of her writings from Esenwein's staff were generally positive, with comments, such as "very well told," "interesting opening," "very creditable," "excellent local color," and "keen character drawing," but also included observations like "sameness of tone," "need of condensation" [up to cutting out one thousand words], "rather slight plot," "cultivate variety."[31]

Two of Susa's best-known stories are "Aunt Fanny's Rocking Chair" and "All is Well! All is Well!" "Aunt Fanny's Rocking Chair" was a three-part story, published in 1905.[32] It tells of the Atwood family, father James, mother Fanny, and son Jamsie. Four other children in the family had already been buried in Kirtland, Far West, and Winter Quarters. The tale describes the family's trip as they journey with the vanguard Mormon pioneer company from Winter Quarters to Fort Laramie. In Winter Quarters James and Fanny argued about what to take with them. James, conscious of the restricted space available in their two wagons, one large and one small, wanted to leave behind the broom, the clock, the looking glass, the dishware, the chest (holding mementos of their deceased children), a big iron pot, and "a small, old, oak rocking-chair," the latter an heirloom from Fanny's aunt; Fanny wanted to bring them all.[33] While James is at a meeting receiving instructions from Brigham Young regarding the next day's departure, Fanny hides the rocking chair among items in the smaller wagon, which she has packed by herself.

Several weeks later, on the banks of the Platte River near Fort Laramie, the company stops for several weeks to make rafts to cross the Platte River. James goes on a hunting trip with Brigham and other men in the company, since the group has had no meat for

---

31. See, for example, the typewritten story with editorial comments, "In the Wilderness," box 100, fd. 16, SYGP (CHL).

32. Gates, "Aunt Fanny's Rocking Chair," *Young Woman's Journal*, 1905, 267–73, 328–32, 371–76.

33. Gates, 272.

over a week. At a distance, James can see the beginning of a cattle stampede, headed straight toward his wife's small wagon, which is open and located at the edge of the wagon train. Suddenly, the stampede stops. James arrives back at camp, only to find out that Fanny had frightened and stopped the animals with "the pinted spikes of the chair or its red and green cushion, or suthing." Brigham and his plural wife Clara had dinner that night with the Atwoods, with the "crowning feature of the whole picture ... [being] the ancient rocking chair." The moral of the story becomes apparent as Brigham compliments James on his sensitivity to his wife, remarking, "These wives are the greatest blessing God ever gave. ... I was so glad to see this comfortable rocking chair which you have brought along. That shows your thoughtful spirit."[34]

"All Is Well! All Is Well!" tells the sad story of a ten-year-old boy named Tommy and his father, English immigrants who are crossing the plains in the 1850s. The story originally appeared in the *Improvement Era* in 1908, but in her correspondence, Susa received multiple requests for copies of the article, and it was therefore reprinted in the *Deseret News* in 1925.

Tommy's mother had died earlier on the trek and was buried along the Missouri River. Tommy's father, described as an "invalid," has difficulty keeping up with the slow wagon train as it moves west. He often lags behind during the day and catches up after the wagons have stopped for the evening. Frequently, during the course of the day, particularly at trying times, members of the group break into song, usually singing the stirring, encouraging words of "Come, Come, Ye Saints," one of Mormonism's most famous hymns. The first three verses were often sung on the trail but not usually the fourth verse, which begins with somber words, although it ends with exultation:

And should we die before our journey's through,
Happy day! All is well!
We then are free from toil and sorrow too;
With the just we shall dwell.
But if our lives are spared again
To see the Saints their rest obtain,

---

34. Gates, 373–75.

Oh, how we'll make this chorus swell—
All is well! All is well!³⁵

One day Tommy's father, who has been ill and struggling for some time, decides at a water stop to rest longer, saying he will catch up. Later that evening, Tommy is worried and asks members of the wagon train to help look for his father. They find him, bring him into camp, and feed him. Tommy falls asleep, and his father begins in a thin voice to sing the first three verses of the hymn. Ultimately, he sings the fourth verse as well. The next morning Tommy wakes to find his father "still and resting." He realizes that his father had died during the night and, like his mother, "was with God."³⁶

The story, dramatic and sentimental, certainly appealed to LDS audiences.

35. "Come, Come, Ye Saints," *Hymns*, 30.
36. Gates, "All Is Well! All Is Well!" *Deseret News*, Aug. 29, 1925.

13
Sisters

Lucy Bigelow Young worried a great deal about her daughters. Spread among the three women were eight marriages in a religion where nothing was more important than marriage. There was much affliction, loss, sadness, and trial in the lives of each of Lucy's children. The lives of Susa's sisters, Dora and Mabel, and their relationship to her, shed light on Susa's personality. She expended great effort throughout her life to help her sisters lead what she believed to be happy, balanced lives, often with less success than more. Much of what is known about her sisters' early lives comes from what Susa wrote about them in her biography of her mother, and what she chose to remember also speaks to who Susa was and what she valued in her family.

Susa enjoyed a close relationship with her two sisters and also with several of her twenty-eight half-sisters, especially, Zina (Card), daughter of Zina D. Huntington; Maria (Dougall), daughter of Clarissa Chase; and Jeannette (Easton), daughter of Lucy Decker. These three half-sisters were each part of the big ten, a group of ten daughters of Brigham Young who were all born between June 1847 and February 1851. Susa's older sister, Eudora "Dora," missed being part of this group by just fifteen months.

In 1877, on the night before Brigham Young was to leave St. George to return to Salt Lake City, he spoke with his wife Lucy, who was forty-seven years old at the time. Lucy asked Brigham if he had any parting words of counsel for her, having no idea that within a few weeks he would die, leaving her a widow. Brigham reportedly told her, "Take care of the girls! Look after the house, and work in the Temple all you can."[1]

This last parting counsel became Lucy's mantra, and during the remainder of her twenty-seven years, her daughters would take first priority in her life. After her daughters moved away from home, working in the temple was always of paramount importance to Lucy. Several times she lost her position of presiding among female ordinance workers in the temple because she was gone to help her daughters in their times of confinement or distress. Lucy's two great spiritual gifts were her powers of healing, for which she always carried with her a bottle of consecrated oil, and her dedication to and knowledge of temple ordinances. John D. T. McAllister, a family friend who was stake president in St. George and later the president of the St. George temple, was asked by church officials to go to Logan in 1884 and Manti in 1888 to train new temple workers. Both times he asked Lucy to accompany him to help train new female ordinance workers, and she spent several weeks in both cities helping with orientation. Susa was also present for the Logan temple dedication. She had been invited by church president John Taylor to act as assistant secretary and reporter for the event.

Eudora Lovina Young Dunford Woodruff Hagan, who was known as Dora for nearly all of her life, or occasionally Dollie, was born on May 12, 1852, in Salt Lake City. She was Brigham Young's thirty-first child, but Lucy Bigelow Young's first. Dora was a great favorite of her father because of her beauty and wit, but she was willful and difficult to discipline. In 1931, ten years after Dora's death, Susa wrote of her sister, "Dear Dora, so beautiful, so gifted, so adorable, she was the idol of her father's, her mother's and little sisters Susa's and Mabel's hearts. And yet, with all her love and loyalty to them personally, there lay in the roots of her character, the corroding weakness of vanity and selfishness."[2] When Lucy moved with Susa for one year to the Young farm in 1862 for Lucy to milk and take care of the cows, Dora remained at the Lion House. Susa also remembered that "Dora was really gifted, both in vocal and instrumental music and she soon became one of the best contralto singers

---

1. Gates, "Lucy Bigelow Young, 89.
2. Gates, 69.

in the family group. She also became very proficient as an organist and pianist." Brigham bought an organ for Dora and Lucy, who had also taken up musical studies.[3]

In adolescence, Dora fell in love with a captivating young man named Frank Morley Dunford, whose convert parents had emigrated from England. Frank, cousin of Alma B. Dunford, Susa's first husband, was described as handsome, industrious, and of a sunny disposition. Brigham tried to break up the romance by sending Dora to school in Provo, where she remained "for a season." But she returned to Salt Lake City "more in love than ever." Brigham decided to send Lucy and her daughters to St. George. But on October 3, 1870, Lucy's fortieth birthday, the two eighteen-year-olds eloped. As recounted in chapter three, Dora walked out of a party at the school house with her sister Susa "as a blind" and met Morley. The three of them went to the home of a Presbyterian minister, where Dora and Morley were married. Many years later Susa remarked, "Let me draw the veil of silence over that terrible time. Mother always did." Two sons were born to the couple, Frank in 1873 and George in 1875. By 1876 the marriage had unraveled due to Morley's alcoholism, and Dora returned to St. George to live near her mother and sisters.[4] There she worked with her mother and Susa as an ordinance worker in the St. George temple immediately after it was completed.

On March 10, 1877, Dora was sealed by her father to Apostle Wilford Woodruff as his ninth wife.[5] Woodruff had just turned seventy, and Dora was not yet twenty-five. Woodruff recorded in his journal, "President Young gave his daughter Eudora Young to me in marriage and sealed us together at the altar in the temple of the Lord this day and I thank the Lord for it." Just under thirteen months later, on April 1, 1878, Woodruff wrote, "I got a telegram saying that Dora had a son born at 3 o'clock and died at 12 o'clock."[6] Woodruff wrote this line in shorthand, and historians who were unable to decipher it have debated who the mother was, often leaning

---

3. Gates, 63.

4. Gates, 71–72.

5. Three of Woodruff's marriages had ended in divorce between 1846 and 1848.

6. Woodruff Journal, Apr. 1, 1878. The shorthand is translated by LaJean Carruth for Dan Vogel's edition of the Woodruff Journals.

toward Dora. In 1878, Woodruff was married to four women of
childbearing age. Two of them had children within nine months of
April 1, 1878. The third wife, Sarah Brown, lived in Cache County
and bore her last child in 1873. Finally, in a letter to Susa, Dora
wrote that she was so sick she was unable to sit up, likely referring
to morning sickness.[7]

Nearly eight months after their newborn child died, Woodruff
and Dora divorced. Woodruff wrote in shorthand, "I signed the bill,"
referring to a bill of divorcement.[8] Perhaps because of the shortness
of the marriage, and because it ended in divorce, several treatments
of Woodruff's life, including a major biography by Matthias Cowley,
do not mention Woodruff's marriage to Dora.[9]

After her second divorce, Dora's life began to take her far from
her Mormon roots, which would be a perennial heartache for her
mother. Although Dora may not have been delighted to marry
Woodruff, who was much older than she, her mother was probably
happy to see her daughter sealed to an apostle and family friend.
Brigham Young did not live to see his daughter's second marriage
fail. Shortly after she left Woodruff, Dora met a married man, a
Catholic attorney practicing in Salt Lake City named Albert Hagan.
Dora and Hagan married on March 1, 1879, either in Salt Lake City
or Seattle.[10] By the next year Dora and "Judge" Hagan had moved to
Denver, but shortly thereafter relocated to Chicago.[11] They had four
children, including two who died in infancy, Albert in 1882 (died
1883) and Lucy Mary in 1891, who died at three months. Two other
children, Harold, born in 1886, and Mabel Clara "May," born in
1889, survived to adulthood. Dora converted to Catholicism, which
was a source of great sadness for Lucy and Susa.

---

7. Dora Woodruff to Susa Young Gates, Aug. 25, 1877, box 31, fd. 1. See also Quinn, "LDS Church Authority," 64, and Alexander, "Apostle in Exile."

8. Woodruff Journal, Nov. 25, 1878. Again, I rely on Vogel's edition of Woodruff's journal with Carruth's shorthand translation.

9. See, for example, Cowley, *Wilford Woodruff*, and the Young family genealogy published in *Utah Genealogical and Historical Magazine*, July 1920, 132.

10. At least one family source says Salt Lake City, while a profile of Dora in the *Salt Lake Herald* says that she and Albert Hagan eloped to Seattle. "Dora Young in Her Youth," *Salt Lake Herald*, Feb. 3, 1905, 8. For the family source, see Dora's entry on familypedia.wikia.com.

11. Gates, "Lucy Bigelow Young," 98.

By the mid-1880s the Hagans had relocated to Coeur d'Alene, Idaho, where Albert was a prominent attorney dealing with mining law. He traveled extensively throughout the Northwest (Washington Territory and Oregon State), often accompanied by Dora. After a year-long illness, Albert died in 1895 at age fifty-two. Dora reported that since the financial crisis of 1893 Albert had had difficulty collecting his legal fees. His death thrust her into penury, from which she never completely recovered.

Soon after Albert's death, Dora relocated to Chicago, because she was "so low in my finances" and the only properties which would provide her any money were there. She did not consider at that time returning to Utah, since living there would mean she "would have to meet people so uncongenial to me."[12]

Shortly before Albert's death in 1895, Dora's son George from her first marriage had become ill and was advised to relocate to California because of its favorable climate. He settled in Pasadena. George's life, like his cousin Bailey's, was filled with tragedy. He was a promising student who had studied at Notre Dame University, where he received a gold medal in his department of 180 young men. He had been nominated for an appointment to the US Naval Academy at Annapolis but failed the physical examination. He married young, and by the time of his death in 1901 at age twenty-six he had fathered three children, who were later left at the Sisters Orphanage when their mother had to relocate to Los Angeles for work.[13] Dora did not stay in Chicago long, and instead moved to Pasadena in 1896 and lived with George and his wife, Marie. Marie took in sewing, and Dora took in roomers. George's employment was sporadic, and they barely made ends meet.[14]

Dora's older son, Frank Dunford, eventually became a bass soloist with the famous Paulist Choir in Chicago. He had had a varied career path before settling on music. He had been expelled from a Catholic school in Oregon for not obeying the rules. After that, he worked for a transportation company in Idaho, spent three months studying at Notre Dame with his brother, attended college briefly

---

12. Dora Hagan to Susa Young Gates, various letters, box 31, fds. 4–5.
13. Hagan to Gates, box 31, fd. 8.
14. Hagan to Gates, box 31, fd. 7.

in Spokane, was a fireman for the Northern Pacific Railroad, and then he temporarily took over management of the Hagan Ranch near Coeur d'Alene. Before settling in Chicago, he had lived in Trail Creek, British Columbia. As a seventeen year old, he lived for a short time with Susa and Jacob in Provo. Eventually, he found his place as a musician. He had been nudged in this direction by Susa.[15]

After several serious illnesses, Dora sustained a major stroke, which crippled her for the last decade of her life. In 1912 she moved to Seattle to live with her sister Mabel. Over the next several years Dora lived with Mabel and Joseph Sanborn, as they moved from Seattle to Portland to Everett, as part of Joe's work with American Express. The Sanborns relocated to Salt Lake City in 1919, at which point Dora, by this time an invalid, lived with her daughter May Farnes. She died at home in Salt Lake City on October 21, 1921, of a cerebral hemorrhage at age sixty-nine.

Dora's obituary in the *Salt Lake Tribune* was brief but telling. She was identified as Dora Mary Hagan, the widow of Albert Hagan. No mention was made of her parents, Brigham and Lucy Bigelow Young. In fact, there was no mention at all of her maiden name. No mention was made of her marriages to Morley Dunford and Wilford Woodruff. No mention was made of her Mormon background. Survivors were listed as Frank M. Dunford of Chicago, Harold R. Hagan of Salt Lake City; and May H. Farnes.[16] Funeral services were held at the Church of Our Lady of Lourdes; she was buried in the Mount Olivet Cemetery.

Susa was greatly exercised by Dora's conversion to Catholicism. For most of Dora's last forty years of life, Susa never reconciled to Dora's defection from Mormonism. Susa was an outspoken, partisan defender of everything Mormon, and much of her adult life was consumed with protecting the Young name and making sure that her actions would be acceptable to her father. Susa later wrote that after Dora's elopement with Dunford, her "mother fasted three days a week, from that day on praying that God would reach and bring back into the Fold of Christ her straying Lamb. And he will!

---

15. Hagan to Gates; Gates to Hagan, various letters, box 31, fds. 4–8.
16. *Salt Lake Tribune*, Oct. 22, 1921, 27.

Someday! Somewhere!" Throughout her typescript of Lucy's life, Susa is unsparing in her negative observations of Dora.[17]

Multiple letters from Dora to Susa over a period of many years express Dora's feelings of being marginalized by Susa. With few exceptions, Susa's letters to Dora are not extant, so it is difficult to determine what provocation Susa may have given to Dora over the years. Six years after her elopement with Hagan, Dora knew that Lucy was sailing with the Gates family to the Sandwich Islands. She wrote to Susa from Chicago, saying, "You will no doubt be anything but pleased at receiving any communication from me but I trust you will excuse me when I plead my anxiety to learn of Mother's safe arrival at her destination."[18]

Four years later, shortly after Susa had returned home, Dora wrote from Hagan Ranch in Idaho to Susa:

> After a silence and total ignoring of my very existence by you, who signs yourself "still your sister," as though time or distance could ever make us aught but "sisters"; comes your very cool letter of date July 15th which I received some time since. ... What has been the cause of this ten years estrangement between us two? had you adaquate cause? And does your heart and conscience approve your conduct? If they do, then Susa I thank God I am not made of the same metal as yourself, for no matter what the provocation, I could never so ignore my own sister. ... I am not only "Still your sister" but I am Your loving sister, Dora.[19]

Time mellowed some of Susa's embarrassment and anger, but she never gave up trying to coax Dora back to the LDS Church. One of the few letters to her sister that Susa did keep a copy of was sent in 1917, when Dora was living in Portland. Susa told her "precious sister" that she wished she "could decide to be rebaptized and renew your covenants in the Church and Kingdom of God." Susa believed that one day she would be "going on the other side to meet father and mother and my beloved children" and she could not bear it if Dora were not "there with them." Susa implored her, "Come back, sweet sister, to our love and arms and to the fold of Christ."[20]

---

17. Gates, "Lucy Bigelow Young," 72.
18. Hagan to Gates, Dec. 6, 1885, box 31, fd. 1.
19. Hagan to Gates, Aug. 4, 1889, box 31, fd. 1.
20. Gates to Hagan, Dec. 6, 1917, box 31, fd. 8.

Dora's response ten days later was stark: "I am so sorry you are so troubled about me. In my spiritual life, I am most happy in my devout belief of the Holy Catholic Church." She told her sister, who was so defensive of her own faith, that "it is wrong for you to harp against my Holy belief—I dont attempt to convert you to my belief, nor can I be … perverted to your belief." Dora asked how she could "feel something I cannot" and wondered why her sister could not "love me as I am." She signed the letter, "Your devoted sister, Dora M. Hagan," then explained the origin of the middle initial M: "You may not know that I took the name of *Mary*, when I was confirmed in the Catholic Church, so this name is dear to me" (emphasis in original). Like her obituary, Dora's death certificate omitted the names Young, Dunford, and Woodruff, but it had the name Mary.[21]

Susa's relationship with Mabel—she sometimes went by May or Rhoda, but her full name after three marriages was Rhoda Mabel Young McCallister Witt Sanborn— was less contentious than with Dora, but was not without its trying moments. Mabel was born in Salt Lake City on February 22, 1863, the third and last daughter of Brigham Young and Lucy Bigelow. She was feisty and in later life described herself as "headstrong," albeit in the past tense.[22] Her early life, before she settled into a comfortable third marriage, was tumultuous.

Mabel moved to St. George with her mother and Susa when she was seven. Nine years later in 1879, she married Daniel Handley McAllister, the son of one of John D. T. McAllister, one of St. George's most prominent citizens.

Mabel's only child with Daniel, a son named Daniel Jr., was born in 1880. The family settled on a ranch in Socorro, New Mexico. In 1882, three years into their marriage, Mabel wrote to Susa that her husband "is so good to me," but fifteen months later wrote to say that she had been very unhappy during the preceding year and vowed to not live another year like it. She apologized for having "deeply wounded your sensitive and delicate spirit," something she repeated on multiple occasions over the ensuing years. Mabel returned to St.

---

21. See Dora's death certificate, which listed her as Dora Mary Hagan. Series 81448, Office of Vital Records and Statistics Death Certificates, Utah Division of Archives.

22. Mabel Sanborn to Susa Young Gates, box 32, fd. 1.

George, and the couple was divorced. A bitter custody battle, which Mabel eventually won, lasted for several years.[23] The fracture between Mabel and Daniel seemed to have little adverse effect on the relationship between the Young and McAllister families.

Like her sisters, Mabel was an accomplished musician. She moved to Provo in 1885 to teach at the Brigham Young Academy. While there, she wrote to Susa, "I am all but expelled from the Academy." She had been caught attending a baseball game with out-of-town friends rather than attending a required meeting. She felt that she was being goaded by Karl G. Maeser, president of the academy, to do better and doubted she would actually be sent away. She had become engaged to a Mr. Smith, whom the family felt was an unsavory character. Lucy threatened to relocate from St. George to Provo to help Mabel put her life in order. Mabel resisted, claiming that Lucy would try to convince her to "give up the one I love so well." She complained, "I am sure Ma would never be happy away from the Temple. Even her children are secondary to her grand, noble, self-denying purpose of saving the ... dead." In her next letter she expressed shame over her comments, said that Maeser was "my true and steadfast friend," and asked Susa to destroy the previous communication.[24]

The new romance was short-circuited when Lucy resolved to take Mabel on a long cruise, perhaps even around the world, to get her away from Provo. Mabel "had become worn out with overwork."[25] Lucy and Mabel made it as far as San Francisco, where they received the news that Jacob had been called on his mission to the Sandwich Islands. They made plans to travel with Jacob to Hawai'i and were delighted when they found out that Susa and their children would be accompanying him as well. Lucy and Mabel remained several months in Hawai'i with the Gateses, and they did not return home

---

23. Mabel McAllister to Gates, various letters, box 31, fd. 9.

24. McAllister to Gates, various letters, box 31, fd. 9. Daniel's father, John, was the temple president in St. George and was called to train new ordinance workers in 1884 in Logan and 1888 in Manti. Both times he asked that Lucy B. Young help him train new ordinance workers, and Mabel accompanied Lucy to Logan, where they remained for six weeks. Susa was also there, having been invited by church president John Taylor to act as assistant secretary and reporter for the dedication ceremonies.

25. Gates, "Lucy Bigelow Young," 104.

to Utah until June 1886. There, Mabel was temporarily reunited with Daniel Jr., who had been living with his father. Lucy and Mabel settled in Salt Lake City for a time so that Mabel could continue her musical studies.

Mabel was much more accepting of Dora's departure from Mormonism than Susa. On numerous occasions Mabel took Susa to task for what she considered Susa's unkindness toward and lack of acceptance of Dora. Dora spent Christmas of 1886 with Lucy and Mabel in Utah. All three of them cried when Susa sent Christmas presents home from Hawai'i for Lucy, Leah, Bailey, sisters Jeannette and Zina, and Mabel, among others, but pointedly left out Dora. Mabel knew that Susa was aware Dora would be in Utah for Christmas. Dora, who was crushed by the omission, said, "She should not have expected anything from anyone who had so long ignored her. ... If that was Christian Charity, I thank God I haven't got it!" Two years later, with Susa still in the islands, Mabel encouraged Susa to write Dora, "I know she cant help but wonder how it is you never send her any word or message."[26]

In June 1887 Mabel moved to Heber, Utah. A month later she wrote to Susa and Lucy, who were both in Hawai'i, that she was getting married the next day to cousin Daniel Brigham "Brig" Witt. She apologized for not waiting to marry until Lucy returned home from Hawai'i, where Lucy had gone to comfort Susa after the deaths of Jacob and Karl. She lamented, "For years my constant prayer has been for death." She could not postpone her marriage, since she had "been buffeted about for many years" without a home. Mabel and Brig's only child, a son named Brigham Winfred (who went by Winnie or Fred) Witt, was born in 1889.[27]

By the summer of 1891 Mabel's second marriage had dissolved, and she was living with Dora and Judge Hagan in Coeur d'Alene, Idaho, where she remained for almost two years. She averred that she had gone through an "awful ordeal again" and was concerned about "scandal and talk."[28] She asked Susa for forgiveness for any pain she may have caused. Mabel took a shorthand course. She said she did

26. McAllister to Gates, various letters, box 31, fd. 10.
27. McAllister to Gates.
28. McAllister to Gates.

not want to return to Utah, since she feared having to deal with Brig. Mabel's behavior caused Albert Hagan consternation. He wrote to Lucy that Mabel was "out at night with persons I consider highly improper characters." Mabel sometimes went to Spokane without explanation, leaving Winnie in Coeur d'Alene. Hagan asked Lucy to come get Mabel before she went elsewhere, but then sent a telegram a few days later that this would not be necessary.[29]

In October 1892 Dora wrote to Susa that Mabel had become a Catholic. Dora felt that Susa would blame her, but Dora insisted that she "had nothing to do with her conversion." Mabel had been attending the Episcopalian Church for several months to sing in the choir. Dora talked of "the [Catholic] church I believe in with all my heart."[30] No further mention has ever surfaced about Mabel and Catholicism, and she died as an active member of the LDS Church.

The following summer of 1893, Mabel was back in Salt Lake City, living with her mother in the Lion House until Lucy's new home was finished. Mabel, assuming $2,000 in financial obligation for the home, moved in with her mother. Mabel's two sons, Dan and Winnie, were living with the Gates family in Provo, where they remained for several years. Mabel sent money to Jacob and Susa for their room and board, despite the fact that she had a difficult time supporting herself by teaching music lessons. In the fall of 1893 Mabel traveled with the Mormon Tabernacle Choir to the World's Fair in Chicago.

Susa approached Mabel to help her with her newfound interest in genealogy, specifically to keep track of the vicarious temple ordinances performed for the Young family. Because no systematic records were kept of what temple work was performed, multiple ordinances were sometimes performed for the same individual. To establish order in the Young genealogy, Susa developed the idea of keeping five record books. Four would be placed in the temples then in existence (St. George, Logan, Manti, and Salt Lake City), and the fifth book would be maintained by the Young family. Ordinances performed for deceased Young family members would be recorded

29. Albert Hagan to Lucy Bigelow Young, July 14, 1892; telegram, July 18, 1892, box 31, fd. 3, SYGP (CHL).

30. Dora Hagan to Susa Young Gates, Oct. 15, 1892, box 31, fd. 3.

in the appropriate book, which would then be cross-checked against the others to avoid a duplication whenever an ordinance was requested. Mabel began indexing several thousand Young family names in 1893 and finished the project four years later.

In August 1897 Mabel married Joseph A. Sanborn, who was not then and would never be a member of the LDS Church, a source of great concern to Lucy and Susa. They both appreciated, however, Joseph's stability and love for Mabel, particularly after her first two unsuccessful marriages. Susa described "his honorable character, his indomitable energy, his high intellectual type of mind, and his refined nobility."[31]

With Mabel's remarriage, Lucy felt that she should leave her house to Mabel and her new husband. This home remained a family focal point, and Mabel lived there for many years. Over time three of Susa's children would live there: Leah for two or three years, and B. Cecil and Emma Lucy each for two years. After giving up her house to economize, Lucy spent the academic year of 1897 and 1898 in Oswego, New York, with Lillian Hamlin Cannon, the young widow of Apostle Abraham H. Cannon. Lillian, who had been an intimate friend of Susa's daughter Leah, was studying pedagogy and needed help with her infant daughter, Marba. Lucy accompanied them as nurse and housekeeper.

Three children were born to Mabel and Joseph: Abbott Young (1898–1901), Lucy Young (1904–43), and Joseph Gilpin Young (1908–85). In numerous letters to Susa, who provided a home for older sons Daniel and Winfred, Mabel lamented her "neglect" of the boys, but felt she had little option but to have Susa care for them.[32]

Mabel's oldest son, Daniel McAllister, served a mission in Great Britain. He arrived in 1899, sailing with his grandmother, Lucy Bigelow Young, who was on her way to chaperone Emma Lucy during her musical studies in Germany after her original chaperones, half-sister Leah and brother-in-law John A. Widtsoe, returned to the United States. Dan later studied at the University of Michigan. Witt spent twenty-two months serving overseas during World

---

31. Gates, "Lucy Bigelow Young," 160.
32. Mabel Sanborn to Gates, various letters, box 31, fd. 13.

War I, which caused Mabel to "feel that he has redeemed himself and repaid me for all my heartaches and disappointments over him."[33]

In 1911 Joseph Sanborn's work with American Express took the family to the Northwest. They lived in Portland, Seattle, and Everett, Washington, for a total of eight years. Dora joined them in 1913 and lived with them until they returned to Salt Lake City. Joseph was eleven years older than Mabel, and his health began to fail. Through Susa's influence, Mabel was able to obtain a position as second assistant librarian in the Genealogical Society of Utah, and in 1919 the family moved back to Salt Lake City. Financially, they had had many difficulties and lost two homes in Salt Lake City because of back taxes.

Mabel supported the family, and Joseph died in 1929. She continued to work at the Genealogical Society. The highlight of her many years of service there was a twelve-country tour of Europe in 1932. She went to pick up her son, Joseph Gilpin, who was finishing his missionary service in Germany. She visited genealogical libraries in the countries she toured, teaching classes along the way. She received half-pay during her absence from work, and her travel expenses were underwritten, in part, by her nephew-in-law, John A. Widtsoe, living in Liverpool at the time as president of the European Mission.

Mabel was the last surviving child of Brigham Young. She died in Salt Lake City on September 20, 1950, at age eighty-seven. As with her sister Dora, Mabel was buried at the Mt. Olivet Cemetery in Salt Lake City.

Knowing of Susa's devotion to the church helps one to understand her attitude toward Dora. Susa spent her life as an advocate for Mormonism, unapologetically sharing her testimony with some of the brightest people in the world. She simply could not understand or accept that Dora could truly find comfort in Catholicism. It is easy to read her letters to Dora encouraging her to return to Mormonism as heavy-handed, but Susa intended them as sincere entreaties to "come home." Susa also felt that she had failed her son Bailey by not keeping him closer to the church. She wrote morality

---

33. Sanborn to Gates, Aug. 28, 1917, box 32, fd. 1.

plays about what happens to people who leave the LDS faith, and the results of leaving were always disastrous in Susa's mind. Her appeals to Dora should be viewed through that lens. Susa may have had tunnel vision when it came to her faith, but she was not guilty of malice or cruelty.

As for Mabel, she developed a close relationship with Susa that transcended any differences. The two sisters worked together on Young family names for temple work, and Susa secured for Mabel a full-time position with the Genealogical Department that allowed her to support her family and join in Susa's work to "redeem" their deceased ancestors. The sisters were close throughout Susa's life, and their letters reflect familial affection and their father's candid way of speaking.

Likewise, regarding the three sisters's marital difficulties, the circumstances each faced were trying. There are at least four considerations mitigating their multiple divorces. First, Dora, Susa, and Mabel were eighteen, sixteen, and sixteen years old, respectively, at the time of their first marriages. This was young, even for the nineteenth century. Women were generally not married during this time in America until their early twenties.[34] There is evidence, especially in Dora's case, that the young women married rashly, perhaps intoxicated by love. Both Dora and Susa married men who struggled with alcohol and possibly gambling. In the 1870s and 1880s, when women had few rights or means of providing for themselves, Morley Dunford's and Alma Dunford's alcoholism was a serious problem. Also, both men may have been abusive.

Second, particularly in polygamous marriages, there was often a significant difference in age between bride and husband. Lucy herself was twenty-nine years younger than her husband, Brigham. Dora was forty-five years younger than her second husband, Wilford Woodruff. Even Mabel, who never entered into polygamy, was eleven years younger than her third husband, Joseph Sanborn.

Third, Lucy's three daughters probably never learned by personal example what constituted a traditional marital relationship. Married in 1847 in Winter Quarters at age sixteen, Lucy was left with her family and finally moved to Salt Lake City with the McMullen

---

34. US Census Bureau, "Estimated Median Age at First Marriage, by Sex: 1890 to Present," Annual Social and Economic Supplement. Chart available online at census.gov.

family in 1848. Dora was not born until 1852, so it is likely that Lucy and Brigham did not enjoy a conjugal relationship for the first several years of their marriage. In the 1860s, Lucy was sent to the Young farm to milk the cows and was gone from the Lion House for a year. After 1870 Lucy was sent to St. George, some 300 miles from Brigham in Salt Lake City. Whenever Brigham did visit St. George, it was in the company of his favorite wife, Amelia Folsom.

Fourth, Brigham Young's attitude toward divorce, particularly in polygamous circumstances, was fairly relaxed: he himself was divorced from ten of his fifty-five wives.[35] Brigham generally granted divorces to polygamous wives without question in the event that they felt "trapped in an unworkable relationship." On the other hand, men were counseled not to seek to divorce "any wife willing to put up with him."[36] Young's daughters grew up in an environment where divorce was more common than it might have otherwise been outside of Utah, and they watched as their father and some others in the upper echelons of LDS leadership were divorced.

All of these circumstances Lucy's daughters faced—youth, lack of traditional modeling of a marriage, age differences in spouses, and a culture that was more tolerant of divorce—created an environment where, in retrospect, it is not surprising that the women struggled, at least initially, in their relationships.

35. Johnson, "Determining and Defining 'Wife,'" 62.
36. Danel Bachman and Ronald K. Esplin, "Plural Marriage," in Ludlow, *Encyclopedia of Mormonism*, 3:1094–95.

Politics and Feminism

14

Susa's life over the next decade took on a frenetic pace that pulled her in multiple directions. She was at the apogee of her influence and power, and she complained that it was difficult to keep up with the demands on her time. In a letter to Jacob, she announced, "The long active years have done their work in my brain, and created a work-microbe that demands more work all the time."[1]

Six major motifs characterize this period of her life: (1) politics, which worried her greatly, but from which she gradually distanced herself; (2) her involvement in Relief Society, including the magazine she initiated, (3) genealogy, to which she devoted increasing amounts of time and which often went hand-in-glove with her Relief Society work; (4) extensive involvement in the National and International Councils of Women, including work to enact the 19th Amendment to the US Constitution, granting women the right to vote; (5) extensive involvement in the lives and careers of her five surviving children, whom she continued to mentor and champion even as adults; and (6) publication of two of Susa's major works of non-fiction, *History of the Young Ladies' Mutual Improvement Association* in 1911 and *Surname Book and Racial History* in 1918. The former was published under the aegis of the general board of the YLMIA and the latter by the general board of the Relief Society with the approval of the board of the Genealogical Society of Utah. Susa's Relief Society and genealogy work are detailed in other chapters.

---

1. Gates to Gates, May 22, 1909, box 11, fd. 1.

Susa's history of the YLMIA was a 488-page tome, which was "revised and published by the General Board of YLMIA."[2] The copyright was obtained in behalf of the general board of the YL-MIA by Martha B. Tingey, general president after the death in 1904 of Elmina S. Taylor, who had served as general president for twenty-four years. The first two-thirds of the book are composed of two parts, the history of the YLMIA itself, which dates from the original meeting held at the Lion House for the daughters of Brigham Young. Interspersed with the history of the association are biographies of fifty-eight women, some that deal with women influential in the organization of the various branches of the YLMIA but who did not serve primarily therein. These women include Eliza R. Snow, Emmeline B. Wells, Sarah Kimball, Mary Isabella Horne, Margaret Smoot, and Jane S. Richards, all of whom were heavily involved in the Relief Society. The last third of the book contains the histories of the YLMIA in sixty-four stakes of the church, extending from western Canada to northern Mexico.

On November 28, 1869, Brigham Young gathered his family in the company of George A. Smith, his first counselor; Smith's wife, Bathsheba, who would become the fourth general president of the Relief Society; and Eliza R. Snow. After evening prayers Brigham, Susa later reported, said,

> All Israel are looking to my family and watching the example set by my wives and children. For this reason I desire to organize my own family first into a society for the promotion of habits of order, thrift, industry and charity; and above all things, I desire them to retrench from their extravagance in dress, in eating and even in speech. The time has come when the sisters must agree to give up their follies of dress and cultivate a modest apparel, a meek deportment, and to set an example before the people of the world worthy of imitation.[3]

The president of the first Retrenchment Association (as the YLMIA was first called) was Ella Young Empey. Many of the presidents of the first Retrenchment Associations had six counselors, as did Ella. All six of them were daughters of Brigham Young: Emily

2. Gates, *History of the YLMIA*, frontispiece.
3. Gates, *History*, 8.

Y. Clawson, Zina Y. Williams, Maria Y. Dougall, Caroline Young, Susa's full sister Dora, and Phebe Young. At the ninth meeting of the Ladies' Cooperative Retrenchment Association on May 28, 1870, Susa was accepted as "general reporter." At the tenth meeting a month later, Susa read an article "of her own composition."[4]

Dora spoke so glowingly of the new organization that her friend, Lona Pratt, daughter of the late Apostle Parley P. Pratt, wanted a similar organization in her own neighborhood. Soon, under the direction of Brigham Young, Eliza R. Snow, with the aid of Mary Isabella Horne, was traveling throughout Utah Territory, organizing the young women into Mutual Improvement Associations. These were administered by local communities until the first official stake MIA was formed in 1878. Spiritual implications of the new organization were recognized. "The one thought of simpler dress, simpler food, simpler habits of life and speech first impressed the girls; but the spiritual meaning of all these things grew with its growth."[5]

The resolutions adopted by the individual units reflected this understanding of the spiritual aspects of the organization: studying the scriptures, "cultivating reverence for sacred things," avoiding gossip, shunning "evil associations," cultivating the mind to "become more enlightened and intelligent," and learning "self-government." The thrust of these resolutions was to cultivate "the mind rather than ministering to the pleasures of the body." Local organizations sprang up throughout the territory. Shortly after the death of Brigham Young in 1877, in accordance with his wishes, the name of the Young Ladies' Retrenchment Association was changed to the Young Ladies' Mutual Improvement Association, bringing it into alignment with the Young Men's Mutual Improvement Association, which had been organized and named under the direction of Brigham Young in 1875.[6]

In 1878 the first organization of the YLMIA on a stake level took place in Salt Lake City under the direction of Eliza R. Snow with Mary A. Freeze named as president. Two years later church president John Taylor chose to form three general heads of the Relief

---

4. Gates, 35–36.
5. Gates.
6. Gates, 60–61.

Society, YLMIA, and Primary. Elmina S. Taylor was called as the first general president of the YLMIA, and the concept of a "central board" was introduced, consisting of other women called to assist the general presidencies. In 1892 the name of central board was changed to general board, which is still used today.[7] Board meetings were initially held irregularly, then quarterly, then monthly (from 1894–98), semi-monthly starting in July 1898, and, finally, weekly beginning in the spring of 1903. Susa became a member of the general board of the YLMIA in 1889 after she returned from Hawai'i and began the *Young Woman's Journal.* In June of that year she spoke on "Women in Foreign Missions" at the YMMIA conference.

In 1892 Susa pushed through a revolutionary proposition: a uniform "guide" of lessons be developed for use in the various YLMIA units throughout the church "to simplify and unify the work done."[8] This was probably the first effort within the church for a uniform set of instruction manuals for any auxiliary organization. As old conflicts over theology gave way, the church would develop a penchant for uniformity in teaching doctrine, and this was a gigantic step. In June of that year the recommendation was adopted, and Susa wrote virtually single-handedly the first two years of the guides. The first guide was printed in 1893, the second in 1896. So popular were the guides that BYA president Benjamin Cluff established a six-week midwinter course in 1893 to teach the principles of Susa's guide, a move quickly adopted at Brigham Young College in Logan and LDS University in Salt Lake City. The first year's guide contained four parts: roster of officers with instructions for use of the guide, a theological department, a historical department, and human physiology and hygiene. It was decided to publish the guide lessons in the *Young Woman's Journal* beginning in 1897.[9]

With few exceptions, the biographies Susa wrote for her *History* were effusive in their praise of these pioneer workers in the YLMIA. Susa's biography was written by Estelle Nell Caldwell, business manager of the *Young Woman's Journal.* Estelle praised Susa's writing skills, "simplicity of style, correctness and vivid illustration adapt her writing

7. Gates, 156.
8. Gates, 181.
9. Gates, 181–87.

to popular audiences." Her *Young Woman's Journal* editorials "show the sympathetic insight into human nature, and the keen perception of human needs, which distinguish the world's great writings."[10]

In July 1897 the offices of the *Young Woman's Journal* moved to the Constitution Building, constructed in 1890 on Main Street in Salt Lake City, with half of the rent to be paid by the *Journal* and the other half by the general board of the YLMIA. Both the Relief Society and the YLMIA became charter members of the National Council of Women. By 1911, Susa had represented the YLMIA at NCW meetings seven times.

Susa lauded the efforts of the YLMIA workers in her *History* for taking the "message of good will out to the world" and in furthering the causes of women's suffrage and world peace. She listed many of the "great women of the world" who had been entertained by the Relief Society and YLMIA general presidencies and general boards in Salt Lake City: "Mrs. Elizabeth Cady Stanton, Miss Susan B. Anthony Mrs. May Wright Sewall, Dr. Anna Howard Shaw, Mrs. Charlotte Perkins Gilman, Mme. L. V. F. Mountford, Lillian M. Hollister, Mary Wood Swift, Fannie Humphreys Gaffney, Mrs. Kate Waller Barrett, Mrs. M. Josie Nelson, Dr. Etta L. Gilchrist, Miss Sadie American, and Mrs. William Todd Helmuth," as well as foreign dignitaries.[11]

Susa continued to serve on the YLMIA general board until 1911, at which time she was called to serve on the general board of the Relief Society. Susa's accomplishments in the early days of the YLMIA are impressive—first editor of the *Young Woman's Journal*, which she launched and led for eleven years; service on the general board for twenty-two years; introduction of uniform study guides for the YLMIA, the first in the church; and visible representation of the women of the church to the luminaries of the world in the National and International Councils of Women. What is more, Susa was aware of her fame in behalf of the YLMIA, and, in true Susa fashion, she was not above a little self-promotion in the *History* she wrote. Although her biography was written primarily by Caldwell, in sections which Susa composed, she said of herself:

10. Gates, 124.
11. Gates, 207–08.

What risk there was the editor [of the *Young Woman's Journal*] willingly assumed, for she was as sanguine financially as she was spiritually. ...

During the eleven years that Mrs. Gates edited the *Journal* there was much creditable advancement made both in the *Journal* itself and by the various writers who gained experience by writing for it. ...

It was gratifying to the long-time editor, Mrs. Gates, to know that the Lord had crowned her labors with partial success, that she had seen the child of her brain and heart grow from a puny weakling to a lusty, well-developed child. She had carried it through the trying sense of early danger and difficulty, and when she at last turned it over to her successor, it bore all the signs of long and vigorous life.

Finally, when Susa resigned as editor, she asked rhetorically, "Was it possible to maintain the standard of excellence, attained through eleven years of experience, when the choice must be made from among those who knew practically nothing of the editorial responsibilities of the magazine."[12]

Susa began the 1910s as an Republican, but she was quick to point out that Jacob was a dyed-in-the-wool Democrat. Their two daughters and three sons were "divided in their politics."[13] Susa and Reed Smoot, a member of the Quorum of the Twelve Apostles and a Republican US senator from Utah, were lifelong friends.[14] Susa worked tirelessly in Smoot's early political campaigns, visited him in Washington, DC, gave receptions for him in Utah, and was a close friend of his first wife, Alpha "Allie" Smoot.

Susa's papers in the Church History Library contain multiple folders of her correspondence with Smoot, and she was not reluctant to seek favors from him for friends and family. For instance, she sought Smoot's help in obtaining a position in the consular service for Rob Easton, a professional singer in New York City and the husband of Susa's half-sister Jeannette.[15] She also wrote Smoot to ask his help in obtaining a position in the New York City law office of J. Reuben

---

12. Gates, 106, 111–13.

13. Susa Young Gates to Arthur Page, Aug. 18, 1913, box 43, fd. 13.

14. Smoot was an apostle from 1900 until his death in 1941 and was a senator until his electoral defeat in 1933, when Democrats were swept into office alongside Franklin D. Roosevelt.

15. Easton was declined for the position because he was over fifty years of age. Gates to Smoot, box 47, fd. 8.

Clark for her daughter Lucy's new husband, Albert E. Bowen. Lucy, increasingly a well-respected performer, was in New York City after signing a recording contract with Columbia Graphophone. Susa tried to persuade Smoot to support Lucy's career by noting that Walter P. Monson, president of the mission in New York City, felt that Lucy was "one of the greatest assets the Church possessed in New York City and he couldn't think of such a thing as losing her."[16]

Susa was heavily involved in elections during the early part of this decade. She failed to see any conflict of interest in her service as a member of the general board of the Relief Society and her political campaigning, since for her the interests of the Republican Party mirrored those of the church. It had been some years since her friend B. H. Roberts was denied his seat in 1900 in the US House of Representatives for being a polygamist and since Smoot had been granted his seat in the Senate after three years of contentious hearings. Although conflict and accusations would continue over church involvement in politics, by the 1910s it had abated somewhat. In addition, since most of the LDS women in Utah were members of the Relief Society, it would be difficult, if not impossible, to have female representation in the political process in Utah if members of the Relief Society were excluded. In fact, Susa commented on the "splendid work" done by Republican women in Salt Lake City following the election of 1912.[17] In addition to Smoot, Susa also carried on extensive correspondence with George Sutherland, US senator from Utah and later a justice of the US Supreme Court, as well as a host of other Utah politicians, including Nephi L. Morris, Ed Callister, and William H. King.

Despite definite views about political issues and candidates, Susa prided herself on never assailing the character of a candidate. In a 1916 letter to Nephi L. Morris, Republican candidate for Utah governor, she wrote, "I have worked a great deal in politics, in this State, since my youth up, and in my labors, I have tried to be open-minded, studious of men and their methods, intelligent in considering

16. Gates to Smoot, Feb. 2, 1917, box 47, fd. 13.

17. Gates to Mrs. James D. Whitmore, Nov. 6, 1912, box 45, fd. 4. Susa's involvement in such partisan politics would almost surely not occur today because of the LDS Church's neutral stand on political issues.

policies, and above all things, I have never, in public, assailed the character or befouled the aspirations and intentions of any political opponent, whatsoever. Principles have always furnished sufficient material for addresses and appeals to voters." The issue for her was always the candidate himself, but she could certainly be vitriolic in her views. "I greatly admire your many and splendid gifts," she wrote to Morris, "and I as greatly deplore your unhappy use of them at certain times and places."[18] Morris would lose the election to Simon Bamberger, Utah's first and only Jewish governor. Susa tended to see political issues like she saw many other issues: in black and white. Her involvement in politics was not for the acquisitions of power. As she wrote to Smoot, "I do not go into politics from purely political motives. Things are right or they are not right to me."[19]

Susa was an ardent admirer of Republican president Theodore Roosevelt, but in 1912 she soured on him. Roosevelt was William McKinley's vice president, and he succeeded him upon McKinley's assassination in 1901. As such, he could have run for another term in 1908, but declined to do so, paving the way for his own vice president, William Howard Taft, to win. But Roosevelt soon became disenchanted with Taft and attempted to recapture the Republican nomination four years later in 1912. When he failed to do so, he launched a third-party bid under the Bull Moose Party. Roosevelt, still popular with voters but not powerful enough to overcome the Republican Party, split the vote with Taft. (Taft won only two states: Utah and Vermont.) Woodrow Wilson, the Democrat, coasted to victory with a large majority of the Electoral College.[20]

Susa had no use for Wilson and blamed Roosevelt for the Republican loss of the presidential election. In "An Address to Women Voters," Susa advised, "If you would have peace, safety and prosperity, you should vote with the old Republican party and for the principles which have brought this nation into existence and ripened it into the full fruitage of power which this country now enjoys. ... A vote for the Bull Moose ticket is a vote for reckless ambition, untried

---

18. Gates to Morris, July 15, 1916, box 47, fd. 2.
19. Gates to Smoot, May 16, 1916, box 47, fd. 11.
20. For more on the 1912 election, see Gould, *Four Hats in the Ring*.

policies, for the rewriting of the Constitution, and is, in fact, a vote worse than thrown away."[21]

Despite working ardently for women's suffrage, Susa did not champion public office for women, opining in 1913, "Given the right to be a complete woman, few women will care for the excitement and the scramble of public life."[22] Susa was herself now moving to remain in the background politically. After entertaining May Wright Sewall in the spring of 1913, Susa wrote to Smoot that Sewall had asked her to renew her association with her. She reported, "But Reed, I am not young any more. And I see so much more to do in temple work and other lines where there is not the strain and the fierce forces to combat that you are now and always have had to meet in your public career. So I must still keep in the background." In 1917, in another letter to Smoot, Susa, complaining of the extravagant expenditures, specifically, a car and a "seven-thousand-dollar rug" of the new Democratic governor of Utah, Bamberger, she insisted again, "I am going to keep out of politics from now on, and I am keeping entirely off from committees in regard to all their patriotic affairs. I am busy with my other affairs." Despite that, she called Bamberger a "shrewd old duck."[23]

Gradually, Susa tired of politics as she became increasingly engrossed in genealogy. Her mind also turned toward her family. In 1913, she wrote, "I find my ambitions, all dropping away from me one by one—except to see all the children settled and happy."[24] When asked for her political support of Herbert Hoover in 1920, she responded, "I cut out politics five years ago and have kept out of it ever since, as my other cares and burdens would not permit me to keep up the work."[25] In the same year, in a letter to Mary Garrett May, Vice Chair, Women's Division, Republican National Committee, Susa reported that she "was at the head of Republican women for fifteen years. I dropped out of the active political work, however, about three years ago and have neither time nor desire to take up the strenuous

---

21. Gates, "Address to Women Voters," box 50, fd. 14, SYGP (CHL).

22. "Prominent English Women Told of Suffrage in Utah," *Deseret Evening News*, Oct. 18, 1913.

23. Gates to Smoot, various letters, box 47, fds. 9 and 13.

24. Susa Young Gates to Jacob Gates, Mar. 1913, box 11, fd. 3.

25. Gates to Gertrude Lane, Apr. 4, 1920, box 45, fd. 4.

labor again."[26] Susa had no problem taking on a myriad of projects, but she could say no with abandon. In 1916 she declined to be the representative of the Republican Women's Club in Utah, recommending instead Sarah Eddington, a single woman with no family.[27]

Susa continued to correspond with Smoot privately about politics. When, in 1919, new LDS Church president Heber J. Grant and his counselors, alongside the Quorum of the Twelve, announced their support for the League of Nations, Susa wrote to Smoot about their mutual opposition to the league. Both agreed amendments to the charter of the league were necessary to guarantee the independence and sovereignty of the United States.[28] But she declined to take any public appointments.

Nonetheless, Susa continued to labor with strong sentiment for causes that could be considered social and political. One issue she vigorously opposed was birth control. In 1916 Susa, as editor of the *Relief Society Magazine,* ran a series of articles denouncing birth control. Susa was responding to the increasingly vocal and prominent birth control movement, led by Margaret Sanger. Sanger, a nurse, pushed for the repeal of Comstock Laws that forbade the dissemination of "obscene" materials, including publications on how to practice birth control. When Sanger opened the country's first birth control clinic in New York City in 1916, she was immediately arrested and the clinic was shut down.[29]

Susa responded to Sanger and the growing birth control movement by printing statements solicited from six members of the Quorum of the Twelve. The strongest response, which mirrored Susa's own feelings, was from Joseph Fielding Smith, son of church president Joseph F. Smith. The younger Smith wrote, "The first great commandment given both to man and beast by the Creator was to 'be fruitful and multiply and replenish the earth' and I have not learned that this commandment was ever repealed. Those who attempt to pervert the ways of the Lord, and to prevent their offspring from coming into the world ... are guilty of one of the most heinous

26. Gates to May, Jan. 2, 1920, box 50, fd. 16.
27. Gates to Grace M. Pierce, Aug. 15, 1916, box 47, fd. 12.
28. Gates to Smoot, Mar. 3, 1919, box 48, fd. 2.
29. See Wallace, *Greater Gotham,* 788–91.

crimes in the category. There is no promise of eternal salvation and exaltation for such as they."[30] These statements drew national attention, causing Susa to seek approval of the comments from the First Presidency. They wrote to Susa, who promptly printed their reply: "We give our unqualified endorsement to these articles, including that of Elder Joseph F. Smith, Jr."[31] Susa then proceeded to present resolutions concerning "birth control or race suicide" to the "Relief Society of the Church of Jesus Christ of Latter-day Saints in Conference Assembled, April 5, 1917, Salt Lake City, Utah":

> Therefore be it Resolved: That we call upon the Latter-day Saint women everywhere to repel this pernicious doctrine. ...
>
> *Resolved:* That we sever all connections with any club, society, or associates who advocate and practice birth-control or race suicide. ...
>
> *Resolved:* That we sustain all laws and law-makers who advocate and maintain laws prohibiting every unnatural and immoral birth-control propaganda. ...
>
> *Resolved, in conclusion,* that we invite the co-operation and support of the Priesthood quorums and auxiliary organizations of the Church in this effort to maintain our high and holy ideals and principles.[32]

In 1913 Susa had been called as the corresponding secretary for the general board of the Relief Society. She was responsible for external communications emanating from the general board and general presidency of the Relief Society. Amy Brown Lyman was general secretary, and would later serve as the general president of the Relief Society from 1940 to 1945. Susa felt that her major contribution to Relief Society work involved genealogy. She had started a newspaper column on genealogy in 1907, and for several years she had simultaneous weekly columns in both the *Deseret News* and the *Salt Lake Herald-Republican* which she continued until 1918. Her

---

30. Joseph F. Smith Jr., "Birth Control," *Relief Society Magazine* (hereafter *RSM*), July 1916, 367–68.

31. First Presidency, Dec. 13, 1916, in "Birth Control," *RSM*, Feb. 1917, 68.

32. Susa Young Gates, "Birth Control," *RSM*, June 1917, 332. LDS policy regarding birth control is vastly different today: "The decision about how many children to have and when to have them is extremely personal and private. It should be left between the couple and the Lord. Church members should not judge one another in this matter." *General Handbook: Serving in the Church of Jesus Christ of Latter-day Saints* (Salt Lake City: Church of Jesus Christ of Latter-day Saints, July 2020), Sec. 38.6.4.

columns often related to individual pioneer histories, which sometimes strayed too far from genealogy, as far as Horace G. Whitney, business manager of the *Deseret News*, was concerned. He instructed Susa in December 1916 that her weekly column needed to stick to "genealogical records" and leave "biographical sketches of pioneers" alone, since they were covered elsewhere.[33]

During this decade Susan traveled extensively as a member of the General Relief Society board, almost always teaching genealogy classes and frequently accompanied by her close friend Elizabeth McCune. In 1910 Susa found herself in Mexico and southern California; in 1913 she traveled to southern Utah and southern Idaho; in 1916 she went to Boise; the next year she made her way to Arizona. In 1918 she spent three weeks in Canada, and as she traveled to Idaho to attend two conferences there, she stopped in Butte, Montana. She made her way to the spot where her oldest son, Bailey, had been killed in an explosion over two decades before. In May 1919 Susa visited the Maricopa Stake in Arizona, as well as the Mexican Mission towns of southern Arizona, traveling with Elder Joseph McMurrin of the Seventy.

Susa had also made another Relief Society trip in 1918, this time with Reed Smoot's sister, Ida Smoot Dusenberry, to Oregon, where she also visited both of her sisters. Dora, who by this time was virtually incapacitated, was living with Mabel in Portland. As she usually did, Susa then spent six weeks in the summer at her beloved cabin in Brighton. By the next year Susa managed to obtain employment for Mabel in the Genealogy Department at church headquarters. Mabel and her husband, Joe Sanborn, who was in poor health, returned to Salt Lake City. Dora also returned to Salt Lake City to live with her married daughter, May Farnes.

Susa enjoyed an active social life. She frequently spent time with a "clique" of four close friends: Elizabeth McCune, Augusta Grant, Edna Smith, and Ann Groesbeck. This heady company included the wife of one of Utah's wealthiest entrepreneurs and the wives of the sixth and seventh presidents of the church. In the summer of 1917, Susa reported a week-long stay of the group at the luxurious new

---

33. Whitney to Gates, Dec. 12, 1916, box 51, fd. 17.

McCune mansion in downtown Salt Lake City. They drove around every night in the McCunes' new Packard automobile.[34] Earlier that same year, Elizabeth McCune, living in New York City at the time, had become very ill. The McCune family solicited Susa's aid at their expense to come East to help take care of her. Susa spent several weeks in January 1917 with Elizabeth and then returned home, stopping briefly in Chicago and Milwaukee on Relief Society business. She delivered a well-publicized speech at the only Mormon chapel in Chicago.[35]

Susa frequently had large and lavish birthday parties, often at the Lion House in conjunction with the "birthday" of the Lion House itself, since she had been the first child born there. Her sixty-third birthday party, held on March 18, 1919, was typical. Clarissa Smith Williams, first counselor in the Relief Society presidency, was master of ceremonies, and the impressive guest list included Charles W. Penrose, second counselor in the First Presidency; Reed Smoot; Joseph Fielding Smith; and the presidencies of the MIA and the Primary organizations, among others. Susa's husband, Jacob, was asked to speak, and he told of the "many great men and women of the earth and of this Church and kingdom" that the Gates family had entertained in their homes, then proceeded to list prominent people inside and outside of the church. In addition to church presidents and apostles, Jacob mentioned prominent women's leaders like Susan B. Anthony and May Sewall.[36] Other guests included Ernest Thompson Seton, F. Marion Crawford, G. Stanley Hall, Susa's friend Charlotte Perkins Gilman, and Judith Allen Foster. John A. Widtsoe, as part of the biographical sketch he wrote of Susa, listed more feminist leaders and famous friends, including Ida Husted Harper, Clara Barton, Anna Howard Shaw, Kate Waller Barrett, Lady Aberdeen, Rebecca West, Peggy Pulitzer (aka Margaret Leech, Pulitzer Prize-winning historian), Susan Ertz, Mary Green, Susanna Dodd, Sadie American, and Lydia Mountford.[37]

---

34. Susa Young Gates to Reed Smoot, July 9, 1917, box 47, fd. 13.
35. Typescript of *Chicago Tribune* article, Feb. 1, 1917, box 52, fd. 1, SYGP (CHL).
36. Susa Young Gates, journal, 1919, box 52, fd. 8, SYGP (CHL).
37. Widtsoe, "Sketch of Susa Young Gates," box 3, fd. 35, SYGP (CHL). Although this box is labeled "autobiographical sketches," it includes biographies of Susa by others.

As Susa's interest in politics began to wane, she started to retreat from her involvement in the National and International Councils of Women. She had been heavily involved in the national and international councils for over two decades. Susan B. Anthony had told her many years before that Susa would become president of the National Council of Women if she would give up her "militant Mormonism," to which Susa replied that "her price was too high."[38]

In April 1914 Susa took her third and final trip to Europe, this time to the International Council of Women meeting in Rome. She had hoped to serve as a delegate, but all delegate positions had already been filled, and Susa was informed by Kate Waller Barrett, president of the NCW, that she could go only as an alternate.[39] She had originally not planned to make the trip because of financial difficulties but was eventually able to marshal the necessary assistance.[40] During this meeting, which was held on the eve of the beginning of World War I, Susa was appointed a member of the International Peace Committee.[41]

In July 1915 she attended the Panama–Pacific Exposition in San Francisco, which included a focus on genealogy. Susa and the church's participation were under the direction of the Genealogical Society of Utah and the Relief Society. She was part of a large contingent, which included all three members of the First Presidency.[42] There was even a Utah Day at the meeting, and Susa taught lessons with Nephi Anderson. Emma Lucy sang *O Ye Mountains High* at the exposition, and the conference was adjudged a success. Susa usually felt that her efforts to promote genealogical work among her fellow Saints was an uphill battle. She felt, however, that a book devoted to genealogy would be helpful, and the result was the publication in 1918 of the *Surname Book and Racial History*.[43]

Five months after the exposition, Lady Ishbel Aberdeen, president of the ICW, visited Utah with her husband. Emmeline B.

---

38. Widtsoe.

39. Barrett to Gates, Apr. 14, 1914, box 43, fd. 13.

40. Gates, "Report of Visit," box 43, fd. 13, SYGP (CHL).

41. Susa Young Gates, "War! War! And Why War?" *Relief Society Bulletin*, Sep. 1914, 3.

42. The presidency was composed of Joseph F. Smith, Anthon H. Lund, who was also president of the Utah Genealogical Society, and Charles W. Penrose, who was vice president of the genealogical society.

43. "Program of Exercises," box 69, fd. 14, SYGP (CHL).

Wells was honorary chair of the welcoming committee, which held a formal function at the Hotel Utah, and Susa was the chair and toast-mistress. But after that event, Susa's involvement in the National and International Women's Councils waned.[44]

By the next year, the general board of the Relief Society asked the First Presidency what relationship the church should have with the national and international women's councils. The First Presidency responded on February 6, 1916, that the affiliation could continue, but that it should be considered a temporary "passing incident in the life of the Society, an incident which may be terminated at any time without affecting in any way the Society itself; and that the Society must be regarded as paramount in importance to everything else now connected with it ... and that its meetings must be conducted in the spirit of a religious organization."[45] Implicit was the under-standing that the day would come when the church would chart its own course. It took over fifty years, but that day came after Belle Spafford, the ninth general president of the Relief Society, had com-pleted her term as president of the National Council of Women from 1968 to 1970.

In November 1918, Joseph F. Smith, president of the church for seventeen years and one of Susa's closest friends, died. He was eighty years old, and both Susa and Jacob were devastated. In a let-ter to Smoot explaining the circumstances of Smith's death, Susa addressed the senator as "My dearest living Friend and Brother now that President Smith has passed away."[46] Because of her long-stand-ing association with the Smith family, Susa was asked to join the family in the Beehive House, where she remained for several days to help the family by answering the door and receiving telephone messages. Susa felt honored to perform this last labor of love for Joseph F. With Smith's passing, Heber J. Grant, also a close friend of Susa and Jacob, as well as the husband of Susa's fellow "clique" member, Augusta "Gusta" Grant, became the seventh president of the LDS Church.

---

44. "Luncheon in Honor of Lady Aberdeen," box 34, fd. 3, SYGP (CHL).

45. First Presidency to Emmeline B. Wells, Feb. 6, 1916, photocopy in author's possession.

46. Gates to Smoot, Nov. 29, 1918, box 48, fd. 1.

Susa's friendships at the highest levels of the church created new opportunities for the Gates family. As Emma Lucy's singing career began to materialize, Jacob lived with her in Germany for a time while she performed there. Even while he was away, Susa began to lobby as early as 1913 for Jacob to obtain a full-time position in church employment as a recorder in the Salt Lake temple. On February 6 of that year she wrote to Joseph F. Smith, recommending Jacob and noting that he would be glad to return home from Germany if necessary. This would provide Jacob a steady income "where he will not be obliged to travel on foot from door to door getting insurance in all kinds of weather."[47] His mining interests had come to naught; his furniture business in Provo had foundered. He had worked hard but had not enjoyed great financial success. His efforts usually depended on the additional income Susa could muster by writing for magazines and newspapers. This, of course, was stressful for Susa, who was often overwhelmed with the demands of her volunteer service. Susa's efforts in behalf of Jacob were successful. In 1915 she wrote to Smith expressing her gratitude that Jacob had been "suggested to work in the Temple."[48] The next year Jacob was offered a position as an assistant recorder, a position he held until his retirement in 1938. The money Jacob earned as a recorder did not make the family wealthy, but it did provide them with something they often lacked: a steady income.

Jacob's efforts to support his wife emotionally in her multiple pursuits had allowed her to spend long periods of time away from home and children. He had maintained stability and peace within the home during her absences. Susa was able to give freely of her time in volunteer service because Jacob had been willing to be a strong, calming influence in a house full of high-performance, high-spirited family members. By their combined efforts and sacrifice, Jacob and Susa gave their children opportunities to further their education, develop their talents, and excel in their chosen fields. Susa always seemed to feel Jacob's support, and she contributed what she could to the financial well-being of the family, allowing them to stretch his modest income to provide opportunities for the development of

47. Gates to Joseph F. Smith, Feb. 6, 1913, box 58, fd. 11.
48. Gates to Smith, Aug. 31, 1916, box 59, fd. 2.

306

their children. Susa advised Jacob that "you are the most eminently successful husband and father I know of," praising him for being "sincere, kind, broad, [and] big-hearted."[49] The Gates family lived a modest life, and granddaughter Lurene Gates Wilkinson never recalls thinking of them as "poor."[50]

Susa commented in a letter to Jacob in 1910 that President Smith "is always so sweet to us, but I often feel that he doesn't quite approve of the way we do with our children."[51] The Gates children enjoyed bounteous educational opportunities, and Susa and Jacob appear to have been fairly indulgent parents. Susa always tried to facilitate her children's pathways by using her considerable influence for their benefit, beginning with Leah. Susa had started the domestic science program at the Brigham Young Academy and kept the program alive until Leah could return from her post-graduate studies at the Pratt Institute in New York and take her mother's place in 1897 as department chair. Leah's husband, John A. Widtsoe, had served on the faculties of both Brigham Young Academy and the Utah Agricultural College in Logan, where he had become president in 1907. In 1916 he was named as the president of the University of Utah, and the couple relocated to Salt Lake City from Logan. Widtsoe remained president until 1921 when he was called as a member of the Quorum of the Twelve Apostles. Leah became president of the Salt Lake City Federation of Women's Clubs in 1919. Leah and John were prominent in Mormon intellectual circles, and published widely in the fields of nutrition and food science. They were especially known as proponents of the Word of Wisdom, the term used to describe the strict Mormon health code, which prohibited the use of alcohol, tobacco, tea, and coffee.[52]

Another of Leah and John's major contributions to LDS theology relates to what historian Kathryn Shirts has called the "priesthood/motherhood model," which had first been enunciated by Susa and which continues to have a large influence in Mormon thought.[53] Joseph F. Smith had mentored Susa during their joint time together

49. Gates to Gates, box 11, fd. 1.
50. Lurene Gates Wilkinson, personal communication with author, Feb. 2009.
51. Gates to Gates, Aug. 24, 1910, box 11, fd. 1.
52. News clipping, box 111, fd. 12.
53. Shirts, "Role of Susa Young Gates."

in Hawaii. For the first two years of the Gateses' mission to Lāʻie in the mid-1880s, Smith was there on the "underground" to escape prosecution for plural marriage. Susa had asked him why she was excluded from the council meetings of the priesthood brethren when she knew more than any of the men there except for her husband and Smith himself. Smith told Susa that it was not a matter of worthiness or capability, but of appointment. Susa seems to have accepted Smith's explanations and later wrote about them. Why women were not given the priesthood was "not because of lack of intelligence, or leadership qualities perhaps—but ever and always because she is the mother of the race." That is to say, Susa and others reasoned, priesthood for men and motherhood for women are parallel and equally spiritual tracks for the two genders. Although she does not hold the priesthood, a mother does share all the blessings of the priesthood. Susa continued, "No woman can be an ideal mother here or hereafter and at the same time assume the heavy tasks and responsibilities which accompany direct leadership." Nonetheless, Susa's entire life spoke to her ardent conviction that, in every way except holding the priesthood, women are the equal of men.[54]

In 1928 Susa and Leah co-authored a pamphlet entitled *Women of the "Mormon" Church*. There they expanded on the priesthood/motherhood model: "Women do not hold the priesthood, but they do share equally in the blessings and gifts bestowed on the priesthood in temple courts, in civic, social and domestic life." For Leah, ideal motherhood involved academic and scientific principles of domestic science, or home economics, which she had studied at the Pratt Institute in New York. Susa and Leah asserted that adding priesthood responsibilities to women already weighed down with other responsibilities was foolish. "No woman could safely carry the triple burden of wifehood, motherhood and at the same time function in priestly orders. Yet her creative home labor ranks side by side, in earthly and heavenly importance, with her husband's priestly responsibilities. ... He is the leader and she follows, not because she must, but because she will. She chooses her sphere as he chooses his."[55]

Leah, heavily influenced by her mother's thinking, later expanded

---

54. Gates, *Why I Believe*, 13–14.
55. Gates and Widtsoe, *Women of the "Mormon" Church*, 5.

these thoughts into a series on "Priesthood and Womanhood" in the October and November 1933 issues of the *Relief Society Magazine*. Leah helped "women of the church understand not only the relevance of priesthood in their lives, but also the equal 'status and opportunity' of motherhood."[56] Furthermore, Leah believed that the qualities of motherhood were not dependent on whether a woman has actually physically borne children, since motherhood is an eternal concept. Just as men holding the priesthood learn to model godly behavior, women without earthly children develop the heavenly traits of motherhood in this life.[57]

Much of what Leah taught and wrote found its way into the chapter on "Priesthood in the Home" in the book authored in 1939 by her husband entitled *Priesthood and Church Government*. Leah and John continued to preach and model the concept of the equality of husband and wife, "The place of woman in the Church is to walk beside the man, not in front of him nor behind him."[58] Decades later, their teachings remain a cornerstone for relationships between men and women in the church.

While Susa and Leah were feminists of their day, they differ, as Kathryn Shirts notes, from modern-day feminists, particularly those who advocate ordination of women to the Mormon priesthood. "Present-day feminists dismiss not only separate spheres for men and women but also the role of men as natural leaders, concepts that both Susa Young Gates and Leah Widtsoe took for granted." Leah "adapted" her mother's beliefs and teachings on motherhood "as a spiritual calling parallel to priesthood office," which "gave women a significant role of their own and provided a rationale for modifying the strictly hierarchical view of the relationship between men and women held in previous generations."[59]

Susa's other surviving daughter, Emma Lucy, who had over the years gone by multiple monikers, namely, Lu, Lule, and Lulu, ultimately became known as Lucy Gates. This was at the insistence of her music managers, who eschewed double names and pushed

56. Shirts, "Role of Susa Young Gates," 132.
57. Shirts, 129–30.
58. John A. Widtsoe, "Evidences and Reconciliations: What Is the Place of Woman in the Church?" *Improvement Era*, Mar. 1942, 35, 62.
59. Shirts, "Role of Susa Young Gates," 138–39.

for simplicity. The shorter the name, the easier for audiences to remember, and for large advertisements in newspapers. After her
unfortunate singing debut in New York City in 1902, she continued
with further vocal training in New York City, Paris, and Berlin. After
mastering multiple major operatic roles at the Royal Opera House
in Cassel (today Kassel), Germany, she had moved to Berlin, where
for two years she was pigeonholed into again performing minor roles.
Always anxious to promote her children, Susa, with some temerity,
wrote in 1912 to Emil Paur, newly appointed director of the Royal
Opera House in Berlin, recommending both Lucy and Susa's son
Cecil to him.[60] Paur, originally from Austria, had enjoyed a distinguished career in America from 1893 to 1910, conducting orchestras
in Boston, New York City, and Pittsburgh before returning to Europe. If he responded to Susa's letter, there is no evidence of it.

In 1912 Lucy contracted typhoid fever and had to return to Utah
to recuperate. Susa spent several weeks taking care of her in Logan.
Susa and Jacob decided jointly that Lucy needed to be accompanied
back to Germany after her recovery. Jacob would live with her and
fulfill an LDS mission at the same time.[61] But upon her return to
Europe with her father, Lucy learned that the prima donna position in Cassel, Germany, had been given to another singer, since the
management was unsure if Lucy would be returning.

Lucy's loss of the role led to a cascade of events that precipitated
a major family fight with Lucy and Jacob on one side, and Susa, who
had remained in Utah, on the other. Susa felt that Lucy should be
ready to return to the Royal Opera House in Berlin and hopefully
replace Frieda Hempel. When it became apparent that Lucy was not
going to sing major roles in Berlin, she and her father decided to
sign a three-year contract in Cassel when the prima donna position
there opened up again. In multiple letters to Jacob and Emma Lucy
in March and April 1913, Susa railed against this decision. Lucy was
too far along in her career to "bury herself in a country town."[62] It
would be unwise to "stay three more dismal hopeless years in Cassel."

---

60. Gates to Paur, 1912, box 58, fd. 10.

61. Susa Young Gates to Jacob Gates, Jan. 5, 1913, box 11, fd. 2.

62. At the time, Cassel had a population of over 150,000, and was considerably
larger than Salt Lake City.

Preferable to staying in Cassel would be coming home, which Susa reported all of Lucy's friends would prefer for her to do.[63]

Susa, ever dedicated to her faith, thought that if Lucy would "come out of her shell of silence" and simply identify herself as a Mormon, a girl from Utah, and a granddaughter of Brigham Young and bear a simple testimony, then things would work out.[64] When Lucy eventually signed a contract for three more years in Cassel, Susa lamented that her hopes had been "dashed into a thousand fragments. ... It was about the worst suffering I have ever endured, except Hal's [early mission release] for some days, or weeks." Susa's harsh words were so painful for Lucy that Lucy became physically ill.[65] Both Jacob and Cecil asked Susa to cease her criticism of what had been a joint decision of Jacob and Lucy, who were both aware of current circumstances in Germany, whereas Susa was not.

Susa was chagrined that nobody in Germany was listening to her advice. In a letter to Jacob, she wallowed in self-pity:

Don't worry. I am done trying to get my children or anyone else to do any one thing on this earth except what they choose to do. I think I have learned my lesson—it has come hard—very hard—for I realize that they all kind of feel that this, that or the other wouldn't have happened to any of them if mother had or had not done this, that or the other. ... I am trying to school myself, and I doubt not I shall succeed, as I did with Dora—to care absolutely nothing about what you all do or leave undone. I suppose in time I can live my *detached* life, doing all in my power to make you happy and comfortable when you are with me, but offering none of you my unwelcome advice and suggestions. Forgive me, dear papa, for you know that I love you and our dear children will all my heart. But I am determined with the help of my Father to overcome my bad habit of giving advice.[66]

Susa's allusion to her sister Dora is telling. Susa was not blind to her own tendency to offer unsolicited advice and opinions. She knew that she could be intense, even harsh, when her beliefs were not shared and her advice not followed. She seemed to regret these

63. Gates to Gates, various letters, box 11, fd. 3.

64. Gates to Gates, May 5, 1913, box 11, fd. 4.

65. Lucy Gates to Jacob Gates, July 5, 1913, box 8, fd. 11.

66. Susa Young Gates, quoted in Jacob F. Gates to Susa Young Gates, July 3, 1913, box 11, fd. 4 (emphasis in original).

lapses, and she longed for her family to understand her intentions. In addition to her criticism of Jacob and Lucy, there were during these months letters full of love and apologies. She was grieved that she had "wounded" Lucy so badly.[67]

Susa, feeling alone and frustrated, drew solace from her service in the temple. "I am sure I don't know what I would have done throughout this lonely and trying winter if I had not been in the temple." A few weeks later, on July 4, 1913, suing for peace, Susa suggested the family "forget all the disagreeable things, for life is not long enough to be spent in making each other unhappy." She had also written to Jacob, in a letter with portions now torn from it, that she was his "sweetheart wife," and she asked him to "keep this little love letter to yourself. The children need not know *all* our secrets, and this is our sweet and sacred secret."[68]

All of Susa's anxiety and worry turned out for naught. The next year in Cassel was a stunning success for Lucy, and she expanded her repertoire substantially. Jacob, perhaps unable to help himself from sharing his version of "I told you so," wrote to Susa in October 1913 that it is "most providential that Lule came back here" to Cassel.[69]

Because Jacob would be living in Germany, arrangements had been made for him to be called as an official LDS missionary. His ministerial certificate, signed by all three members of the First Presidency, was issued January 7, 1913.[70] Just over a year later, he left for home. He could barely proselytize, given harsh laws against Mormons and other groups.[71] Mormon elders were routinely imprisoned, and mission president Hyrum Valentine in Basel, Switzerland, warned Jacob that his "stay in Berlin will be fraught with great danger to you and your children should they appear in our meetings or even associate with our Elders. Under the circumstances you may feel at liberty to move about as you choose and any service which you may render us will be greatly appreciated."[72]

---

67. Susa Young Gates to Jacob Gates and children, various letters, box 11, fd. 4.

68. Gates to husband and children, various letters, box 11, fd. 4.

69. Gates to Gates, Oct. 9, 1913, box 8, fd. 12.

70. In box 5, fd. 13, SYGP (CHL).

71. See, for example, Nelson, *Moroni and the Swastika*. See also letters from Jacob Gates to Susa Young Gates, box 8, fds. 12 and 14.

72. Valentine to Gates, Mar. 10, 1913, box 58, fd. 11.

During his year in Germany, Jacob mostly attended operas. He rode in a zeppelin balloon and wrote an article about his experience for the newspapers in Salt Lake City. Susa asked him why he had not contacted Apostle Rudger Clawson, president of the European Mission in Liverpool, since after all, he had been officially called as a missionary. A month later, Susa wrote again to Jacob, urging him to put himself under Clawson's charge. Several weeks after that, Susa suggested a three-month mission for Jacob during the summer in England. There is no evidence that Jacob contacted Clawson.[73]

Jacob's separation from Susa for over a year was more difficult for Susa than for Jacob. He missed Susa, but wrote her, " I am having a fine, a pleasant, a glorious time in this my first real trip out into this big world."[74] Susa, on the other hand, was very occupied at home with her temple, genealogy, and Relief Society work. She also felt great tension because of the internecine battles among the Relief Society general board regarding the writing of lesson manuals and preparations for the new *Relief Society Bulletin*. The battles among the general board became so intense that Joseph F. Smith threatened "that if we could not behave ourselves better than we were doing he would dissolve the whole Board and put in a new one."[75]

Jacob worried about Susa, perhaps because of her health scare a decade earlier and perhaps because he knew how fully she threw herself into her work. In a letter in the fall of 1913, he advised her to not confine her pleasures to Relief Society and temple work "and looking after the welfare of the great public. I have been generous of my dear wife's strength and talents, and I have no great cause to complain, but I want her to remember to keep her feet on the earth and her heart also for I am still here. But I love you too dearly to see you undertake anything too seriously, too strenuously."[76]

While Jacob was in Germany, he watched over Lucy, as well as Romania Hyde, a close family friend who was studying violin in Berlin. When she was not performing in operatic roles, Lucy traveled extensively giving concerts, most often in Scotland, where she

---

73. Gates to Gates, various letters, box 11, fds. 2–4.
74. Gates to Gates, May 1, 1913, box 8, fd. 9.
75. Susa Young Gates to Jacob Gates, Dec. 13, 1913, box 11, fd. 6.
76. Gates to Gates, October 27, 1913, box 8, fd. 12.

was a particular favorite. Lucy's three-year contract in Cassel was aborted following the outbreak of World War I. In August 1914 Lucy found herself in England, unable initially to return to America because of the war. She arrived in New York City in September. While there, she sang for the Rubenstein Club, where she saw Enrico Caruso, famed soprano Geraldine Farrar, and Arturo Toscanini. Reportedly, Caruso told her that she had the "clearest, purest voice, and the most perfect intonation he had ever heard."[77]

When she returned to Utah, Lucy formed, with brother Cecil, the Lucy Gates Grand Opera Company. By this time she had learned forty-five operatic roles. In Salt Lake City Lucy and Cecil staged two full-scale operas, *La Traviata,* in 1915, and *Faust* in 1916. Lucy and Cecil took these productions on the road to Ogden, Logan, and Provo as well. Lucy was always a favorite with her Utah audiences, from whom she invariably received rave reviews.[78]

In June 1916 Lucy married Albert E. Bowen, a prominent widowed attorney from Logan with twin sons. She signed a contract with Columbia Graphophone and enjoyed a prominent career as a coloratura. She and Albert never had children of their own. Albert was called to the Quorum of the Twelve Apostles in 1937. Had Susa lived, she would have witnessed both of her sons-in-law becoming apostles.

Cecil fulfilled a mission to the New England States from 1907 to 1910, where he was active in musical circles. Susa visited him during his missionary service. He spent a year studying at the New England Conservatory of Music before departing in 1910 with Lucy for Germany, where he spent three years studying music at the Schwarenka Conservatory in Berlin. He returned home and lived with Susa, who once again used her considerable influence to secure a teaching position for him in Utah.

Cecil, or "Pete," as he was often called, became head of the music department at the LDS University in the fall of 1913, staying until 1925. In 1916 he was named second assistant conductor of the Mormon Tabernacle Choir. He remained with the choir until 1935, becoming one of the most famous and prolific of Mormon composers. In addition, he served as a member of the general board of the

77. Lucy Gates to Susa Young Gates and Jacob Gates, Sep. 29, 1914, box 59, fd. 1.
78. News clippings, box 107, fd. 11, SYGP (CHL).

Young Men's Mutual Improvement Association from 1918 to 1929. He was also one of the thirteen members of the original General Church Music Committee formed in 1920. Unfortunately, beginning in 1929 Cecil developed a progressive neurological disease and spent the last decade of his life as an invalid. He died in 1941 at age fifty-four, survived by his widow Gweneth Gibbs Gates, with whom he had five children.[79]

Harvey, who was always called "Hal" by family and friends, was the one child, at least since the death of Bailey, who remained largely outside of Susa's influence. He had served a mission to the Northwestern States, based in Portland, Oregon, from 1907 to 1909. He served another very brief mission to England, beginning at the end of 1911. It appears that he did little, if any, missionary work during his short stay in Britain, and he was released suddenly a few months later. His release from missionary service was a source of great consternation to his parents, who exchanged notes about their concern for him.[80]

After Hal left England, he traveled to Germany and then went on to New York City, where he found employment at Universal Studios. While there, he married a young woman named Lucie Jeanne "Bichette" Genez from New Jersey. Susa's half-sister Jeannette Easton, who lived in New York City, attended the wedding at the Genez home in Hoboken. The marriage, which occurred quickly, was a shock. Jacob wrote candidly to Susa about their inability to control Hal now that he was an adult:

> This is another of the surprises that our boy has sprung on us. What next. We will have to take all as patiently as possible, and make the best of it. … It may be better for Hal to marry, than to drift about and perhaps do something worse. … Our suggestions, and our councils have never appealed to him very much. We have prayed for him, wept over him, pleaded for him and to him. The Lord only knows what the end will be. I shall not upbraid him. I shall continue to love him the best I may, and commit him to the care of the good Father, whose son he is.[81]

---

79. "Death Removes Leading Utah Music Figure," *Salt Lake Tribune*, Aug. 30, 1941, pgs. 17, 25.

80. Susa Young Gates to Jacob Gates, May 1913, box 11, fd. 4.

81. Gates to Gates, Dec. 17, 1912, box 8, fd. 4.

Jacob, en route to Germany, visited with Hal and his new wife in New York City in January 1913.

By 1915 Hal and his wife were living in Los Angeles, where he became a well-known scriptwriter, with over 200 screenplays to his credit. He worked for several film companies, as well as a freelance writer. Hal was the one adult child of Susa and Jacob who did not practice Mormonism later in life. He smoked heavily and died in 1948 at fifty-nine. He would still return to Salt Lake City to visit with family. Susa, as usual, was less impressed by secular success, and she worried deeply about Hal's drift away from the LDS Church.

Franklin was the youngest of the Gates siblings to marry. He had studied at the Utah Agricultural College, where he had been observed by his brother-in-law, John A. Widtsoe, president of the institution, to be brilliant, but perhaps not as focused as he could be. Franklin fell in love with diminutive Florence Keate, and they were married in August 1913 when Franklin was twenty years old. Franklin's bishop had talked with Joseph F. Smith prior to the marriage about several young men in his ward. The bishop said perhaps Franklin could go on a mission with his wife, to which Smith assented. On their wedding night the newlyweds were informed by their bishop that they were being called on a mission. The news was not well received, after which Susa explained to Jacob, who was still in Germany with Lucy, "We had a scene here." Florence's parents were particularly anguished over the call.[82]

Nonetheless, the young couple left within two months for Hilo, Hawai'i, where they served for almost two years, supported by $10 a month from Susa and Cecil. Franklin and Florence returned home, and with the influence of his family, he obtained a position as janitor in the Logan temple. Soon thereafter, however, he quit his job and returned to school at the University of Utah, subsidized by Susa and Jacob. Susa noted that Franklin received less financial assistance than any of his siblings, and she and Jacob were anxious for him to complete his education. In 1920 she and Jacob were paying $75 per month for Franklin to continue his education; by that time, he and Florence had three children.[83]

---

82. Susa Young Gates to Jacob Gates and Lucy Gates, Aug. 20, 1913, box 11, fd. 5.
83. Susa Young Gates to Mrs. Gilbert H. Grosvenor, Jan. 26, 1920, box 44, fd. 6.

After finishing at the University of Utah, Frank attended Harvard University for one year of post-graduate studies. He later worked for Warner Brothers Studios in Hollywood, KSL radio station in Salt Lake City, and the Federal Radio Commission in Washington, DC, before settling in Salt Lake City, where he directed his own acoustics business. He died in 1979 at age eighty-six. Of Susa's five adult children, only Leah, who died at ninety-one in 1965, lived longer.

Best and Truest of Friends

The triumvirate of men most consequential in Susa's life were her father, Brigham Young, her second husband, Jacob Gates, and her beloved friend and "brother," Joseph F. Smith, sixth president of the LDS Church. The importance in Susa's life of her relationship with Smith cannot be overestimated.

Smith had been an acquaintance of the Young family for as long as Susa could remember. He was seventeen years older than Susa, and she could not recall life without him. Joseph F. was the son of Hyrum Smith, older brother of the Prophet Joseph Smith, and Hyrum's second wife, Mary Fielding. He was born on November 13, 1838, in Far West, Missouri, just days after his father had been imprisoned in Liberty Jail in present-day Independence, Missouri, after Missouri governor Lilburn Boggs had issued the so-called "extermination order" for Mormons. Joseph F. lost his father when Hyrum and Joseph were assassinated in Carthage, Illinois, in June 1844. Joseph F. went west with his mother. Mary Fielding Smith was a force to be reckoned with, and she took not only her own two children, but the six children of Hyrum from his deceased first wife, Jerusha Barden.

Mary Smith lived a hard-scrabble life with her children and died in 1852 in Salt Lake City when Joseph F. was not yet fourteen years old. He would later write of the "boiling" rage he felt as a young man, due, he said, to the loss of both his parents at so young an age.[1] He was

---

1. Smith, "Recollections," *Juvenile Instructor*, Mar.-June 1871.

rudderless, probably used alcohol and tobacco, and got into trouble. Two years after his mother died, young Joseph F. was called as a missionary to Hawai'i, after he assaulted a teacher at school.[2] The mission changed his life. Life on the islands was hard, and as a young orphan, he received almost no mail. But he learned to control his temper better and eventually became knowledgeable in the native language.

In February 1858 he returned to Salt Lake City, where he thereafter was a frequent guest in the Brigham Young home. Susa and Joseph F. shared a lifelong friendship. Susa developed a youthful crush on him at age fourteen, which she confessed to him in writing on at least two occasions, first in 1887 when Susa was in Hawai'i on her own mission with Jacob, and later in 1906, after Smith was president of the church. In her many letters to him, Susa addressed him as her "Dear beloved brother,"[3] and Joseph F. referred to Susa and Jacob as "among the truest and best and most beloved" of friends.[4]

By 1866, at twenty-seven, Joseph F. had become an apostle, serving as second counselor to Brigham Young in the First Presidency of the church until Young's death in 1877. He would subsequently serve as second counselor to three more church presidents: John Taylor, Wilford W. Woodruff, and Lorenzo Snow, before becoming president himself in 1901.

Smith had become a polygamist at the urging of Brigham Young. By 1885 he had married six women, and fled to Hawai'i with his second wife, Julina Lambson, to avoid prosecution. Smith and his first wife, cousin Levira Smith, divorced in 1868 after she had become disillusioned with polygamy. During the years 1885 to 1887, within the very small community of La'ie, the Smiths and the Gateses became particularly close friends. Joseph F. was a great comfort to Susa and Jacob as they dealt with the deaths of their two young sons, Jay and Karl. It was Joseph F. who reportedly had seen in a dream two gravesites side by side several weeks before the deaths of the two young boys.

Joseph F. and Susa's relationship was close enough to allow both to speak candidly to one another and share personal feelings that

---

2. Kenney, "Before the Beard."

3. See various letters in both Susa's papers and Joseph F. Smith's papers.

4. See, for example, letters from Smith to Gates while in Hawai'i, box 46, fd. 32.

might have caused offense in others. When Susa, always headstrong, had a conflict with another person in the community—the details of the incident are unknown—Joseph F. wrote to her that she had a "right to speak when and where you please," but advised her that next time she "do so with a little more wisdom." He admitted that he himself had a very impetuous nature and that it would be foolish for Susa to take offense at "earnest reproof."[5]

Eight months later, when twenty-one-year-old Elizabeth Noall was called as president of the local Relief Socity, Susa took umbrage. She scribbled a letter to Joseph F., full of hurt and embarrassment. "I would like to ask you as a friend, the reason of the slight which has been put upon me tonight in the appointments which have been made." Why had Noall, "a young girl," been "placed over my head ... when age has generally had its weight in these matters here." Susa insisted that "it is not office that I care for," but it was rather the embarrassment that Noall's calling had caused her. "I could not but see how all the boys and even [mission] President Farr rejoiced in my apparent humiliation." She asked her friend to "tell me please whose appointment it was."[6]

Smith's response to Susa was quick and blunt, and it sheds light on the depth of their friendship:

My dear Sister Susa,

Your letter of enquiry just handed me has been read, with surprise. I cannot see why you should ask me any such question. Bros. Farr and King are the Authorities here, and could no doubt answer better than I can. Be that as it may, I will answer for myself. When the question was submitted to me by Bros. Farr & King, I suggested Sister King for the position, but my suggestion was not accepted. Sister Noall was the choice, and I had no more to say. That you were not the choice or that Sister King was not, is not my fault, if it be the fault of anyone.

Nor do I see that you should raise the question at all. Indeed, I think it out of place for you to do so, inasmuch as it is not office that you care for. As to age, if *it* is a qualification, then Sister Madsen, and not you, should feel aggrieved. If ability only then *you* might feel aggrieved, altho Sister Noall has good ability. But these are not factors in this question

---

5. Smith to Gates, July 25, 1886, box 46, fd. 32.
6. Gates to Smith, Apr. 1, 1887, box 14, fd. 32, Smith Papers.

at all. Either you or Sister Noall have as good ability as the former presidents have had, and you are both of age.

My wife came here when Sister Farr did but Sister F. was chosen President, and my wife did not complain about it, altho her ability and judgement was at least in all respects equal to Sister F.'s.

If you had said nothing about it no one would have suspected that you care one whit. And all would have admired your respect for the decision of the Council and your alacrity to work where they assigned you. As it is at least I am apprised of your disappointment, and disagreement with the voice of the Council. I voted for it, and consented to it before it came to Council knowing it was the choice of all I had heard refer to the subject. That was enough for me, and should have been sufficient for you.

With love and sympathy in your bereavements, in the loss of your precious little boys, I am your friend and brother, Jos. F. Smith.

P.S. permit me to suggest, that if the [missionary] boys whispered and bro. F. exulted, disappoint them by disarming them of their apprehensions, by never letting know that you did not make the suggestion yourself. Otherwise you put yourself in their power and confess they were right.[7]

Susa accepted the rebuke; she and Joseph F. continued their lifelong friendship. Susa also accepted her place as a woman among priesthood holders in the church.

A few months later in the summer of 1887, as Joseph F. and Julina Smith were preparing to return to Utah, Susa expressed concern that he might be apprehended as a polygamist as soon as he reached American soil. She questioned whether it might be better for them to go to Australia or New Zealand. She lamented that church members in Hawai'i would need to "learn to stand alone," after having "leaned so much on you, who have been to us a rock of strength." She confessed that their friendship had been a blessing for her since she was an adolescent. "I am not going to try and tell you how I individually felt and feel, for I am so grateful for the blessed priviledge my husband and myself have enjoyed of seeking and gaining your friendship, a friendship aye an affection that I have longed to call mine ever since I was a girl of fourteen." She assured him that "two loving friends [Susa and Jacob] will watch your shining course from

7. Smith to Gates, Apr. 1, 1887, box 46, fd. 32.

one pinnacle of greatness to another with true and faithful hearts."[8] She sought forgiveness for her misdeeds and hoped that Joseph F. would remember only the good.

Frequent correspondence continued between Susa and Joseph F. Because of his status as a wanted man under anti-polygamy legislation, Susa addressed her letters using pseudonyms, including President J. F. Speight, J. F. Spaight, or most often Smith's preferred alias, Jason Mack. Susa's communication seeking permission and blessings for beginning the *Young Woman's Journal*, directed to Elmina Taylor and President Wilford Woodruff, were channeled through Joseph F. She also kept him informed about family members. In September 1889, shortly after returning to Utah from Hawai'i, Susa advised Joseph F. that Jacob's father, "Pa Gates," seventy-eight years old and living in Provo, had been arrested for adultery—for being a polygamist—and taken by deputies to court.[9] Two years later, and one year after the Woodruff Manifesto, Joseph F. wrote to Susa and Jacob that he was able to return to Salt Lake City for the first time in over seven years.[10] He had been pardoned on September 10, 1891, by US president Benjamin Harrison for infractions of anti-polygamy bills. They were able to resume correspondence free of aliases.

Susa and Joseph F.'s relationship weathered several more reproofs from him, especially around controversies involving the *Young Woman's Journal*. One article in the September 1891 issue discussed menstruation and ovulation, which upset George Q. Cannon, first counselor in the First Presidency, because he thought it an inappropriate topic for a church magazine. Cannon's son, Abraham, was the publisher of the *Journal*, and he said he allowed the article to be printed because he believed that Joseph F. had approved it. For his part, Joseph F. said he knew nothing about it until he learned of George Q. Cannon's displeasure. Joseph F. told Susa that the less said, the better. The issue blew over, but Susa was advised, "Go right ahead and do better." A few months later, in February 1892, Joseph F. emphasized that in the bitter falling out between Susa and Ellen

8. Gates to Smith, June 27, 1887, box 14, fd. 4, Smith Papers.
9. Gates to Smith, Sep. 3, 1889, box 16, fd. 23, Smith Papers.
10. Smith to Gates and Gates, Sep. 22, 1891, box 46, fd. 33.

Jakeman over business affairs of the *Young Woman's Journal*, "I am not a party between you and Sister Jakeman and have nothing to do with such matters." Susa frequently reprinted in the *Young Woman's Journal* discourses given by her father. But Joseph F. Smith advised in 1890, because of tense relations between the US government and the LDS Church, that it would be "impolitic" to publish references in one of Brigham's talks to "a political kingdom."[11]

Despite the general feeling that Susa was liberal in her advice to church leaders, in the extant correspondence between Susa and Joseph F., the reverse is true: In almost all cases, Susa sought instruction from him. In 1891, in response to a question about physicians and medicine, Joseph F. distinguished between "surgeons" and "doctors": "speaking of *Doctors* as a rule, they are a curse to the world." Susa inquired if Latter-day Saints should call on physicians and surgeons not of our faith? Joseph F. replied only if LDS physicians cannot be found. She asked if elders should keep "brandy and whiskey" in the house? Only for medicinal purposes, came Joseph F.'s response. Is it wise to buy and use beer, Susa wondered? "No!" was Joseph F.'s emphatic reply.[12]

Over the years Susa consulted Joseph F. regarding a plethora of personal issues. One that was particularly important to her was getting a cancellation of sealing from Alma Dunford. Even though she had obtained a divorce through civil courts, in the eyes of the church and God, she and Alma remained married after death for all eternity. Almost immediately after she returned home from Hawai'i in 1889, she wrote to Joseph F., "I wish to consult the Presidency in relation to getting a church divorce."[13] Apparently, this was either never granted or, if the cancellation did take place, it was not appropriately recorded. In 1918 Jacob, working in the Salt Lake temple as a recorder, looked to see if church records "showed a *cancellation* or *annullment*" of Susa's first marriage. When he found no record of a temple divorce, he asked now-church president Joseph F. Smith to fix the problem. In Smith's handwriting on Jacob's letter, there is a

---

11. See chapter ten. Joseph F. Smith to Susa Young Gates, various letters, box 46, fd. 33.
12. Smith to Gates, various letters, box 46, fd. 33.
13. Gates to Smith, May 7, 1889, box 16, fd. 23, Smith Papers.

note to George Reynolds, secretary to the First Presidency, "Please see to this. Let the record be cancelled. J. F. S."[14]

In May 1911 Susa was named to the general board of the Relief Society by Joseph F. Emmeline B. Wells had been named general president of the Relief Society the preceding year at age eighty-two. Susa and Emmeline, who had been thrown together in a host of common endeavors over many years, had a checkered history. By December of that year Susa was thoroughly disgusted with Emmeline's administration of the Relief Society, and in her customary way of dealing with issues head-on, she wrote a rough draft of a letter to Joseph F. outlining her concerns. There is no evidence that this letter was ever sent, received, or answered. Amid their ongoing conflict, Susa offered to resign but continued to serve on the general board until 1922. (For more, see chapter sixteen).

In the summer of 1912 Emma Lucy was dangerously ill at the Gateses' summer home in Brighton Canyon. She was so sick that the family, who usually eschewed doctors, sent for Dr. Clarence Snow. Heber J. Grant, who would become president of the church in 1918, wrote to the family that both the First Presidency and the Quorum of the Twelve Apostles felt that Emma Lucy should not return to Europe to fulfill her ongoing contract with the Cassel Opera House in Germany. Susa knew that Joseph F. was vacationing in southern California. At Emma Lucy and Jacob's insistence, she wrote to Smith, asking him if it were his opinion also that Emma Lucy should not return to Germany. Susa detailed that Emma Lucy owed about $5,000 to Joseph F. and three other unidentified men who had helped finance her musical career and that Susa and Jacob owed about $3,000 on their home for Emma Lucy's debts. Not only had Smith loaned the Gateses money, but Susa sought him out for advice on major and minor family decisions.

Emma Lucy's plan was to finish her contract in Europe, return to America, and make it big in New York City for one season, thus paying off all her debts. Then, she wanted to start a music conservatory in Salt Lake City with her brother, Cecil. Jacob ended up accompanying Emma Lucy back to Europe that fall and remained with

---

14. Jacob Gates to Joseph F. Smith, June 7, 1918, box 3, fd. 14, SYGP (CHL).

her throughout the year, fulfilling his church mission at the same time. During her darkest moments Emma Lucy informed Susa that if anything were to happen to her that she wanted to be sealed to "Uncle Joseph F."[15] Emma Lucy recovered, and four years later she married Albert E. Bowen.[16]

In 1916 Susa wrote to Joseph F. to promote her son Cecil's appointment as assistant director of the Mormon Tabernacle Choir. Smith, in turn, wrote to Professor Anthony Lund, son of Anthon H. Lund of the First Presidency. Anthony had recently been appointed conductor of the choir. Susa offered her opinion, "If he will hold his appetites in restraint, there is much good and brilliant work for him to do." If Lund is going to have assistants, perhaps he should take Cecil, who would not expect a salary.[17] Susa praised Cecil as "a boy of clean life, good faith, modest and retiring in his ways and of a genial disposition." Cecil did serve as assistant director of the Tabernacle Choir from 1916 to 1935.[18]

One aspect of Susa and Joseph F.'s relationship that has puzzled historians revolves around two effusive letters of adulation Susa sent to the LDS Church president at the end of 1906, then again at the beginning of 1907. The first, received by Smith on New Year's Eve, 1906, reads:

My Brother—

Thou art a poet, an artist, a musician. A musician because the best and highest expression of the great masters finds an echo in thy soul. The great paintings are alive to you; and your words, written and spoken, often betray the very soul of poetry. The precious note I have of yours breathes poetry in every line. It is too precious to me for other eyes than mine, ever to rest upon.

I have written you a hundred letters recently (in my mind!) but your last sentence of caution sunk deep in my heart.

When I think of who and what you are—one of the greatest historical characters of this Church and of this world—and when I remember that some day every scrap of your own writing, as well as all letters written to you will be eagerly searched for historical purposes, I am simply

15. Susa Young Gates to Joseph F. Smith, box July 27, 1912, box 47, fd. 2.
16. See chapter fourteen for more on this marriage and Emma Lucy's singing career.
17. Gates to Smith, Aug. 4, 1916, box 22, fd. 7, Smith Papers.
18. Gates Journal, box 105, fd. 4, SYGP (CHL).

frightened out of all further speech. Why, brother mine, I have been writing to you out of the very core of my heart! And when, in fancy, I see men like Bro. A. M. Musser or Andrew Jenson[19] poring over these letters of mine, heavens above me! What a thought! But that last sentence of yours sounds in the very ears of my soul! "Write nothing others may not read." Dearly beloved, this shall be my very last "core of my heart" letter. But, even if I draw close the door into the chambers of my soul, that chamber, closed fast since I was a girl of fourteen, it will be there! …

Oh, if you knew what an inspiration your true, wise friendship has been to me, these past few years. … And sometimes—daring thought—I fancy that you are sufficiently interested in me to remember me in your prayers. … Such a thought makes me willing to bear all other troubles and afflictions, while it makes me fearful lest I cannot be worthy of such divine friendship. …

May the emblems of your affection always shine on.

Susa signed the letter, "Your Sister," then added, "Dont you think this letter better be destroyed? Think of Andrew Jenson and be merciful! This is the very last core of my heart letters."[20]

A second letter, also undated but written very shortly afterward, begged Smith to

Please destroy that letter, and forget and forgive it. It should never have been written. God in Heaven knew, and no one else should ever have known. Let it be buried away forever. I am your true, good sister, and the hourly prayer of my heart is to keep me in purity and truth to all the holy covenants I have made. … Am I forgiven and still your sister? And I often wonder, will God and my good, true, loving husband be merciful also? They will, when they know how I have suffered and struggled—and how godlike you have been![21]

Joseph F. would usually scribble a small note in the corners of correspondence to indicate when he responded, and although he wrote that he answered these letters on January 21, 1907, no answers have been found. Given Susa's pleading with him to destroy her letters, it is likely she destroyed his answer.

19. Amos Musser and Andrew Jenson were both Assistant Church Historians. Jenson in particular had an encyclopedic mind, and he wrote about major and minor events in LDS Church history.
20. Gates to Smith, undated, box 3, fd. 1, Kenney Collection.
21. Gates to Smith, undated, box 3, fd. 1, Kenney Collection.

What to make of such intimate, personal letters, that Susa asked to be destroyed, and would have been mortified to know they are now housed in church archives? In 1870, when Susa was fourteen years old, Joseph F. was a handsome thirty-one-year-old counselor in the First Presidency to her father, Brigham Young. She felt she was in love with him at that time. There is not a scintilla of evidence that her affection for him was ever acted upon physically in any way, or that Susa was ever unfaithful to Jacob. Given her tender feelings for Joseph F., it would appear that Susa simply wanted him to know of her deep and abiding love for him. Throughout her life she constantly expressed this brotherly love for him. Others, including Jacob and her friend Reed Smoot, knew of her affection for Smith. But Susa clearly came to feel that her confessions of love for Joseph F. in these letters would probably better have been left unwritten. And her worries have since proven correct, since the letters have given rise to some speculation regarding their meaning.

The spiritual apogee of Susa's relationship with Joseph F. occurred on the evening of November 5, 1918, exactly two weeks prior to his death. Susa and Jacob had stopped by the Smith residence at the Beehive House to visit Joseph F. and his wife Julina, and to pick up some apples.[22] The president, who had been ill for several months, asked Susa and several other people to gather around his sick bed, where he asked her to read what was later canonized as Section 138 of the Doctrine and Covenants. He had received this revelation on October 3, a month prior. Although he had appeared at general conference the next day, he did not feel good enough to present it to the gathered audience. He dictated it to his son, Apostle Joseph Fielding Smith, several days later. It was unanimously approved on October 31, by the counselors in the First Presidency, the Quorum of the Twelve Apostles, and the Patriarch. The revelation seems to have been prompted, in part, by World War I (Germany would surrender on November 11) and the unexpected death ten months earlier of Joseph F.'s forty-five-year-old son, Apostle Hyrum Mack Smith. According to Joseph F.'s revelation, missionary work is actively being performed in the spirit world with those people who

---

22. Tait, "Susa Young Gates," 315.

had not had the opportunity to receive and accept the gospel of Jesus Christ during their earthly sojourn. Jesus Christ personally visited the spirits of the dead while his body was in the tomb.[23]

When Susa and Jacob stopped by to visit, the vision had not yet been published, although plans were underway to do so in the church's *Improvement Era* periodical in December. In the company of Jacob and Julina, Joseph F. gave Susa a transcript of the revelation to read. There were four points that particularly impressed and thrilled Susa: First, "to know the heavens are still opened"; second, "to be permitted to read a revelation before it was made public."[24] Third, Susa was especially excited to know that "our glorious Mother Eve, with many of her faithful daughters," (D&C 138:39) had been mentioned in the vision, indicating God's concern for women and confirming "the noble standard of equality between the sexes which has always been a feature of this Church."[25] Finally, and *"above all,* to have this given at a time when our Temple work and workers & our genealogy need such encouragement. No words of mine can express my joy and gratitude" (emphasis in original).[26] By this time, after a lifetime of other endeavors, Susa's major focus in life had become genealogy and temple work.

The Gates-Smith friendship was a significant, positive, overarching, lifelong relationship for both Susa and Joseph F. The year after leaving Lā'ie in 1887, Joseph F. wrote to Susa as "one for whom I have so much respect, and sincere and affectionate brotherly regard." He spoke of their shared experiences as "an inseparable part of my own … life," and then continued, "You and Jacob are and ever shall be, cherished in my heart as among my best and truest friends."[27] Those tender feelings were shared by both Susa and Jacob as well.

---

23. See heading to D&C 138.
24. Gates Journal, box 105, fd. 4, SYGP (CHL).
25. Susa Young Gates, "In Memoriam: President Joseph F. Smith," *Relief Society Magazine,* Jan. 1919, 21.
26. Gates Journal, box 105, fd. 4, SYGP (CHL).
27. Smith to Gates, July 7, 1888, box 46, fd. 30.

The Relief Society

16

In May 1911 Susa was called as a general board member of the LDS Relief Society. She was released from the general board of the YL-MIA, where she had served since 1889. The venerable Emmeline B. Wells had been sustained seven months before as fifth general president of the Relief Society at age eighty-two. Her counselors were Clarissa Smith Williams, daughter of Apostle George A. Smith, and Julina Lambson Smith, a polygamous wife of church president Joseph F. Smith. Susa and Julina had become close friends as a result of having lived in Hawai'i at the same time, from 1885 to 1887.

Susa learned of her calling in a letter from Wells. These two women, so influential in Mormonism, had had a prickly relationship for many years, dating back to at least 1888, when Susa wrote to Emmeline and proposed that she be made associate editor of the *Woman's Exponent*. The journal, a publication dedicated to instructing and uplifting Mormon women, had started in 1872 with Lula Greene Richards, a great-niece of Brigham Young, as editor. In October 1875 Lula was joined by Emmeline, who became the editor two years later in 1877. For many years Emmeline had jealously guarded control of the journal, which she owned, and she could not have appreciated Susa's impertinence at suggesting a role for herself at the magazine.

Despite the twenty-eight-year difference in age between Emmeline (b. 1828) and Susa (b. 1856), they had been affiliated in common causes for most of Susa's adult life. They had traveled together to multiple meetings of the National Council of Women. They had attended a presidential inauguration together. They had both supported women's suffrage for decades. They had both encouraged writing among the women of the church. They were both driven, ambitious, stubborn women whose strivings had allowed each the opportunity to rise to prominent positions among Mormon women.

In public and in print, Susa was typically polite to and laudatory of Emmeline. In 1917 Susa wrote of Emmeline as "among the most precious human possessions of the Relief Society today." She described Emmeline as "dedicated, great-minded … yet with fierce independence." Susa praised Emmeline's "ineffable spirit … fixed integrity to the truth … gentle refinement … appealing charm … gentle, tender innocence … power and majesty of her spirit … sensitively pure spirit … lovely dignity … clear music of her voice … like a mountain peak in the midst of her valleys of affliction."[1] In two editorials a month apart in the *Relief Society Magazine*, Susa asked the members of the society, in their prayers, to "remember mercifully the President of this Society in her unflinching testimony and constant avowal of thy purposes," who she then described as "this great and worthy heroine in Zion."[2] And on Wells's ninety-first birthday, Susa again rhapsodized over Wells's "extremely long and constantly active service … her gifted mind, her facile pen … her generosity and her sympathy with womanhood everywhere; her unselfish devotion … and, living worthy of this great calling [as president of the society], she commands our respect and reverence."[3]

Privately, however, Susa had ambivalent feelings about Wells. With Susa's penchant for time management, efficiency, prioritization of goals, and willingness to speak her mind, it did not take long for Susa to lock horns with Wells in board meetings over the direction of the Relief Society. Two months after beginning service on the general board, Susa wrote to Wells while she was on a Relief Society assignment in Manti. She explained that she knew that Emmeline had not expected Susa to come "into this work," but that,

1. Gates, "Our Lovely Human Heritage," *Relief Society Magazine*, Feb. 1917, 74–75. Hereafter the magazine is cited as *RSM*.
2. Gates, "The New Year Relief Society Prayer," *RSM*, Jan. 1918, 46; "President Emmeline B. Wells," Feb. 1918, 106.
3. Gates, "Our General President," *RSM*, Feb. 1919, 112–13.

having been called, she was "anxious" to do her best. If Emmeline wanted, Susa would "build you up, to stimulate others to be loyal and true to you and to keep very close to you in all your labors. … Trust me and dont be sharp … with me, and I will be your best and truest friend, your most loyal supporter, and when I write of you in future years—as I surely shall—my pen will be tipped with reverence and my words shall be mellowed with absolute devotion."[4]

By December, however, just seven months after beginning her service, Susa was frustrated. In her papers is a rough draft of a letter to church president Joseph F. Smith. It is unclear whether this letter was sent since there is no evidence of a reply. It is five typed, double-spaced pages, with multiple edits and corrections. Susa begins with a sense of "most profound regret," despite the "great honor" of being named to the board. Notwithstanding "the deepest affections for Aunt Emmeline," Susa complained that the affairs of the board "are very unsystematically managed; there is no order, no real liberty of speech allowed, and there is but one woman on the Board who does things, and she only does what she wants to, and when she wants to. That woman is Sister Emmeline B. Wells." Susa had "loved her for her integrity … and her long and faithful service." But she was also aware of "her indomitable and invincible will, her determination to have her own way." Previously, Susa had simply acquiesced to Emmeline, but since becoming a board member, Susa had found it "almost impossible to do or say anything which come in opposition to her [Emmeline's] desires."[5]

Susa had voiced opposition to the board's purchase of hospital supplies from an outsider's store, rather than church-owned ZCMI, which Susa felt the Relief Society should treat with "patriotism and … loyalty." After a fervent appeal, Susa and Elizabeth McCune both voted "in opposition to all others present" and in favor of ZCMI, whereupon Emmeline "most severely chided" them and remarked that she "guessed the Board knew what to do without having Susa Gates come there to preach to them about it—and ended by saying that our votes were the first contrary votes cast in the history of the Board."[6]

---

4. Gates to Wells, July, 1911, box 81, fd. 23.
5. Gates, unsent letter to Joseph F. Smith, Dec. 23, 1911, box 81, fd. 25.
6. Gates.

Susa listed her complaints in her letter. First, the schedules for visits of board members to stake Relief Society conferences were made "in a secret and arbitrary way." With sixty-three conferences requiring attention, Susa thought that the board secretary should improve the schedule, since she and her traveling companion had been sent out twice on the wrong date and on another occasion did not realize until arriving at the train station that they were there on the wrong date. Susa proposed a "conference committee" at one meeting, but was forced back to her seat by Wells. Second, Susa recommended that the general board develop an outline for lessons presented in the Relief Societies throughout the church. Wells responded with the observation that "outlines prepared by the Board is not the best thing for the [local] Societies," even though the priesthood quorums and "all other auxiliary organizations" have them. Finally, Susa felt strongly that the Relief Society ought to have its own magazine, which would "have the dignity, regularity, and prestige which such a publication ought to have." Over the years Wells had jealously protected her *Exponent*, which served as her primary source of income, and had rebuffed attempts to start a journal specific to the Relief Society, despite the urging of wards and stakes to do so. Only Julina Smith and Susa had dared to raise the matter in general board meetings. Some members believed that Clarissa Smith Williams and Alice Merrill Horne were trying to take over Emmeline's paper for Horne to run, and others felt that Julina and Susa were trying to take it over for Susa to oversee. Susa refused to tiptoe around the issue and confronted the gossip at a board meeting, where she said that such talk was a "disgrace" to the women of the board, whereupon "pandemonium reigned."[7]

Susa felt that she had only two choices—"to remain on the Board, and keep perfectly quiet,[8] allowing Aunt Em to have her own way unchecked and unhampered, or to resign and let her go her own way without having me there as a reminder." She expressed her willingness to resign and asked Joseph F. Smith, "Shall I go or shall I stay?"[9] No reply is extant, if indeed the letter was ever sent, and Susa

7. Gates.
8. Susa misspelled *quiet* as *quite*.
9. Gates to Smith.

remained on the board for over ten more years. Although some of Susa's objections were resolved, feelings at the general board meetings became sufficiently acrimonious that Smith confided to his wife Julina "that if we could not behave ourselves better than we were doing he would dissolve the whole Board and put in a new one."[10]

On at least two of Susa's points of complaint she prevailed. The *Woman's Exponent* ceased publication in 1914, the same year that the *Relief Society Bulletin* began, with Susa as its first editor. The name was changed the next year to *The Relief Society Magazine*. Susa's goal was to "have this magazine filled with the Spirit of the Lord from cover to cover.[11] Her view of the role of the society was expansive: "The scope of our work, the possibilities of our development, are bounded only by woman's capacities and woman's eventualities. The Relief Society is as broad as eternity."[12]

The first edition of the *Relief Society Bulletin* carried lesson outlines for ward Relief Societies, which continued throughout Susa's eight-and-a-half-year editorship and beyond. The general board, in a "circular of instruction," stressed that the lessons it provided "should all be taken." If the various stakes could use all the lessons of the general board and still have time for "other lines of study," fine, as long as this information was communicated to the general board. "But it would be a mistaken policy" for the stakes and wards to provide their own materials "and to reject that which has been prepared by the proper authority."[13]

Susa wrote many of the lesson outlines herself and, as the chair of the Genealogical Committee of the Relief Society, wrote the monthly lessons on genealogy. By this time in her life, genealogy had become her passion, and she felt strongly that she needed to champion it among her Relief Society sisters, many of whom considered genealogy confusing, labyrinthine, and difficult. On several occasions comments were made that genealogical work needed to be simplified for the general membership of the Relief Society. Susa wrote to her friend, Elizabeth McCune, "We have had, however,

---

10. Susa Young Gates to Jacob Gates, box 11, fd. 6.
11. Gates, "Editorial," *RSM*, Jan. 1915, 38. This issue is misdated as January 1914.
12. Gates, "The Scope of the Relief Society," *RSM*, Apr. 1915, 198.
13. "Circular of Instructions," box 81, fd. 6, SYGP (CHL).

several difficult sessions of the Guide Committee in which I have had to take the part of the genealogical work against all others present. ... I think the Guide lessons in genealogy are once more established for this year."[14]

This letter followed the general Relief Society conference of October 2 and 3, 1918, in which, as summarized by Amy Brown Lyman, "Mrs. Susa Young Gates explained more fully the plan of work to be taken up in Genealogy ... every effort would be made to simplify the lessons ... genealogical work is especially helpful as a foundation for Temple Work."[15] Susa appeared on many occasions to be weighed down by the often negative feelings of the general Relief Society board regarding the importance of genealogy.

In addition to chairing the Genealogical Committee and editing the *Relief Society Magazine*, Susa also served as the corresponding secretary of the general board from September 1913 to April 1921. Janette A. Hyde, who wrote a monthly article on the Home Science Department, was the business manager, and Amy Brown Lyman, who wrote a monthly column called Notes from the Field, containing reports from component Relief Societies around the world, was the assistant manager. The magazine, which was published monthly, contained articles, biographies, poems, dramas, editorials, stories, and lesson guides. It continued until 1970, when all auxiliary magazines were discontinued and three magazines, the *Friend* for children, the *New Era* for youth, and the *Ensign* for adults were introduced. Regular features of the *Relief Society Magazine* included the editorials, usually one to two pages long; the lesson guides, usually ten to sixteen pages long; Notes from the Field; Home Science Department; and Current Topics.

Susa, in the maiden issue of the *Relief Society Magazine* (after it was rechristened from the *Relief Society Bulletin*) in January 1915, wrote, "Let me be true to the counsel of my husband, loyal to my bishop, obedient to the Prophet of the Lord, and quick to take their counsel or reproof, and I shall be safe and at peace, though the heavens fall, and the earth rolls up as a scroll." She was featured alongside other board members, who also had a quote and a portrait in the magazine.[16]

---

14. Gates to McCune, Oct. 4, 1918, box 41, fd. 2.
15. Lyman, "General Conference of Relief Society," *RSM*, Dec. 1918, 662.
16. Gates, [Untitled], *RSM*, Jan. 1915, 6.

Respect for and obedience to the priesthood was a hallmark of the magazine during Susa's tenure as editor. Susa claimed that "many a woman has saved her own soul through thrift and obedience to the priesthood."[17] A second hallmark, according to Susa, was that women in the church "choose to be womanly."[18] Susa spoke frequently about women being "womanly." She wrote of "obedience to the priesthood in whatever rank of life we live and struggle! This is our mark."[19] The lesson guides provided outlines for genealogy, health and hygiene, literature, art and architecture, work and business, testimony, theology and testimony, home ethics and art, home economics, Bible lessons, and the Book of Mormon.

Besides her extensive writing as corresponding secretary and editor of the *Relief Society Magazine,* Susa took an active role as a general board member. In April 1916 she proposed the reinstitution of the Penny Fund to provide income for the construction of the Lā'ie, Hawai'i, and the Cardston, Alberta, temples, the first such edifices built outside the continental United States. By this program, which was approved by Joseph F. Smith, each Relief Society member was asked to voluntarily donate a penny a week for the temple fund. This program had originally been instituted in 1842 by Smith's mother, Mary Fielding Smith, and her sister, Mercy R. Thompson, to aid in construction of the Nauvoo temple, which was finished in 1846. The Relief Society "sisters" in Illinois had donated hundreds of dollars, including money for all the nails and glass used in that structure. In 1916–17 Relief Society sisters donated $13,588.90 to the Penny Temple Fund.[20]

Part of Susa's responsibilities took her throughout the state to visit local ward Relief Societies. Her travel was not as extensive or glamorous as it had once been, but it involved issues important to her. She would attend stake Relief Society conferences, often speaking or teaching. For example, in 1921, Susa visited meetings in Kanab, St. George, South Davis County, and Cache Valley, all in Utah.

Susa also dedicated some time to writing about World War I,

17. Gates, "Editorial," *RSM*, Feb. 1915, 80.
18. Gates, "Address," *Relief Society Bulletin*, Feb. 1914, 2.
19. Gates, "Keep Your Eyes on the Mark," *RSM*, Apr. 1918, 165.
20. Annual reports, box 81, fd. 4, SYGP (CHL).

which raged in Europe from 1914 to 1918. US president Woodrow Wilson had tried to avoid American involvement, but as Germans sank more and more US ships, the country inched toward war. By 1917, it was clear the United States would join the fight. Fervid American citizen that she was, Susa, in her editorial pages, encouraged the purchase of Liberty Bonds by those who are "patriotic and able." She pointed out that the church itself was buying $250,000 of such bonds.[21]

Susa, in addition to her other responsibilities, was part of the Teachers Committee of the Relief Society general board. She wrote out a list of duties of visiting teachers—members of the Relief Society assigned to visit with and fellowship other members:

> Teachers should get and keep the spirit of the Gospel. ... As they feel in entering a home so will the hostess feel after their visit.
>
> Avoid gossip of every kind. Talk about principles not people. Enquire kindly into the health of those visited, but never pry into private or personal affairs.
>
> Bring a spirit of cheerfulness and good cheer with you. Everybody needs encouragement and happiness. No one wants criticism, argument, or depressing suggestions.
>
> Pray in secret, and with your companion before entering on your monthly visits. The power of prayer is beyond compare.
>
> Be faithful in your visits; when impossible to go, acquaint the President in time for her to secure a substitute.
>
> Get well acquainted with the sisters in your district. Love them, and they will be bound to respond in kind.
>
> Visit the sick, even if it be out of your time and turn.
>
> Be first in the house of mourning. Offer help and comfort, but refrain from much talk at such times.
>
> Attend all R.S. meetings. These and your sacrament meetings are the supply depots where your spiritual essence will be renewed. ...
>
> Keep your books carefully, and report regularly.[22]

One of Susa's major skirmishes as a member of the general board related to the administration of charitable assistance to the poor. Her opponent was Amy Brown Lyman (1872–1959), a pioneer in the

21. Gates, "Liberty Bonds," *RSM*, Nov. 1917, 643–44.
22. Teachers Plan, box 81, fd. 20, SYGP (CHL).

professionalization of social work. Lyman graduated from Brigham Young Academy and taught school in Provo and Salt Lake City. After her marriage to future apostle Richard R. Lyman, she encountered social work during summer school in 1902 at the University of Chicago as she and her husband were preparing to move to Ithaca, New York, where he would finish a doctorate at Cornell. While in Chicago, she took a sociology course and met Jane Addams of Hull House fame.[23]

During the ensuing years, Amy studied at the University of Utah and the University of Colorado, where she earned a certificate in social services. She became proficient in the implementation of modern social work methods, including the case method system. In 1909 she was named to the general board of the Relief Society, and in 1913 she became the general secretary. In this position, she worked with Susa. Amy was "not afraid to speak her mind," and she was "businesslike" and "outspoken," not unlike Susa, who, because of their sixteen-year age difference, treated her more as a daughter.[24] Susa has been described as standing at one end of the Bishops Building and hollering to the other for Amy, who came running.[25] In 1918 Amy's husband was named as an apostle. Amy had in the meantime become a close associate of both Emmeline B. Wells, who served as president until 1921, and Clarissa Williams, who became president thereafter. Surely, Susa's lack of tact must have irritated Amy, although Amy's secretary, Vera Pohlman, later said that she never noted a "strain" in Susa and Amy's relationship.[26]

In 1913 Joseph F. Smith asked Amy to conduct a "thorough study of modern social work methods."[27] Six years later Amy started the Social Services Department of the church. (In 1973 this became LDS Social Services, now called Family Services.) Amy's Social Services Department became "a corps of dedicated professionals," and Susa became "an early and outspoken critic of Lyman's efforts to modernize the church's charity work." Susa feared that older women in the church would be marginalized in this newer set-up of

---

23. Hall, "Anxiously Engaged," 76.
24. Hall, 75; Tait, "Review: Dave Hall, *A Faded Legacy*," 180.
25. Hall, *Faded Legacy*, 83.
26. Hall, "Anxiously Engaged," 81.
27. Hall, "Anxiously Engaged," 77.

"commercialized charity," because they would be unable to perform according to the "new more rigorous standards."[28]

Some board members suggested the possibility of streamlining and professionalizing how charitable assistance to the poor was administered by the Relief Society. Susa, strongly opposed to these changes, emphasized that the Relief Society has "the most perfect social and religious machinery known to mortal man for the carrying out of all our social and religious work."[29] In addition, the charity of the Relief Society had always been administered without cost. It was a voluntary organization, and she saw no need to pay outsiders or hire church members to do the work. For these reasons Susa opined in an address to the presidency and board of the Relief Society in December 1919 that "as long as my own views are not exactly in accordance with what I can glean are those of some members of the Board, it is right and fitting that we all should have the privilege of expressing our points of view, and then, when the majority rules on the matter, let us all unite, or at least keep a discreet silence after that action has been taken." Some changes and modifications might be necessary, but she spoke against "fundamental changes" to what she considered a "perfect and wise" method of administering relief.[30]

Ultimately, because they both held tenaciously to their positions, Susa and Amy met in January 1920 with President Heber J. Grant, who had replaced Joseph F. Smith as president of the church. They were unable to work out a compromise, and Grant referred them back to the general board for a resolution. Eventually, Amy won, though Susa continued to decry the "professional, salaried bureaucracy" with its overhead. Amy's husband claimed that even after she left the general board in 1922, Susa continued to campaign against the professionalization of social services. Several years later, in 1928, Annie Wells Cannon, one of Emmeline Wells's daughters, observed that "the spirit of the gospel and religion seem to have disappeared [from the Relief Society], and it seems to be a social welfare organization."[31]

---

28. Hall, "Anxiously Engaged," 80, 81.
29. Address to the Relief Society board, 1919, box 81, fd. 3, SYGP (CHL).
30. Administration of Eliza R. Snow, box 81, fd. 1, SYGP (CHL).
31. Hall, "Anxiously Engaged," 81–82.

Susa wrote numerous articles for the *Relief Society Magazine* between 1914 and 1922 under her own name. She published *The Prince of Ur* in serial form in 1915–16 under her long-standing pseudonym of Homespun. In addition, she wrote many unattributed articles. In addition to her strong stance against birth control, she wrote on a plethora of topics, including Mothers in Israel, which included the life story of Mary Fielding Smith, mother of Joseph F. Smith. She wrote biographies of Charles W. Penrose, counselor in the First Presidency and avid supporter of women's suffrage in Utah, and of Alexander Neibaur, the first Jewish convert to the church.[32] She probably wrote the biographies of Lucy Mack Smith, Emmeline B. Wells, and Eliza R. Snow.[33]

Susa wrote eulogies for Lydia von Finkelstein Mountford, who died in 1917; for Apostle Hyrum M. Smith, who died on January 23, 1918, at age forty-five; for Joseph F. Smith, who also died in 1918, at age eighty; and for May Wright Sewall, leader in women's rights, friend of Mormon women and former president of both the National and International Council of Women, who died in 1920.[34] Susa praised "Our Relief Society Stake Presidents" in April 1918, for their "self-reliance, independent thinking, and humanitarian development, [which] have been beyond price."[35]

Susa wrote articles—some quite lengthy—on topics as disparate as "The Temple in Jerusalem" (Aug. 1918, 427–34), "Sacred Vestments of Ancient People" (Sep. 1920, 502–06), "Suffrage Won by the Mothers of the United States" (May 1920, 251–75), and "The International Council of Women" (Jan. 1921, 21–31). This council, formed in 1888, had several LDS representatives and both the Relief Society and the YLMIA were charter members. She wrote on "Church School Education" (Sep. 1921, 497–502), "Presiding Patriarchs of the

---

32. "Mothers in Israel," *RSM*, Mar. 1916, 123; "President Charles W. Penrose," Feb. 1922, 63; "Alexander Neibaur," Mar. 1922, 132.

33. "Mothers in Israel," *RSM*, Jan. 1916, 3; "Mothers in Israel," Feb. 1916, 63; "The Mother of Mothers in Israel," Apr. 1916, 183.

34. "Madame Lydia von F. Mountford," *RSM*, Feb. 1921, 71–77; "The Passing of Apostle Hyrum M. Smith," Mar. 1918, 125–27; "In Memoriam: President Joseph F. Smith," Jan. 1919, 3–10; "Mrs. May Wright Sewell [sic]," Sep. 1920, 499–501.

35. Gates, "Our Relief Society Stake Presidents," *RSM*, Apr. 1918, 187.

Church" (Jan. 1922, 3–7), "Relief Society Beginnings in Utah" (Apr. 1922, 184–96), and "Our Hymn Book" (July 1922, 349–56).

In 1921, Susa was invited by prominent railroad executives to be part of a group taken on a tour of southern Utah as part of the railroad's "See America First" campaign. Also invited were church president Heber J. Grant, his counselor Anthony W. Ivins, Grant's wife and close friend of Susa, Augusta, and Ivins's daughter Fulvia. Several other prominent church leaders and members were also part of the group.[36] The party left on September 5 and attended church conferences in Kanab and St. George. They were accompanied by several railroad executives, and their stops included Little Grand Canyon, Little Zion, Bryce and Grand Canyons, the Kaibab Forest, St. George, and Kanab. Susa penned a lengthy writeup of the trip and published it in the magazine.[37]

Two months later Susa reiterated the editorial policy of the journal: "To print articles, poems, stories and departments written by Latter-day Saint women [rarely men] for Latter-day Saint readers."[38] Indeed, perhaps Susa's greatest talent was as an editor. She had spent years editing the *Young Woman's Journal*, and now she handled the *Relief Society Magazine*. Her own tour-de-force during her tenure was the approximately 100 editorials she wrote. Since these one- to three-page communications allowed her free rein to express her personal feelings, they offer insight into some of Susa's thoughts.

Above all, Susa emphasized righteousness, spirituality, covenant-making, commandment-keeping, following God, and obedience to priesthood holders. She wrote early on that she "would have this magazine filled with the Spirit of the Lord from cover to cover" so that it might be "a beacon light of hope, beauty and charity." She wove belief in self-control and self-discipline together with peace, happiness, and righteousness. Obedience to God's commands were the way to joy and tranquility. Susa warned against "self-pity

---

36. They were Grant's son-in-law Robert L. Judd; Apostle George Albert Smith, his wife, and their daughter Emily Smith Stewart; LeRoi Snow and his wife, Burma; and Ruth May Fox.

37. Gates, "A Memorable Journey to the Scenic Glories of Southern Utah," *RSM*, Nov. 1921, 617–32.

38. Gates, "How Do You Do, New Year?" *RSM*, Jan. 1922, 49.

and self-indulgence," and taught that it was impossible "to travel our own way and the Lord's way at one and the same time." She, who knew all too well that words can sting, told her readers that, "If we can acquire the mastery of our thoughts, our words will be our servants." Regardless of other circumstances, "No man or woman is ... a failure who has striven to do good and struggled to overcome individual temptation." She knew that temptation and life's challenges were real, and while she could be rigid, she also felt that "if life has permitted you measurable health, measurable opportunity to work, to strive, to overcome, and you have measurably overcome, then you may consider yourself a measurable success. It is not what you achieve in worldly paths, it is what you overcome in spiritual matters that counts for success."[39]

Susa lived her life with stoicism in the face of adversity, and she believed that "opposition and the discipline born of that opposition will strengthen us if we accept it for what it is and intelligently turn it to best account." She encouraged submitting one's will to God. "Blessed the man who learns early to subdue his own will without allowing people or conditions to break his spirit." Individual will was "the chief cause of all our suffering, as of all our joy."[40]

Susa pushed obedience unceasingly in her life and in her editorials. By focusing "on the fundamental principle of obedience to the authority of the priesthood," Latter-day Saints would "be the captain of your soul, not the slave of your impulses or your undisciplined desires." Obedience should come "because you want to be so, not because someone threatens or demands that obedience." She counseled the members of the Relief Society to not pursue "spiritual gifts and manifestations in excess," but instead to "just keep your eye on your file [priesthood] leader." These leaders, Susa believed, were inspired, and that when "instruction comes through the channels of the priesthood ... we shall do well to become willing pupils, eager students." She was certain that "there are fixed moral laws, as perfect

---

39. "Editorial," *RSM*, Jan. 1915, 38; "Climbing," June 1916, 355; "Discipline Our Thoughts," July 1920, 425; "Am I a Failure?" Feb. 1921, 112; "The Measure of Success," June 1922, 345.

40. "The Discipline of Opposition in this Newest Year of 1920," *RSM*, Jan. 1920, 48; "The Discipline of Obedience," Mar. 1920, 163; "Will Conquering," Aug. 1916, 465.

and as rigid as are the laws of light and heat," and she could not understand those who she felt flaunted those moral laws.[41]

She put tremendous emphasis on the daily and weekly activities Latter-day Saints ought to be engaged in. She believed that Sunday testimony meetings "are our most exhaustless sources of strength and power." Personal study and prayer were also essential: "It is next to impossible for men and women to grow and progress in this Church without daily, regular, secret and family prayer." In addition to personal activities, "there are still gospel principles to study, and homes to visit, meetings everywhere to attend."[42] The work of the church was just that: work.

She also loved the temple and pushed readers to dedicate their time there. "The most glorious way to spend your remaining months or even years is in the temple." Susa, the daughter of a church president but never herself materially wealthy, saw the temple as a great equalizer: "The temples open wide their portals for all who care to enter therein," and she underlined the point when she wrote that "all men and women of whatever age or educational training can take an active part in this vital temple labor." Susa knew that some were born with advantages that others lacked. "We are never equal in opportunities, in gifts, nor in worldly position, but we are all equal before the Lord," and this was especially true, she believed, in the temple. She felt that "men should be equalized in environment and opportunity," and that only the Latter-day Saints "have the right ideals and the experience to make those ideals practicable." But the temple was not to be taken lightly. The covenants made there were sacred to Susa, and she urged readers, "Keep them, and you get the blessing; break them and you pay the price."[43]

The *Relief Society Magazine* was written, after all, for the Relief Society, which was made up exclusively of women. Susa wrote

41. "The Discipline of Obedience," *RSM*, Mar. 1920, 164; "Spiritual Manifestations," Apr. 1917, 228–29; "Teachers' Training Course," July 1919, 427; "Are We Always Honest?" Sep. 1919, 546.

42. "Our Testimony Meetings," *RSM*, June 1918, 358; "Prayer," Mar. 1922, 166; "Vital Questions," June 1921, 371.

43. "The Year's Old Age," *RSM*, Dec. 1921, 721; "Vital Questions," June 1921, 371; "Jealousy," Feb. 1922, 106; "The Social Unrest in the World," Mar. 1919, 176; "Girlhood's Dangers," Aug. 1921, 475.

often on motherhood, womanhood, being a wife, and keeping a home. "Mormonism," she said, "has given to the modern world a virile conception of the home." She was simultaneously gentle and strident when she wrote about the challenges women faced. Women should not overburden themselves or try to be perfect, but Susa was clear that a woman's job was to cultivate a home of peace for her husband and children. "Who are the successful wives? They are not necessarily the women who have kept their houses scrupulously clean and who are the best bread makers in the neighborhood. ... The successful wives are not the women who give all their time and strength and thought to their ... children. The successful wives are the women who learn to balance their lives so that they can give ... themselves ... with loving generosity in personal ministrations to their husbands." Under the subheading "Do What You Can, and What You Can't Do, Don't Do," to an editorial she titled "Are You Conserving Yourself?" Susa counseled, "The woman who has a home to keep, a husband, and a family of children on her hands, is doing quite all that the heavens and the earth ought to require of her."[44]

She told readers not to over-extend themselves, since their "full duty" is to "guard and guide your little ones and make home a haven of rest for husband and family." Women were expected to bear their burdens quietly, and Susa passed that on to the readers of the magazine. "Remember your husband, your children, your friends, all have troubles of their own, and the recital of yours will not make theirs easier to bear." She believed that "women who have learned to regulate their own affairs ... are, as a rule, qualified for a wider usefulness, a broader sphere of activity." Indeed, women who learned how to manage themselves and their homes would learn how to perform church service more effectively. "We can all minister as understanding Relief Society teachers, if we will train ourselves first to speak kindly words to our every-day associates in the home."[45]

44. "Thank God for Our Homes," *RSM*, Nov. 1915, 512; "Success," *Relief Society Bulletin*, July 1914, 4; "Are You Conserving Yourself?," *RSM*, Oct. 1917, 581.

45. "Are You Conserving Yourself?," *RSM*, Oct. 1917, 581; "Selfishness," Nov. 1918, 646; "Efficiency," Feb. 1916, 110; "If I Were a Relief Society Teacher," Mar. 1921, 172.

Susa revered womanhood, and she wrote about it often. She was grateful to be a woman, but she had not always felt that way. "Let us all give thanks for wifehood, motherhood, and most of all, for tender, gentle, helpful womanhood." But, she continued, "When youth and high ambitions claimed my life, I thought I was dissatisfied with womanhood and all its limitations. ... Gradually there came to me a joy that I was just a woman. ... At last my prison changed ... into a moated castle where peace and safety dwelt." During this tumultuous social time, as the fight for women's suffrage reached its crescendo, Susa told her readers, "When women receive the vote they receive with it a heavy responsibility to use it according to their best judgment."[46]

She addressed contemporary issues, notably World War I. At the start of the war, she encouraged women to store food such as flour, fruit, and beans, and to have a supply of clothing. They should also, she wrote, keep "a check on all lines of needless expenditures." As the fight dragged on and her own country was pulled into war in 1917, she noted that "our good Mormon boys" would go to battle. "Let us pray that they go as on a mission." Then, as the war wound down the next year, she felt that, despite the violence, the uncertainty, and the turmoil, "our young people—all are drawing nearer to God than ever before." As always, she turned to her faith, and she preached that only one thing could safeguard the lives of all people. "Make democracy safe for the world by preaching the gospel of Jesus Christ." The ills of the world, Susa believed, could not be cured by war. In the midst of the fighting, she turned to the last days, and wrote, "Every effort we put forth to build up righteousness ... will help the Savior that much in this final upheaval of world events."[47]

She preached hard work, honest work, and service to others. Susa, responding to an obituary in a Salt Lake City newspaper that characterized the deceased as a "scrub-woman," decried the label and wrote, "There is no occasion for anyone to shrink from honest work

---

46. "Let Us Give Thanks," *RSM*, Nov. 1920, 657–58; "What Women Will Do with the Suffrage," May 1920, 292.

47. "Conserving Our Resources," *Relief Society Bulletin*, Oct. 1914, 2; "The Battle is On," *RSM*, Aug. 1917, 461; "O War, Where Is Our Fear of Thee?" Feb. 1918, 104; "Democracy Must Be Made Safe for the World," Apr. 1918, 232; "Editorial," July 1917, 408.

of any kind." She encouraged community and church service, and praised "choosing always the difficult, unselfish things to do, climbing hard paths of self-control and of devotion to community duties." She said that service brought women closer to God: "A test of the measure of divinity within us is our understanding and willingness to give Christlike unselfish service to others."[48]

Susa, who had seen much death in her life, wrote about it as well, sometimes in conjunction with temple work. In addition to work for the living, it was essential for Latter-day Saints to "work for the dead—to redeem our kindred who have been waiting in their prison houses." She reminded readers that "life has no graduation but death." Further, "only God may matriculate our souls and only eternity encompass our commencement." She did not despair as she wrote about death, which she said was "an open door to a better life." Instead, "death, a glorious, honorable death, is far more to be preferred than an ignoble, impure, pusillanimous life."[49]

Finally, Susa wrote about finding peace, sometimes with simple encouragement:

> Laugh at yourself. Make light of ordinary troubles.
> The most valuable piece of property this nation possesses today is YOU, yourself.
> Peace is the harmony of the human soul with the infinite will.
> Friends, love, peace, salvation—these are the glorious rewards which come from serving God; they are ours no matter how poor, how sick, or how humiliated we may be.[50]

Her last editorial appeared in the June 1922 edition of the *Relief Society Magazine.*

In addition to her responsibilities with the magazine, Susa spoke at numerous general Relief Society conferences. Usually her talks dealt with genealogy, but among her noteworthy addresses was one given in October 1917, after America's entry into World War I,

---

48. "The Dignity of Toil," *RSM*, Mar. 1915, 158; "Paying the Price," May 1916, 284; "Modern Society," Sep. 1918, 532.

49. "Destruction upon the Waters," *RSM*, July 1915, 337; "Life and the School," Oct. 1918, 589, 591; "The Church Militant," Nov. 1916, 649.

50. "Self-Pity," *RSM*, Sep. 1916, 524; "Are You Conserving Yourself," Oct. 1917, 580; "Peace," *Relief Society Bulletin*, May 1914, 4; "What Does the Church Owe Me?" *RSM*, May 1921, 310.

when she "appealed to the mothers to write letters to their own sons and to the sons of other mothers; not to preach too much to them; not to worry or nag them; but to influence them by kindly sympathy. She felt that everybody should strive for that broad sympathy and generous love, that spiritual insight, all of which help people to appreciate and understand each other."[51]

In April 1921, with the call of Clarissa Williams as the new general Relief Society president, Susa was released as corresponding secretary and as a member of Emmeline Wells's general board. She was then immediately reappointed to the new general board, along with a number of younger sisters, who, it was felt, would bring a renewed vigor to the organization, and she continued as editor of the magazine.

However, when Clarissa was called as general president, she announced that the offices of editor and business manager of the *Relief Society Magazine* were "annual appointments," which came as a "shock" to Susa, since she had been "appointed ... and set apart" for this assignment in 1913 by Joseph F. Smith. By May 1921 the masthead of the *Relief Society Magazine* listed Amy Brown Lyman as the secretary and treasurer. Gone were the names of Susa Young Gates as corresponding secretary and Emma A. Empey as general treasurer. Furthermore, Clarissa announced that "Sis. Lyman was her Third Counsellor, and the General Manager of all the activities of the Board," including the magazine.[52]

One year later, at the end of May 1922, a meeting was called of the *Relief Society Magazine* committee, and Susa felt a premonition. Susa had disagreed with Amy's views on "Social Service," namely, "hiring charity professionals" to administer to the poor (see above). In addition, Susa noted privately that she believed Lyman had "shown ... a disrespect (inwardly) to the priesthood" and lacked "real humility and unselfishness," showing "her real ignorance of the fundamentals of the Gospel."[53] Publicly, Susa said nothing about her differences with Lyman, and, not surprisingly, she resigned on June

---

51. Amy Brown Lyman, "General Conference of Relief Society," *RSM*, Dec. 1917, 673.

52. Gates Journal, undated entry written upside down on p. 200, box 105, fd. 6, SYGP (CHL).

53. Gates.

28, 1922, from the general board of the Relief Society and as editor of the *Relief Society Magazine*.

Susa's lengthy resignation letter to Williams began, "Will you kindly accept my resignation as editor of the Relief Society Magazine?" She explained that it would be very difficult for her to continue as editor in view of the "exceedingly explicit, yet not ungentle ... recital of criticisms you [and Lyman] have indicated against me and my past labors." Susa then summarized the concerns Clarissa and Amy had lodged. First and foremost, they "find it necessary to censor my own articles and editorials." Susa pointed out that she had not had free rein before. Edward H. Anderson had been appointed by Joseph F. Smith to review her work, and he sometimes also deleted and censored her work. But apparently, Susa observed, Anderson's edits were "inadequate and unsatisfactory" to the general Relief Society presidency.

Next, Williams and Lyman "wish to choose the authors of articles, especially designating our leaders as possible contributors." Susa insisted that she had tried on multiple occasions to have the "brethren" (the church's male priesthood authorities) write articles for the *Relief Society Magazine,* but their busy schedules made this a "futile" endeavor. What is more, Susa was expected to let Williams and Lyman "select title and scope of articles to be solicited or used," and they asked her to "bring all my material into your council for reading and approval before acceptance or rejection." But, even if these issues were resolved, it seemed there was no way forward. Susa wrote that the duo objected "to the general tone and policy of the Magazine, expressing the wish to have it become more modern."

Susa defended her tenure by pointing out that the *Relief Society Magazine* had the largest circulation of any church publication—24,000. Still, she was conciliatory:

> I am quick to acknowledge that you and Sister Lyman are the final arbiters of the destinies of the Relief Society, together with the official organ, the Magazine. ... No one knows better than I, the duty of obedience I owe to my superior officers in this Church. When you express the desire to do all the work of editing the Magazine, I can but conclude that you would like to dispense with my services, however tactfully you may express that desire. It has been a grief to me that in all the years

I have labored in this capacity, I have received no encouragement or approval from you. ... I will close up this July number of the Magazine, with your permission, now halfway completed, and then remove myself and my belongings from the office. In all this, my loving prayers are for you personally and for all those associated with you in the General Board, and the Relief Society.[54]

There was no editorial in the *Relief Society Magazine* edition that July, but the cover article in August was a three-page homage to the retiring editor that included some telling words and did not shy entirely away from the internal conflict. Susa's forte, the unsigned editorial read, "is in creating, not in polishing thoughts and sentences; in originating, not in smoothing ideas and expressions." Her success in writing "has come rather from her ability to do things vigorously than from a more quiet and toilsome work of editing other peoples' efforts in literature." Perhaps most revealing was the observation that "a nature like hers chafes under restraint and longs for original expression." Still, the new editors regretted "that she has seen fit to resign as editor of the *Relief Society Magazine,* which she has so ably edited since its beginning in 1914–1915. ... The policy she pursued in the choice of matter was always favorable to womankind." An additional two pages eulogize Susa's many accomplishments.[55]

The Relief Society presidency announced Susa's resignation in a separate notice in the same issue, which was "as great a surprise to our numerous readers, and all readers of the Relief Society, as it was to the presidency and members of the General Board." The presidency assured readers that they "deeply appreciate the efficient and faithful work Sister Gates has accomplished, and our prayers and good wishes go with her in whatever field of activity she may decide to enter, or wherever she may be."[56]

Susa's "Farewell" on the next page was a gallant departure in what was surely a trying event for her. She wrote, "To the Latter-day Saint, there is no such word as farewell or finish, for to us life and effort, expression and development, go right on ever

---

54. Gates to Williams, June 6, 1922, box 48, fd. 5.
55. "Our Retiring Editor," *RSM,* Aug. 1922, 401–03.
56. "Resignation of Mrs. Susa Young Gates," *RSM,* Aug. 1922, 440.

and forever. We may part from friends for a time ... but you and I, friends, we do not say good-bye at any time, for we go right on developing, achieving." Susa pled for the same love, patience, and loyalty for the new editor that she had received. She left "without one shade of regret for I have done wisely in this separation and have taken counsel." She returned, as always, to her faith and stated, "If we love God, and desire greatly to bring to pass righteousness, we shall be assured that there is always a place, a labor that only we can do." Finally, she pledged her public loyalty to her leaders: "Our President Clarissa S. Williams agrees entirely with this parting of ours and I bear you my testimony that she is the one chosen of God through his servant for her high and exalted position."[57] Susa once again demonstrated her lifelong public support of church leaders called through priesthood channels.

Multiple letters arrived from readers, contributors, and church leaders, all universally lamenting Susa's departure and wishing her well in her new endeavors. To Ruth May Fox, first counselor in the general presidency of the YLMIA, Susa wrote, "I think if I have suffered about anything it is from a sense of my own weaknesses. ... I have stood up against billows of discouragement and storms of misunderstandings. I dont want my will or rather, my self-respect to get flabby. I want to keep my spiritual and mental muscles firm and healthy."[58] As must have been expected, word leaked out about the reasons for Susa's departure. Heber Q. Hale, president of the Boise Stake, wrote her that there had been "some little speculation" regarding the cause of the resignation, but that "we certainly admire your position in this matter, and the high and noble attitude you take in reference thereto."[59]

Despite feeling "humiliated and chagrined" by Clarissa Williams's words, Susa believed Williams "was chosen by President Grant through the inspiration of the Lord to be the elect lady of this Church, and my only desire is that she may be blessed and comforted and inspired in all her future work." She even acknowledged that "perhaps I needed the discipline which she so frankly administered.

57. Gates, "Farewell," *RSM*, Aug. 1922, 441.
58. Gates to Fox, Aug. 7, 1922, box 81, fd. 25.
59. Hale to Gates, Sep. 1, 1922, box 81, fd. 25.

You know I have had a great deal of discipline in my life, and when it has come from those over me in the Church I have accepted in the spirit of meekness." Susa's real complaint was with Clarissa's "selfish and ambitious adviser," Amy Brown Lyman.[60]

Susa had written in April 1918 in an article on stake Relief Society presidents, "There is a time to labor and a time to quit. How few of us laborers know when the right time comes to quit."[61] It took several more months before Williams herself was appointed as editor of the *Relief Society Magazine*, with Alice L. Reynolds, a professor at Brigham Young University, as associate editor.[62]

---

60. Gates to Charles W. Penrose, July 29, 1922, box 52, fd. 10.
61. Gates, "Our Relief Society Stake Presidents," *RSM*, Apr. 1918, 189.
62. Mary E. Connelly, "Clarissa Smith Williams," *RSM*, Apr. 1923, 162.

Genealogy

Genealogy had long held a fascination for Susa. In 1895 she said, "Once taken up, it is impossible to ever lay it down again."[1] Two decades later, she wrote that "the study of genealogy is the dearest to me of anything outside my religion."[2] The Young family had engaged in genealogical research and temple work very early; reportedly, the first known family meeting ever held in the church was on January 8, 1845, in Nauvoo at the direction of Brigham Young and his cousin, Jesse Haven.[3]

Susa's *Report of Temple Committee of the Young Family Association* of June 1, 1910, outlines the early history of genealogy work in the Young family.[4] Shortly after the death of Brigham Young, his nephew Franklin W. Young was commissioned by the family to travel east to obtain as many family names in Massachusetts as he could. They found names of family members through both Brigham Young's father, John Young, and his mother, Abigail ("Nabby") Howe Young. He and his family then performed vicarious temple work in Manti for the Young family members they could identify.[5] The first meeting of the proto-Young family association in Utah occurred in 1884

---

1. Gates, "Report of Mission and Labors of Susa Young Gates to the Young Family Association," Apr. 12, 1895, box 65, fd. 6, SYGP (CHL).

2. Susa Young Gates to W. Farrand Felch, Aug. 25, 1914, box 73, fd. 18.

3. Young Family Association Minutes and Reports, Nov. 28–29, 1921, box 65, fd. 13, SYGP (CHL). Hereafter cited as Minutes and Reports.

4. The report is in box 65, fd. 14, SYGP (CHL).

5. Gates, *Report of Temple Committee.*

at the time of the April general conference of the church, but little came of it at that time.[6]

In the fall of 1890 Susa accompanied her mother, Lucy, to the Bigelow family reunion in Northborough, Massachusetts, where they stayed a week at the home of Gilman Bigelow Howe, a distant cousin and professional genealogist. For over thirty years Susa and Howe carried on correspondence.[7] She and her mother also visited the genealogical library in Boston.[8] Two years later Susa spent the summer at Harvard University (1892), and during her time in Boston she again attempted genealogical research but without much success.[9] As early as 1894, Susa was writing to Howe to request genealogical information.[10]

After the Young sisters performed the temple work for most of the names of Nabby Howe's ancestors collected by Franklin Young, they decided to resurrect the Brigham Young family organization that they had tried to form in 1884.[11] The formal organization of the Young Family Association took place on April 19, 1894, and Apostle Brigham Young Jr. was elected president. Other officers included Seymour B. Young, vice president; William B. Dougall, secretary; Susa Young Gates, corresponding secretary; and Susa's younger sister R. Mabel Young, recorder.[12] Susa became the informal genealogist of the family, and was assisted by her sister Mabel. Seymour Young soon succeeded Brigham Young Jr. as president of the family organization because Young Jr.'s apostolic responsibilities required most of his attention.[13]

In an unpublished manuscript from April 1895, Susa detailed her earliest experiences with genealogy. She spent a month in Logan in the spring of 1895 recovering from an illness. She visited the Logan temple, where she heard her second cousin Apostle Franklin D. Richards offer a "stirring sermon" on vicarious work for the dead.

---

6. Young Family Association reports, box 65, fd. 17, SYGP (CHL).

7. See their correspondence in box 61, fds. 9–10, SYGP (CHL).

8. Gates, "Lucy Bigelow Young," 144.

9. Susa Young Gates, "Young Family Association," *Utah Genealogical and Historical Magazine*, Oct. 1921, 166.

10. See various Gates and Howe correspondence, box 61, fd. 9.

11. Minutes and Reports.

12. Officers of Young Family Association, box 65, fd. 14, SYGP (CHL).

13. Minutes and Reports.

Susa wrote that she had a vision of her father. "He visited me in that Temple, and planted in my heart the desire and longing to attend to such work." On the train home to Provo, where she was living at the time, she met Frank Farnsworth, recorder in the Manti temple, who asked her why she and her sisters did not take up the work of the Brigham Young and Howe lines "and do the work for these people."[14] Within a few weeks, some of Susa's half-sisters, including Maria Dougall, Fanny Thatcher, Jeannette Easton, Phebe Beattie, Myra Rossiter, along with Susa, decided to pursue genealogy work on the Howe and Young lines.[15]

Still, from 1896 to 1904 work in Young family genealogy languished. But in 1902 life took a turn for Susa, and thereafter genealogy became a consuming passion during the last three decades of her life. She grew gravely ill after attending the International Council of Women meeting in Copenhagen that summer.[16] She received two blessings from church leaders, including one from Apostle Francis M. Lyman (see chapter 11). Lyman initially blessed Susa to pass on peacefully, but then paused for several moments and instead told Susa that a council had been held in heaven, and the decision had been made that Susa should remain on earth, but with a new mission, that of redeeming the dead through genealogy and temple work, "a greater work than you have ever done before."[17] After this life-altering blessing, Susa donated 10 percent of her income to genealogy and temple work, in addition to her 10 percent for tithing.[18]

When Susa returned home from Europe, she weighed only eighty-five pounds, but slowly recuperated. In 1904, shortly after the Gates family moved from Provo to Salt Lake City, Susa met Joseph Christenson, who asked her why she did not frequent the library operated by the Genealogical Society of Utah (GSU). Susa confessed that she had never even heard of the library.[19] She soon thereafter visited the genealogical library—and spiritually never left it.

---

14. Gates, "Report of Mission."

15. Minutes and Reports.

16. For more on Susa's travel to Europe, her subsequent illness, and the blessing from Lyman, see chapter eleven.

17. Minutes and Reports.

18. Allen, Embry, and Mehr, *Hearts Turned to the Fathers*, 61.

19. Gates to members of the general board of the GSU, Apr. 26, 1923, box 70, fd. 10.

The Genealogical Society of Utah had been organized in November 1894 with Apostle Franklin D. Richards as president.[20] In addition to Richards, other church luminaries were among the charter members of the Society, including LDS president Wilford Woodruff; his counselors in the First Presidency, George Q. Cannon and Joseph F. Smith; and apostles Lorenzo Snow and Abraham H. Cannon. Other prominent men who were original members of the society were John Nicholson, Amos Milton Musser, James H. Anderson, James Walkley, George Reynolds, John Jaques, and Duncan M. McAllister.[21] The purposes of the society were "benevolent, educational and religious" and described as four-fold:

> To provide genealogical books which might be placed at the disposal of members of the Society.
> To assist the Saints (members) in acquiring information concerning their dead ancestors.
> To teach them how to record that information and how to prepare the records thus obtained, for temple work.
> To act as a clearing house for all genealogical and temple labor.[22]

Franklin D. Richards had amassed about 100 books on genealogy and donated them to the LDS Church. By 1915 the number of books had increased to over 8,200.[23] These volumes served as the nucleus for what eventually became one of the largest genealogical libraries throughout the world. All of the directors were male; the only female listed during Susa's lifetime on the masthead of the Genealogical Society of Utah was Lillian Cameron, assistant librarian.[24] The GSU started its own quarterly publication, the *Utah Genealogical and Historical Magazine*, in January 1910. Susa was a frequent contributor thereafter.[25]

Susa further promoted genealogy and historical memory in 1901 when she helped organize the Daughters of the Utah Pioneers

20. "Duncan M. McAllister," biographical sketch, box 61, fd. 22, SYGP (CHL).

21. Charles W. Penrose, "The Genealogical Society of Utah," typescript of speech given at the convention of the GSU, July 27, 1915, San Francisco, California, box 69, fd. 7, SYGP (CHL).

22. "Handbook of Genealogy and Temple Work," box 74, fd. 4, SYGP (CHL).

23. "McAllister."

24. GSU enrollment card, box 75, fd. 7, SYGP (CHL).

25. See Penrose, "Genealogical Society."

(DUP). She was pressured to accept the presidency of the organization but said that the only way she would do this would be if the DUP adopted a genealogy program. The officers of the organization agreed to this condition, and Susa became president of the Daughters of the Utah Pioneers in 1905. By 1908 a difference of opinion regarding the role of genealogy in the DUP had arisen. Susa was concerned that the DUP program was not taking into account the essentially religious work of LDS genealogical research: supplying names for vicarious ordinances in the temples for people who had died. The DUP, conversely, felt that the program was too oriented toward religious purposes. Susa and some of her friends went to Anthon H. Lund of the First Presidency, LDS Church Historian, and president of the GSU to ask for direction.[26] The women were invited to bring their genealogy work with them to the Genealogical Society of Utah, which they did.[27]

Joseph Fielding Smith, secretary of the GSU, announced that on July 21, 1908, a resolution was passed by the board of the GSU requesting that the newspaper articles on genealogy appearing under the auspices of the DUP be published thereafter under the direction of the GSU. Susa and her genealogical associates promptly resigned their positions within the DUP. A Woman's Committee of the GSU was appointed, with Susa as chair and Alice K. Smith, Ann D. Groesbeck, Elizabeth C. McCune, Zina Y. Card, Maria B. Winder, Augusta W. Grant, and Isabel Whitney Sears as members, and Annie Lynch as secretary and treasurer.[28] The first meeting of the committee was held on September 4, 1908.[29]

Anthon Lund, for one, recognized the yeoman's work performed by the Woman's Committee. At a committee meeting held in May 1912, he praised the work of the committee, "naming especially Susa Young Gates as deserving of supreme credit." At the end of the meeting, Susa demurred, asking Lund not to refer to the women's work and her part in it for two reasons. First, jealousies might arise

---

26. For details of the dispute with the DUP, see Allen and Embry, "Provoking the Brethren," 122–23.
27. "Report of Woman's Committee," box 69, fd. 18, SYGP (CHL).
28. "Report of Woman's Committee."
29. Allen and Embry, "Provoking the Brethren," 126.

among the committee members.[30] One of the officers of the committee, Annie Lynch, felt "discrimination against her" and, according to Susa, was known for her "ungovernable temper."[31] Second, Susa felt that the priesthood should " not only direct the affairs, control the activities, but also ... be given the credit and praise."[32]

Circumstances changed once again when Susa and Elizabeth McCune were called to the general board of the Relief Society in 1911. The Woman's Committee was dissolved in 1914, the year after much of its work had come under the aegis of the Relief Society. This had occurred at the behest of church president Joseph F. Smith, who, when he called Susa and Elizabeth to the general board, asked them "to advocate the formation of genealogical studies" within the Relief Society.[33]

Despite a male-dominated leadership within the GSU, most of the genealogy work itself was performed by women. Susa developed the mantra, "Let us provoke the brethren to good works, yet not provoke the brethren while we work."[34] During her many years of genealogical research, Susa articulated another saying: "Do not expect God nor the spirits behind the veil to do that which you can do yourself."[35]

Transferring much of the genealogical work from the GSU to the Relief Society was not without its problems, particularly on the part of the Relief Society. There had been pointed discussions regarding several questions: Should the Relief Society develop uniform lesson guides to be used by all branches of the Relief Society everywhere? All of the other auxiliaries had done so, and the Relief Society would become the last organization to adopt churchwide lessons. Indeed, the general board of the Relief Society had dug in its heels against doing so for years, even in the face of pressure by Joseph F. Smith. According to historians James Allen and Jessie Embry, "The Women's Committee knew that convincing the Relief Society to adopt

---

30. "Genesis of Classwork in the G.H.S.U.," undated typescript, box 69, fd. 22, SYGP (CHL).

31. Susa Young Gates to John A. Widtsoe, Aug. 13, 1913, box 69, fd. 14.

32. "Genesis of Classwork."

33. "Genesis of Classwork."

34. Allen and Embry, "Provoking the Brethren," 115.

35. Gates, "Report of Mission."

the genealogical lessons would be a giant step toward achieving the committee's goal of genuine church-wide participation." Should the lessons be unduly technical, or would lessons with a theological bent be better suited to the general membership of the Relief Society? Eventually, uniform genealogical lessons were adopted, and the second weekly meeting of the Relief Society each month was devoted to genealogy instruction.[36]

Allen and Embry, along with historian Kahlile B. Mehr, give credit for "the early accomplishments of the Genealogical Society of Utah" to "two forceful advocates" who "doggedly pursued" their visions of the possibilities of the Genealogical Society: Susa Young Gates and Joseph Fielding Smith, apostle and future tenth president of the church.[37] Much of Smith's work was administrative and doctrinal in nature, but Susa has left her personal imprint on the practical aspects of genealogical work in the church. Everyone in the tight-knit genealogy community knew Susa. Over the years she visited genealogical libraries across America and Europe. She corresponded extensively with well-known genealogists. Her membership in genealogical societies included the Society of Genealogists of London, the New England Historic Genealogical Society, the National Genealogical and Historical Society of Washington, DC, and the California Genealogical Society.[38]

Susa frequently felt the hand of God directing her labors in genealogy. During her visit to New York City to help nurse Elizabeth McCune back to health in January 1917, Susa visited a genealogy bookstore in Brooklyn. She was perusing the shelves when she saw it: a copy of a rare book on Young family genealogy published in 1869 and out of print for forty years. She had copied information from this book from time to time when she had seen it in genealogical libraries, but she thought the opportunity to buy her own copy a real treasure.[39] Susa, defensive of her father but also accustomed to how non-Mormons thought of him, may have laughed when she

36. Allen and Embry, "Provoking the Brethren," 127–29.

37. Allen, Embry, and Mehr, *Hearts Turned to the Fathers*, 59.

38. For details of Susa's enrollment and participation in these societies, see box 71, fds. 12 and 16, and box 73, fd. 10, SYGP (CHL).

39. Minutes and Reports. The book was I. Gilbert Young, comp., *Fragmentary Records of the Youngs* ... (Philadelphia: William S. Young, 1869).

reached page seventy-one. The author, without providing any firm evidence that Brigham Young was even part of his own Young family line, concluded a three-page diatribe against Brigham with these words: "With such a Turk as Brigham Young, we claim not even the most distant cousinship, and 'by these presents,' we read him out of the great Young family."[40]

Susa developed procedures for indexing names, wrote columns for newspapers, developed the earliest manuals for genealogical work, taught classes throughout the church in the United States and Canada, authored a genealogical book on surnames, and promoted "Genealogy Sunday." She researched 20,000–30,000 Young names and wrote letters to thousands of Youngs throughout the country to determine possible family connections. She became one of the first women in the LDS Church to speak on the radio when she gave talks on genealogy. She organized temple excursions and performed temple work for several of her prominent feminist friends who had passed away. Her list of achievements in genealogy is long and continues to influence LDS temple work to the present.

Susa not only worked tirelessly in the organized genealogy endeavors of the church, but she was also intimately involved with all aspects of genealogy work associated with the Young family. In 1906 the Young Family Temple Committee was formed, with Susa as chair. Other members were Richard W. Young, Willard Young, Zina Card, Afton Young, Persis Richards, and Josephine Beatie Burton, secretary and treasurer.[41] Later John M. Young, Mabel Sanborn, John A. Widtsoe, Maria Dougall, and Jeannette Easton were added as honorary members.[42] Over time, Susa collected the names of 30,000 Young family members for temple work and developed methods to avoid duplication in performing ordinances.[43]

Susa wrote genealogy columns in both the *Deseret News*, beginning in January 1907, and in the *Salt Lake Herald-Republican*, beginning in 1908. She had developed the idea of a weekly genealogy

---

40. Young, *Fragmentary Records*, 71.

41. See Officers of Young Family Association.

42. "Report of Young Family Association," 1921, box 65, fd. 17, SYGP (CHL).

43. See, for example, "Report of Young Family," and Susa's ongoing correspondence with Gilman Howe in box 61, fd. 8, SYGP (CHL).

column and approached the *Deseret News* to assess management's interest. They approved her recommendation, and Susa started writing. The columns were helpful to workers in genealogy and contained "reports from temples, from conventions, notes of meetings, calls for information and lists of books purchased for the library."[44]

Susa developed multiple types of genealogy classes. She obtained a room in the Lion House for instruction, which she began in 1906. Over the years these classes grew. Genealogy training began in Provo at BYU in 1909 with Susa teaching some of the original classes. Susa was officially appointed in October 1912 as director of class work in the GSU.[45] She and Elizabeth McCune went on the road and spent the summer of 1913 teaching methods of doing genealogy to LDS stake representatives in western Canada and southern Utah.[46] In April 1917 Susa traveled to teach genealogy classes in the stakes of northern Arizona, and in 1918 she took a long trip to northern Utah to teach there.[47] Most genealogy classes were taught at the stake level, and Susa not only prepared the lectures, but in many cases taught the local stake instructors their responsibilities.[48]

Susa was instrumental in the inauguration of semi-annual genealogical conventions in April 1914. These meetings lasted for three days and were held after the general conference of the church.[49] The first convention had 500 delegates present from sixty-five stakes.[50] On January 22, 1914, a few months prior to the first convention, a standing committee of genealogy and temple work on the general board of the Relief Society was formed. Members of the committee were Elizabeth C. McCune, Susa Young Gates, Janette A. Hyde, Sarah Jenne Cannon, Priscilla P. Jennings, Carrie S. Thomas, Edna May Davis, Sarah M. McClelland, and Amy Brown Lyman.

---

44. Lofthouse, "History of the Genealogical Society," 17.

45. "Genesis of Classwork."

46. Susa Young Gates, "Genealogy in the Relief Society," *Utah Genealogical and Historical Magazine*, Jan. 1916, 41–45.

47. For the trip to Arizona, see, for example, correspondence from Gates to German and Mary Ellsworth, Apr.–May 1917, box 62, fd. 10, and for northern Utah, see Gates to Charles Whittier, Sep. 24, 1918, box 63, fd. 5, SYGP (CHL).

48. Lofthouse, "History of the Genealogical Society," 18.

49. See "Genealogical Conventions," *Utah Genealogical and Historical Magazine*, Jan. 1916, 21.

50. Allen and Embry, "Provoking the Brethren," 131.

Susa, along with Nellie T. Taylor and Mabel Y. Sanborn, developed genealogy instruction for departing missionaries, which began in 1925. At that time the decision was made for new missionaries to undergo one hour of instruction in genealogy with a visit to the Genealogy Library during their one week of preparation in the Mission Home in Salt Lake City. The missionaries would visit "places of interest, obtaining their endowments [in the temple]."[51] Questions the missionaries needed to consider included, "Why should missionaries and converts undergo training in genealogy?" "Where shall missionaries and converts find genealogical training?" and "How should new converts prepare their genealogical information?"[52] Susa continued to teach the classes for four years, until Archibald Bennett took them over, and the classes continued with different teachers until the 1940s.[53] After she stopped teaching missionary classes, Susa continued to teach genealogy classes for the Relief Society until 1929.[54]

Susa wrote one of the first, if not the first, genealogy instruction books in 1912. She was listed as the author, and the book contained eight lessons:

Introduction
The Genealogist at Work—Materials and Sources of Information
The Genealogist at Work—Approximating Dates and Method of
    Recording
Method of Recording
Heirship with Temple Work
Numbering
Work in the Library: Some Standard Books
Work in the Library: Some Standard Books (continued)[55]

Seven more editions appeared between 1912 and 1928.[56] Susa wrote

---

51. See mission correspondence and lessons for 1925–26, box 68, fds. 9–10, SYGP (CHL).

52. Mission lessons, 1926, box 68, fd. 10.

53. See "Genesis of Classwork," and Lofthouse, "History of the Genealogical Society," 20.

54. Gates, "Susa Young Gates and Genealogical Research," undated typescript, box 70, fd. 4, SYGP (CHL).

55. "Genesis of Classwork."

56. "Genesis of Classwork."

most of the manuals through 1924, although, at her insistence, her name did not appear as author after the original 1912 edition.[57]

Everywhere she went, Susa visited genealogy libraries. In North America she visited libraries in Boston, Washington, DC, New York City, Philadelphia, Chicago, Omaha, Toronto, and Montreal.[58] She became well-acquainted with the librarians of the great American genealogical collections.[59] In Europe she visited libraries in London multiple times, as well as in Copenhagen and Berlin.[60] When Susa and Elizabeth McCune traveled to Rome for the 1914 International Council of Women, they visited genealogy libraries in London, Cassel, Basel, and Rome, in addition to multiple American genealogical libraries. On her way home to Utah, Susa, traveling with Ida B. Smith, spent two weeks doing further research in London.[61]

Susa played a key role in the LDS Church's participation in the International Congress of Genealogy held July 28–30, 1915, in conjunction with the Panama–Pacific Exposition in San Francisco. She urged every stake genealogical committee to send at least one member to California for the meeting. She chartered a separate railroad car, and almost 250 members of the church made the trip from Salt Lake City to San Francisco. It was also one of the few trips Jacob took with Susa. Many of the attendees also took the optional tour to Los Angeles and San Diego.[62]

Both the Genealogical Society of Utah and the National Woman's Relief Society Genealogical Extension Division were among the sixty-six official delegations to the congress.[63] Susa and Nephi Anderson gave lessons on genealogy at the Utah Day of the fair, which

---

57. Archibald Bennett to Los Angeles and Hollywood Stakes, Oct. 25, 1928, box, 73, fd. 26, SYGP (CHL).

58. Gates, "Susa Young Gates and Genealogical Research."

59. See, for example, Susa's correspondence with various libraries, 1913–14, box 73, fd. 18.

60. "The Story of the Genealogical Society of Utah," undated typescript, box 69, fd. 6, SYGP (CHL).

61. "Genealogists Abroad," *Utah Genealogical and Historical Magazine*, July 1914, 125–33.

62. "The Genealogical Society of Utah at the International Congress of Genealogy," *Utah Genealogical and Historical Magazine*, Jan. 1916, 1–33. Hereafter cited as "GSU at International Congress." See also Allen and Embry, "Provoking the Brethren," 131–32.

63. "International Congress of Genealogy," *Utah Genealogical and Historical Magazine*, Oct. 1915, 157–228.

took place the day before the official opening of the three-day convention. Utah governor William Spry, Salt Lake City mayor Samuel C. Park, and LDS Church president Joseph F. Smith all attended. Susa's daughter Emma Lucy Gates sang, and the Ogden Tabernacle Choir performed.[64]

At the congress Susa was named to three different standing committees: the Committee on Program, the Committee on Permanent Organization, and the Committee on Establishment of a National Bureau of Vital Statistics. Joseph Fielding Smith was named to the Committee on Permanent Organization as well.[65] The congress authorized the *Utah Genealogical and Historical Magazine* to publish the official proceedings of the congress in its October 1915 and January 1916 issues.[66]

Susa also moved to address some of the complaints newcomers had relating to the technical difficulties of genealogical research. With the approval of the Relief Society and the GSU, she edited and had published a 576-page tome, *Surname Book and Racial History*, using information largely culled from other sources.[67] The book was widely distributed and used among genealogy workers; even as she neared the end of her life, Susa still received queries about how to obtain the book.

Even as Susa attended conferences and taught others how to research their own genealogy, she continued to work on her own family lines. One of her great frustrations was her inability to delineate the Young family beyond her great-grandfather William Young, who had lived in Boston and eventually died in Hopkinton, Massachusetts. There were four William Youngs worshipping at the same church in Boston during the years of 1721 to 1725, and two of them were married to a woman named Hannah, which made tracing her ancestors nearly impossible.[68] Susa was never able to determine exactly when or where her particular William Young was born.

---

64. "GSU at International Congress," 2–3. See also agendas and programs in box 69, fd. 14, SYGP (CHL).

65. "International Congress of Genealogy," 164.

66. Allen and Embry, "Provoking the Brethren," 132.

67. "Surname Book and Racial History," *Utah Genealogical and Historical Magazine*, Jan. 1919, 29–34.

68. See Susa's extensive correspondence trying to trace William Young, in box 63, fd. 2. Since Susa's time, the Young family genealogy has been traced back six generations

Generally speaking, church members were discouraged from performing vicarious temple ordinances for non-relatives. Susa, however,
had been told by then-president Wilford Woodruff that, despite
not being able to trace the Young line beyond William and despite
not knowing which Youngs were related to Brigham, that Brigham
"would stand at the head of all the Young families in this generation
and dispensation." Woodruff therefore gave the Brigham Young family "permission to gather up all Young names that related to other
Young families in the Church."[69] The Young family thus had the prerogative to perform temple work for any deceased persons with the
surname Young, whether they were related to Brigham or not.

There were obviously thousands of Americans with the surname
Young, and Susa tried diligently over the years to see if and how these
different families were related. She got one idea from German Ellsworth, an LDS mission president in Chicago, to copy down names
from city directories and then mail questionnaires to see if common
ancestors could be found. Susa called this the Ellsworth Plan, and at
her own expense she sent out over 2,000 surveys to Youngs found in
multiple phone books throughout the country.[70] Despite Susa's enthusiasm, not much useful information was obtained, and nearly all
of the people who responded to the questionnaire were not related
to Brigham and his descendants.

Beginning in about 1921 Susa organized a "benefit night session" at the temples in Utah, wherein patrons would attend a session
in behalf of a deceased Young family member, in this way working
through the hundreds of names for whom the temple work had not
yet been performed.[71] These "benefits" occurred on the day the temple
was open which was closest to Brigham Young's birthday on June 1.
Susa later added the Lā'ie, Hawai'i, and the Cardston, Canada, temple
presidents in her correspondence. The cooperation demonstrated by
the temple presidents in these events in every available piece of correspondence is a tribute to Susa's sway in matters related to genealogy

---

from William Young Jr. (1695–1747), Brigham's great-grandfather, to Duncan Young
(1514–83), who was born in Edinburgh, Scotland.

69. Young Family Association reports.

70. Young Family Association reports.

71. See, for example, Susa Young Gates to Joseph R. Shepherd, June 3, 1921, box
63, fd. 1.

and temple work.[72] Susa continued to orchestrate these annual temple events honoring Brigham Young throughout the remainder of her life.

Susa promoted uniformity among Relief Society sisters in their genealogical research. She discouraged initiation of new programs without the approval of the GSU, declaring in a Relief Society general conference address, "You will never get anywhere by going at it alone, only trying to be a law unto yourself. ... Our motto is: It is better to be united on an inferior plan than divided over a superior one."[73]

In order to involve more women in temple work, Susa helped to encourage temple excursions for them. By 1916 the Relief Society sisters were asked to spend one day a year working in the temple.[74] One Sunday in September was set aside as "Genealogy Sunday," devoted to teaching all members of the church regarding genealogy. As one of the first Latter-day Saint women to talk on the radio, Susa spoke on "The Spirit of Genealogy" on March 29, 1929, on KSL Radio in Salt Lake City to promote genealogy.[75] On another occasion she spoke on "Patriotic Societies and Genealogy."[76]

Susa took it upon herself personally to perform temple work for several of her friends in the women's movement. On October 19, 1920, she wrote to Joseph R. Shepherd, president of the Logan temple, requesting that the names of May Wright Sewall, Anna Howard Shaw, and Rachel Foster Avery, all of whom had died recently, be reserved for her to perform their temple work. Susa wrote that both Sewall and Shaw had specifically requested that Susa undertake this labor for them after she had explained to them the nature of temple work for the dead.[77] Susa also made similar requests of the temple presidents in St. George and Manti and of the temple recorder in Salt Lake City.[78]

Not unexpectedly, given her forceful personality, Susa ran into

---

72. See, for example, correspondence in box 72, fd. 15.

73. Amy Brown Lyman, "General Conference of Relief Society," *Relief Society Magazine*, Dec. 1918, 676. See also Allen and Embry, "Provoking the Brethren," 133.

74. Allen and Embry.

75. The talk was printed as Gates, "The Spirit of Genealogy," *Latter-day Saints' Millennial Star*, Sep. 19, 1929, 602.

76. Gates, "Patriotic Societies," copy in box 70, fd. 8, SYGP (CHL).

77. Gates to Shepherd, Oct. 19, 1920, box 63, fd. 1.

78. See Susa's correspondence to the St. George and Manti temple presidents in box 72, fd. 21, and to the Salt Lake Temple recorder in box 73, fd. 23.

occasional challenges. After meeting with "responsible parties" at the *Deseret News,* Joseph Fielding Smith counseled "Aunt Susa" that the GSU "are going to meet with trouble if we publish too much in the nature of advice for the student," rather than "a few short pedigrees, answers to genealogical questions, etc."[79] In December 1916 Horace G. Whitney, business manager of the *Deseret News,* recommended that Susa leave out "biographical sketches of pioneers" from her genealogical columns, since they are covered elsewhere, and confine herself strictly to "genealogical records."[80] A few months prior, Susa had taken Whitney to task in a letter relating to confusion of dates regarding Young family members in an article she had written. "Your rules concerning care in comparing dates are no more rigid than my own. I think if you will take the trouble to examine the material which I have furnished you so cheaply during the past ten years, you will find that accuracy has been the keynote of the work."[81]

In 1918 the *Deseret News,* in Susa's words, "crowded out" her weekly genealogy column.[82] For several weeks in August of that year, the column did not appear. Susa thought that the column had been discontinued; the *Deseret News* editorial staff, however, maintained later that American involvement in World War I had created a paper shortage, requiring a condensed version of the column.[83] After consulting with the board of directors of the Genealogical Society of Utah, Susa waged a campaign to have the genealogy column reinstated. She sent 1,000 circulars to Relief Societies throughout the church, urging the members to protest to the newspaper staff against the cessation of the column in the *Deseret News.* After hundreds of letters poured into their office, the newspaper editors said that they were simply changing the format of the column and urged these same sisters to inform whoever had encouraged them to send letters to the *Deseret News* office that they were not planning to cancel the column. Susa's office in turn received hundreds of letters. The *Deseret News* management, presumably Whitney, snapped in a letter to the

---

79. Smith to Gates, July 15, 1910, box 69, fd. 12.
80. Whitney to Gates, Dec. 1916, box 51, fd. 12.
81. Gates to Whitney, Aug. 27, 1916, box 73, fd. 20.
82. Susa Young Gates to Charles Whittier, Oct. 12, 1918, box 63, fd. 5.
83. Allen and Embry, "Provoking the Brethren," 123.

Elwood Ward in Utah, that those who oversee the newspaper are "the best judge of what should and should not appear in its columns in these days of stress and government regulations."[84]

Susa's genealogical column in the *Herald-Republican* was discontinued after a decade. She decided that, after the debacle over the mix-up of the column in the *Deseret News*, a male editor would wield greater influence and turned the department over to Nephi Anderson, who served until his death in 1923, at which time Susa resumed editorship.[85]

On several occasions the general board of the Relief Society tried to do away with genealogy lessons in Relief Society, since they were technically difficult. Susa's frustration is obvious in two letters written to Anthon H. Lund. In September 1915 she wrote, "We have just scratched the surface, as it were, of this work in our Relief Society." She complained that she had "considerable difficulty with certain members of my Board concerning the genealogy lessons in my Society" and that these board members "would be glad to throw the whole thing out and substitute various attractive club subjects and studies." Susa felt, though, that "we have succeeded, I hope, in establishing the work for a time at least on a broad sure foundation"[86] In a second letter two years later, Susa confided to Lund that were it not for a conversation the two had, "I doubt whether I could have withstood the onslaught I received this morning from the same sisters on our Board whom I mentioned to you who repeated the criticisms of those who say, 'There is a Genealogical Society of Utah; why not let them take over all this lesson work and leave the Relief Society to take up other fields of activities.'"[87]

Joseph Fielding Smith wrote to Susa on behalf of Lund and the board of directors of the GSU a letter which was reprinted in the *Relief Society Magazine*. He said that they were "very greatly pleased with your labors in instructing the sisters of the Relief Society, in matters pertaining to genealogy." He continued, "We feel that it would be a deplorable thing should you, for any cause, discontinue

84. Allen and Embry, 124.
85. "Genesis of Classwork," and Allen and Embry, "Provoking the Brethren," 124.
86. Gates to Lund, Sep. 14, 1915, box 73, fd. 19.
87. Gates to Lund, June 25, 1917, box 73, fd. 21.

the work in this direction. For we consider the work in the interest of the salvation of the dead ... the most important labor with which we have to do."[88]

Nevertheless, by 1920 the decision was made to transfer virtually all of the genealogy workload back to the Genealogical Society of Utah.[89] By that year only temple excursions exclusively for the sisters and annual temple days for them were still under the direction of the Relief Society.[90] These changes did not bother Susa, since she had always felt that genealogy was a priesthood responsibility which should operate under the direction of priesthood leadership.[91] The Relief Society decided to continue genealogy lessons for the time being only on a theological basis and not on a practical or technical basis. Eventually, the genealogy classes were phased completely out of the Relief Society.[92]

Susa lamented on multiple occasions that she felt like a lone voice in the wilderness preaching the gospel of genealogy and temple work. At the annual Young Family Association meetings, family members were so "indifferent to temple work" that she was not given time to report on the temple work she was doing.[93] On numerous occasions Susa complained about lack of help and support in this work from other family members. In a letter to Logan temple president Joseph Shepherd in 1923, thanking him for his support of the Brigham Young Memorial Day, Susa wrote, "The rest [of the family] are too engaged in social affairs to bother about temple work. It is a great blessing that people love Brigham Young well enough to help him with his dead even if his family do not."[94] To another temple president, Edward J. Wood of the Cardston temple, Susa wrote in 1926, "I struggle along alone almost in this work. ... If it were not for

88. Joseph Fielding Smith, "Communication," *Relief Society Magazine*, Aug. 1918, 475–76.
89. Allen and Embry, "Provoking the Brethren," 133.
90. "Notice to Genealogical Committees," *Relief Society Magazine*, Dec. 1920, 731.
91. "Genesis of Classwork."
92. See Allen and Embry, "Provoking the Brethren," 134, and Susa's correspondence over the decision in box 2, fd. 7, SYGP (UDSH).
93. Susa Young Gates to David H. Cannon, May 16, 1921, box 72, fd. 21.
94. Gates to Shepherd, July 5, 1923, box 70, fd. 23.

our yearly benefits, Brigham Young's dead would lie in their prison houses, I don't know how long."[95]

Despite the fact that Susa cared a great deal about genealogy, she could be disingenuous about her involvement. In April 1919 Susa wrote to her friend in genealogy, Charles C. Whittier of Boston, averring, "You know this genealogical quest is but a by-product of my busy life, for I not only edit a magazine [*Relief Society Magazine*] and occupy other prominent public positions, am in my office from half past eight in the morning until six at night, but I do the house work at home for my husband, my son and myself even to the old-fashioned labor of washing and ironing. I cannot afford to hire help as we are still putting our boys through college. So I pick up my genealogy as a side issue."[96]

In 1923 Susa was appointed head of the genealogical research bureau for the GSU. She was thrilled with the assignment and wrote to Charles W. Penrose, First Presidency counselor and president of the GSU, "I wish I might be able to express to you the joy and gratitude that fills my heart in this appointment. It is something which I have longed for for many years."[97] In writing to a genealogy colleague, Susa declared, "I am now devoting myself exclusively to genealogical work."[98] However, in the male-dominated leadership of genealogical work, it was decided within a few months that this responsibility belonged to a priesthood holder. Susa was accordingly relieved of the task, and in 1924 Andrew K. Smith, son of Joseph F. Smith, was named as head of the newly established Research Bureau.[99]

By the beginning of the 1920s, Susa and Jacob had settled into a comfortable routine. Jacob was employed full-time as an assistant recorder at the Salt Lake temple. Susa spent mornings at the temple and the rest of the day at the genealogy library. Over the last decade and a half of her life, Susa wrote hundreds of letters to individuals, usually in response to requests for help in their genealogical

---

95. Gates to Wood, July 9, 1926, box 72, fd. 15. By "prison houses," Susa means that they would not be able to enter the celestial kingdom because they lacked the necessary temple ordinances.
96. Gates to Whittier, Apr. 1919, box 63, fd. 5.
97. Susa Young Gates to Charles W. Penrose, Apr. 26, 1923, box 70, fd. 10.
98. Gates to Pierson W. Banning, May 1, 1923, box 71, fd. 4.
99. Allen, Embry, and Mehr, *Hearts Turned to the Fathers*, 105.

endeavors. Susa was also not hesitant to initiate correspondence about genealogy with prominent figures, even people she did not know. In June 1924, for example, she wrote to Charles Gates Dawes to ask about his Gates genealogy. Later that year Dawes was elected as vice president to President Calvin Coolidge. In her letter to Dawes, she pointed out once again that she had largely left politics behind, although she did participate as a private citizen: "I have turned over my political duties five years ago to Janette A. Hyde, who is also a dear friend, yet I don't propose to neglect my private opportunities of helping the cause [Republican] along this fall."[100]

Susa ascribed her longevity and health to her involvement in genealogy and temple work: "The life and health and happiness which has been given back to me because of this Temple work, is beyond my command of language to even faintly express."[101] Nevertheless, her genealogy and temple work were sufficiently taxing that in December 1916, she wrote to acquaintance Evelyn Clark, "I am so busy these days that I fear I am not courteous to anyone, but I do feel very anxious to spend the time remaining to me on this earth in helping everybody to save the souls of the dead and thus insure their own salvation."[102]

Archibald F. Bennett, secretary of the Genealogical Society of Utah from 1928 to 1961 and popularly known as "Mr. Genealogy,"[103] paid this tribute to Susa in 1928:

> Sister Gates is a real pioneer in genealogical work, and her mission for many years has been to arouse the Saints to the urgency of this work and teach them methods of doing so. Her contribution to the literature of the cause has undoubtedly been greater than that of any other individual in the Church. She compiled the first lesson book in genealogy, so far as I know ever published. Besides several lesson books she has contributed the Handbook of Genealogy and Temple Work and the Surname Book and Racial History, both filled with most valuable and vital information. Past volumes of the Relief Society Magazine and the

---

100. Gates to Dawes, June 17, 1924, box 60, fd. 16.
101. Susa Young Gates, "Report of the Temple Work Done in Behalf of the Young Family," Apr. 20, 1906, box 65, fd. 18.
102. Gates to Clark, Dec. 1916, box 51, fd. 17.
103. Allen, Embry, and Mehr, *Hearts Turned to the Fathers*, 95.

Genealogical Magazine contain most inspiring articles from her pen on genealogical subjects."[104]

For the foreseeable future, Susa will likely remain the predominant LDS woman in the annals of genealogy and temple work.

---

104. Bennett to Los Angeles and Hollywood Stakes.

The Life of an Ascetic

Susa's focus changed dramatically during the 1920s. By this decade, gone were the far-flung travels, personal participation in politics, and standing at the forefront of national and international women's movements. Her editorship of two churchwide women's periodicals, which had covered nineteen years of her life beginning in 1889, ended in 1922. Susa, always passionate about genealogy and temple work, made these endeavors the centerpiece around which her life now revolved.

Along with genealogy and temple work, two other pursuits formed the triumvirate of the final years of her life. First, she wrote two major works. A biography of her father, *Life Story of Brigham Young*, was published. A second major work on women in the LDS Church remained unpublished. Second was Susa's emergence as the *grande dame* of *belles lettres* in Utah. Mostly remaining in Utah, she met and entertained many distinguished literary figures in the world. Because of the physical demands of her work in the temple, social life outside the home at night diminished, and she spent almost all evenings quietly at home with her husband.

Accolades continued to accumulate. She enjoyed several "firsts"— she was the first, and possibly the only, woman to have her own office in the new Church Office Administration Building at 47 East South Temple Street, which had been completed in 1917. In October 1922, several months after resigning from her Relief Society duties, she was welcomed into the Historian's Office by Anthony W.

Ivins, second counselor in the First Presidency, and Apostle Joseph Fielding Smith.[1] She expected to work on her history of the women of the church, but she fretted, "When that is done, what then?" Two months later, in December 1922, Susa was given by Apostle Smith and Assistant Church Historian William Lund the vacant office of B. H. Roberts, who was then living in New York City as he presided over the Eastern States Mission. She was told to "keep still about it and get out before ever the owner came home to conference" and discovered she was there.[2] Sure enough, on April 2, 1923, Susa wrote Elizabeth McCune that Roberts was coming home for the April general conference, so her things were moved back to the Historian's Office temporarily.[3]

In addition to giving radio addresses on genealogy, Susa spoke on other topics. Her first speech, delivered at the invitation of David A. Smith, counselor in the Presiding Bishopric, was given on May 17, 1925, entitled "Opening the Gates Beautiful for Women."[4] On June 1, 1929, her topic was "Brigham Young: Patriot, Pioneer, Prophet." In this address Susa described Brigham Young's forefathers' service in the Colonial army during the Revolutionary War, his role in the settlement of Utah, his associates—both male and female—in his pioneering endeavors, his family life, and several of his prophecies. Susa recorded what she remembered her father had told her in the last year of his life: "If it had not been for the Gospel of Jesus Christ as revealed by the Prophet Joseph Smith, I would have been, today, but a carpenter in a country village. I am what Mormonism has made me."

Susa had been the first Utah woman to be listed in Marquis *Who's Who in America* in 1906, which continued to include her. During the 1920s she received numerous requests for information for various biographical collections, including *The International Blue Book, Who's Who Among North American Writers, National Cyclopedia of American*

---

1. Gates Journal in box 105, fd. 4, SYGP (CHL). During the last eighteen years of her life, Susa sporadically kept a journal, often crossing out the pre-printed dates in the diary books and adding her own. She did not write chronologically—entries from 1918 might appear alongside entries from 1927. It was not until the last two years of her life that she recorded more consistently, and two journal books filled with hundreds of entries exist for 1932–33.
2. Gates Journal, under date, box 105, fd. 6.
3. Gates to McCune, Apr. 2, 1923, box 40, fd. 3.
4. Gates Journal, under date, box 105, fd. 4, SYGP (CHL).

Biography, Women of Today, Utah's Distinguished Personalities, The Yearbook and Directory of the National Council of Women, Women of the West, Outstanding Women, and *Principal Women of America.*[5]

Early in the decade, Susa continued to be chosen for important positions and assignments. In 1920 she was appointed to the executive committee of the Utah State Historical Society, and in January 1922 she was appointed by Utah governor Charles R. Mabey to the Federal Legislative Committee to help "develop the scenic attractions of this State."[6] Susa was also one of two women chosen to represent Utah in Chicago in February 1920 to celebrate the 19th Amendment, which granted universal suffrage to women in America. Her traveling companion was Donnette Smith Kesler, daughter of President Joseph F. Smith and roommate of Susa's daughter Leah at the Pratt Institute a quarter of a century previously. Susa herself was "the earliest pioneer voter present in Chicago, she having married at sixteen and cast her vote in 1872." Susa later claimed, as noted below, that she voted in 1870. Three Utah women, Emmeline B. Wells, Emily S. Richards, and Susa Young Gates, received gold honor pins for longevity of service in women's suffrage.[7]

After their time in Chicago, Susa and Donnette traveled to New York City, Brooklyn, Boston, and Lynn, Massachusetts. They went on to Philadelphia, Baltimore, and Washington, DC, where they met with Senator Reed Smoot and Kate Waller Barrett, former president of the National Council of Women. In all of these cities Susa and Donnette conducted Relief Society business for the general board.[8]

About this time was published a picture of five generations of female voters in Susa's family, starting with Susa's grandmother Mary Gibbs Bigelow and continuing with her mother Lucy Bigelow Young, Susa herself, Susa's daughter Leah Dunford Widtsoe, and Susa's oldest granddaughter Anna Gaarden Widtsoe.[9] Susa's official

---

5. See Susa's correspondence with these publications in box 49, fds. 15–17, 19, 26, and 28.

6. Charles R. Mabey to Susa Young Gates, Jan. 10, 1922, box 59, fd. 3.

7. Susa Young Gates, "Suffrage Won by the Mothers of the United States," *Relief Society Magazine,* May 1920, 254.

8. See Susa's correspondence and newspaper clippings of this trip in box 50, fd. 16, SYGP (CHL).

9. *Deseret News,* undated clipping, copy in author's possession.

position was that she had first voted as a married woman in 1872,[10] but she confessed that she had actually sneaked into the voting precinct in 1870 at age fourteen with a large group of women and gotten lost in the crowd. Looking older than her age, she had voted.[11]

In March 1920, about a month after her trip to Chicago, Susa was involved in an automobile accident, causing her to miss several weeks of work. Her son-in-law, John A. Widtsoe, was driving on South Temple Street in Salt Lake City when his car collided with a streetcar. Because of automobiles parked in the street, Widtsoe did not see the oncoming westbound street car until it was almost upon him, nor did the streetcar engineer see the Widtsoe vehicle in time. Widtsoe almost outran the streetcar, but it clipped the rear end of his auto, turning it around. Widtsoe's aunt, Petroline Gaarden, was hospitalized with minor injuries, and Susa was "badly shaken up" but not hospitalized. Thereafter, however, Susa reported suffering a "nervous sickness," which she said was worse than the accident. In a letter to her daughter Lucy, Susa said that after nine weeks she was just beginning to feel like herself.[12] Leah, Jacob, and Susa's friend Elizabeth McCune were also in the car, but were unharmed.

In March of the following year John Widtsoe was named a member of the Quorum of the Twelve Apostles, which required his resignation as president of the University of Utah. Susa continued her collaboration with daughter Leah, and John became involved with the publication of Susa and Leah's biography of Brigham Young, particularly after the Widtsoes were assigned to head the European Mission in 1927 in Liverpool, England.

Susa traveled infrequently during the 1920s, especially compared to her previous world tours. She traveled through southern Utah with church leaders for her article in the *Relief Society Magazine* (see chapter sixteen) and with Jacob in 1923 to the Grand Canyon, where they met their son Hal. Later that year she attended the Cardston temple dedication in Canada, where she recorded the proceedings of the dedicatory services, as she had done previously with

---

10. See, for example, Susa Young Gates to Mrs. Cyrus Beard, Aug. 18, 1925, where she says she first voted in 1872, in box 50, fd. 18.

11. Susa Young Gates to Grace Raymond Hebard, Nov. 26, 1930, box 50, fd. 18.

12. Gates to Lucy Gates Bowen, May 23, 1920, box 22, fd. 13.

the temples in Utah.[13] In 1927 she reported on a trip to Yellowstone National Park.[14] She wrote about the Mesa, Arizona, temple dedication in 1927.

Susa did not avoid a good battle or showdown when she thought her cause was just. In 1922 she and three of her siblings (Willard Young, Zina Card, and Maria Dougall) sent a letter to church president Heber J. Grant and the board of BYU to protest the "somewhat concerted movement to call the school simply the Young University." They continued, "The school might as well be called any name or no name as to be left without the distinctive first name of Brigham Young," which they felt was honorable enough to be perpetuated.[15]

Susa also wrote an angry letter to her old friend and well-known church historian B. H. Roberts.[16] Roberts had credited the Mormon Battalion for introducing irrigation into the Salt Lake Valley. Susa, ever defensive of her father's legacy, pointed out that three days before Brigham Young's arrival into the Salt Lake Valley on July 24, 1847, Young had sent Orson Pratt and a few other men into the valley. He then sent Erastus Snow with instructions to plant seeds as soon as they arrived. As Susa later wrote, when asked how to deal with the parched land, Young replied, "Throw up a dam in the stream, flood a few acres of ground, and then you can plant your potato and other seeds."[17] Thus began, according to Susa, modern-day irrigation, pioneered by Brigham Young. At that time, she said, the Mormon Battalion was still in California. Susa threatened to not give a penny to the construction of the Mormon Battalion Memorial unless a correction in the history were made.[18]

Susa, still against birth control, was outraged when she received a form letter from Margaret Sanger of the American Birth Control League asking for a donation. She fired off an angry reply to tell Sanger "how unhappy" she was with Sanger's endeavors. "I do very

---

13. Gates autobiographical sketches, box 3, fd. 35, SYGP (CHL).

14. See, for example, Gates to Carol Dunn, July 30, 1927, box 35, fd. 8.

15. Young siblings to Grant and BYU board, Sep. 18, 1922, box 35, fd. 19, SYGP (CHL).

16. Gates to Roberts, Jan. 7, 1920, box 41, fd. 11.

17. Susa Young Gates, *Brigham Young: Patriot, Pioneer, and Prophet*, 10, originally an address on KSL radio given June 1, 1929, then published as a pamphlet.

18. Gates to Roberts.

gravely question the righteousness of your fundamental principles." Susa explained her feelings: "Alien races are propagating their species rapidly and the genuine american is dying out. What a pity for the future of humanity." Sanger, accustomed to much worse mail than Susa's, appears to have never replied.[19] Susa filed her copy of her letter in a folder labeled "unimportant" correspondence.

Susa also railed against Democrats. Even though her husband was an ardent Democrat, Susa in 1924 characterized them as non-taxpaying renters, compared to home-owning Republican taxpayers.[20] Susa did acknowledge, in a letter to Reed Smoot, that only two people could sway her political opinions: "my dear husband" and the president of the LDS Church.[21]

There had been a long-standing discussion in American history regarding which state (or territory), Wyoming or Utah, first allowed suffrage for women. Susa engaged in an extended but positive exchange of information with Grace Raymond Hebard of the University of Wyoming regarding the question. Wyoming first passed legislation on December 10, 1869, granting women the vote, but the first statewide election there was not held until the first week in September 1870. Utah, on the other hand, did not pass legislation allowing women suffrage until February 1870, but there was an election held there on February 21. Historians and state residents of Wyoming and Utah, proud of their heritage, have often split hairs over which state granted the right first. Some have even noted that the February election in Utah was only a municipal election, so the commonly touted first female vote in America, cast by Seraph Young, a great-niece of Brigham Young, did not really count as the first female vote. However, the first general territory-wide election in which women voted in Utah was held on August 1, 1870. Wyoming, then, was the first territory to enact suffrage for women, but Utah was the first territory to hold a territorial election in which women voted.[22]

With few exceptions, Susa did not engage in politics after the

---

19. Gates to Sanger, June 9, 1921, box 44, fd. 20.

20. See, for example, Susa's correspondence during the 1924 Republican campaign in box 46, fd. 5, SYGP (CHL).

21. Gates to Smoot, Sep. 6, 1928, box 46, fd. 5.

22. In addition to Susa's ongoing correspondence over this in box 50, fd. 18, see Van Wagenen, *Sister Wives and Suffragists*.

elections of 1916. In January 1920 Susa wrote to Mary Garrett May, vice-chair, Women's Division of the Republican National Committee, that she "was at the head of Republican women for fifteen years. I dropped out of the active political work, however, about three years ago and have neither time nor desire to take up the strenuous labor again."[23] She indicated that she had turned over her political work to Janette Hyde, business manager of the *Relief Society Magazine*. A few months later Susa declined a request of Gertrude B. Lane of the Hoover National Republican Club to join a committee in behalf of promoting Herbert Hoover for president. "I cut out politics five years ago and have kept out of it ever since, as my other cares and burdens would not permit me to keep up the work."[24] However, Susa felt strongly enough in 1928 that J. Reuben Clark should be the Utah Republican candidate for the US Senate that in the summer she sent out a letter to "Fellow Citizens," detailing "an issue ... which demands immediate action from all those who wish right and good government to prevail." Clark was then undersecretary of state in US president Calvin Coolidge's administration, and Susa championed him as representing "that which is best in the traditions and in the fundamental principles of this great American Government."[25] Ultimately, Ernest Bamberger emerged as the Republican candidate, losing to incumbent Democrat William H. King.

In 1926 Susa, with the help of her daughter Leah Widtsoe published a pamphlet entitled *Women of the "Mormon" Church*, which was supposed to be a prelude to Susa's magisterial work on the same topic. In the thirty-four-page work, the name of Emma Smith, wife of LDS founder Joseph Smith, was not mentioned once, which seems unusual, given the panoply of women who were named, some of whom are largely forgotten by now, such as Phebe Cousens and Georgia Snow, Utah's first two pioneer women lawyers.[26] Emma was, after all, the first general president of the Relief Society, which had been organized in Nauvoo in March 1842 under the direction of Joseph Smith himself. Lillie T. Freeze, a prominent leader active

---

23. Gates to May, Jan. 2, 1920, box 50, fd. 16.
24. Gates to Lane, Apr. 2, 1920, box 45, fd. 4.
25. Gates circular to "Fellow Citizens," July 4, 1928, box 46, fd. 5, SYGP (CHL).
26. Gates and Widtsoe, *Women of the Church*, 9.

in both the Primary and Young Ladies' Mutual Improvement Association, took Susa to task for this omission, to which Susa responded that she would "try to remember to put" Emma's name in a new edition. She added, "I would not be unjust to anyone for all the world. I think you know that as well as I do."[27]

Susa's father had periodically clashed with Emma Smith in Nauvoo, following Joseph Smith's murder. Susa, in correspondence with Frederick M. Smith, president of the Reorganized Church of Jesus Christ of Latter Day Saints (now Community of Christ) and grandson of Joseph and Emma Smith, justified Brigham's treatment of Emma after Joseph's death. Emma spoke disparagingly of polygamy and claimed that Joseph had not accepted it as a tenet of the church he established. Susa wrote of "the courtesy of silence which marked my own father's attitude toward your grandmother [Emma Smith] and all those who remained behind. President Joseph F. Smith told me that after the people came out here father had President George A. Smith and himself go over all of the stories and memoirs, historical and biographical, which were obtainable at that time and weed out everything of a controversial nature or that might reflect [poorly] upon any of the Prophet's descendants who were left behind." Only "historic facts" that were "wise and judicious" remained, and the "rest were either destroyed or put away from casual searchers."[28]

In the revised chapters of her "History of Women" files, Susa first commended Emma for her "splendid physical force ... invincible courage, deep mothering instincts, and a temporary adherence to her husband's mission." The women in Nauvoo "had followed her dominant leadership for years ... had admired her courage, her devotion to her husband, and her hospitality to rich and poor alike." But Emma had been warned against "vanity," and Susa lamented Emma's failure to "measure up to" her "high destiny." According to Susa, Emma was unwilling to join with the Quorum of the Twelve Apostles, particularly Brigham Young; she would not humble herself to go west with the remainder of the Saints; she refused to help complete the temple and prepare for the final exodus from Nauvoo.[29]

---

27. Gates and Freeze various correspondence, March 1927, box 83, fd. 3.
28. Gates to Smith, May 1926, box 46, fd. 22.
29. Gates, chapter drafts in box 86, fds. 9, 11, 18, SYGP (CHL).

These actions were unfavorably compared by Susa to those of Emma's sister-in-law, Mary Fielding Smith, widow of Joseph's brother Hyrum, who had been martyred at the same time as Joseph. Mary followed Brigham Young, and both her son and grandson became general authorities of the church—Joseph F. Smith was the sixth church president, and Joseph Fielding Smith would become the tenth. Brigham, despite his tense relationship with Emma, nonetheless sent Apostle George A. Smith multiple times to visit Emma in an attempt to convince her to come west, promising "every help and assistance possible to convey herself and family out of Nauvoo." Young also sent Presiding Bishop Newel K. Whitney to plead with Emma to join the Saints in their move westward. All of Smith's and Whitney's attempts were met with a "curt refusal."[30]

Susa felt that Joseph Smith's family would have been treated with "respect, nay reverence," had Emma been able to bow "her dominant will" and submit "her feelings humbly." She was unable to "conquer self and follow where duty led," thereby closing "the gates to her spiritual advancement on earth." Susa concluded, "Joseph might weep as would the heavens" for Emma. These words are harsh and have often been held against Susa.[31]

Such lack of charity toward Emma Smith was the prevailing sentiment of the times among members of the LDS Church until the seminal work of Linda King Newell and Valeen Tippetts Avery, *Mormon Enigma: Emma Hale Smith*, was published in 1984. Since then history has dealt with Emma in a much kinder, less partisan light. Furthermore, Susa saw the difficult later years of Emma, when she was married to a rough river captain, Lewis Bidamon, as a result of Emma's unwise decisions. Susa recognized Emma's many strengths but was deeply offended by what she considered Emma's "apostasy."[32]

In Salt Lake City society, an exclusive group ranging at times from five to six women calling themselves "the clique," dating from at least 1915, enjoyed a unique and close friendship. The members were an impressive group of women, including two who were wives of presidents of the church: Augusta Winters Grant, wife of Heber J.

30. Gates, chapter drafts, box 86, fds. 11 and 18.
31. Gates, chapter drafts, box 86, fds. 11 and 18.
32. Gates, chapter drafts, and Newell and Avery, *Mormon Enigma*.

Grant, and Alice Kimball Smith, wife of Joseph F. Smith. The other four women were Elizabeth Snow Ivins, wife of First Presidency counselor Anthony W. Ivins, Elizabeth McCune, Ann Dilworth Groesbeck, and Susa Young Gates.

Susa had known Elizabeth Snow Ivins since childhood in St. George, and Elizabeth Claridge McCune had been perhaps her closest friend for many years. Susa and Elizabeth had served together on the general boards of the YLMIA, the Relief Society, and the Utah Genealogical Society. They had served at the same time on the Utah State University board of regents. They had traveled together to inspect universities in the East. In addition, they had made multiple other trips with each other, including to the temple dedication in Cardston, Canada. Susa cherished their friendship, and wrote to Elizabeth, "If you only knew what an inspiration your life and your example are to me and to thousands of others you would be grateful for the spirit and testimony which you have so consistently borne throughout your life."[33]

Elizabeth McCune died at age seventy-two of stomach cancer on August 3, 1924. From her wealth, Elizabeth had left a contribution to the Genealogical Society of Utah, as well as a sum of money for Susa to do genealogy work.[34] After Elizabeth's death, Susa authored a 119-page monograph to honor her.[35] Elizabeth's death was difficult for Susa, who kept in touch with Alfred McCune until his death in 1927 in Cannes, France. Alfred, thought by many Utahns to be a non-Mormon, was a lapsed member of the LDS Church. He and Elizabeth had been married in the Endowment House in Salt Lake City in 1872.[36] Shortly before Alfred McCune's death, Susa made yet another plea to him to put his spiritual life in order: "Oh! Alfred, there is nothing that will comfort the human heart except the spirit of God, which gives us best and helps us to be reconciled both to ourselves and to our fellow creatures during circumstances which life thrusts upon us." Susa went on to report that the "clique" had met together two weeks earlier for the first time since Elizabeth's death.[37]

33. Gates to McCune, undated, box 41, fd. 3.
34. Hal Gates to Susa and Jacob Gates, Aug. 21, 1924, box 26, fd. 10.
35. Gates, *Memorial to Elizabeth Claridge McCune.*
36. Gates, 24.
37. Gates to McCune, Oct. 13, 1926, box 41, fd. 4.

Susa continued to correspond extensively with another lifetime friend, Reed Smoot. Susa not only supported Reed politically but gave him advice unstintingly about a wide range of topics, from his wife's health to his diet to his re-election campaigns. Ever the powerbroker, Susa never stopped asking him for favors for friends and family. She asked for help for Gilman Howe, a distant cousin employed in an underpaid position by the Census Bureau in Washington, DC. On multiple occasions, she wrote asking for assistance for Lucy's new husband, attorney Albert E. Bowen. Could Smoot help Albert get a position in the New York office of J. Reuben Clark; could he help with a position for Albert on the Tenth Circuit Court of Appeals? Grandson-in-law Lewis Wallace, husband of Anne Widtsoe Wallace, needed a calling on a church auxiliary. Could Reed help? Archibald Bennett, an employee at the Genealogical Society of Utah, was planning post-graduate studies in Washington, DC. Could Reed help him obtain a position at the Library of Congress? Rey L. Pratt, long-time president of the Mexican Mission of the church, had a son who needed a job in DC. Susa's son Franklin applied to be a radio technical adviser with the Federal Communications Commission. Could Reed put in a good word for him? Susa's nephew Joe Sanborn, son of sister Mabel, needed both to have a new military assignment and later, with the death of his father, to get out of the service. How could Reed help Joe? And could Reed get an invitation for daughter Lucy Bowen to sing at the Warren Harding White House? How about on the day of Herbert Hoover's inauguration in 1929?[38]

These requests showcase Susa's loyalty and persistence. She was always apologetic and polite in her requests of Smoot, expressing concern at disrupting his busy schedule. Reed's aplomb was never ruffled, however, and in his multiple responses he never showed any reaction other than accommodation and courtesy. Her letters to Smoot occasionally indicated a fawning adulation, and her language was reminiscent of what she used in her "love letters" to Joseph F. Smith in 1906. In February 1922 she wrote, "You know how I love

---

38. See Susa's extensive correspondence with Smoot, esp. box 47, fd. 13, and box 48, fds. 4 and 7.

you, Reed."[39] In June 1928 she penned, "There are a few of your own who really do appreciate and love you with their whole heart and soul. Of them you know one of them is your loving sister. Always lovingly yours."[40]

Famous personalities regularly filed in and out of Susa's office during these years, and in her rare travels she met many more. Susa usually asked her illustrious friends for a picture, which she would frame and put in the "rogues' gallery" in her office. Granddaughter Lurene Gates, daughter of Franklin and Florence, worked as a secretary for Susa several days a week during her freshman year at the University of Utah (1932–33), which was the last year of Susa's life. Lurene remembers a roomful of pictures of famous people.[41] In a letter to Lady Aberdeen, herself internationally famous, Susa listed some of her "distinguished and loved friends" whose pictures with "signed sentiments" graced her office walls, including "Theodore Roosevelt, Clara Barton, Aunt Susan B. Anthony, Charlotte Perkins Gilman, Dr. Anna Howard Shaw, May Wright Sewall, Carrie Chapman Catt, Senator Reed Smoot, Caruso and others."[42]

Susa also corresponded with a range of literary friends as well, some of whom she had known for many years. She made sure that whenever any famous author surfaced in Salt Lake City, she had the opportunity to meet and greet them, show them the sights of the area, and on several occasions introduce them to church authorities. She confided to W. C. Glass, a lecture-booking manager in New York City, that she would be happy, with restrictions, to entertain his clients appearing in Salt Lake City. "I am quite willing to assist in enlightening some strangers regarding our misunderstood people and religion; but I am not willing to be patronized under any circumstances, as I think you will readily understand."[43]

With several visiting celebrities, Susa managed to forge personal relationships, such as, for example, Charlotte Perkins Gilman; Margaret Leech, also known as Peggy Pulitzer; and Ida Husted Harper. Other visiting luminaries included Fannie Hurst, Ida Clyde Clarke, Ada

---

39. Gates to Smoot, Feb. 20, 1922, box 48, fd. 5.
40. Gates to Smoot, June 26, 1928, box 48, fd. 7.
41. Lurene Gates Wilkinson, personal communication with the author, Feb. 2009.
42. Gates to Lady Aberdeen, Jan. 7, 1930, box 34, fd. 2.
43. Gates to Glass, Jan. 23, 1925, box 38, fd. 16.

Patterson, Idah Strobridge, Rebecca West, Susan Ertz, Upton Close (Josef W. Hall), Clarence Drinkwater, and Tagore Rabindranath.

Although these names may be largely unknown today, they were at the time considered "heavy hitters." Margaret Leech (1893–1974), a member of the Round Table group of authors meeting at the Algonquin Hotel in New York City, married Ralph Pulitzer, the second son of publisher Joseph. An accomplished historian, Peggy, as she was commonly known, later won two Pulitzer Prizes in history. She sent the used clothes of her daughters to Susa's son and daughter-in-law, Franklin and Florence Gates, who were financially strapped at the time.[44] Ida Husted Harper (1851–1931), prominent suffragist and author, wrote the authorized three-volume history of Susan B. Anthony. She collaborated with Anthony on the fourth volume of *History of Woman Suffrage* and wrote volumes five and six by herself after Anthony's death in 1906. Susa had known Harper since the 1890s.

Fannie Hurst (1885–1968), probably the most-widely read American female author of her time (novels and short stories) and one of America's most highly compensated authors, helped Susa in her efforts to have the biography of Brigham Young published. Ida Clyde Clarke (1878–1956) was a prominent journalist, suffragist, associate editor of the *Pictorial Review*, and wrote both fiction and non-fiction. She read an early manuscript of Susa's biography of Brigham Young and offered helpful suggestions.[45] Ada Patterson (1867–1939) was a famous journalist and wrote at one time for the *Salt Lake Herald*. She covered several famous murder trials and became one of the so-called "sob sisters," so named for their sentimentality. Susa shared a common interest in genealogy with Los Angeles-based Idah Strobridge (1855–1932), who was an expert "in Puritan lines." Idah had grown up in Nevada and written the *Sagebrush Trilogy*, a collection of tales and folklore of pioneering days in that state.[46]

The most unlikely friendship, however, was that between Susa and Charlotte Perkins Gilman, a grand-niece of author Harriet Beecher Stowe and famous clergyman and abolitionist Henry Ward Beecher.

---

44. Gates to Pulitzer, May 11 and June 5, 1931, box 45, fd. 16.
45. See Clarke and Gates's correspondence in box 37, fd. 5.
46. Idah Mecheam Strobridge business card, box 48, fd. 16, SYGP (CHL).

Susa and Perkins first met in the 1890s. Charlotte was considered by many to be the most literate woman of her day in America. She was a social reformer, feminist, humanist, and free thinker. She wrote extensively in multiple genres, including novels, short stories, and poetry, and she lectured throughout the nation. She and Susa failed to agree on almost every issue, but Susa called her the "most remarkable woman I ever knew in my life."[47] On another occasion Susa praised Perkins "as the greatest woman I have ever known in the outside world."[48] And in response to a query from *Liberty Magazine* in 1925 to name the three most interesting people she knew, Susa responded with the names of Charlotte Perkins Gilman, Ida Clyde Clarke, and Fannie Hurst.[49] Susa arranged for Gilman to lecture several times at the three major universities in Utah—the University of Utah, BYU, and Utah State University.

There was mutual admiration between Susa and Gilman, who wrote Susa in February 1924, expressing gratitude to Susa for "your deep sincerity, your profound faith, your genuinely religious life." In the same letter, however, Gilman wrote of her new book, indicating, "You won't like my new book, even though you like me."[50] Two years later Gilman wrote to Susa, "It is really very interesting the enormous differences between our beliefs and theories, and the similarities of purpose."[51]

Gilman even attended Susa's lavish seventieth birthday party on March 18, 1926, in the Lion House in Salt Lake City and widely attended by the LDS glitterati of Salt Lake City society. Husband Jacob, usually somewhat retiring, was considered with his wit and wisdom as master of ceremonies to be "the star performer of the evening."[52] Speakers, besides Gilman, included all three members of the First Presidency, Apostle Orson F. Whitney, and Maud May Babcock. Susa's son Cecil provided music from his own compositions. Three of Susa's brothers and five of her sisters were also in attendance. Susa's most lavish birthday present was a "closed car"

47. Gates to Gilman, Nov. 1, 1923, box 38, fd. 11.
48. Susa Young Gates to Katherine S. Chamberlain, Sep. 8, 1928, box 36, fd. 13.
49. Gates to "Gentlemen," Aug. 27, 1925, box 37, fd. 5.
50. Gilman to Gates, Feb. 16, 1924, box 38, fd. 11.
51. Gilman to Gates, Mar. 27, 1926, box 38, fd. 12.
52. *Deseret News*, Mar. 19, 1926.

purchased by her son Harvey, who was at the time one of Hollywood's most successful "scenarists" (screenwriters).[53] Hal had visited Susa and Jacob at New Year's "riding around in a six-year-old second-hand Dodge open touring car" and sent them money to buy a "closed in upholstered Chevrolet."[54]

Susa was fearless in sharing her witness of the truthfulness of Mormonism, called a "testimony" in Mormon parlance, even with her sophisticated literary friends. For example, to John Drinkwater (1882–1937), she wrote, "We are, those of us who are converted Latter-day Saints, conscious that our church rests upon the solid foundation of Revelation from God himself and his son Jesus Christ. To me these glories are as real and as perfect as are my own father and brother. When I look out into the world of doubt and cynicism I marvel that I retain my childlike intensity of Faith in the simple things of the Gospel of Jesus Christ, but I do, I do."[55] To Charlotte Perkins Gilman she wrote, "O, how I wish you would turn your brilliant [mind] into a study of the Gospel of Jesus Christ as we teach it. However, no amount of study can give the testimony. But I must not preach to you; I love you too well to bother you with propaganda."[56] Perkins, speaking of Mormonism in a later missive to Susa, wrote, "There is so much I utterly disagree with, but there is also much that I admire and respect."[57] Susa had informed Gilman that she intended to have vicarious LDS temple ordinances performed for her if Susa outlived her. Gilman wrote to Susa, partly in jest, "Now don't you go and bounce off to Heaven before I manage to see you again! Remember you've got to see me out and make a good Mormon of me 'behind my back' as it were. You'll never do it while I'm alive I'm afraid."[58]

When Peggy Pulitzer's young daughter died unexpectedly in Europe, Susa wrote to her, "Of course I would love it if you could come to know the truth concerning the Gospel of Jesus Christ as revealed to the Prophet Joseph Smith in latter days, for the Lord taught him

---

53. Elizabeth Cannon Porter, "A Daughter of Brigham Young," updated newspaper clipping, box 3, fd. 30, SYGP (CHL).
54. Susa Young Gates to Alfred W. McCune, Feb. 3, 1926, box 41, fd. 4.
55. Gates to Drinkwater, Mar. 11, 1926, box 37, fd. 20.
56. Gates to Gilman, Mar. 24, 1927, box 38, fd. 13.
57. Gilman to Gates, Dec. 30, 1930, box 38, fd. 14.
58. Gilman to Gates, Dec. 31, 1931, box 38, fd. 14.

concerning both pre-existence of spirits and the after existence of our resurrected bodies. Moreover, he gave him the keys of the Priesthood which seals on earth as it is sealed in heaven."[59] Susa wrote to Idah Strobridge, "How I wish you could see the truth while you live upon this earth, for you are so noble and so intelligent." Susa promised Idah that she would have her baptized vicariously in the temple, if Susa survived her. But, "If not, I will leave word for some of my dear ones to do this for you and me."[60]

To be sure, Susa encountered disappointments in this decade of her life. The furor over her departure from the general board of the Relief Society and as editor of the *Relief Society Magazine* was disheartening, and Susa and Jacob with their limited financial means must surely have missed Susa's modest salary. Susa finished the first draft of her biography of Brigham Young in 1925, but the book was not published until 1930. Her papers include rejection letters and at least one complaint that the book "is not very well written."[61] In 1929 the *Young Woman's Journal*, which had required so much of Susa's efforts at a difficult time in her family's life, ceased publication. Susa was rather philosophical, however, noting in an article entitled "Hail and Farewell," which appeared in the last edition of the journal:

> Who may sound its death knell?
> Not I! Life is my concern, not death. ...
> Yet I wonder if I would not choose a less strenuous path to travel were I again to choose.[62]

In 1929 Susa's son Cecil developed a significant neurological problem that rendered him wheelchair-bound within a few years, and ultimately led to his death in 1941. In the summer of 1929, he moved with his wife, Gweneth, to southern California in hopes that the milder weather would improve his health. Thereafter, their children joined them, and the family remained in California for over a year without much improvement in Cecil's condition.[63]

---

59. Gates to Pulitzer, Sep. 16, 1930, box 45, fd. 16.

60. Gates to Strobridge, May 21, 1930, box 48, fd. 16.

61. See letters from publishers, especially Harry C. Black to Fannie Hurst, Jan. 7, 1926, in box 91, fd. 21, SYGP (CHL).

62. Susa Young Gates, "Hail and Farewell," *Young Woman's Journal*, Oct. 1929, 657, 678.

63. See Susa and Jacob's correspondence with their son Hal, who was also living in Southern California, box 26, fd. 14.

At the end of the 1920s, after the stock market crash that would lead to the Great Depression, all three Gates sons were unemployed. Hal wrote to his mother that he was "more or less out of work for quite a while." Franklin had been hired as a consultant for the Federal Radio Commission in Washington, DC, in 1928, but was lured to Hollywood shortly to work in sound research for the Vitaphone Corporation before the economic downturn of October 1929, which caused him to lose his position.[64] Canceled checks indicate that Susa and Jacob provided financial assistance from their own limited means to Cecil and Franklin and their families during this time.[65]

Susa lived the life of an ascetic. In the late 1920s she wrote an article titled "What My Life Taught Me about Health and Hygiene." Susa had a simple diet, which she monitored carefully, consisting of only two meals a day. "For twenty years, pecans, almonds, filberts, walnuts, and brazil nuts, together with fresh fruit or raisins, figs or prunes, form one complete meal for me. ... The other meal, if I eat meat, and I usually do, is comprised mostly of vegetables and fruit."[66] She avoided white bread, potatoes, starch, and sweets. She ate all meat except pork, a habit adopted from her father. She drank up to a gallon of water a day. She started with one lemon a day but eventually used three lemons a day. Susa's suspicions of medicine did not change, and she continued to eschew medical care. In a discussion on diet and health of her children, Susa reiterated that there was never a doctor with the family.[67]

She and Jacob exercised on a daily basis, swam on a weekly basis, and ran up and down stairs. They had settled into a simple, but reassuring lifestyle. Four mornings a week they arrived at the temple at 7:00 a.m. Jacob was a full-time temple employee. Susa served as an ordinance worker and then went to her office at the genealogical department later in the morning, where she continued to write. At home she would do her own housework, since she had no domestic

---

64. See various correspondence with Hal Gates and Franklin Gates, box 26, fd. 14, and box 29, fd. 5, respectively.

65. See financial records in box 2, fds. 6–8, SYGP (CHL).

66. Susa Young Gates to Ada Patterson, Sep. 24, 1925, box 37, fd. 9.

67. For Susa's views on health, see her correspondence and writings in box 37, fd. 9, SYGP (CHL).

help. In the evenings she and Jacob remained home, where they dined and retired by 9:00 p.m.

Susa routinely turned down invitations for activities at night. She responded to an evening invitation in 1926, "I do not try to go out where I am obliged to spend the evening anywhere."[68] To young groom David J. Smith, Susa explained why she could not attend his wedding reception. "I am so sorry I cannot attend your charming reception. I do not go out evenings. I find when I do go out I cannot sleep afterwards and the next day's work cannot be done."[69] Susa said that movies bored her or made her tired and nervous. She had stopped writing romance, but did "take time every evening to read it." She wrote of her love of reading: "My evenings are spent with my friends who talk with me from magazine pages and out of the lids of good books."[70]

---

68. Gates to Fannie C. Woodruff, Mar. 31, 1926, box 37, fd. 17.
69. Gates to Smith, Sep. 20, 1926, box 52, fd. 13.
70. Susa Young Gates to Harold Wright, Apr. 21, 1924, box 51, fd. 6.

Later Writings

19

During the last fifteen years of her life, Susa worked on three major writing projects. One, *The Life Story of Brigham Young*, written in collaboration with her daughter Leah D. Widtsoe, was published in 1930 in both England and America. The second and third works, "The History of Women" and "Lucy Bigelow Young," although Susa worked on them for several years, were never published.

Susa's purpose in writing her father's biography was to set the world straight on the life of Brigham Young. She wrote to her author friend Ida Clyde Clarke in October 1925 that "one of the big reasons I want to print it, is to get over the truth of Mormonism as my father saw it, and as it made him what he was." The work was not meant to be unbiased. Susa's goal was to offer an intimate look into the home and church life of Young, whom she referred to numerous times throughout the book as "the Leader." A month later she wrote again to Ida and said, "You know there is a lot of propaganda in the book, and I would not care to take it out."[1]

Part of Susa's protection of the name of her father resulted from the publication in 1925 of *Brigham Young*, a biography by M. R. Werner, who was lambasted by Susa, because she felt that Werner was inaccurate and deprecatory. Werner's book had been preceded by several articles he wrote for the *Ladies' Home Journal*. Generally, however, Werner is fairly even in tone, and his volume probably

---

1. Gates to Clarke, Oct. and Nov. 17, 1925, box 37, fd. 5.

represents the best historical treatment of Brigham to that point.[2] He was straightforward in saying that he does not accept Mormon theology. He wrote of Joseph Smith's deceit and his "pecuniary interest" in founding a new religion.[3]

Werner spent almost half of his book dealing with Smith, rather than Young. He alleged that Smith seduced young women in Kirtland. Sacred temple ordinances were characterized as "sexually symbolic," and polygamy was "only a violent form of adultery." Government under Young was a "theocracy" in which "the Mormons controlled justice." Young exercised "as much intimidating control over the dissatisfied as possible, and this control ... extended sometimes to murder." Also, Young, according to Werner, was "indirectly responsible" for the Mountain Meadows Massacre. But, quite even-handedly, Werner in the last chapter of his book, concluded, Brigham

> showed himself a man of resourcefulness and sturdiness, and his personality contributed as much as that of any one man to the development of the western half of the United States. He indicated to Americans of the eastern states what could be done with their unexploited frontier, and by successfully dominating his band of faithful disciples in the wilderness, he demonstrated that a wilderness could become paradise enough. Beset by the opposition of the government, competing creeds of Christianity, the force of ridicule, and the power of intolerant prejudice, he built his scattered and insecure community into a compact body of self-supporting people, who were soon able to dominate their section of the world by their industry and their faith.[4]

Against this backdrop, Susa inveighed against Werner and sought to place articles about her father in various magazines, as well, including *Good Housekeeping*, the *Atlantic Monthly*, and *Woman's Home Companion*, all of which turned her down.[5] Susa was sufficiently irate with Werner that when given a copy of his book, she referred to it as "libelous" and sent it on to A. Rex Johnson at the BYU library with the comment, "I don't want anything to do with it, and so send it on to you."[6]

2. True, Werner characterizes Mormonism as "religion carried to its illogical conclusions." Werner, *Brigham Young*, vii.

3. Werner, viii, 31, 63.

4. Werner, 95, 285, 297, 376, 400, 415, 455.

5. See rejection letters in box 83, fd. 11, SYGP (CHL).

6. Gates to Johnson, Aug. 21, 1925, box 35, fd. 6.

Susa worked on her father's biography for several years. It is difficult to determine how much of the final product is Susa's writing, since she had substantial editorial assistance from Leah Widtsoe, Harold Shepstone, and John A. Widtsoe. Often, there is little correlation between what Susa wrote in a rough draft and the final product. Susa frequently wrote in effusive terms. Consider, for example, her description in a rough draft of Brigham's birth, "On a beautiful first June day, 1801, the angel of birth entered the little Vermont homestead, leaving in the mother's arms a large-framed, viril male infant whose announced advent proved the strength of his tiny lungs and the joy of conquest over the hushed air."[7] Compare this with the final product of the American edition of the book: "Here [in Whittingham, Vermont] a log house was built, and a delicate wife, Abigail Howe Young, was located, and soon thereafter her ninth child and fourth son, Brigham, was born on June 1, 1801."[8]

By 1925 Susa had apparently finished her rough draft. She wrote to Lady Aberdeen in February of that year that she had just completed the biography of her father and that the manuscript was in the hands of publishers,[9] and in May she wrote to her daughter-in-law Bichette, Hal's wife, that she had just written the last chapter of the book.[10]

An additional five years passed before the book was finally published, and its advent followed a somewhat circuitous pathway. The book was turned down by multiple publishers. Susa enlisted the aid of her friend, Fannie Hurst, to help circulate the manuscript in New York publishing circles. One assessment from Harry C. Block of the editorial staff of Alfred A. Knopf, Inc., to Hurst was less than flattering: "While it contains a great deal of original and probably valuable material, it is less a biography of Brigham Young than a history of the beginnings and a very partisan defense of the Mormon Church." The material would have probably been of "great value" to M. R. Werner in his book, but "as it stands, it is entirely unsuited for publication, particularly, as it is not very well written. I do not really see how we could possibly have used the book."[11]

---

7. Gates, "Birth and Parentage," chapter draft, box 92, fd. 5, SYGP (CHL).
8. Gates and Widtsoe, *Life Story of Brigham Young*, 2.
9. Gates to Lady Aberdeen, Feb. 3, 1925, box 34, fd. 2.
10. Gates to Bichette Gates, May 26, 1925, box 26, fd. 11.
11. Block to Hurst, Jan. 7, 1926, box 91, fd. 21, SYGP (CHL).

Throughout the lengthy process of getting the book published, Susa's daughter Leah was a substantial help, to the point that Leah eventually became a coauthor. In a letter to Minerva P. Young after the book was published, Susa said that "if it had not been for her [Leah] and John [Widtsoe], the book would never have been printed; she read the proof over four times over in England, correcting, recorrecting, over and over, adding to and taking from."[12] The title page lists Susa Young Gates as the author "in collaboration with Leah D. Widtsoe."

A seminal figure in the biography's publication was Harold J. Shepstone, a prominent English author, editor, and press agent. Shepstone had become a close friend of Apostle George Albert Smith, who would become the eighth president of the LDS Church after the death of Heber J. Grant in 1945. Shepstone and George Albert Smith met during Smith's stay in England in the early 1920s. During a visit to Salt Lake City, Shepstone met Susa at a birthday party for Anthony W. Ivins, first counselor in the First Presidency. They spoke about Susa's writing, and she gave Shepstone several chapters of her manuscript to read. In the foreword to the British edition of her biography, Shepstone described his reaction: "I was amazed at the wealth of detail they contained and recognising the importance of the work and believing it should be given as wide a publicity as possible I offered to render any assistance I could towards its publication."[13] Shepstone felt he could get the book published in England. After Susa's unsuccessful efforts in America, this was welcome news. Serendipitously, John Widtsoe was assigned this same year (1927) as president of the European Mission, based in Liverpool, and he and Leah moved to England, where they remained until 1933, taking Susa's manuscript with them. Susa turned over to John all business decisions and arrangements regarding publication of the book.[14]

Susa's manuscript was so unwieldy that it was obvious it would require two volumes. The decision was made by the Widtsoes and Shepstone that a single-volume edition would find a larger and more

---

12. Gates to Young, July 2, 1931, box 91, fd. 28.

13. Gates and Widtsoe, *Life Story of Brigham Young* (British ed.), 14.

14. See various correspondence between Susa and the Widtsoes, box 91, fd. 23. See also Parrish, *John A. Widtsoe*, 407.

general audience. Shepstone and the Widtsoes devised a plan for Shepstone to edit the manuscript into numerous articles to be serialized in British newspapers to promote the upcoming book.

This plan did not materialize, however, and only one newspaper, the *Sunday Sun* in Newcastle, carried just five of Shepstone's articles. Newspaper staffs felt that the articles were not sensational enough, and they wanted more coverage of polygamy.[15] Also, the fact that several ministers had complained about the articles may have led to their cessation.[16] John and Leah, however, were adamant in their dealings with Shepstone about not emphasizing polygamy. They wrote to him, "We're to stress the epoch-making contribution of the man [Brigham Young] to the conquest of the West. Give the other [polygamy] a rest."[17] Shepstone also wanted to use a photograph of Young and his wives, which he thought would stimulate interest in and increase sales of the book. The Widtsoes replied unequivocally, "We object absolutely to the use of Brigham Young and his wives," laying out their multiple objections, which included "undue prominence" of a single phase of Young's life, unnecessary offense to "sensitive readers," and a tendency to turn active LDS Church members against the book.[18]

The Authors' Note in the American edition explained that Shepstone "undertook the task of condensing the original two-volume manuscript into a series of interesting articles. From his condensation the present volume has been prepared."[19] After Shepstone finished his articles, Leah spent a great deal of time to increase their length to prepare the manuscript for publication. John wrote to Susa and Jacob in May 1930 that Leah went to work the previous Christmas preparing the manuscript for publication. She worked night and day for several weeks to meet printing deadlines. Shepstone's chapters were in many cases almost doubled in length. Because of Leah's work, Susa had said, "I am not going to be satisfied to have my name only appear on the history of my father. Your name [Leah's] must follow mine both in the newspapers and in the book." It was largely because

15. Parrish, *John A. Widtsoe*, 410–11.

16. See Gates and Widtsoe correspondence in box 91, fd. 23.

17. Parrish, *John A. Widtsoe*, 410.

18. Parrish, 413.

19. Gates and Widtsoe, *Life Story of Brigham Young*, v.

of Leah's efforts that John convinced her to accept Susa's offer to be listed as a co-author and to accept 50 percent of the profits.[20]

Susa desperately wanted the sanction of LDS Church president Heber J. Grant regarding the biography of her father and her work on the history of women in the Church. She asked the First Presidency if they would appoint a committee to review the manuscripts. The First Presidency "did not feel it was wise to approve publication of manuscript they have not read,"[21] and no committee was ever formed, although, upon learning that Widtsoe was reviewing the entire manuscript and excising most of the material on polygamy, the Presidency did give its tacit blessing to the project. However, no First Presidency approval or blessing, either explicit or implicit, ever appeared in print in either the American or the British editions of the biography.

Shepstone was able to arrange for the printing of the manuscript in England through the publishing house of Jarrolds under moderately favorable conditions. No advance was made to the authors, but the percentage of proceeds was according to standard protocol, and it was the first time, according to Susa, that a work on Mormonism by a Latter-day Saint author had been printed by a major publishing house without a "substantial guarantee from the Church."[22] Shepstone's agent in New York City, Francis Arthur Jones, was in the meantime trying to promote interest in the manuscript among American publishers. He was finally able to commit the MacMillan Company to accept the manuscript, having negotiated for reasonable royalties to the authors and agents, as well as a $500 cash advance.[23] Initially, Jarrolds had wanted worldwide publishing rights, but since they were slow in making arrangements for distribution in America, Jones had signed up Macmillan, and Jarrolds gave up their rights to publish in America.

John and Leah were exhausted, but relieved, with the resolution of the arrangements to publish the biography, since they had devoted so many hours to their editing efforts, at the risk of their health and

---

20. Widtsoe to Gateses, May 1, 1930, box 92, fd. 2.

21. Widtsoe to Gateses.

22. Gates, handwritten notes on the publication history of *Life Story of Brigham Young*, ca. 1930, box 91, fd. 23.

23. Parrish, *John A. Widtsoe*, 412

their time-consuming new responsibilities in the European Mission, which was composed of ten separate components all over Europe.

The English foreword was written by Shepstone, while the American foreword was attributed to Reed Smoot, although it was written by John Widtsoe.[24] The English edition has 282 pages of smaller print, while the American version, with virtually identical text, has 380 pages with a larger size print. The thirty-one chapters are fairly uniform in length, generally consisting of ten to fifteen pages each in the American printing.

In the British edition, which was printed seven months before the American, Susa spoke frankly and negatively about Ann Eliza Webb, Brigham Young's so-called "twenty-seventh wife," who became disaffected with polygamy, left Young and the church, and then made a living giving anti-polygamy lectures throughout the country. Although Webb had died in 1917, she had two sons. Despite lack of knowledge of the sons' whereabouts, there was concern by editors at the Macmillan Company that a suit for libel from Ann Eliza's family members might ensue if Susa's negative comments were published in America.[25]

The printing plates had already been made in England and were planned for use in the American edition, so the staff at Macmillan was adamant that as few changes as absolutely necessary be made in the American copy. The idea arose to substitute two passages of equal length, describing Brigham's family life, for the American edition, to replace the expunged aspersions regarding Ann Eliza Webb in the British edition. The original passages from the British edition are found on pages 238 and 262–63; the replacement text in the American edition is located on pages 316 and 351–52.

While the British version says Ann Eliza Webb "chose to disgrace herself" with her "puerile claims" and then "made a great deal of money for herself and her exploiters," the US version replaces these lines with details of how "Aunt Eliza Snow" would solve "domestic tension" by inviting "the unhappy wives into her own sitting room." As British readers got the details of Ann Eliza's "extravagant claims for alimony" before she "sank out of sight, as such persons

24. John A. Widtsoe to H. J. Shepstone, May 6, 1930, box 92, fd. 2, SYGP (CHL).
25. Susa Young Gates to H. S. Latham, July 2, 1930, box 91, fd. 23.

usually do," American readers took in the details of how domestic squabbles were solved by singing hymns and prayer, which "filled the soul with divine love and peace." Eliza Snow's sitting room hosted "women's public activities and projects, such as suffrage," and other activities. The choice to expunge these paragraphs in the American edition worked seamlessly.

An amusing typographical error on page 281 of the British edition which stated, "By their faults ye shall know them," was corrected to "By their fruits ye shall know them" on page 379 of the American version. The two texts are otherwise identical, except for the fact that sums of money in American dollars are divided by five and expressed as British pounds in the Jarrolds edition. Susa insisted that her portrait, which appeared opposite the title page in the British edition, be replaced in the American edition by a portrait of Brigham Young. There are minor differences in the illustrations used in the two editions as well.

Sales were sluggish, primarily because of the Great Depression, and because of the relatively high price of the book, $5.00 in America and 18 shillings in Britain.[26] The book was not a financial hit for Susa or Leah, or for agents Shepstone and Jones. Susa reported that she collected over 300 reviews of the biography.[27] The reviews on both sides of the Atlantic were mostly positive, although the book was admittedly "biased," since it had been written by Brigham's daughter. There were some negative comments about the work, but fewer than might have been expected for a biography of the world's most famous polygamist written by his daughter.

By 1930 Brigham's gigantic contributions to settlement in the American West were recognized, and, despite plural marriage, he was viewed generally as an impressive historical figure. In the *Saturday Review* of London, the reviewer opined "that with the object of vindicating her father's memory ... she ... has been unexpectedly successful. ... As to the tenets of Mormonism, by stating them with a minimum of argument she has gone far to disarm criticism. ... But allowance made for filial partiality, the biographer has done her work well."[28]

26. See Jarrolds statement of sales, and Susa Young Gates to Francis Arthur Jones, Oct. 14, 1930, both in box 91, fd. 25. Twenty British shillings equal £1, which was worth about $5.00 USD in 1930.
27. Susa Young Gates to Kenneth Roberts, Jan. 6, 1931, box 41, fd. 6.
28. Copies of all of the quoted reviews are in box 11, fds. 3–4, SYGP (USDH).

The unknown reviewer for *The Bookman* in London produced a poison-pen note in July 1930, claiming that Susa and Leah's biography "presents no new materials of importance, and because of its sustained loyalty to the subject cannot be regarded as a serious addition to the literature of Mormonism. ... The quite remarkable success of Utah was due to the commercial, not spiritual genius of Brigham Young." He lauds the "altogether admirable biography" of M. R. Werner, which Susa had declared anathema, and then concluded, "Mormonism as a driving faith has long been in decay, and as a creative emotion it has, apart from the charlatan who founded it and the subject of this book who made it a power, produced nothing of aesthetic value to preserve its memory against the slow challenge of the ages." A left-handed compliment came from the reviewer of *The Sphere* (London) on May 17, 1930: "The book, being written by a daughter is in the nature of a vindication, but indeed polygamy is the only thing in his career that needs vindicating. The courage, the endurance, even political wisdom and organizing ability of the Mormon leader can hardly be called in question."

Reviews that Susa collected from US publications were similarly positive, though with some criticisms. The *Tulsa World* published on October 19, 1930, that "Mrs. Gates is anything but detached ... and is, in fact, intensely partisan." The biography is "a dramatic story, vividly told," although "Mrs. Gates digresses continually to sketch in a broad and compact background against which the figure of her father moved." The September 28 review in the *State Journal-Register* (Springfield, Illinois) stated, "The author has written a very forceful account of this interesting life and this much maligned group of people. ... She was not blind to his faults, which she discusses with equal frankness as she does his virtues." In fact, chapter twenty-six of *The Life Story of Brigham Young* is titled "Persecution and Some Faults." The review in the *St. Louis Post Dispatch* of September 29 declared, "the dominant tone of the book is not defensive. Although the point of view is, naturally, quite orthodox, there is no effort to preach the Mormon doctrine to the world. ... What emerges from this ... work of the famous Mormon leader ... is one of the most astonishing stories of successful human heroism in all history." Despite its lackluster sales, *Life Story* remained influential for many years, and Susa impressed her fellow Latter-day Saints for publishing a biography of a Mormon prophet with national publishing houses in the United States and England.[29]

Although Susa worked tirelessly on her "History of Women" manuscript, it was probably her biggest project in life that never came to fruition. In 1915 Susa was selected by the Relief Society general board to serve as historian of the society "to gather historical data" and prepare "an extensive history of the Relief Society."[30] Julina Smith, second counselor in the Relief Society general presidency, said that this action was taken with the knowledge and blessing of her husband, church president Joseph F. Smith. Nonetheless, Susa reported in her journal that Emmeline B. Wells, "Aunt Em," general president of the Relief Society, was "terribly upset," because she and her daughter, Annie Wells Cannon, were themselves planning to write such a history.[31] At the October 1915 conference of the Relief Society, Susa reported on her plans. "She gave an outline ... of the Chapters which would take up the positions women have held in the history of the world, both ancient and modern; how the dawn of woman's equality appeared when the Prophet Joseph Smith organized this Church and the Relief Society. Brief mention was made of the other topics to be included which would cover all the activities of women in this Church."[32]

Susa wrote a work of sixty chapters over the next decade and a half. There are drafts with dates ranging from 1916 to 1930. Work was slow, and the manuscript was tucked away for years at a time. During this time Susa published the *Surname Book and Racial History* in 1918 and *The Life Story of Brigham Young* in 1930. She was also heavily involved in temple and genealogy work. She frequently mentioned that she was working on her history of women. But by 1922, when she resigned as editor of the *Relief Society Magazine,*

---

29. Susa's biography has since been succeeded by the more scholarly oriented, nationally published studies of Leonard J. Arrington, *Brigham Young: American Moses* (New York: Alfred A. Knopf, Inc., 1985), and John G. Turner, *Brigham Young: Pioneer Prophet* (Cambridge, Massachusetts: Harvard University Press, 2012).

30. Gates, "Chapter 23, 1910–1921," revised chapter, box 86, fd. 29, SYGP (CHL).

31. Gates Journal, Mar. 25, 1915, box 105, fd. 4, SYGP (CHL).

32. Gates, "Chapter 23, 1910–1921."

work was far from complete, and she took her work with her to her new office in the Genealogical Library.

By now Susa had also obtained new church president Heber J. Grant's blessing. Grant wrote to her, "I read your letter with interest and think Bro. [Edward H.] Anderson's suggestion to you about writing a history of the work of the women of our church have done, is a very good one. I know of none of our writers among our good sisters who would take greater interest in writing such a history or who would be more diligent in hunting up the facts than yourself."[33]

Susa had recently complained to Anderson that in his new edition of *The Brief History of the Church* he had ignored the work of the women in the church. Anderson had responded that he would like to see a women's history written and suggested that Susa do it. Susa had sent that letter, with her own, to Grant. Grant's counselors, Charles W. Penrose and Anthony W. Ivins, had added to Grant's letter in a postscript, "The Presidency considered the matter referred to in this letter and [is] united in the opinion that Sister Gates proceed with the work."[34]

With this mandate, Susa soldiered on, albeit slowly. Several versions of Susa's files on the "History of Women" exist in her papers at the LDS Church History Library. The revised chapters, 1–60, in boxes 86 to 88 are the most complete. Susa's coverage of women's history is far-reaching. Over one-third of the chapters are devoted to histories of the Relief Society, the YLMIA, and the Primary Association. Other topics included the organization of the church, the history of the church from Joseph Smith to settlement of the Great Basin, women in canonized books of scripture, as well as women in genealogy, education, temples, literature, suffrage, Utah statehood, medicine and related fields, industrial enterprises, grain storage, silk culture, professional life, patriotism, and national and international relations.

The revised chapters are not particularly well edited, and there are multiple redundancies and irrelevancies, though they show the depth of Susa's interests and how she could meander off on various topics. For example, Brigham Young's health measures for his family and Shoshone Indian mating and birthing practices have little to do

---

33. Grant to Gates, Feb. 15, 1922, box 45, fd. 1.
34. Grant to Gates, Feb. 23, 1922, box 45, fd. 1.

with the chapter on LDS women in medicine.[35] A lengthy treatment of sericulture in ancient China is not particularly germane to silk production in Utah.[36] Music among Hebrew women seems like an unnecessary filler for nineteenth- and early twentieth-century female musicians in Utah.[37]

Susa wrote again to Heber J. Grant five years after their first correspondence on the women's history. She asked for a blessing from the First Presidency to continue her women's history as well as their endorsement of her work on the Brigham Young biography. She outlined that when she was still on the Relief Society general board, she had completed sections devoted to the Relief Society, the YLMIA, and the Primary, which sections had been approved by the appropriate presidents of the auxiliary organizations at the time, namely Emmeline B. Wells, Martha H. Tingey, and Louie B. Felt, respectively. She expressed her intention to update the materials on these organizations. There is no evidence extant that any action was taken on providing approval for the manuscript on women's history.[38]

After Leah and John Widtsoe had taken the Brigham Young manuscript with them to England, Susa turned again to the history of women. In March 1928 she wrote to her friend, Charlotte Perkins Gilman, that she was trying to resurrect her lengthy treatise on women, working on it from "seven to seven."[39] In an article by Olive Woolley Burt on Susa in the January 1930 issue of *The Westerner*, Susa indicated that she was "putting the finishing touches on a 400,000 word volume dealing with women, especially the history and the work of Mormon women."[40]

Susa also corresponded with the general board of the Relief Society, inquiring whether the organization would use her book as a lesson manual for the Relief Society. Whatever hopes she may have had were dashed when the general secretary of the Society, Julia A. F. Lund, wrote, "It was the consensus of opinion that your book was,

35. Gates, "Women in Medicine, Hygiene and Nursing," revised chapter, box 88, fd. 4, SYGP (CHL).

36. Gates, "Sericulture," revised chapter, box 88, fd. 7, SYGP (CHL).

37. Gates, "Women in Professional Life," revised chapter, box 88, fd. 8, SYGP (CHL).

38. Gates to Grant, Apr. 2, 1927, box 38, fd. 21.

39. Gates to Gilman, Mar. 21, 1928, box 38, fd. 13.

40. Copy in autobiographical sketches, box 3, fd. 35, SYGP (CHL).

no doubt, most excellent, but that the Relief Society could not use it as a lesson text. It was, therefore, the unanimous decision not to accept your proposition."[41] Hugh J. Cannon, editor of the *Improvement Era*, wrote to Susa six days later his own reservations about printing the book: "My great fear has been that this material, if put into one volume, would make a book too large to be sold at a price which our people would be willing to pay. That of course would cause serious loss and would defeat your purpose." Cannon suggested some edits and gave some encouragement. "There are some repetitions which might well be eliminated, thereby reducing the length and then if the very valuable material which you have could be unified, somewhat more than it is, you would have a work of which you might well be proud and which could be a real contribution to the literature of the Church. It should inspire women to live up to their highest possibilities."[42]

Susa had hoped to use profits from the Brigham Young biography to fund the publication of the "History of Women." This appears not to have occurred, but Susa did have $1,000 remaining from money left to her from Elizabeth McCune's estate. Susa worked with James Kirkham, manager of the *Deseret News*, and Albert Hooper, manager of the Deseret Bookstore, and negotiated a deal whereby "I will give into your hands the manuscript book, together with $1,000 in cash, and that you two will take over the details of the business of printing and selling the book. If there is a loss, finally, neither myself nor my children ... will be held financially responsible. On the other hand, if there should be any profits made, all three of us will share and share alike." In the eventuality of Susa's death, the copyright and Susa's share of profits would revert to Leah, without whom the book, Susa asserted, would never have been written.[43] This deal was not consummated. Ultimately, the project never materialized, and Susa's "History of Women" never saw the light of day.

In addition to her voluminous papers at the LDS Church History Library that include drafts of her writings, some of Susa's papers were donated to the Utah State Historical Society (now the

---

41. Lund to Gates, Nov. 1, 1929, box 83, fd. 11.

42. Cannon to Gates, Nov. 7, 1929, box 83, fd. 11.

43. Gates to Kirkham and Hooper, Nov. 12, 1929, box 83, fd. 11.

Utah Division of State History) in 1966 by John and Leah Widtsoe's daughter, Eudora Widtsoe Durham, and her husband, G.
Homer Durham, and Eudora's sister, Anna Widtsoe Wallace. Susa's
biography of her mother, "Lucy Bigelow Young," an unpublished,
243-page, rough-draft manuscript, is located in these papers.[44]

Susa began the biography of her mother stating, "I have told you
about my honored and revered father and his people, now I wish to
relate some genealogical and historic facts about my dear mother
and her progenitors."[45] The manuscript has numerous omissions,
and it is riddled with hand-written additions and corrections by
Susa, but it nonetheless gives interesting, unknown insights not only
into Lucy's life, but into her daughters' lives as well. The manuscript
totals about 75,000 words and concludes with, "Susa Young Gates,
in my office 408, Church Offices, 47 East South Temple Street, Salt
Lake City, Utah, August 29, 1931," to which her sister added, "A
faithful chronicle and a blessed tribute to our adored Mother. Mabel
Y. Sanborn."[46] Other than Ann Eliza Webb Young (whose life story
added substantial scandal to the Young family name), Eliza R. Snow,
and Zina Huntington Young, no other wife of Brigham has had a
more complete biography than Susa's treatment of her mother.

---

44. See Gates, "Lucy Bigelow Young." The manuscript is in box 1, folder 6.
45. Gates, 1.
46. Gates, 243.

Death

During the last years of her life, Susa settled into a routine. Every weekday by 7:00 a.m. she was in the Salt Lake temple with Jacob, who worked in the recorder's office, where she sometimes assisted him. Usually, she attended an endowment session. Thereafter, she made her way to her office at the Church Administration Building, where she worked on her numerous projects. These included continuing genealogical research; the biography of her mother; the revision of her "History of Women"; and classes on biography offered to women through the Genealogical Society of Utah. There were no more international travels or evening social events. Susa and Jacob spent nearly all their evenings at home and were in bed by 9:00 p.m.[1] Jacob still did occasional work in his insurance business.[2]

Susa had kept a journal sporadically beginning in 1870, when she and her mother and sister were "banished" to St. George in the aftermath of Susa's assistance in her sister Dora's elopement with Morley Dunford. She kept a journal fairly regularly on her and Jacob's mission to Hawai'i, 1885–89. Entries between 1915 and 1925 occurred occasionally. But on April 8, 1932, Susa began again to write regularly in her journal, a practice she continued until her last entry on May 3, 1933, three weeks before her death.

On January 5, 1930, Susa and Jacob celebrated their 50th wedding

---

1. See the brief autobiography Susa wrote in a letter to Ada Patterson, Sep. 24, 1925, box 37, fd. 9.

2. See, for example, Gates Journal for 1932–33, box 105, fd. 8. Hereafter cited as Gates Journal.

anniversary. As described by Olive Woolley Burt for a contemporary account in the *Westerner*, the event, although "extraordinary ... was not, as is so often the case, rejoicing over work done, over a life practically completed. It was more nearly a reunion of a number of distinguished people, moving forward in high careers, who paused to celebrate the fact that two of the number had been happy partners for fifty years."[3]

Susa and Jacob worried chronically about their children, particularly their sons. At the beginning of the Great Depression in 1930, all three men were unemployed. As noted in previous chapters, Cecil became acutely ill in 1929, suffering from what was probably multiple sclerosis and soon was unable to work full time, either in Salt Lake City as assistant director of the Mormon Tabernacle Choir or in Logan as a music faculty member at Utah Agricultural College. Harvey was between jobs as a screenwriter but he soon switched studios and continued a successful career. Franklin, after teaching for several years at BYU, went to Washington, DC, with the Federal Trade Commission and then joined his brother in Hollywood, with promises of generous financial remuneration. After his research position in Hollywood fizzled, he was unable to return to his previous position in Washington, DC. He came home to Salt Lake City, where he headed the F. Y. Gates Company (electronics) until his retirement in 1972.[4]

The depression made life difficult. Franklin and his wife, Florence, struggled with finances, and Susa and Jacob talked of depleting their savings in order to prevent foreclosure on both Franklin and Cecil's homes. Susa and Jacob, at an age when many couples could finally enjoy financial security after a lifetime of hard work, were instead trying to help their children. Susa wrote that she and Jacob "are so mixed up with our finances and the debts of Cecil and Frank that we don't know where we are at."[5] Susa and Jacob moved to Lucy's home, around the corner from their own, in 1930 so that Cecil and his family could live in their home. Because of Cecil's "nervous

3. Burt, "Susa Young Gates," *The Westerner*, Jan. 1930, clipped copy in box 3, fd. 35, SYGP (CHL).

4. See Susa and Jacob's correspondence with Hal, who kept them abreast of Frank's time in California, box 26, fd. 14.

5. Gates Journal.

breakdown," Jacob and Susa continued to provide financial assistance to him and his family.[6]

Cecil was eventually taken by his sister Lucy to the Battle Creek Sanitarium in Michigan for his progressive neurologic disorder. They left for Michigan on December 3, 1932, with the likelihood that Lucy would deplete her savings to pay Cecil's medical bills, which Susa estimated would cost between $500-$1,000. Susa felt herself unable to provide the care Cecil needed. She wrote in her journal, "My only hope of avoiding a breakdown myself has been to leave all the care of Cecil to others."[7] Lucy returned to Utah in January 1933, but Cecil remained at the sanitarium until April. His wife, Gweneth, now responsible for supporting the family, opened a restaurant and relied on extended family to watch their children.

Susa lamented Hal's inactivity in the church until her death. On his birthday, Susa wrote in her journal, "O, that's our real tragedy! Hal out of the Church with his dear wife and wonderful children! If I can only live to see him repent and come back into the Fold of Christ! That is my constant, daily prayer!"[8] On Leah's birthday a month later, Susa made a rare reference—though not by name—to her ex-husband, Alma Dunford. "Leah's birthday today—God bless her. What a joy she has been to me all her life—my reward for my tragic life with her father for five years."[9]

Susa continued her association with BYU, where she was the longest-serving member of the board of directors. She carried on an extensive correspondence with Franklin Harris, president of the university, expressing great concern about what she considered the lack of religiosity of several BYU faculty members. She participated each January with genealogical lessons in the annual Education Week, which presented her an opportunity to give frank advice freely to Harris, which he seems to have accepted good-naturedly.[10] Susa, fifty-three years after her father's death, remained protective of him and the school bearing his name.

Susa, who felt that Harris allowed his faculty too much freedom

---

6. Susa Young Gates to Charlotte Perkins Gilman, Nov. 3, 1930, box 38, fd. 14.

7. Gates Journal.

8. Gates Journal, Jan. 19, 1933.

9. Gates Journal, Feb. 24, 1933.

10. See their correspondence for 1930–33 in box 35, fds. 11–12.

in matters of religion, wrote, "I don't want to tell you nor anyone else what they should think, but I do expect men in your position and those associated with you in the B.Y.U., when they discuss religious matters, to do it from the positive side and not from the negative. You, yourself, are alright; there is no question about that; but you are so loyal and so broad-minded that you let some of your teachers go too far it seems to me."[11] This was in follow-up to an earlier letter in which Susa compared BYU negatively to LDS University in Salt Lake City. She declaimed, "Outside of yourself and one or two others, my most potent suggestions would be to get a new class of teachers; real Latter Day Saint men instead of philosophers and theorists. However, I don't want to be sarcastic."[12]

Susa also loved and worried about her grandchildren, especially Leah and John Widtsoe's daughters, Anna and Eudora. Anna visited her grandmother frequently and relied on her for moral support through marital problems and a painful divorce. Eudora, thirteen years younger than her sister, tried living with Anna in Utah, but her parents ultimately decided that it would be better for her to return to live with them in England, where Widtsoe was serving as mission president.

Susa, although no longer directly active in politics, remained staunchly Republican and was devastated by the 1932 election losses of US president Herbert Hoover and of Senator Reed Smoot. Smoot, after surviving contentious hearings to gain his seat, had served in the Senate for nearly thirty years. Susa had spent the weekend before the election in Provo with Smoot and his guest, US vice president Charles Curtis. After this bitter defeat, Susa mentioned to Anthony W. Ivins of the First Presidency that it would be wonderful if Smoot, still serving as an apostle, could replace Widtsoe as president of the European Mission. Ivins passed this idea onto church president Heber Grant, who warmed to the suggestion.

Susa, however, had second thoughts. She remembered Smoot's second wife, Alice Sheets Smoot, and what Susa considered to be her heavy-handed personality, and recanted. Both Grant and Ivins then chastised Susa for meddling in priesthood affairs, which depressed

---

11. Gates to Harris, Mar. 8, 1930, box 35, fd. 11.
12. Gates to Harris, Feb. 27, 1930.

her.[13] The Widtsoes remained in England until August 1933. Although Susa missed Leah, her other daughter, Lucy, was a great comfort during Leah's absence in England. Lucy had no children of her own, and her twin stepsons were studying at Stanford University. By now Lucy had largely quit performing as a singer. She was extraordinarily generous to her brother Cecil, expending a great deal of her means to pay for his medical care.

Susa continued to work in her office until the last several weeks of her life. She became fast friends with author Susan Ertz, who had been recommended to her by Rebecca West. Four and a half decades after Susa had communicated with Leo Tolstoy's oldest daughter, Tatiana, in Russia, she hosted his youngest daughter, Alexandra, in Utah in 1932. Alexandra was in the state to lecture at BYU; she later became an American citizen.[14]

In April 1932 Susa began a weekly series of lessons on writing biography held Thursday afternoons, sponsored by the Genealogical Society of Utah. She began with 87 enrolled students.[15] At her seventy-seventh birthday party, her last, held at her beloved Lion House, she actively promoted her last two projects. One was her project of gathering histories of Women of Utah and the church. The other was a discussion of plans for an appropriate monument for the pioneer women of Utah.[16]

Susa had intermittently sat in the press section of the Salt Lake Tabernacle during the church's semiannual general conference since 1868, recording the proceedings in shorthand. In 1916 she prevailed upon church leaders to have the general board members of the Relief Society, YLMIA, and Primary sit in front of the crowd alongside the men. After her release from the general board of the Relief Society, she had returned to the press section, where she had her own special chair. A brass nameplate had been placed on her chair by David A. Smith, first counselor in the Presiding Bishopric of the church.[17]

As death approached, Susa ruminated about her sister Dora, who

13. Gates Journal.

14. See Susa's correspondence with Alexandra Tolstoy in box 49, fd. 5.

15. Susa's class notes, correspondence about the class, and lesson materials are in box 75, fd. 18, SYGP (CHL).

16. "Birthdays Are Work Days," *Salt Lake Telegram*, Mar. 18, 1933, 7.

17. See, for example, Gates Journal.

had died twelve years earlier. She wrote in her journal that her father had once said it had been revealed to him that every wife and child "would get back to him sometime, somewhere." Brigham Young's sorrow came from knowing "what some of them would have to go through before they got back. Poor, tragic, selfish, vain Dora—where are you?" Susa wrote.[18]

Susa remained optimistic until the end of her life. In anticipation of turning seventy-seven, she said, "I have no fear for the future, either economically or spiritually." Her advice to the younger generations had not changed since her days as editor of the *Young Woman's Journal*: "Get married and have your families just as your parents did before you. Don't be discouraged. Have faith and by all means attend to your religious duties."[19]

Famous people often have rumors emerge over alleged deathbed confessions, and Susa was no exception. According to one unsourced account—and subsequently repeated in other accounts—Susa supposedly said, "May the Lord forgive me for any wrong I may have done Dr. [Alma] Dunford—unknowing." It would be a shocking admission by Susa after a lifetime of anger and sadness over her first marriage. The line asking for forgiveness first appears in a 1951 master's thesis, and has no basis in fact.[20] But unfortunately this story has been perpetuated in at least two other publications.[21] The thesis claims that Susa told her granddaughter, Anna Widtsoe Wallace, that she could die happy if Hal were to return to activity in the church and if Leah could be sealed to her in the temple: "She then had her granddaughter destroy a letter she had previously written to Leah. The contents of this letter she [Susa] revealed to no one, but it is thought by her family to have had some reference to her life with Dr. Dunford, because, at about the same time ... she ordered the letter burned."[22] It was then that she purportedly asked for forgiveness, but the thesis provides no source for this assertion.

There is no evidence in any of Susa's voluminous papers that the

---

18. Gates Journal, Mar. 13, 1933.

19. "Noted Utah Woman Claimed by Death," *Salt Lake Telegram*, May 27, 1933, 1–2.

20. See Cracroft, "Susa Young Gates," 38.

21. See Person, "Susa Young Gates," 201, and a reminiscence in the *Salt Lake Tribune*, July 23, 1995, J-4.

22. Cracroft, "Susa Young Gates," 38.

thought of having wronged Dunford ever crossed her mind. On the contrary, Susa's journal entries just weeks before her death tell a very different story. Her granddaughter Anna told Susa she wanted to place a picture of Dunford next to one of Susa in her Book of Remembrance.[23] Susa was horrified. She recorded, "I have just written a cruelly tragic letter to Leah, here in the Temple, explaining to her why I object to having my picture put side by side with that of her cruel, brutal, selfish father in Anna's Book of Remembrance. I have told her things she never knew for I have kept silent on all that tragedy of my early life!" In a second entry that afternoon, Susa wrote, "Anna read the letter and *begged* me not to send it because of what it would do to her mother. She promised me she would not go against my wishes in the matter" (emphasis in original). Susa wrote that she put the letter away, and there is no written evidence that she asked Anna to "destroy" it.[24]

The letter no longer exists, or at least it has never been found, and it is likely that Anna destroyed it, but probably not on Susa's orders. Susa, with the exception of the letter she wrote to her half-sister Zina (see chapter five), never mentioned the name of Alma B. Dunford after her divorce. Her granddaughter Lurene, who was with Susa almost daily during the last year of her life, said that she never once heard Susa mention her first husband, and certainly never mentioned a plea for forgiveness.[25]

Susa did, however, engage in some last-minute deathbed repentance or, at least, some apologies. She called J. Reuben Clark, sustained the previous month, as the new second counselor in the First Presidency, and her son-in-law, Albert E. Bowen, to her bedside. She apologized for the way she had maligned Apostle James E. Talmage, chair of the LDS Church's Radio Commission.[26] Susa

---

23. Church members had been encouraged to maintain a personal "Book of Remembrance." This record contains religious papers of importance, including certificates of ordinances such as baptism and confirmation and ordinations to priesthood offices, patriarchal blessings, photographs, family history and genealogy, and personal spiritual accounts, including blessings which a person may have received. Latter-day Saints have been promised that these records will not only help them to remember their covenants but may also guide their posterity in futurity in spiritual matters.

24. Gates Journal, Mar. 29, 1933.

25. Lurene Gates Wilkinson, personal communication with the author, Feb. 2009.

26. Gates Journal, May 3, 1933.

had tried to convince Talmage to give her air time on church-owned KSL radio station to promote her biography class and history of women project. Susa, turned down by Talmage, wrote privately in her journal, "He's a *hard* man and a vain one," then days later wrote, "O these self-centered men." She added, "I hope I haven't [the same attitude]—I don't think I have."[27] Susa had complained to Clark and Bowen as well, and before she died, she wanted to apologize to them for speaking ill of an apostle. She also sent for a Brother Mertz, who sat by Jacob in the temple recorder's office. Susa had been "snooty" to him, but "I knew he yearned for my friendship." Mertz brought flowers, and Susa apologized. It was a tender moment for her.[28]

Susa may have known her time was coming to an end. About six weeks before, she had developed influenza. She died at 3:45 a.m. on Saturday, May 27, 1933. Her official cause of death listed was "chronic myocarditis," with "chronic valvular heart disease" of ten years duration as a contributory factor. Susa had complained of multiple symptoms of abdominal, bladder, and back pain for several months. She was survived by Jacob, her five children, fifteen grand-children, and three great-grandchildren.

Her funeral was held two days later on May 29 in the Assembly Hall on Temple Square. Services were conducted by Bishop Gordon T. Hyde of Jacob and Susa's ward. It was attended by prominent Utahns and church leaders, but Leah, still in England, missed her mother's funeral. The speakers included her son-in-law, Albert E. Bowen, who would be ordained an apostle four years later; Joseph Christenson, who worked with Susa for almost forty years in temple and genealogy work; Anthony Ivins, lifelong friend and first coun-selor in the First Presidency; and Heber J. Grant, president of the church. Praise for Susa's rich, full life was effusive.

Bowen spoke of Susa's "justice, resolution, independent judg-ment, veneration [of] ... the men who stood at the head of this Church," devotion, sincerity, and "loyalty." Christenson called her "Aunt Susa" and said that "she always accepted meekly that word [of rebuke] which was spoken" by "those who presided." Her "first and only thought" was "the advancement of this great work that has

27. Gates Journal, Nov. 1932.
28. Gates Journal, May 3, 1933.

been given to us," yoked with generosity toward other people. Ivins praised her as an exemplar of Latter-day Saint values: "The principal thing in life, the one thing which most expresses it all is this, that if we have done our duty, if we have lived righteously, virtuously before the Lord, and if we have dealt justly with our fellows, if we have been considerate, merciful, forgiving, there can be little doubt as far as our future life is concerned. And all of these things she has done." Heber J. Grant, who was twenty years old when Brigham Young died, intoned: "President Brigham Young had no child who more perfectly and thoroughly honored him than did Sister Gates." The LDS Church president knew "of no more loyal, devoted Latter-day Saint than was Sister Gates. ... Integrity and devotion to the work of the Lord are the most wonderful and blessed traits that anyone can possess, and our dear sister possessed them in the highest degree. She wanted to know what to do for the best good of the work here on earth, and the very best that was in her was given on all occasions for the advancement of that work."[29] It was a succinct and accurate summary of a remarkable life.

---

29. Quotes are from *Funeral Services of Sister Susa Y. Gates*, typescript copy in author's possession.

Epilogue

Susa always felt that her first family responsibility was to her husband. In July 1914 she asked rhetorically, "Who are the successful wives? They are not necessarily the women who have kept their house scrupulously clean and who are the best breadmakers in the neighborhood. ... The successful wives are not the women who give all their time and strength and thought to their ... children. The successful wives are the women who have to balance their lives so that they can give ... with loving generosity in personal ministrations to their husbands."[1]

The love affair between Susa and Jacob served each well. Jacob survived for almost nine additional years after Susa. He died on January 22, 1942, at age eighty-seven. Susa was a larger-than-life figure and could hardly be contained. She was loved and revered, and most within the LDS community who were younger than she was called her "Aunt Susa." Jacob was a tower of strength for her, secure in his own masculinity and assured that Susa would be deferential to him in matters of priesthood authority. She was a feminist, but she believed there were clear differences between men and women, and she would surely not have agreed with some of today's LDS feminists who call for female ordination to the priesthood. And she would no doubt disappoint them with her willing subservience to priesthood authority.

It took Susa many years to embrace her gender. Earlier in her life

---

1. Gates, "Success," *Relief Society Bulletin*, July 1914, 4.

she had wanted to be a boy. In Hawai'i, she had difficulty under-standing why she was not consulted in ecclesiastical matters given her superior intellect and leadership skills compared to the men around her, except her husband and Joseph F. Smith. But by 1920 she exulted: "I am so glad that I am a woman. It was not always so! When youth and high ambitions claimed my life, I thought I was dissatisfied with womanhood and all its limitations. ... Let us all give thanks for wifehood, motherhood, and most of all, for tender, gentle, helpful, womanhood."[2]

Susa took pride in Jacob's leadership of the family. One almost detects in her writings that her deference to priesthood authority is a little too strident, perhaps forced. Susa wrote, "I was once jok-ingly referred to by one of the Church authorities as the Thirteenth Apostle. He told me that if he could just put breeches upon me, he would put me in the quorum." Another friend and apostle, Francis M. Lyman, delighted Susa with his "keen sense of humor." He used to sometimes greet Susa with, "'Jacob still boss, Susa?' 'He certainly is,' I would answer, 'if he were not, I would have left him long ago. No man with wishbones instead of backbones for me.'"[3] Late in life, Susa ascribed her success to following priesthood counsel. She told Har-old H. Jenson," I think what little success I have made is because I have never disobeyed my husband or the counsel of those over me."[4]

On only two occasions did Jacob ask Susa, during her long, busy professional life, to stay home and not fulfill an assignment she had accepted. They were living in Provo at the time, and completing the tasks would have required a round-trip train ride to Salt Lake City and leaving young children at home. Near the time of her seventieth birthday, she described the circumstances.

> I was appointed to represent father's daughters at the unveiling of his monument at the head of Main street [in Salt Lake City in 1897]. ...
> "I don't want you to go," he said. "But Jacob, it's father's monument," I insisted.
> "I don't want you to go," he persisted.
> "What did you do?" ...

2. Gates, "Let Us Give Thanks," *Relief Society Magazine*, Nov. 1920, 657–58.
3. As quoted in the register of Susa's papers, SYGP (UDSH).
4. Jenson, "Susa Young Gates," 135.

"Stayed home."

The other time was when I was scheduled to speak in the Tabernacle with Susan B. Anthony, the Rev. Anna Shaw and other famous suffragists [in 1895].

"I am one of the speakers," I exclaimed when he objected to my going.

"I don't care," he countered.

"What did you do?"

"Stayed home."[5]

Jacob said that, although it was a great honor for Susa to have been invited by an international luminary like Susan B. Anthony to share the podium with her, there were "so many others" who could speak, including Emmeline B. Wells. Susa later commented on the give-and-take in her marriage, and it demonstrates her ability to pick her battles. She noted, "If I were to have my liberty in the future in big things, I must be wise enough to give way in this matter, which after all was comparatively unnecessary." She reasoned that she was only invited because Anthony had "to please me" since she was "dealing with Brigham Young's daughter."[6]

Despite the fact that Susa was a Republican and Jacob a Democrat, she apparently even listened to Jacob regarding political matters. She wrote in a letter to Reed Smoot in 1928, "Only two men can influence my political decisions; one is my dear husband, the other is the leader of this Church."[7]

Susa was often grounded in reality by Jacob's sound advice. A favorite family story relates Susa's anger over being slighted. She had been asked to direct a play for an "entertainment." Another unidentified woman took over the last two rehearsals, as well as the entertainment itself, thus getting all the glory for its success and angering Susa. It bothered Susa that somebody else got the credit for the project. Jacob wisely noted that the important thing was that the work got done. Jacob asked Susa if she did the project "for the furtherance of the cause of the Church" or for her own honor? If the

---

5. Elizabeth Cannon Porter, "A Daughter of Brigham Young," undated newspaper clipping in box 3, fd. 30, SYGP (CHL).

6. Susa Young Gates to Ida Husted Harper, Dec. 13, 1926, box 38, fd. 25.

7. Gates to Smoot, Sep. 6, 1928, box 46, fd. 5.

former, then she would eventually receive her reward. If the latter, "then it served you just right."[8]

Jacob took great pride in Susa's accomplishments, and he was almost always willing to remain at home and take care of his boys and the home fires. Having Susa referred to as the thirteenth apostle did not seem to daunt him at all. It was almost a perfect union, and over the years Susa was able to explain their happy chemistry. Susa always believed that a woman's first responsibility was to her husband, second, to her children.[9]

Susa gave identical advice to two young men, Clifford G. Snow and David J. Smith, in 1926 regarding marital "peace and domestic comfort. ... Set aside a certain sum each month for the unquestioned use of your wife's expenses." Having done this, however, "I suggest you never ask your wife how she spends the money she has. If she tells you that is quite all right; but her earnings and expenses in the home are as much a personal matter to her as your earnings and expenses outside of the home are to you."[10]

The ultimate secret for marital bliss was a certain degree of detachment. Certainly, the degree of freedom afforded Susa by Jacob was a huge factor in the feats Susa achieved. In an undated autobiography she sent to her friend Susan Ertz, Susa wrote: "My husband has solved the marital problem of the ages. He leaves me to my own labors and devices—unmolested and unquestioned. ... His detachment permits me to seek my literary and political counsel from wise men trained in these lines, while my husband and I meet on the common ground of family and domestic problems."[11]

Of Susa's many strengths, her primary one was, without doubt, loyalty. Susa's loyalty extended to everything in her life—loyalty to her parents, loyalty to the church, loyalty to priesthood authority, loyalty to friends, loyalty to spouse and children. Without fail, she tried to do what she felt God would want her to do—and what would

---

8. Gates biographical sketches, box 3, fd. 36, SYPG (CHL).

9. Susa expressed this sentiment frequently, but see especially advice given in her correspondence to Peggy Pulitzer after Pulitzer married and had children, box 45, fd. 16.

10. Gates to Smith, Sep. 20, 1926, box 52, fd. 13.

11. Untitled, undated autobiography, box 38, fd. 3, SYGP (CHL).

make her father proud of her. She lamented, "So many of us want to travel our own way and the Lord's way at one and the same time."[12]

It is impressive to realize how much she accomplished in her seventy-seven years. Except for a couple of years at the turn of the twentieth century, when poor health overtook her, she never gave up trying to make the world a better place. Unlimited enthusiasm characterized her life. She did not expect God to do anything for her that she could do for herself. In 1918 she wrote, "The Lord does not perform miracles for His children when He has provided natural ways by which they can achieve results."[13]

Susa was charismatic; she held audiences spellbound as she spoke. Susa's granddaughter Lurene Gates Wilkinson described the electrifying scene when she was a young schoolgirl in Provo, and Susa spoke to a group of students at BYU. The occasion was a student assembly on September 28, 1923, and Susa's topic was "The Contribution of Women to the Church Schools." She said, "[Woman] conserves those things that make life worth living. The woman should carry the ideal of home where ever she goes."[14]

> When I [Lurene] was a little girl I was going to the BYU grade school. I was in ... third grade, and my teacher said to me, "Your Grandma is going to be the speaker today at the BYU Devotional. Would you like to go over and hear her?" and I said, "Oh, yes!" I went over into the assembly hall, and I sat there in my little girl dress and low heels and looked at the girls around me, and they were wearing high heels and lipstick, and I could remember feeling just like a little wallflower, and oh, my goodness, I don't belong here. Then Grandmother came in and sat on the stage. ... She always wore old-fashioned clothes. [The students'] skirts were short, heels were high, lipstick was bright, but she sat up there with her usual dress, which was high-necked with a little ruffle around it, and it would either be black or gray or purple, and long sleeves and long skirts with petticoats underneath and low heels that laced up. ... Her white hair drawn up with combs in it ... everybody else in short hair. As I sat there and looked at her, I thought, "Oh, my goodness, she looks so old-fashioned." Everyone around me ... was so fashion-conscious, and I sort of scrunched down.

---

12. Gates, "Climbing," *Relief Society Magazine*, June 1916, 355.

13. Gates, "Inspiration Versus Information," *Utah Genealogical and Historical Magazine*, July 1918, 131–32.

14. "Susa Y. Gates Talks on Woman," *Y News*, Apr. 4, 1923, 4.

Then they introduced her, but the moment she stepped forward to the podium to speak, it was like a spell came over the audience. They were absolutely in awe ... they were just enchanted with her. They'd lean forward on their seats to hear every word. All at once I thought, "Oh, that's my grandmother up there," and I sat up straight. I almost wanted to stand up and point to her and say, "That's my grandmother up there!"[15]

Susa was fearless in preaching the gospel because she believed it was true. But it was not always so. Susa describes as a youngster feeling that she lacked the "burning testimony" her father and mother had. She asked herself how she could "get that flame and fire" for herself. Her father had told her that if she wanted a specific blessing, she would need to pray for it on a daily basis. The confirmation would come via the Holy Spirit. At length, Susa received her affirmation, which she described in detail: "During one year I was nearly 40 years old, I disciplined my taste, my desires and my impulses—severely disciplining my impulses—severely disciplining my appetite, my tongue, my acts, for one whole year, and how I prayed." One day, at the end of that year, approximately sixteen years after the death of her father, Susa was sweeping the floor, and there came a "soul enlightening voice," which spoke to her spirit, "You know it is true! Never doubt it again!" "I never have!" she said. Thereafter, it became a straightforward task to measure spiritual matters. If a "theory" agrees with the truths of the gospel, "it is mine! If it does not, I cast it out."[16]

Susa wrote to an autograph seeker, "I am truly converted to my religion and am a natural propagandist even as was my father."[17] As she wrote to great literary luminaries, she did not hesitate to tell them how much they would gain from accepting the LDS Church, which she equated with the true gospel of Jesus Christ. Susa even promised some that if she survived them, she would have vicarious baptisms performed for them in the temple.[18]

---

15. Lurene Gates Wilkinson, interview by the author, Nov. 21, 2010. Lurene was in the third grade in 1922–23.

16. Gates, *Why I Believe*, 27.

17. Gates to Katie Lowe Kendrick, Feb. 25, 1933, box 41, fd. 8.

18. See Susa's correspondence with Gilman (box 38, fds. 14 and 20), Hurst (box 39, fd. 10), Pulitzer (box 45, fd. 16), McCune (box 41, fd. 4), and Strobridge (box 48, fd. 16), in her papers at the CHL.

There was great magnanimity in Susa's soul, which demon-strates two competing aspects of her personality. She frequently had differences of opinion with people, often entering pointed comments into her journal or other writings. Always, however, in public, she gave praise to these same people, who were for the most part very accomplished. Examples include Emmeline B. Wells, with whom Susa sometimes scrapped. Wells had ignored Susa's suggestion that she help as an associate editor with the *Woman's Exponent* in 1888. In 1915 Emmeline became "terribly upset" to find out that Susa had been asked by church authorities to begin work on a women's history of the church, since she and one of her daughters had planned such an undertaking.[19] Yet in 1917 Susa referred in print to Emmeline as "the Morning Miracle." She praised "Our beloved President Emmeline B. Wells who is among the most precious human possessions of the Relief Society today," and then singled out her many virtues, including her "fierce inde-pendence," "ineffable spirit," "fixed integrity to the truth," " power and majesty of her spirit," "sensitively pure spirit," "lovely dignity," "the clear music of her voice," and "the truths which fall one by one from her precious lips."[20] Susa had reason to dislike Clarissa Smith Williams and Amy Brown Lyman, general Relief Society officers whose actions had led Susa to resign from the general board of the Relief Society and the editorship of the *Relief Soci-ety Magazine* in 1922. Yet Susa later wrote glowingly of Clarissa, "whose knowledge of every phase of Relief Society development was only equaled by her faith and integrity to the principles which she so nobly exemplified."[21] In 1932 Susa wrote of "our brilliant First Counselor Amy Brown Lyman."[22]

Susa left voluminous papers in which she often expressed her most intimate thoughts. That she thought one thing about a given person but spoke about them differently is due to several factors. First, she had strong opinions and often wrote them down. For the

19. Gates Journal, box 105, fd. 4.

20. Gates, "Our Lovely Human Heritage, President Emmeline B. Wells," *Relief So-ciety Magazine*, Feb. 1917, 74–75.

21. "The Female Relief Society," box 3, fd. 33, SYGP (CHL).

22. Gates, "Sketch of the National Women's Relief Society," Jan. 27, 1932, box 44, fd. 3, SYGP (CHL).

most part, these written confidences were never destroyed, so we may easily see how Susa felt at the moment and what she later said publicly. For instance, she expressed negative comments privately about three of her future children-in-law before marriage: John A. Widtsoe, Gweneth Gibbs, and Florence Keate. But she came to love each without reserve. Second, Susa valued the "womanly life" and did not engage in behavior she would have found to be "unladylike." She might skewer politicians in private, for example, but she never attacked them in public. Third, Susa was a master at controlling the public's perception of herself. She would certainly not want to say anything that would reflect poorly on herself or on the Young family. Finally, Susa harbored little, if any, jealousy. She seemed able to acknowledge and express appreciation for the talents and accomplishments of her contemporaries.

Susa understood her ability to irritate other people, usually from a well-intentioned but sometimes overbearing attitude. Before the Utah Genealogical Society group left for the Panama Pacific Exposition in San Francisco in 1915, President Joseph F. Smith held a meeting in his office, at which he said, "If I had the enthusiasm, the energy, etc., etc., of my sister Susa, I could do many things." Susa replied, "If you were like me you would be one of the most unpopular persons in the Church, instead of being what you are, beloved & honored of all men." Smith and his counselor Charles Penrose replied that "when you do get corrected & sat down on you get right up and try again." A year later Susa described another meeting with President Smith, in which he told her "that a lot of the 'big' women are afraid of her [Susa]—worried over all these things you are doing, the changes you are instituting; they are pretty worried."[23]

Susa, after initial frustration, tended to meet criticism with submission and humility. She wrote in 1918, "Try to love me and be patient with my mistakes, kind to my faults and let us love and serve each other truly."[24] Susa, for all her frank assessments of others, seems not to have harbored grudges. Shortly after her resignation from the Relief Society general board, she wrote to Charles W. Penrose, "You

---

23. See Gates Journal, box 105, fd. 4.
24. Gates, "Little Children, Love One Another," *Relief Society Magazine*, Dec. 1918, 706–07.

know I have had a great deal of discipline in my life, and when it has come from those over me in the Church I have accepted it [in] the spirit of meekness, realizing that after all life is short and it will be the better for the training which my spirit has received from both friends and those who feel unkindly to me."[25]

Susa understood the role and blessing of adversity in her life. In 1905, after her life had seen a nasty divorce, serious illness, and the deaths of eight children, she wrote, "The human being most to be pitied is the one who has few if any trials, the one who lives out a mildly contented, self-satisfied life, prosperous and uneventful."[26]

In one of her letters to Reed Smoot, Susa wrote, "There are some of our leaders whose characters and temperaments are not naturally agreeable to me, but I have been so trained by a respectful father and a reverential mother that I would hold off all possible comment concerning those I do not like naturally, and try to cultivate a real and inspiring friendship for them all. I endeavor to select the best traits in each and every one of them and reflect upon that side of their characters."[27]

Susa's opinions were usually arrived at after careful thought imposed on strong feelings based on her religious ideals. She was partisan, a fierce champion of her children, although she realized their imperfections. She was strong-willed, but acquiesced graciously to church leaders. She suffered fools poorly, but she never intended to be mean-spirited. She could be impatient but would always go the extra mile to be of service to her fellowmen.

Paul Cracroft, who wrote a master's thesis on Susa, aptly summarized the reasons for Susa's importance as one of Mormonism's grand women. He wrote, "But to judge Mrs. Gates' greatness, we must look at her as something more than a writer. The rearing of her thirteen children, her brilliance in the Woman's Suffrage movement, her vigorous political career, her indefatigable work in Mormon temples, her desire always to be a part of the growth of her small Mormon community—all these things consumed time which might

---

25. Gates to Charles W. Penrose, July 29, 1922, box 52, fd. 10.
26. Gates, [Untitled], *Young Woman's Journal*, 1905, 296.
27. Gates to Smoot, Dec. 26, 1922, box 48, fd. 5.

otherwise have gone into the self-criticism which makes for more distinguished writing."[28]

Historians write often about the influence of turn-of-the-century leaders on the LDS Church today. To the names of Joseph F. Smith and Heber J. Grant, I believe we must add that of Susa Young Gates. She left an imprint on virtually every aspect of Mormonism. Almost everything Latter-day Saints do has been influenced by Susa. We study from lesson manuals, the writing of which Susa pioneered. She started two major publications, and although these two journals have since been folded into different publications, her journalistic standards continue. The way the Young Women and the Relief Society conduct their business, with different literary, homemaking, and religious pursuits, shows her handiwork. Even in our digital age, how we perform genealogical research and keep records accord with guidelines she established. Her emphasis on the importance of temple attendance has been echoed by every church president since Joseph F. Smith. Susa could accurately be called "the mother of family history," one of its handful of major advocates in our time. Principles expostulated by Susa continue to be preached today from the pulpit—tithing, Word of Wisdom, chastity, proselytizing, marrying within the faith, marital fidelity, and family unity, among others.

Charles A. Callis, who would become an apostle four months after Susa's death, wrote a fitting tribute when he summarized Susa's life with these words: "You have the faculty of doing common things in an uncommon way. With your great ability you have acquired the habit of doing big things, and you have the spirit of lifting your fellow creatures on to higher spiritual lines. The good work you have done with your pen, voice and example of constant devotion will never pass away."[29]

More than four decades after her death, Susa received another accolade, which would have pleased her immensely. In 1975 she was chosen by a committee representing the American Mothers Committee as the "most outstanding mother in Utah history."[30]

---

28. Cracroft, "Susa Young Gates," 139.

29. Callis to Gates, Oct. 19, 1932, box 41, fd. 10.

30. Ten outstanding mothers from each state were selected. The other nine mothers chosen from Utah included Ivy Baker Priest, Belle S. Spafford, Emmeline B. Wells, and Amy Brown Lyman, among others. "Susa Y. Gates 'Outstanding Utah Mother,'" Deseret News, Sept. 6, 1975, W1, 6.

Photographs

Susanne (or Susannah) Amelia Young, age 8, ca. 1856, Salt Lake City.

Mary Gibbs Bigelow and Nahum Bigelow, Susa's maternal grandparents.

Emma Forsberry Gates and Jacob Gates,
parents of Jacob Forsberry Gates and Susa's parents-in-law.

Lucy Bigelow and Brigham Young, Susa's parents, about the time they were married in 1847. Creases in Brigham's photo are from Lucy's carrying the picture in a small purse.

Lion House (left) and Beehive House (right). Several Young families lived in the Lion House, completed in 1856. Brigham conducted business from the Beehive House.

Lion House, ca. 1878. Susa lived in the Lion House for her first fourteen years.

Union Club, organized in 1876 in St. George by Susa, who is seated in the middle of the front row. Sister Mabel is seated next to her, second from right.

Susa as a young woman.

Susa Y. Dunford, age 20, 1876.

Susa, 1870s, Salt Lake City.

Jacob F. Gates, age 22, January 1877, San Francisco California,
en route to first mission in Hawai'i.

Susa, ca. 1896.

Lucy Bigelow Young, with daughters Susa Y. Gates (left) and Dora Y. Hagan
(right), ca. 1904, Salt Lake City.

432

Zina Y. Williams Card (half-sister) and Susa Young Gates, ca. 1898.

Young Sisters, (left to right) Mabel, Susa, Dora.

Gates Family, Honolulu, 1886. Jacob (standing), front row, Jacob (Jay), Susa, Joseph, Karl, Emma Lucy. This is the only known photograph of Jay and Karl.

Jacob F. Gates, age 34, Laie, Oahu, Sandwich Islands, 1888.

Susa Young Gates

Lucy Bigelow Young, 1889, San Francisco, returning from Hawai'i with Gates grandchildren, (left to right) Joseph, Cecil, Harvey, Emma Lucy.

Jacob F. Gates, age 40, 1894.   Susa Y. Gates

Gates Family, 1897. First row, Franklin, Sarah Beulah.
Second row, Susa, Cecil, Jacob F., Harvey (Hal), Brigham.

Susa Young Gates, 1895, Salt Lake City.

Madame Lydia Finkelstein Mountford (seated) with (left to right) Emma Lucy
Gates, Franklin Y. Gates, Beulah Gates, and H. Giles, 1896, Provo.

Jacob F. Gates (standing) with four sons, (left to right) Cecil, Franklin, Brigham Young, Harvey, ca. 1898, Utah.

Susa Young Gates (center) with three daughters, (left to right) Emma Lucy
and Sarah Beulah Gates, Leah (Dunford), 1897, Salt Lake City.

Gates and Snow Boys' Band, 1902, Provo. First row, far left,
Franklin Y. Gates. Second row, third from left, B. Cecil Gates with trombone;
third from right, Harvey Gates with snare drum.

Gates home in Salt Lake City, Nov. 1907.

Jacob F. Gates, 63 years old, Jan. 1918.

Susa Young Gates, 50 years old, 1906.

Jacob F. and Susa Young Gates, at mountain cabin in Brighton, Utah, 1920s.

"The Clique," McCune Mansion, Salt Lake City, July 1917,
(left to right) Ann Groesbeck, Augusta W. Grant, Elizabeth C. McCune,
Alice K. Smith, Susa Young Gates.

Extended Gates family, Brighton, Utah, ca. 1919. Left to right, back row,
Albert E. Bowen, Lucy Gates Bowen, Leah Widtsoe, Franklin Y. Gates (partially
obscured by wife Florence), B. Cecil Gates (holding baby) and wife Gweneth,
John A. Widtsoe, Jacob and Susa Gates.

Gates family at "Old Provo Home," 1924, with various grandchildren in front.
Back row, left to right, B. Cecil and Gweneth Gates, Harvey and Bichette Gates,
Jacob and Susa Gates, Florence Gates, Lucy Gates Bowen, Franklin Gates.

Jacob F. and Susa Young Gates, ca. 1930, Salt Lake City.

Gates family, ca. 1925. Center, seated, Jacob F. and Susa Young Gates. Seated left, Albert E. Bowen, seated right, John A. Widtsoe. Standing, left to right, Lucy Gates Bowen; Harvey Gates; Gweneth and B. Cecil Gates; Florence and Franklin Gates; Anna, Eudora, Marcel, and Leah Widtsoe.

Susa Young Gates, February 1920, Chicago, at celebration of
passage of universal women's suffrage in the United States.

Jacob F. Gates

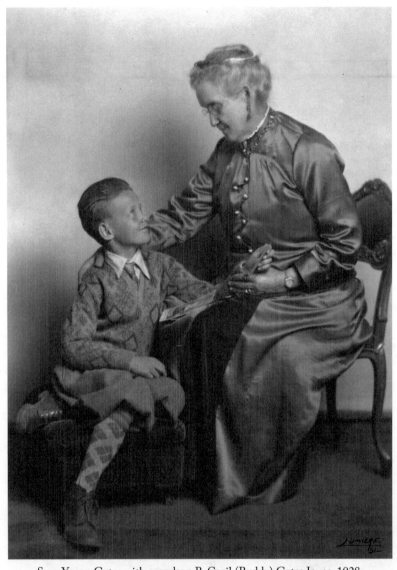

Susa Young Gates with grandson B. Cecil (Buddy) Gates Jr., ca. 1928.

Susa Young Gates (second from right) in Hollywood, late 1920s. Left, three
unidentified women in film industry. Back row, Harvey Gates, Augusta W. and
President Heber J. Grant, Bichette Gates, Susa, and granddaughter Susan.
Courtesy of Utah State Historical Society.

Last known Gates family photo, 1931, Salt Lake City. Jacob F. and Susa Y. Gates,
right foreground. Four adult children present. Front row, Franklin, far left;
Back row, B. Cecil, second from left; Lucy Gates Bowen, fourth from right;
Leah Widtsoe, second from right. Harvey absent.

Five generations of voting women. Susa Young Gates (center), surrounded by (clockwise from left upper) grandmother Mary Gibbs Bigelow, mother Lucy Bigelow Young, granddaughter Anna Widtsoe Wallace, daughter Leah Dunford Widtsoe.

Bibliography

Alexander, Thomas G. *An Apostle in Exile: Wilford Woodruff and the St. George Connection*. St. George, Utah: Dixie College, 1996. Lecture originally given as part of the Juanita Brooks Lecture Series, 1994.

———. *Brigham Young and the Expansion of the Mormon Faith*. Norman: University of Oklahoma Press, 2019.

———. *Things in Heaven and Earth: The Life and Times of Wilford Woodruff, a Mormon Prophet*. Salt Lake City: Signature Books, 1991.

———. *Utah: The Right Place*. Salt Lake City: Gibbs Smith, 1995.

———. "The Word of Wisdom: From Principle to Requirement." *Dialogue: A Journal of Mormon Thought* 14, no. 3 (Fall 1981): 78–88.

Allen, James B., and Jessie L. Embry. "'Provoking the Brethren to Good Works': Susa Young Gates, the Relief Society, and Genealogy." *BYU Studies* 31, no. 2 (Spring 1991): 115–38.

Allen, James B., Jessie L. Embry, and Kahlile B. Mehr. *Hearts Turned to the Fathers: A History of the Genealogical Society of Utah, 1894–1994*. Provo, Utah: BYU Studies, 1995.

Allen, Joseph. *The Worcester Association and Its Antecedents: A History of Four Ministerial Associations*. Boston: Nichols and Noyes, 1868.

Anderson, Devery S., ed. *Salt Lake School of the Prophets, 1867–1883*. Salt Lake City: Signature Books, 2018.

Arrington, Leonard J. *Brigham Young: American Moses*. New York: Alfred Knopf, 1985.

———. *Great Basin Kingdom: An Economic History of the Latter-day Saints, 1830–1900*. Cambridge, Massachusetts: Harvard University Press, 1958.

———. "Women as a Force in the History of Utah." *Utah Historical Quarterly* 38, no. 1 (Winter 1970): 3–6.

Arrington, Leonard J., Feramorz Y. Fox, and Dean L. May. *Building the City of God: Community and Cooperation Among the Mormons*. Salt Lake City: Deseret Book Co., 1976.

Arrington, Leonard J., Susan A. Madsen, and Emily M. Jones. *Mothers of the Prophets*. 3rd ed., revised and updated. Salt Lake City: Deseret Book Co., 2009.

Beecher, Maureen Ursenbach, and Lavina Fielding Anderson, eds. *Sisters in Spirit: Mormon Women in Historical Perspective*. Urbana: University of Illinois Press, 1987

Beeton, Beverly, and Ray R. Canning, eds.. *The Genteel Gentile: Letters of Elizabeth Cummings, 1857–1858*. Salt Lake City: University of Utah Press, 1977.

Bergera, Gary James. "Identifying the Earliest Mormon Polygamists, 1841–44." *Dialogue: A Journal of Mormon Thought* 38, no. 3 (Fall 2005): 1–74.

Bigelow, Mary Gibbs. "Autobiography of Mary Gibbs Bigelow." Edited by Maurine Carr Ward. *Nauvoo Journal* 6 (Spring 1994): 32–37.

Bigler, David L. *Forgotten Kingdom: The Mormon Theocracy in the American West, 1847–1896*. Spokane, Washington: Arthur H. Clark Co., 1998.

Bitton, Davis. "The B. H. Roberts Case of 1898–1900. *Utah Historical Quarterly* 25, no. 1 (Jan. 1957): 27–46.

———. *George Q. Cannon: A Biography*. Salt Lake City: Deseret Book Co., 1999.

Bitton, Davis, and Linda P. Wilcox. "Pestiferous Ironclads: The Grasshopper Problem in Pioneer Utah." *Utah Historical Quarterly* 46, no. 4 (Fall 1978): 336–55.

Black, Susan Easton. "How Large Was the Population of Nauvoo?" *BYU Studies* 35, no. 2 (1995): 91–94.

Black, Susan Easton, and Larry C. Porter. "Martin Harris Comes to Utah, 1870." *BYU Studies* 57, no. 3 (2018): 143–64.

Booth, Edith Young, Phyllis B. Phillips, and Beverly L. Allred. "History of Harriet Elizabeth (Cook) Young." Typescript, copy available at familysearch.org/tree/person/memories/K2M4-JPP.

Bradley, Martha Sonntag. *ZCMI: America's First Department Store*. Salt Lake City: ZCMI, 1991.

Buerger, David John. "'The Fulness of the Priesthood': The Second Anointing in Latter-day Saint Theology and Practice." *Dialogue: A Journal of Mormon Thought* 16, no. 1 (Spring 1983): 10–44.

Burgess-Olson, Vicky, ed. *Sister Saints*. Provo, Utah: Brigham Young University Press, 1978.

Bushman, Claudia, ed. *Mormon Sisters: Women in Early Utah*. 2nd ed. Logan: Utah State University Press, 1997.

Butler, Anne M. *Daughters of Joy, Sisters of Misery: Prostitutes in the American West, 1865–90*. Urbana: University of Illinois Press, 1987.

Cannon, George Q. The Journal of George Q. Cannon, 1849–1901. Typescript. Salt Lake City: Church Historian's Press. Online at churchhistorianspress.org/george-q-cannon

Cannon, M. Hamlin. "A Pension Office Note on Brigham Young's Father." *The American Historical Review* 50, no. 1 (Oct. 1944): 82–90.

Carter, Kate B., ed. *Our Pioneer Heritage*. 20 vols. Salt Lake City: Daughters of Utah Pioneers, 1958–77.

Carter, D. Robert. "Fish and the Famine of 1855–56." *Journal of Mormon History* 27, no. 2 (Fall 2001): 92–124.

Christensen, Louise Jensen. "History of Thomas and Elizabeth Higgs." Unpublished paper submitted to the Centerfield, Utah, Camp of the Daughters of the Utah Pioneers, 1989. Copy available at the Daughters of Utah Pioneer Museum and online at familysearch.org/tree/person/memories/KWNR-93S.

Coakley, Robert W. *The Role of Federal Military Forces in Domestic Disorders, 1789–1878*. Washington, DC: Center of Military History, 1988.

Compton, Todd. *In Sacred Loneliness: The Plural Wives of Joseph Smith*. Salt Lake City: Signature Books, 1997.

Cornwall, Rebecca. *Brigham Young's Forest Farm*. Salt Lake City: Utah State Division of Parks and Recreation, April 1979.

———. "Susa Young Gates: The Thirteenth Apostle." In Burgess-Olson, *Sister Saints*, 61–93.

Cowley, Matthias. *Wilford Woodruff, History of His Life and Labors*. Salt Lake City: Bookcraft, 1964.

Cracroft, Paul. "Susa Young Gates: Her Life and Literary Work." Master's thesis, University of Utah, 1951.

Davidson, Karen Lynn, and Jill Mulvay Derr. *Eliza: The Life and Faith of Eliza R. Snow*. Salt Lake City: Deseret Book Co., 2013.

Derr, Jill Mulvay. "'Strength in our Union': The Making of Mormon Sisterhood." In Beecher and Anderson, *Sisters in Spirit*, 153–207.

Dirkmaat, Gerrit J., Brent M. Rogers, Grant Underwood, Robert J. Woodford, and William G. Harley, eds. *The Joseph Smith Papers: Documents Volume 3: February 1833–March 1834*. Salt Lake City: Church Historian's Press, 2014.

Dunford, Alma. "The Letters of Alma Bailey Dunford." Transcribed by Jill W. Dunford. Unpublished typescript, 1996, copy in author's possession.

England, Eugene. "Mormon Literature: Progress and Prospects." In *Mormon Americana: A Guide to Sources and Collections in the United States*, edited by David J. Whittaker, 455–505. Provo, Utah: BYU Studies, 1995.

Erekson, Keith A. "Elvis Has Left the Library: Identifying Forged Annotations in a Book of Mormon." *BYU Studies* 57, no. 4 (2018): 51–77.

Fetzer, Leland A. "Tolstoy and Mormonism." *Dialogue: A Journal of Mormon Thought* 6, no. 1 (Spring 1971): 13–29.

Flake, Kathleen. *The Politics of American Religious Identity: The Seating of Senator Reed Smoot, Mormon Apostle*. Chapel Hill: University of North Carolina Press, 2004.

Gates, Susa Young. "Family Life among the Mormons," *North American Review* 150, no. 400 (Mar. 1890): 339–50.

———. "From Impulsive Girl to Patient Wife: Lucy Bigelow Young." Edited by Miriam B. Murphy. *Utah Historical Quarterly* 45, no. 3 (Summer 1977): 270–88.

———. *History of the Young Ladies' Mutual Improvement Association*. (Salt Lake City: Deseret News, 1911.

———. "How Brigham Young Brought Up His Fifty-Six Children." *Physical Culture*, Feb. 1925, 29–31, 138–44.

———. *John Stevens' Courtship*. Salt Lake City: Deseret News, 1909.

———. "Lucy Bigelow Young." Unpublished manuscript in author's possession.

———. *Lydia Knight's History*. Salt Lake City: Juvenile Instructor Office, 1883.

———. *Memorial to Elizabeth Claridge McCune: Missionary, Philanthropist, Architect*. Salt Lake City: by the author, 1924.

———. "Notes on Young and Howe Families." *Utah Genealogical and Historical Magazine* 11 (1920): 180–87.

———. Papers, 1852–1932. MSS B 95, USHS.

———. Papers, ca. 1870–1933. MS 7692, CHL.

———. "Utah." In *History of Woman Suffrage*, edited by Ida Husted Harper, vol. 6, 644–50. New York: National American Woman Suffrage Association, 1922.

———. *Why I Believe the Gospel of Jesus Christ*. Salt Lake City: Deseret News Press [ca. 1931].

———. "The Young Family." *Utah Genealogical and Historical Magazine* 1 (1910): 66–70.

Gates, Susa Young, and Leah D. Widtsoe. *The Life Story of Brigham Young*. New York: Macmillan, 1930. British edition published in London: Jarrolds Publishers, 1930.

———. *The Prince of Ur*. Salt Lake City: Bookcraft, 1945.

———. *Women of the "Mormon" Church*. Independence, Missouri: Press of Zion's Printing and Publishing, 1928.

Gildire, Richard P. *The Profane, the Civil, & the Godly: The Reformation of Manners in Orthodox New England, 1679–1749*. University Park: Pennsylvania State University Press, 1994.

Givens, Terryl L. *People of Paradox: A History of Mormon Culture*. Oxford: Oxford University Press, 2007.

Gordon, Sarah Barringer. *The Mormon Question: Polygamy and Constitutional Conflict in Nineteenth-Century America*. Chapel Hill: University of North Carolina Press, 2003.

Gould, Lewis L. *Four Hats in the Ring: The 1912 Election and the Birth of Modern American Politics*. Lawrence: University Press of Kansas, 2008.

Hales, Brian C. *Joseph Smith's Polygamy*. 3 vols. Salt Lake City: Greg Kofford Books, 2013.

Hall, Dave. *A Faded Legacy: Amy Brown Lyman and Mormon Women's Activism, 1872–1959*. Salt Lake City: University of Utah Press, 2015.

Hall, David. "Anxiously Engaged: Amy Brown Lyman and Relief Society Charity Work, 1917–45," *Dialogue: A Journal of Mormon Thought* 27, no. 2 (Summer 1994): 73–91.

Hardy, B. Carmon. *Solemn Covenant: The Mormon Polygamous Passage*. Urbana: University of Illinois Press, 1992.

Harper, Reid L. "The Mantle of Joseph: Creation of a Mormon Miracle." *Journal of Mormon History* 22, no. 2 (Fall 1996): 35–71.

Hatch, Robert Duane. "The Pratt–Newman Debate." Master's thesis, Brigham Young University, 1960.

Herman, R.D.K. "The Aloha State: Place Names and the Anti-Conquest of Hawai'i." *Annals of the Association of American Geographers* 89, no. 1 (Mar. 1999): 76–102.

Hilton, Hope A. *"Wild Bill" Hickman and the Mormon Frontier.* Salt Lake City: Signature Books, 1988.

Historian's Office. Journal, 1844–2012. CR 100 1, CHL.

Holzapfel, Richard Neitzel. "Thomas and Elizabeth Higgs: 1856 Mormon Pioneers from Iowa." *Nauvoo Journal* 8, no. 2 (Fall 1996): 29–38.

Hymns of The Church of Jesus Christ of Latter-day Saints. Salt Lake City: Church of Jesus Christ of Latter-day Saints, 1985.

Isaac and Leah Dunford Family Association. *The Isaac and Leah Bailey Dunford Family Story.* 2nd ed. Snellville, Georgia: Gloucester Crescent, 2006.

Ivins, Stanley S. "Notes on Mormon Polygamy." *Western Humanities Review* X (1956): 229–39.

Jessee, Dean C., ed. *Letters of Brigham Young to his Sons.* Salt Lake City: Deseret Book Co., 1974

———. "'A Man of God and a Good Kind Father': Brigham Young at Home." *BYU Studies* 40, no. 2 (Apr. 2001): 23–53.

Jenson, Andrew. *Encyclopedic History of the Church of Jesus Christ of Latter-day Saints.* Salt Lake City: Deseret News Publishing, 1941.

Jenson, Andrew. *Latter-day Saint Biographical Encyclopedia.* 4 vols. Salt Lake City: Andrew Jenson History Co. and Deseret News Press, 1901–36.

Jenson, Harold H. "Susa Young Gates—True Pioneer Stories." *Juvenile Instructor*, Mar. 1929, 135–37.

Johnson, Catherine M. "Emma Lucy Gates Bowen: Singer, Musician, Teacher." *Utah Historical Quarterly* 64, no. 4 (Fall 1996): 344–55.

Johnson, Jeffery Ogden. "Determining and Defining 'Wife': The Brigham Young Households." *Dialogue: A Journal of Mormon Thought* 20, no. 3 (Fall 1987): 57–70.

Johnson, William E. "The Educational Views and Practices of Brigham Young." Master's thesis, Brigham Young University, 1968.

Journal of Discourses. 26 vols. Liverpool: Latter-day Saints' Book Depot, 1854–86.

Kane, Elizabeth Wood. *Twelve Mormon Homes: Visited in Succession on a Journey through Utah to Arizona.* Introduction and notes by Everett L. Cooley. Salt Lake City: Tanner Trust Fund/University of Utah Library, 1974.

Kenney, Scott G. "Before the Beard: Trials of the Young Joseph F. Smith." *Sunstone*, Nov. 2001, 20–42.

———. Collection, 1820–1984. MS 0587, Special Collections, Marriott Library, University of Utah.

Loeffelbein, Robert. "Dio Lewis: He Started American Physical Education." *Improving College and University Teaching* 14, no. 1 (1966): 41–42.

Lofthouse, Merrill S. "A History of the Genealogical Society of the Church of Jesus Christ of Latter-day Saints to 1970." Master's thesis, Brigham Young University, 1970.

Ludlow, Daniel H., ed. *The Encyclopedia of Mormonism.* 4 vols. New York: Macmillan, 1992.

Lund, Jennifer L. "Out of the Swan's Nest: The Ministry of Anthon H. Lund, Scandinavian Apostle." *Journal of Mormon History* 29, no. 2 (Fall 2003): 77–105.

Lyman, Edward Leo. *Finally Statehood! Utah's Struggle, 1849–1896.* Salt Lake City: Signature Books, 2019.

Macfarlane, L. W. *Yours Sincerely, John M. Macfarlane.* Salt Lake City: by the author, 1980.

MacKinnon, William P. *At Sword's Point: A Documentary History of the Utah War.* 2 vols. Norman, Oklahoma: The Arthur H. Clark Co., 2008–16.

Madsen, Carol Cornwall, ed. *Battle for the Ballot: Essays on Woman Suffrage in Utah, 1870–1896.* Logan: Utah State University Press, 1997.

———. *Emmeline B. Wells, An Intimate History.* Salt Lake City: University of Utah Press, 2017.

Mak, James. "Creating 'Paradise in the Pacific': How Tourism Began in Hawaii." Working paper no. 2015-1, uhero.hawaii.edu, accessed Mar. 27, 2020.

Mariger, Marietta M. *Saga of Three Towns: Harrisburg, Leeds, Silver Reef.* Panguitch, Utah: Garfield County News, 1951.

Maxwell, Margaret Finlayson. "A Particular Favorite: Sara Alexander of the Old Salt Lake Theatre." *Journal of Mormon History* 32, no. 2 (Summer 2006): 87–110.

Mueller, Max Perry. *Race and the Making of the Mormon People*. Chapel Hill: University of North Carolina Press, 2017.

Neilson, Reid L. *Exhibiting Mormonism: The Latter-day Saints and the 1893 Chicago World's Fair*. New York: Oxford University Press, 2011.

Nelson, David Conley. *Moroni and the Swastika: Mormons in Nazi Germany*. Norman: University of Oklahoma Press, 2015.

Newell, Linda King, and Valeen Tippetts Avery. *Mormon Enigma: Emma Hale Smith*. 2nd ed. Urbana: University of Illinois Press, 1994.

Noall, Matthew Frederick, and Claire Wilcox. Papers, 1805–1970s. Ms 0188, Special Collections, Marriott Library, University of Utah.

Park, Benjamin E. *Kingdom of Nauvoo: The Rise and Fall of a Religious Empire on the American Frontier*. New York: Liveright, 2020.

Parrish, Alan K. *John A. Widtsoe: A Biography*. Salt Lake City: Deseret Book Co., 2003.

Paulos, Michael Herold, ed. *The Mormon Church on Trial: Transcripts of the Reed Smoot Hearings*. Salt Lake City: Signature Books, 2008.

Person, Carolyn W. D. "Susa Young Gates." In Bushman, *Sister Saints*, 199–224.

Petersen, Wanda Snow. *William Snow, First Bishop of Pine Valley*. Provo, Utah: Community Press, 1992.

Peterson, Paul H. "An Historical Analysis of the Word of Wisdom." Master's thesis, Brigham Young University, 1972.

———. "The Mormon Reformation of 1856–1857: The Rhetoric and the Reality." *Journal of Mormon History* 15 (1989): 59–87.

Philbrick, Nathaniel. *Mayflower: A story of Courage, Community, and War*. New York: Viking, 2006.

Pye, Mary F. Kelly. "Utah Women's Press Club History,"

Quinn, D. Michael. "LDS Church Authority and New Plural Marriages, 1890–1904." *Dialogue: A Journal of Mormon Thought* 18, no. 1 (Spring 1985): 9–105.

———. *The Mormon Hierarchy: Wealth and Corporate Power*. Salt Lake City: Signature Books, 2017.

Radke-Moss, Andrea G. "Mormon Women, Suffrage, and Citizenship at the 1893 Chicago World's Fair." In *Gendering The Fair: Histories of Women and Gender at World's Fairs,* edited by J. T. Boisseau and Abigail M. Markwin, 97–112. Urbana: University of Illinois, 2010.

Robinson, Kari Widtsoe Koplin. "Susan Amelia 'Susa' Young Dunford Gates." In Isaac and Leah Dunford Family Association, *Dunford Family Story.*

Sessions, Gene Allred. *Latter-day Patriots: Nine Mormon Families and their Revolutionary War Heritage.* Salt Lake City: Deseret Book Co., 1975.

Shirts, Kathryn H. "The Role of Susa Young Gates and Leah Dunford Widtsoe in the Historical Development of the Priesthood/Motherhood Model." *Journal of Mormon History* 44, no. 2 (Apr. 2018): 104–39.

Sillito, John. *B. H. Roberts: A Life In the Public Arena.* Salt Lake City: Signature Books, 2021.

Smith, George D. *Nauvoo Polygamy: "... But We Called it Celestial Marriage."* Salt Lake City: Signature Books, 2008.

Smith, Joseph F. Papers, 1854–1918. MS 1325, CHL.

Spencer, Clarissa Young, and Mabel Harmer. *Brigham Young at Home.* Salt Lake City: Deseret News Press, 1947.

Stenhouse, Mrs. T.B.H. *Tell It All: The Story of a Life's Experience in Mormonism.* Hartford, Connecticut: A. D. Worthington & Co., 1875.

Stromberg, Alex. "Brigham Young's Forest Farmhouse: Space and Power in 19th Century Agricultural Utah." *Historia: A Journal of the Epsilon Mu Chapter of Phi Alpha Theta and the Eastern Illinois University History Department* 2019, 72–88, digitized copy at www.eiu.edu/historia/Stromberg2015.pdf.

Stuy, Brian H. "'Come, Let Us Go Up to the Mountain of the Lord': The Salt Lake Temple Dedication." *Dialogue: A Journal of Mormon Thought* 31, no. 3 (Fall 1998): 101–22.

Tait, Lisa Olsen. "Mormon Culture Meets Popular Fiction: Susa Young Gates and the Cultural Work of Home Literature." Master's thesis, Brigham Young University, 1998.

———. "Review: Dave Hall, *A Faded Legacy: Amy Brown Lyman and Mormon Women's Activism, 1872–1959.*" *BYU Studies Quarterly* 55, no. 4 (2016): 177–82.

———. "Susa Young Gates and the Vision of the Redemption of the Dead." In *Revelations in Context*, edited by Matthew McBride and James Goldberg. Salt Lake City: Church of Jesus Christ of Latter-day Saints, 2016. Also available online at Revelations in Context, churchofjesuschrist.org.

———. "Thank God That I Have Been Counted Worthy: Susa Amelia Young Dunford Gates, 1856–1933." In Turley and Chapman, *Women of Faith*, 3:57–68.

Tebbel, John, and Mary Ellen Zuckerman. *The Magazine in America, 1741–1990*. New York: Oxford University Press, 1991.

Turley, Richard E. Jr., and Brittany A. Chapman, eds. *Women of Faith in the Latter Days*. 4 vols. Salt Lake City: Deseret Book Co., 2012–17.

Turner, John G. *Brigham Young: Pioneer Prophet*. Cambridge: Harvard University Press, 2012.

Ulrich, Laurel Thatcher. "Give Us an Expanding Faith." In Turley Jr. and Chapman, *Women of Faith*, 3:1–12.

———. *A House Full of Females: Plural Marriage and Women's Rights in Early Mormonism, 1835–1870*. New York: Alfred A. Knopf, 2017.

Utah History Encyclopedia. Online encyclopedia maintained by the Utah Education Network at www.uen.org. Originally published as Allan Kent Powell, ed., *Utah History Encyclopedia* (Salt Lake City: University of Utah Press, 1994).

Van Wagenen, Lola. *Sister Wives and Suffragists: Polygamy and the Politics of Woman Suffrage, 1870–1896*. Provo, Utah: BYU Studies, 2003.

Van Wagoner, Richard S. "The Making of a Mormon Myth: The 1844 Transfiguration of Brigham Young." *Dialogue: A Journal of Mormon Thought* 28, no. 4 (Winter 1995): 1–24.

Vogel, Dan. *Early Mormon Documents*. 5 vols. Salt Lake City: Signature Books, 1996–2003.

Walker, Charles Lowell. *Diary of Charles Lowell Walker, 1830–1904*. Edited by A. Karl Larson and Katherine Miles Larson. Logan: Utah State University Press, 1980.

Walker, Ronald W. "Martin Harris: Mormonism's Early Convert." *Dialogue: A Journal of Mormon Thought* 19, no. 4 (Winter 1986): 29–43.

———. *Wayward Saints: The Social and Religious Protests of the Godbeites against Brigham Young*. Provo, Utah: BYU Studies/Brigham Young University Press, 2009.

Wallace, Mike. *Greater Gotham: A History of New York City from 1898 to 1919*. New York: Oxford University Press, 2017.

Werner, M. R. *Brigham Young*. New York City: Harcourt, Brace and Co., 1925.

White, Richard. *The Republic for Which it Stands: The United States during Reconstruction and the Gilded Age, 1865–1896*. New York: Oxford University Press, 2017.

Whitehead, George F. "Sketch of the Life of Adolphus Rennie Whitehead and Diary of Mary G. Whitehead." Unpublished typescript of family reminiscences, 1992. Copy in author's possession and at Harold B. Lee Library, Brigham Young University.

Whitley, Colleen, ed. *Brigham Young's Homes*. Logan: Utah State University Press, 2002.

Whitney, Orson F. "Home Literature." In *A Believing People: Literature of the Latter-day Saints*, edited by Richard H. Cracroft and Neal E. Lambert. Reprint edition. Pleasant Grove, Utah: Liahona Publishing, 2000.

Widtsoe Family. Widtsoe Family Papers, 1866–1966. MSS B92, Utah State Historical Society.

Widtsoe, John A. *In a Sunlit Land: The Autobiography of John A. Widtsoe*. Salt Lake City: Deseret News Press, 1952.

———. *Priesthood and Church Government in The Church of Jesus Christ of Latter-day Saints*. Salt Lake City: Deseret Book Co., 1939.

Wilkinson, Ernest L., ed. *Brigham Young University: The First One Hundred Years*. 4 vols. Brigham Young University Press, 1975.

Wilkinson, Ernest L., and W. Cleon Skousen. *Brigham Young University: A School of Destiny*. Provo: Brigham Young University Press, 1976.

Wood, Dale Glen. "Brigham Young's Activities in St. George during the Later Years of his Life." Master's thesis, Brigham Young University, 1963.

Woodruff, Wilford. Journals and Papers, 1828–1898. MS 1352, CHL.

———. *Wilford Woodruff's Journal*. Edited by Dan Vogel. 7 vols. Salt Lake City: Benchmark Books, 2020.

Young, Ann Eliza. *Wife No. 19, or the Story of a Life in Bondage ... and Sufferings of Women in Polygamy*. Hartford: Dustin, Gilman & Co., 1875.

Young, Emily P. Diary and Reminiscences, Feb. 1874–Nov. 1899. Typescript. MS 2845, CHL.

Index

N-O

National Association of Colored Women, 240

National Council of Women, 31, 186, 194, 235, 239, 243, 291, 304; annual conference, 176–77, 189–90, 230

National Household Economic Council, 170, 226

Nauvoo, Illinois, 29, 36, 37

Neff, Estelle, 183

New York City, 164, 178, 180, 229, 232, 233

Noall, Elizabeth, 154–55

non-Mormons, 58n54, 148, 213, 215–16

Old Tabernacle, 48n6

P

Panama–Pacific Exposition, 304, 363–64, 422

Panic of 1893, 170

Park, John R., 62

Pearl of Great Price, 262

Penrose, Charles W., 249, 303, 341, 370, 401

People's Party, 129

Pioneer Day, 80

plural marriage, 14, 63, 67, 116–17, 129, 180; LDS defense of, 161–62, 170, 246–47; prosecution and raids, 81, 114, 135–36, 152, 156, 190, 203, 221, 323; Second Manifesto, 246

poetry, 264–70; see also Susa Young Gates: writings

polygamy. See plural marriage

Pond, James B., 227–28, 229, 233, 234

Pratt, Orson, 65, 67–68

Pratt, Romania B., 201, 202, 209

prayer, 6–7, 18, 49, 188

priesthood, 308–09, 337, 369

Prince of Ur, 262–64; see also Susa Young Gates: writings

Puritans, 18, 19, 20, 31, 39, 260

Q-R

Queen Lili'uokalani, 147; see also Sandwich Islands

Queen Victoria, 196, 211, 218, 236

Quorum of Twelve Apostles, 29, 30, 300

radio, 360, 374

railroads, 66, 126

Rawlins, Joseph L., 227

Republican Party, 31, 130, 227, 298, 299

Relief Society, 176, 199, 291, 295, 297, 331; Magazine, 335, 336, 340–52, 376; and Susa Young Gates, 302, 305, 325, 334–35, 336–38, 340–41

Revolutionary War, 22

Reynolds, Alice, 250

Reynolds, George, 136, 356

Richards, Lula Greene, 166, 191, 199, 331

Roberts, B. H., 180, 192–93, 244, 297, 374, 377

Rock Canyon, Utah, 179, 251

Rogers, Aurelia, 176

Roosevelt, Theodore, 232, 298

S

Salt Lake Tabernacle, 67, 95, 409; see also Old Tabernacle

Salt Lake temple, 169, 306

Salt Lake Theatre, 55, 59

Salt Lake Herald–Republican, 360, 368

Salt Lake Tribune, 78

Sanborn, Mabel Young, 75, 95, 134,

University of Deseret, 62

University of Utah, 62, 166, 167

US National Council of Women Press Committee, 182

Utah War, 15–17, 258

Utah Women's Press Club, 159, 166s

W

Webb, Ann Eliza, 10, 51, 227, 404

Wells, Emmeline B., 149, 166, 176, 187, 189, 292, 305, 400; editor of the *Exponent*, 200–01; relationship with Susa Young Gates, 228, 234, 252–53, 331–33, 421; Relief Society president, 199, 226, 339

Wells, Junius F., 199

Widtsoe, John A., 159, 167, 169, 181, 232, 241, 403, 446–47; apostle, 307, 376; education, 188; marriage to Leah Dunford, 186; relationship with Susa Young Gates, 167–68, 242, 303; teacher, 182, 185; university president, 254, 307

Widtsoe, Leah, 104, 150, 160, 174, 182, 188, 241; birth, 86; children, 194, 232, 408; education, 169; marriage to John A. Widtsoe, 168, 185, 186; photographs, 442, 446–47, 451–52; relationship with B. H. Roberts, 180–82, 185; relationship with her mother, 104, 112–13, 175–76; writing, 208–09, 307, 376; see also *Life Story of Brigham Young*

Wilkinson, Lurene K. Gates, 251, 269–70, 307, 384, 419; secretary to Susa Young Gates, vii, 108, 411

Willard, Frances E., 176

Williams, Clarissa Smith, 303, 348, 351–52, 421

Wilson, Woodrow, 298, 338

Winter Quarters, 39

Woman's Exponent, 166, 199, 212, 331, 334

Women's Christian Temperance Union, 160

women's rights, 19, 129, 176, 190, 191, 221–22, 416; and priesthood, 308–09; suffrage, 227, 232, 295, 378, 448; *see also* National Council of Women; International Council of Women

Woodruff Manifesto. *See* plural marriage

Woodruff, Wilford, 13, 90, 95, 100, ; approves founding the *Young Woman's Journal*, 201–03; marriage to Dora Young, 98

Word of Wisdom, 60, 142, 145, 217–18, 307

World's Columbian Exposition. *See* Chicago World's Fair

World War I, 338, 346

Y–Z

Young, Brigham, 1, 2, 5, 13, 15, 36, 427; ancestry, 20–27; birth, 25; childhood, 26–27; conversion to Mormonism, 28; death, 92, 95–96; early church years, 28–30; family life, 4–11, 47–50, 54–55, 68–69, 85; farm, 50–53, 56; first home in Utah, 43; health, 73; and polygamy, 1, 14, 42; president of the church, 30; siblings, 24–25, 28; St. George homes, 73, 77

Young, Brigham, Jr, 75, 77, 354

Young Family Association, 353–54, 369

Young, Harriet Cook, 57–59

Young, John, 22–28

Young Ladies' Mutual Improvement Association, 159, 168, 176, 202–03, 212, 214–15; general presidency, 205, 206; history, 292–96; see also *Young Woman's Journal*

ABOUT THE AUTHOR

Romney Burke was born in Safford, Arizona, and graduated from high school in Fairbanks, Alaska, with many family moves to other western states along the way. He graduated from Stanford University and then obtained his MD from Yale University School of Medicine, with post-graduate work at the University of Utah Hospital and Yale–New Haven Hospital. He was a practicing surgeon (urologist) in Portland, Oregon, for thirty-two years before he retired and taught English at Ocean University in China, through the BYU China Teachers Program. He and his wife, Mary Sue, a great-granddaughter of Susa Young Gates, served missions to Brazil and Hong Kong where they acted as medical advisers. Romney has had a lifelong interest in history and Mormon studies. He and Mary Sue have ten children and live in West Linn, Oregon.